FINANCIAL RECORD KEEPING
An active-learning approach

E. Lee M.A. **& R. Jarvis** BA, FCCA

Edward Lee was formerly a Senior Lecturer at Thames Polytechnic, and is now a full-time educational consultant and writer.

Robin Jarvis is an author of accounting texts, and a Reader in the School of Accounting and Finance, Kingston Business School.

DP PUBLICATIONS LTD
Aldine Place
London W12 8AW
1991

Acknowledgements

VAT and other tax forms and tables are reproduced with permission of the Controller of Her Majesty's Stationery Office.

A CIP catalogue record for this book is available from the British Library

ISBN 1 870941 75 6

Text copyright E. Lee & R. Jarvis © 1991

Design and illustrations copyright DP Publishing Ltd © 1991

Typesetting and design by Elizabeth Elwin for DP Publications Ltd

Printed in Great Britain by
    Loader Jackson Printers
    Arlesley
    Bedfordshire

Contents

Section 2: The information bank – 67

Section 3: Practice and development of skills and knowledge – 295

Section 4: Useful forms and documents – 359

Preface

Aim

This book provides a course of study in the handling of the main financial documents used in business. The student progressively acquires the competences required by NVQ Levels I and II Business Administration (Finance).

It is intended to be used, in the classroom, on the following courses:

BTEC First Certificate

RSA and LCCI Office Practice/Bookkeeping

City and Guilds (organisation and management qualifications)

GCSE Accounting

Secretarial Courses (Office Practice requirements)

Courses offered by organisations such as the **Training Commission**.

Need

There are other books on the market that deal with the topics covered. However, no other book fully satisfies the need for material that is genuinely **activity-based**. *Financial Record Keeping* enables students to meet the NVQ requirements through realistic simulations of business activities. The unique structure ensures that students acquire skills and knowledge through the necessity of solving problems that engage their interest.

Approach

The book is carefully structured to **support** and encourage the reader. There are three main sections:-

Section 1: Entering the world of business - scenarios and related tasks
This section consists of a unified sequence of activities, simulating aspects of business operations. The scenarios are created out of a single story-line, describing the setting up of a business as a sole trader, and building up to a larger scale enterprise which is at the stage before it becomes a limited company. Tasks encourage the student to arrive at the key points of financial record keeping on their own, and refer them on to the appropriate parts of the Section 2 Information Bank when they need help with specific techniques and principles. This structure enables students who already have some experience or knowledge of the subject to attempt practical activities without having to read through topics they already understand.

Section 2: The information bank
This provides all the necessary information on the handling of financial documents and facilities, as well as help for students having difficulty with understanding formal texts and writing business letters. Its overall style and clear summaries make it easily accessible to students who are less skilled at interpreting such information. Students consult The Information Bank, in order to carry out the activities in Section 1, according to their needs. It does not preclude students from obtaining information by consulting works of reference, other texts, or by personal enquiry.

Section 3: Practising and developing knowledge and skills

This section allows the student to gain wider understanding and skills through short simulations and scenarios encompassing the range of variables for each of the relevant NVQ competences eg the 'paying in' procedure can be performed with cash, postal orders, cheques and credit card payments. The whole section is ordered according to the NVQ elements 20.1 to 23.1 so that lecturers can easily test students understanding, and students themselves can identify areas that they need to work further on. If students have difficulty with a particular task, they are referred back to the Section 2 Information Bank to reread the relevant summary. The tasks in this section can also be used for revision purposes.

Section 4 : Forms Bank

A selection of blank forms are provided at the end of the book, which can be photocopied for use in student activities.

Lecturers' Supplement

An extremely comprehensive lecturers' guide enables the book to be incorporated easily into a lesson plan. It provides answers for all the tasks and assignments in the text, and gives suggestions for role play, simulation and group work. The Lecturers' Supplement is available free to lecturers recommending the book as a course text.

How to use this book

The book may be used entirely as a classroom workbook, as material for directed but unsupervised learning, as follow up to formal teaching or as a mixture of the above (for the purpose, for instance, of variety).

In all cases, Section 1 of the book is the driving force of the learning process. The student learns via the experiences of Eve Adams, who leaves her job in an office and sets up as a freelance gardener. As her business develops she comes across different problems of financial record keeping, which the student is asked to solve.

Section 1

ENTERING THE WORLD
OF BUSINESS

How to use this section

1. This section is organised into sequential *units*. Complete each unit in *sequence*.

2. **Read the scenario**
    This tells you about the main stages of the development of Eve Adams' business.

3. **Read and carry out the *Tasks***
    These are tasks to develop your competence at the sorts of activity which you will require on most (if not all) courses dealing with financial record keeping.

4. If you need to, **consult *The Information Bank* (Section 2), as directed**
    This book is designed so that you only have to read information if and when you need it. If you already have the knowledge to carry out a task, you go straight ahead and do so.

5. **Carry out *Extension Tasks* which need to be done**
    The extension tasks give an opportunity for further activity on the subject matter which you have just studied. Whether you undertake any of these tasks will depend on what course you are studying, the advice of your lecturer, time available and your own interests.

Section contents

Section contents continued

Unit 1 – Eve Adams goes into business

Use of banks; savings and transferring money; deposit slips; the business and financial year.

> Eve Adams has a job in an office which she finds boring. She also finds the journey to work very stressful; she is fed up with waiting for hours in bus queues. But she is very fond of gardening, and she is often asked by friends and neighbours for advice. They will tell you that Eve can always suggest the ideal pot plant for a present.
>
> One day she meets a friend, Debora, for lunch. It is a rainy day, and the bus journey was even worse than usual. Not surprisingly, Eve says how much she wishes she could leave her job. Debora points out that there is a great need for gardeners, and that Eve could make a living from gardening. Lots of people need jobs doing. Eve is not sure that she knows enough about the subject, but Debora says that Eve would learn quickly, once she had work to do. There are lots of ways to find out about a subject: Eve can go to the library, she can buy books, she can go on courses, she can ask other people.
>
> As often happens in life, events decide things for Eve. Her employer needs to make economies, and offers Eve a redundancy payment of £2 000. Urged on by Debora, she accepts. She is now a self-employed gardener.
>
> She realises that her first task will be to make arrangements with the bank.

● Tasks

Eve starts her affairs on Monday April 5th; conveniently, this is the first day of the financial year. She goes to the town centre of Codlington to the Sheep Market branch of the Mercia Bank. She has her redundancy cheque of £2 000, and cheques for her birthday from her grandmother and parents, for £50 and £75 respectively. She also wants to deposit £40 in ten pound notes, collected for her at work when she left. The bank's sort code is 70-64-69, and they give Eve the account number 05400780.

1. *Decide what Eve will need to know about using a bank in order to start up her business. Also decide what things she will need to do during this first visit.*

   Things to consider:

   a) Eve already has a personal account. She will need a business account.

   b) Will she need a savings account, a current account, or should she open both?

   c) How will she deposit her redundancy cheque in her new account?

   Help ?

   See **Section 2: The Information Bank**

   Banking facilities: uses of banks, page 98; types of account, page 98; transfer of money, page 99.

   Final accounts: definition of 'year', page 148.

2. *Fill in the deposit slip below as though you were Eve.*

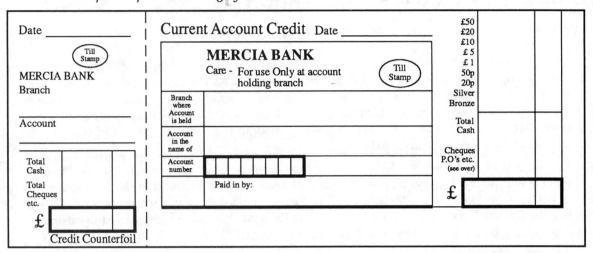

Help ?

See Section 2: The Information Bank

Bank documents: deposit slips, page 91.

● Extension tasks

E1. *Obtain leaflets from a local bank on (a) types of account available (b) services for small businesses. Also obtain a deposit slip and compare it with the example given.*

Help ?

See Section 2: The Information Bank

If you find any difficulty in reading the material, it may be useful to study *Texts: Reading and understanding,* page 248.

Unit 2 – Eve makes a quotation

Making a quotation; quotation or estimate; costing; goods and services.

Debora rings to say that at work she has met someone who has just moved to the area. His name is Henry Nicholson. He has bought a house in Hillcroft, a suburb on the other side of town. There is a large garden which has been neglected, and Mr Nicholson wants someone to clear it up and make it pleasant to sit in. Debora thought this was just the sort of work which Eve needed and has recommended her.

Eve rings up Mr Nicholson. He is not unpleasant, but he obviously likes to handle business quickly and firmly. He says that he has heard of her from Debora and that she sounds the sort of person who could handle the work. He then goes on to ask 'Can you quote me a price?'. Eve is quite flustered and says that she hadn't really thought – she's only just started in business – can she ring back a little later when she's thought about it?

As soon as Mr Nicholson rings off, Eve goes to see an old friend of the family, Tom O' Neill. Tom is a plumber and has worked for himself for years. After Eve has explained her problem with Mr Nicholson, Tom tells Eve she has come about one of the most important aspects of being in business – the handling of costing, estimates and quotations. Before he gives her advice he asks her a question: 'You have got to arrive at a price which you will name ('quote') to a customer. To decide on the price ask yourself "What have they got to pay me for?" '.

● **Tasks**

3. *Decide what price Eve will quote.*

   Things to consider:

   a) Is this a quotation or an estimate?

   b) What price should Eve quote?

   Eve notes of her costs are as follows:

   ```
   garden needs digging - 2 days;
   needs fertiliser (4 bags mulch and mix, £6.15 a
                     bag), 2 bags bone meal @ £2.75;
   1 bag lawn feed and weed (£3.23);
   1 day to apply this; hedge cutting, tree pruning,
   lawn mowing, plant roses - 1 day; roses (6 plants,
                                            £4.20);
   bedding plants (lobelia 5 strips, £2.00 per strip;
   begonias (10 plants, £1.60 per plant;
   french marigolds - 5 strips, £1.90 per strip;
   ```

```
    marguerites - 5 plants, £1.70 per plant);
-----------------------------------------------------------------
    1 day to put in plants;
-----------------------------------------------------------------
    travel bus 65p each way;
-----------------------------------------------------------------
    start 8-30 finish 4-30 - one hour for lunch.
-----------------------------------------------------------------
```

Help ?

*See **Section 2: The Information Bank***

Quotations – the process, page 227; *costing*, page 230.

● Extension tasks

E2. *As Eve develops her business, what sorts of cost will she have?*

Unit 3 – Eve uses her cheque book

How to fill in a cheque; using a cheque to obtain cash; cheque guarantee cards.

Eve goes to do the work. It progresses well but there are a few unforeseen problems. One of the shrubs she is supposed to remove is deeply rooted and takes much longer than expected. The ground is hard after a long dry spell and she has to buy a pick. She also has to replace a fork which her family have had for years, which finally falls apart.

At the end of the week, Mr Nicholson is pleased though, and hands her the fee of £250 in cash saying 'I thought you'd prefer cash to a cheque – oh, and keep the change!' Eve is heartened to receive the money, as it is the first she has earned in her new life, and takes her leave. She calls in at her bank, and puts half the money into her business account, keeping the rest for her personal expenses. Now she can go to Sainsbury's and buy things for the meal she's going to give Debora to celebrate.

● Tasks

4. On April 23rd Eve goes into Awl and Mallet, Codlington's leading hardware shop. She buys her new fork costing £20.66 and and edging knife for £18.45. *Fill in the cheque below which Eve uses to make her purchases.*

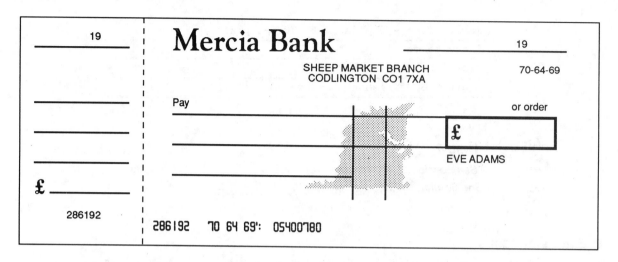

Help ?

See Section 2: The Information Bank

Bank documents: how to fill in a cheque correctly, page 84.

5.   The hardware store, Awl and Mallet, require Eve's cheque to be supported by a cheque guarantee card (see below). *What does the assistant need to do?*

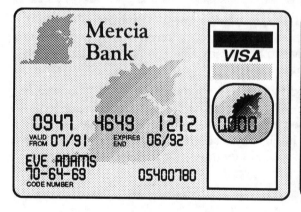

Help ?

See Section 2: The Information Bank

Cheque guarantee cards, page 89.

6. *Using a copy of the document on page 5, deposit Eve's cash at her bank, after she has been paid.*

● Extension tasks

E3. Eve needs to get £20 out of the bank to pay for her travel, and for something for lunch. She forgets to do this until she breaks off for lunch. The only bank which is nearby is a branch of the Wessex and Cornwall Bank; this has no cash dispenser. *Using a copy of the cheque on page 8, do whatever Eve has to do.*

Help ?

See Section 2: The Information Bank

Cheques: using a cheque to obtain cash, page 85.

Unit 4 – Eve begins to set up her books

Basic approach to record keeping; two column accounts; balancing an account.

When the friends meet for the meal, Debora reminds Eve that at school she got on well with Lucy Luca, whose parents run the Italian restaurant in Orchard Street. For a while Eve and Lucy were quite close, because they both used to be in the school netball team, but they have rather lost contact. Debora points out that Lucy went into accountancy, and must now be well advanced in her training. Wouldn't it be an idea to meet up with her and ask her advice about money matters?

Eve rings Lucy, who is delighted to hear from her. Lucy says she will be glad to give Eve free advice until the business begins to thrive – then she can become a client!

Lucy explains that at present she is very busy – her final exams are coming up. However, she tells Eve that she should start to set up her accounts. You will find the main points of her comments in *The Information Bank* reference for Task 7 below. Lucy also gives Eve two things to do – these are to be found in Task 8 and Task E4 below.

● Tasks

7. *Summarise Lucy's advice.*

Help ?

See Section 2: The Information Bank

Accounts: nature of accounts, page 70, *bank accounts,* page 71.

8. On different sheets of paper (one for cash dealings, and one for cheques), record the following information which Eve notes down during the next week. Use a two column system. Total the columns.

> May 3 sent off cheque for £16.60 for plants;
> ---
> took bus to gardening job (Mr West)
> ---
> return fare £1.60;
> ---
> May 4 bought 2 bags of lawn seed – £6.46 in cash;
> ---
> May 5 job in Eastcote (Mrs Harris) bus fare £1.60;
> ---
> May 6 Mrs Harris called to pay £30 cash;
> ---
> cheque for £20 arrived from Mr West;
> ---
> bought fertiliser (£13.54) – paid by cheque.
> ---

Help ?

See Section 2: The Information Bank

Accounts: basic approach to record keeping, page 74.

● **Extension tasks**

E4. *Alter your accounts to include balancing them.*

Help ?

See Section 2: The Information Bank

Accounts: balancing, page 77.

Unit 5 – Eve makes some payments

Bank giro credit transfer; paying in and withdrawing money; direct debit.

Eve finds that there is quite a lot of work for her. Codlington, the town where she lives, is prosperous, as several companies have relocated there, and one large computer company, Azure, has set up a factory and research centre in the area. Some of Eve's work comes through personal recommendation, some from advertising, both on newsagents' notice boards, and in the local paper.

Some people pay in cash, which means that Eve can have largish sums of money in her bag. One day, while depositing cash at her bank, she mentions to the clerk, John Dewey, that it makes her very uneasy to carry so much money about. He suggests that she should use the bank giro system to deposit money at a bank which is more convenient for her.

That evening, Lucy rings. She is still not able to spend any time on Eve's accounts, but has thought of one thing. As Eve is self-employed, she will not receive sick pay if she is ill. However, there are schemes run by insurance companies to safeguard against such times. Eve follows up the suggestion, decides on a policy and is asked to pay by direct debit.

● Tasks

9. Eve has a job on the far side of town. She is paid in cash and uses the bank giro system to deposit her money. *Fill in the form below accordingly.*

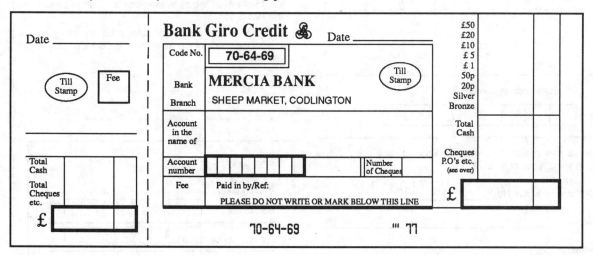

Details:

Same as previously. Eve deposits £125 in cash (five £20, two £10, one £5).

Help ?

See Section 2: The Information Bank

Bank documents: bank giro, page 79.

Banking facilities, paying in and withdrawing money, page 100.

10. *Fill in this direct debiting mandate for Eve's insurance policy, according to the following details:*

CATHEDRAL LIFE INSURANCE PLC
INSTRUCTIONS TO YOUR BANK TO PAY DIRECT DEBITS

Please complete parts 1 to 5 to instruct your bank to make payments directly from your account. <u>Then send the form to your bank.</u>

Originator's Identification Number

1	8	6	4	2	7

To The Manager,

Bank,

4 Please write Customer Account No. in box below

M	S	V	G	-	1	0	3	-	1

1 Please write the full postal address of your bank branch in the box above.

2 Name of Account Holder

5 Your instructions to the bank, and signature

* I instruct you to pay direct debits from my account at the request of Cathedral Life Insurance plc

* The amounts are variable and may be debited on various dates

* I understand that Cathedral Life Insurance plc may change the amounts and dates only after giving me prior notice.

* I will inform the bank in writing if I wish to cancel this instruction.

* I understand that if any direct debit is paid which breaks the terms of this Instruction, the bank will make a refund.

Signature(s) ....

Date ....

3 Bank account number

Banks may refuse to accept instructions to pay direct debits from some types of account.

Customer Account No.   MSVG 103 1

Name

Address

To New Policies Division
Cathedral Life Insurance plc
Spire House
The Close
Undercroft
UC2 4EL

FOR BANK USE ONLY

Branch title ....

Sort Code   ☐☐ - ☐☐ - ☐☐

A/c no.   ☐☐☐☐☐☐☐☐

A/c name ....

(Maximum 18 characters)

Direct debits in respect of our customer's Instruction under the reference number quoted should be made out as above.

For .... Bank

Manager .... Date ....

After completion the bank branch should detach the lower part of the form and return it to Cathedral Life Insurance plc.

Help ?
See Section 2: The Information Bank
Bank documents: direct debit, page 92.

● **Extension tasks**

E5. *List the options which Eve has for obtaining cash other than at her own bank. Which will be the most convenient method? Enquire at your local bank what practical obstacles there are to obtaining cash. When are banks and cash dispensers open? Take especial note of what sort of identification is required.*

Unit 6 – Eve has some problems with cheques

Validity of cheques; postal orders.

During the first few weeks Eve has to handle quite a few cheques. Not only does she have to pay for tools and materials; more importantly, she has to accept cheques in payment for her work. She finds that this is less simple than it might seem. In particular, she must examine carefully any cheque which she is offered. If she doesn't do this, she may well not get paid. It is surprising how many people make errors when filling in a cheque; and occasionally, of course, there are those who try to pass off cheques which are not valid. Eve soon learns, too, that it is wise to ask for a cheque to be supported by a cheque guarantee card, whenever possible.

● **Tasks**

11. Below are some of the cheques which Eve has been offered. *Examine them carefully, and decide whether Eve should accept them or not.*

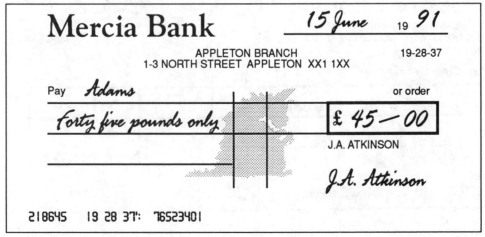

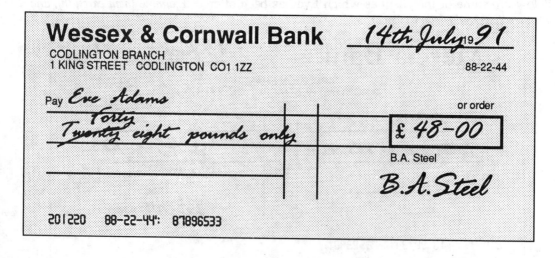

12. *(a)* *Which of the cheque guarantee cards (if any) should Eve accept in support of the cheque below?*

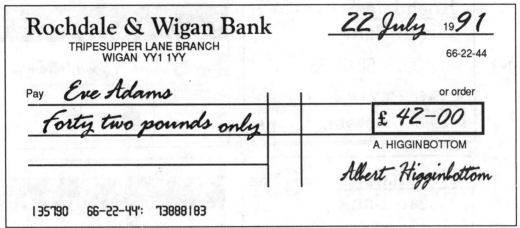

Rochdale & Wigan Bank

TRIPESUPPER LANE BRANCH
WIGAN YY1 1YY

22 July 19**91**

66-22-44

Pay *Eve Adams*　　　　　　　　　　　　　　　or order

Forty two pounds only　　　£ 42-00

A. HIGGINBOTTOM

Albert Higginbottom

135790　66-22-44⁚　73888183

Front of cheque ⟋↗　　　　　　　　　　　　Back of cheque ⟍↘

7733 5012 33

Card 1

Rochdale & Wigan Bank

CHEQUE
GUARANTEE
CARD

7733 5012 33

VALID FROM 05/90　EXPIRES END 04/91

A. HIGGINBOTTOM

66-22-44　73888183

CODE NUMBER

SIGNATURE *Albert Higginbottom*

Please keep this Cheque card in the wallet provided. If this card is found please hand it to a branch of the Mercia Bank plc.

£50

Card 2

Card 3

(b) Here is another cheque which was presented to Eve earlier in the year; card 1 was offered to support it. *Should Eve have accepted it?*

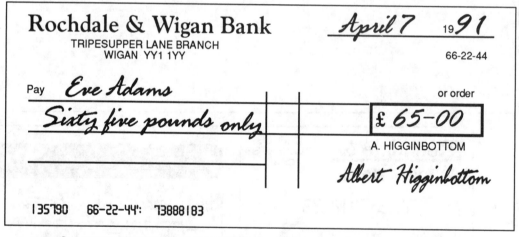

Help ?

*See **Section 2: The Information Bank***

Bank documents: cheques, page 83.

● **Extension tasks**

E6. Here are two more cheques which Eve is offered. *What special features are there? Should she accept them?*

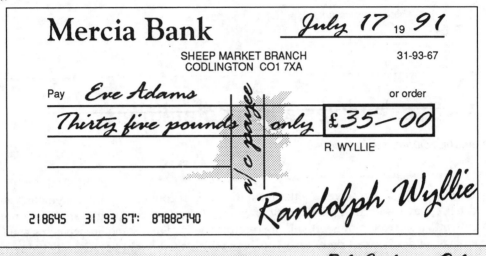

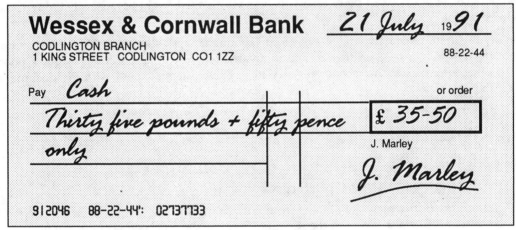

Help ?

*See **Section 2: The Information Bank***

Bank documents: crossing of cheques, page 86.

E7. Mrs Winterton is an old lady who can no longer manage the heavier work in her garden. She is also rather old fashioned, and sends Eve a postal order with the details:

payee: Eve Adams
Office to be paid at: Codlington

She also crosses it for safety in the post.

What should Eve do?

Help ?
See Section 2: The Information Bank
Methods of payment: postal orders, page 201.

Unit 7 – Eve receives a bank statement

Bank statements; clearance of cheques.

About once a month Eve receives a letter from the bank: it contains a bank statement. As Lucy has told her to save everything, until they have set up Eve's accounting system, Eve puts the statements into a drawer, along with all the receipts she is given, some French coins she found in her change, and a book of petty cash vouchers which she bought because she thought they might be useful.

One day it is raining heavily, and she has to postpone the work she was going to do that day. So she decides to sort out her drawer, and to do anything which needs doing. A quick phone call to Lucy informs her that she should 'try to reconcile the statement with the documents' which she has.

● Tasks

13. Given below are:

    ❏ the first page of Eve's second bank statement; and

    ❏ the information which she obtains from going through her cheque book and deposit slip counterfoils She also refers to the 'Cheque' account she has been keeping at Lucy's suggestion (Unit 4), together with a few notes she has made.

    Find out if Eve's records and the bank statement agree. Then list and explain any differences.

    ❏ **Eve's notes:**

        Cheque counterfoils

Date	Description	Cheque no.	Amount
2 May	plants	no 724350	48.70
7 May	living expenses	724351	100.00
11 May	hoe	724352	15.50
21 May	living expenses	724353	100.00
Total spent			264.20

```
Deposit slips
--------------------------------------------------------------
6 May       Mrs Fox (£30); Mr Otter (£20); £50.00
--------------------------------------------------------------
9 May       Mr Stanton (paid in at Eastcote) £77.00
--------------------------------------------------------------
10 May      Mr Edens £140.00
--------------------------------------------------------------
27 May      Mrs Fox (37.50);
--------------------------------------------------------------
            Bluebird Minimarket (£150); 187.50
--------------------------------------------------------------
Total deposits £454.50
--------------------------------------------------------------
Balance at end of April was £2394
--------------------------------------------------------------
Should now be 2394 + 454.50 - 264.20 = £2584.30
--------------------------------------------------------------
```

❐ **The bank statement:**

	IN ACCOUNT WITH
	BANK Mercia
TITLE OF ACCOUNT Eve Adams	**BRANCH** Sheep Market, Codlington
ACCOUNT NUMBER 05400780	STATEMENT NUMBER 2

	DATE	PARTICULARS	PAYMENTS	RECEIPTS	BALANCE
	1 May	Opening balance			2394.00
	2 May	724350	48.70		2345.30
	4 May	Cathedral DD	37.50		2307.80
	6 May	Sundry Credit		50.00	2357.80
	7 May	724351	100.00		2257.80
	9 May	BGC		77.00	2334.80
	10 May	A. Edens		140.00	2474.80
	11 May	724352	15.50		2459.30
	16 May	Charges	10.00		2449.30
	21 May	724353	100.00		2349.30
	27 May	Sundry Credit		187.50	2356.80

Help ?

See Section 2: The Information Bank

Bank documents: bank statements, page 81.

● Extension tasks

E8. One Monday Eve goes to the bank to take out some money. The clerk who serves her says that he is sorry, but Eve cannot draw any money out, as she is well above her overdraft limit. Eve is surprised. Last week she had about £300 in the account. It is true that she had to pay a supplier, for a new job she is taking on. But she has been also been paid by a customer, so that what she has laid out should easily be covered. John Dewey comes over to help, and says it must be a problem of clearance. They arrange for Eve to have the cash she wants, but she feels that she needs to get clear why the problem arose.

In order to map out what has happened, Eve first notes down the following information:

```
On Thursday 28th she had £200 in her account.
-------------------------------------------------------
   On the Friday she took out £100 in cash, but put in
   a cheque for £200.
-------------------------------------------------------
   She signed a cheque on Wednesday for £500, which she
-------------------------------------------------------
   knows was paid in on the same day.
-------------------------------------------------------
```

She then draws up this information as it would appear on a bank statement. *Can you explain the source of the difficulty?*

Help ?

See Section 2: The Information Bank

Banking facilities: clearance of cheques, page 100.

Unit 8 – Eve makes a quotation for a contract

Giving a quotation; documents used in more formal business situations.

So far Eve's work has come on a fairly informal basis. Arrangements could be made and agreed on the phone, and payments made in cash, by cheque (or even postal order!) as soon as the work was completed.

However, once any business takes on work which is more complex, involves large outlay on both sides, or is undertaken for an organisation rather than an individual, a more formal system of negotiating and handling the arrangements is needed. Eve now finds that she has to begin to arrange her affairs in this way.

cont/...

You will remember that her first job was for Henry Nicholson. He regularly plays golf with Matthew Arnold, the Headmaster of Longmeadow School, a well known local public school. One day Eve receives the following letter:

LONGMEADOW SCHOOL

Phone:
Longmeadow
0936 4124

Headmaster:
Matthew Arnold
(MA Oxon)

2 May 1991

Dear Miss Adams,

You have been recommended to me by Henry Nicholson as the person who might be suitable to undertake work at this school.

After fifty-three years of excellent service our resident gardener, Mr Hodge, has finally decided to retire. He will be leaving the district so as to live near his daughter on the coast.

In view of the considerable economic pressures which now obtain, the Governors have decided not to appoint another full-time gardener, but instead to have the work carried out on a contract basis. This will also release accommodation for a new house master.

The Governors feel also that the contracts should for the time being run for the period of one term only. Their reasoning is that the nature and amount of work to be done will fluctuate seasonally. It also seems sensible for there to be a trial period, during which both sides can discover whether the arrangement is satisfactory.

I would therefore be grateful if you could let me have a quotation for undertaking the work for the Autumn Term (ie the period 1 September – 31 December) in time for the Governors' meeting on the 24th of this month.

If you care to ring my secretary, Mrs Gregg, she will arrange for Mr Hodge to show you the nature of our requirements.

Yours sincerely,

Matthew Arnold

Matthew Arnold
(Headmaster)

This is a letter of enquiry initiating the formal process of issuing quotations, receiving orders and issuing invoices.

● Tasks

14. Eve visits the school and makes an assessment of the work. Her notes are as follows:

```
Work needed:
---------------------------------------------------------
   ---------------------------------------------------------
   Regular: mow lawns and playing fields (1/2 day
   ---------------------------------------------------------
   fortnightly); hedge cutting 1/2 day monthly; flower
   ---------------------------------------------------------
   bed weeding and maintenance (1/2 day weekly); cut
   ---------------------------------------------------------
   and prepare herbs for kitchen (1/2 day fortnightly)
   ---------------------------------------------------------

   Projects: bedding plants (11/2 days); re-seeding
   ---------------------------------------------------------
   pitch 7, 3 days; herb garden re-design and replant
   ---------------------------------------------------------
   6 days; fruit picking (3 day); fruit trees
   ---------------------------------------------------------
   maintenance (1 day); plant tree windbreak (playing
   ---------------------------------------------------------
   fields) 3 days
   ---------------------------------------------------------

   Costs: bedding plants (100 approx @ average £1.80);
   ---------------------------------------------------------
   grass seed 10kg - £47; herbs (40 @ average £2);
   ---------------------------------------------------------
   trees (20 @ average £25 apiece)
   ---------------------------------------------------------
   Travel: 1 gallon a day (say £2.50)
   ---------------------------------------------------------
   Labour: £30 a day
   ---------------------------------------------------------
```

Sketch out the quotation that Eve sends to Mr Arnold.

Help ?

See Section 2: The Information Bank

Quotations: preparing a quotation, page 234.

Invoices: function of documents, page 164.

(Ignore any information about discount or terms of business.)

15. *Write a suitable covering letter.*

Help ?

See Section 2: The Information Bank

Letters, page 195.

Quotations: covering letter, page 237.

● Extension tasks

E9. *Decide which of the documents listed in* The Information Bank *entry on* Invoices, *page 164, will be necessary in this transaction.*

Unit 9 – Eve receives an order

Ordering goods; order forms; acknowledgement of order.

The Governors decide to give Eve the contract for the Autumn Term. They ask Eve not to provide herbs at this point, as they are considering making some major changes to the school grounds and garden in the Spring Term.

As far as the contract with Eve is concerned, the school handles its accounts in two ways. Services will be paid for in one payment on satisfactory completion of the work. The invoice should also include agreed expenses, in this case travel. The goods that Eve needs for the job are to be ordered by means of an order form. In this case a discount is not expected. No VAT will be chargeable, as Eve is not registered.

Mr Arnold writes to Eve to set matters in motion.

● Tasks

16. *Draw up an order form for the goods which Eve will supply.*

Help ?

See Section 2: The Information Bank

Orders: ordering goods, page 211; order form, page 212.

17. *Write a covering letter, formally asking Eve to undertake the work according to the agreed conditions.*

● Extension tasks

E10. As this is her first big contract, Eve decides to make an acknowledgement of order. *Prepare the document you think she should send.*

Help ?

See Section 2: The Information Bank

Orders: acknowledgement of order, page 213.

Unit 10 – Eve issues her invoice

Invoices; remittance advice.

> Eve carries out the work. There are no problems, and the school renews the contract. But first Eve must request payment.

● Tasks

18. *Draw up an invoice for the goods which Eve has supplied. (Use the appropriate blank form from the selection in* The Forms Bank, *page 359.)*

Help ?

See Section 2: The Information Bank

Invoices, page 161.

19. *Draw up an invoice for the services which Eve has supplied. (Use the appropriate blank form from the selection in* The Forms Bank, *page 359 or devise your own document.)*

20. The school is prompt in payment. *Draw up a remittance advice itemising both aspects of the contract.* (Use the appropriate blank form from the selection in The Forms Bank, *page 359.)*

Help ?

See Section 2: The Information Bank

Invoices: remittance advice, page 172.

21. *Make out a cheque to Eve for the amount due.*

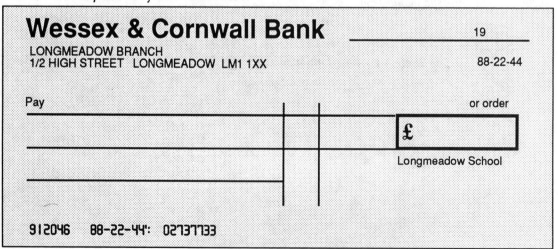

● **Extension tasks**

E11. *Make out the documents (taken from* The Forms Bank, *page 359) which are exchanged for Eve's contract for the Spring Term.* Eve's notes are as given below. On this occasion there are no amendments.

```
mow lawns and playing fields (1/2 day fortnightly);
hedge cutting 1/2 day monthly; flower bed weeding
and maintenance; cut and prepare herbs for kitchen
(1/2 day fortnightly)

Projects: plant annuals (3 days); re-seeding pitch
4; cut down dangerous tree (1/2 day); re-design and
plant herb garden (6 days)

Transport
Materials: various fertilisers (£45); annual plants
(40 @ £2.25); grass seed (10kg £47); herbs
(30 approx @ £5 average)
```

Help ?

See Section 2: The Information Bank

Invoices: similarities between documents, page 164; *invoice – summary,* page 174.

Unit 11 – Eve learns more about business accounts

Personal and business expenses; financial obligations of the self-employed.

Soon after Eve is approached by Longmeadow School, Lucy finishes her examinations. She arranges to meet Eve and go over the process of setting up Eve's accounts. She is a little amazed by Eve's assortment of papers but congratulates her on what she has done so far. She begins by making various points as follows.

❒   Eve needs first to realise that she now has a split personality. One part of her is personal – the real Eve whom everyone knows. The other part of her exists when she is carrying out her business. This will become important when dealing with income tax and VAT. She must separate out her business records from her personal finances.

cont/…

- ❏ She is now self-employed, so she will pay tax under a different scheme (Schedule D) from the one which applied when she was in her job.

- ❏ She will still need to pay National Insurance contributions, but she will now pay in the way which applies to the self-employed.

- ❏ At present Eve is what is called a sole trader. This is in contrast to other forms of business structure, such as partnerships and companies, which are separately legally constituted and regulated.

- ❏ When she comes to draw up her accounts for tax and other purposes, Eve will need to distinguish (a) her income from (b) her expenses.

  She can only count as expenses money laid out in pursuit of her business.

- ❏ Eve is right to have kept all her receipts as these are evidence of her expenses. But she must now separate out personal and business expenses.

- ❏ Eve asks about VAT. Lucy advises that she need not worry about this at present.

● Tasks

22. Among the things in Eve's drawer are:
    - ❏ a cheque for her birthday from Aunt Agatha;
    - ❏ a cheque, a fee from St Aidan's School, Eastcote;
    - ❏ some French coins;
    - ❏ a letter from Mrs Winterton thanking Eve;
    - ❏ a copy of the quotation for Longmeadow school;
    - ❏ some receipts from Sainsbury's;
    - ❏ a £20 note; the receipt for her garden fork;
    - ❏ her latest electricity bill;
    - ❏ a receipt for books from Cullions, including Undershaft and Fields' classic work.

    Which of these are personal and which go to her business file?

23. *Fill in the direct debiting mandate form on the opposite page to enable Eve to pay Class 2 National Insurance contributions.*

Help ?

See Section 2: The Information Bank

Wages and salaries: the self-employed, page 272.

Bank documents: direct debit, page 92.

Department of Social Security

INSTRUCTIONS TO YOUR BANK TO PAY DIRECT DEBITS

Please complete parts 1 to 5 to instruct your bank to make payments directly from your account. <u>Then send the form to your bank.</u>

To The Manager,						
			Bank,			

1 Please write the full postal address of your bank branch in the box above.

2 Name of Account Holder

_____

3 Bank account number

Originator's Identification Number

1	9	2	8	7	6

4 Please write Customer Account No. in box below

C	O	X	S	-	2	6	2	-	4

5 Your instructions to the bank, and signature

* I instruct you to pay direct debits from my account at the request of the Department of Social Security

* The amounts are variable and may be debited on various dates

* I understand that the Department of Social Security may change the amounts and dates only after giving me prior notice.

* I will inform the bank in writing if I wish to cancel this instruction.

* I understand that if any direct debit is paid which breaks the terms of this Instruction, the bank will make a refund.

Signature(s) ....

Date ....

Banks may refuse to accept instructions to pay direct debits from some types of account.

Customer Account No.   *COXS-262-4*

Name _____

Address _____

_____

To	Contributions Section
	Department of Social Security
	Workhouse Lane
	Codlington
	CO2 2XX

After completion the bank branch should detach the lower part of the form and return it to Department of Social Security.

FOR BANK USE ONLY

Branch title ....

Sort Code ☐☐ - ☐☐ - ☐☐

A/c no. ☐☐☐☐☐☐☐☐

A/c name

....

(Maximum 18 characters)

Direct debits in respect of our customer's Instruction under the reference number quoted should be made out as above.

_____

For .... Bank

Manager .... Date ....

● Extension tasks

E12. *Obtain and study leaflets from your local Inland Revenue and DSS (National Insurance) offices explaining*

   a)   *Schedule D taxation*

   b)   *NI contributions for the self-employed.*

E13. *Find out from a suitable source the main differences between*

   a)   *sole traders*

   b)   *partnerships and*

   c)   *limited companies.*

E14. *Make a list of things on which Eve might spend money. Then classify them as*

   a)   *personal expenses*

   b)   *expenses laid out solely in the pursuit of her business*

   c)   *expenses which are split between personal and business expenditure.*

Unit 12 – Eve's first cash book

Purpose and use of the analysed cash book.

> The discussion of Eve's accounts continues. Lucy advises that, in Eve's position, the best formal way to keep her accounts is probably to use an analysed cash book.
>
> Lucy says that they will summarise Eve's trading so far in a simple statement of her earnings and expenses for that period at the end of the tax year. They will therefore only enter her most recent transactions. They begin by dealing with the first week in June.

● Tasks

24.   *Using the details given, make the first entries in Eve's cash book opposite. Then total and balance the columns.*

Eve gives details for the week Monday to Friday, June 1–5 inclusive. On Monday (1 June) she was paid £10 for cutting lawns and hedges; her travel cost £2.50. On Tuesday she had a busy day, and had to travel to two jobs (cost £3.10). She was paid by cheque for a replanting job (£45). Another lawn and hedge job brought in £20 cash. Before doing the first job she fetched the plants (cost £15.60), and called in at Awl and Mallet to get some Number 6 secateurs (cost £28.95). They were for a job the next day. She had been asked by Ashbury's the big department store to look after all their store plants. They paid her £370 by cheque – but she nearly didn't have enough change for her bus fare of £1.80. Thursday and Friday were spent at Mrs Fox's. She wanted the garden of her new house landscaping, and Eve said it should have a treatment of fertiliser at the same time. She got a cheque for £65 for the work, and laid out £42 on fertiliser, to be paid for when she finishes the work. Travel was £2.50 a day. At the start of the week she had no cash in hand, but her bank balance was as shown on her statement (Unit 7).

Debit

Date	Details	Cash	Bank	Lawns & hedges	Replanting	Land-scaping

Left-hand side (above)

Right-hand side (below)

Credit

Date	Details	Cash	Bank	Plants	Fertiliser	Equip-ment	Expenses

Help ?

See Section 2: The Information Bank

Cash book: analysed cash book, page 118.

Extension tasks

E15. *Consult the remaining part of the entry in the Information Bank in order to be able to state in what respects Eve's cash book will differ from the type which would be used in a larger organisation.*

Help ?
See Section 2: The Information Bank
Cash book, page 115.

Unit 13 – Eve checks her bank statement

Cash book: bank reconciliation statement.

Eve's long first encounter with formal record keeping is not yet over. Lucy explains that there is one more procedure to learn. This is the reconciliation of the cash book with bank statements. Fortunately for Eve, this turns out to be a very profitable exercise.

● **Tasks**

25. *Reconcile Eve's first cash book entry with the following extract from her June bank statement.*

				IN ACCOUNT WITH	
			BANK	Mercia	
TITLE OF ACCOUNT Eve Adams			**BRANCH**	Sheep Market, Codlington	
ACCOUNT NUMBER 05400780			STATEMENT NUMBER	3	

	DATE	PARTICULARS	PAYMENTS	RECEIPTS	BALANCE
	1 May	Opening balance			2394.00
	2 May	724350	48.70		2345.30
	4 May	Cathedral DD	37.50		2307.80
	6 May	Sundry Credit		50.00	2357.80
	7 May	724351	100.00		2257.80
	9 May	BGC		77.00	2334.80
	10 May	A. Edens		140.00	2474.80
	11 May	724352	15.50		2459.30
	16 May	Charges	10.00		2449.30
	21 May	724353	100.00		2349.30
	27 May	Sundry Credit		187.50	2356.80

Help ?
See Section 2: The Information Bank
Bank documents: bank statements, page 81.
Cash book: bank reconciliation statement, page 122.

● **Extension tasks**

E16. *Eve decides that, even though she has no one to answer to, she needs to keep a written note of any problems which arise. Draw up her bank reconciliation statement for this accounting period.*

(Note that a period of one week is taken to make the task more manageable. Eve would normally draw up such a statement for the whole month covered by the bank statement).

Unit 14 – Eve sets up a market stall

Standing orders; retail trading; giving change; end of day procedures.

While she was still in paid work, Eve had often thought how nice it would be to run a flower shop. One day she attends a broadcast of the BBC Gardeners' Question Time programme. Afterwards Eve gets talking to Henry Meadows, the longest serving member of the panel. He is enthusiastic about her new career, but advises her against trying to run a flower shop at this stage. He points out that cut flowers are highly perishable, and are very much a luxury. Eve's small savings could not stand a loss through bad weather, or a lack of sales. Also a shop will have many overheads – rent, electricity, etc. But he goes on to suggest that pot plants could be a good idea, because they will keep indefinitely with a little care. And perhaps she could try a market stall? Then she'd only have to pay rent one day a week. Eve thinks this could be a good idea as the stalls in Sheep Market and Pippin Lane on a Saturday are always very busy.

Eve goes along to the local Council Offices, and finds that a stall will be available very shortly. Since it is Council policy to encourage new businesses and especially those started by young people and by women, she will be given a high priority. The rent will be payable monthly, and they will require her to make out a Standing Order to cover this.

The stall soon becomes available. As Eve has lived in the town all her life, and as she herself was so recently a customer of similar plant stalls, she has a good sense of what will sell.

● **Tasks**

26. *Make out the Standing Order using the following details:* Eve should write to the Manager of her bank. She wants a standing order to be arranged so that she can pay Codlington Borough Council, whose account number is 17453920. The Council have given her the reference MS/1328E. The payment should take place on the 1st of every month, starting on August 1st. The money is to come from her business account, number 05400780. The Council bank with the Wessex and Cornwall Bank, Codlington branch, (sort code 88-22-44). *(Use the appropriate blank form from the selection in* The Forms Bank, *page 359.)*

Help ?

See Section 2: The Information Bank

Bank documents: standing orders, page 94.

27. The running of the stall requires Eve to become quite skilful at giving change. *In the following transactions*

1) *what change should she give, and*

2) *what is the cash analysis (breakdown into note and coin values) which will involve the least number of coins?*

Sale number	Price of goods	Total due	Amount tendered by customer	Change due	Analysis of change
1	£3.00		£10		
	£2.50				
2	£8.10		£20		
	£4.40				
	£1.25				
3	£1.10		£5		
	£0.87				
4	£0.45		£50		
	£0.97				

Help ?

See Section 2: The Information Bank

Methods of payment: giving change, page 204; end of day procedures, page 205.

● **Extension tasks**

E17. *What procedure could Eve adopt for dealing with her money at the end of the day?*

(Note: she does not have an electric till, and so has no till roll.)

Help ?

See Section 2: The Information Bank

Methods of payment: end of day procedures, page 205.

Unit 15 – Eve is offered a customer account

Customer accounts; statement of account; credit notes; ledger cards; letters making and answering a complaint.

Eve soon realises that she is going to need regular supplies for her stall, though it is not clear exactly what the demand will be. She therefore takes a trip to Hoxted Horticulture, a very large garden centre about fifteen miles from Codlington. They have an enormous stock of plants of all types – you can even buy quite large trees.

There she explains her position, and is offered a customer account, subject to obtaining a banker's reference. She does so.

● Tasks

28. Eve's purchases in the first month are as follows:

Aug 4 bedding plants £24; Aug 6 fertilisers £42.50; Aug 10 trees £35.50; Aug 12 bedding plants £16; Aug 17 rose bushes £8.50; Aug 22 4 young trees £80 (£20 each) – one damaged and returned with comment on that delivery note; Aug 24 bedding plants £28.50; Aug 26 small tools £23.55

At the end of the month she receives the statement given below. *Check the statement to see if it is correct.*

She has received invoices for all the above. The Hoxted reference numbers are CT112/01 forward.

HOXTED HORTICULTURE ·

LITTLE ACRE, HOXTED

Credit limit: £300

Account no: CT 112
Date: 31 August 1991
Terms: 30 days

STATEMENT OF ACCOUNT

Date	Reference	Description	Debit	Credit	Balance
Aug 4	CT112/01	bedding plants	24.00		24.00 DR
Aug 6	CT112/02	fertilisers	42.50		66.50 DR
Aug 10	CT112/03	trees	35.50		102.00 DR
Aug 12	CT112/04	bedding plants	16.00		118.00 DR
Aug 17	CT112/05	rose bushes	85.00		203.00 DR
Aug 22	CT112/06	young trees	80.00		283.00 DR
Aug 24	CT112/07	bedding plants	28.50		311.50 DR
Aug 26	CT112/08	small tools	23.55		335.50 DR
			Amount now due		335.50 DR

Please note you have exceeded your credit limit. Failure to remain within the agreed limit will oblige us to withdraw this facility

29. *Make out a cheque (copy the one on page 8) for what is owed and write Eve's letter to Hoxted Horticulture.*

Help ?

See Section 2: The Information Bank

Invoices: customer accounts, page 166; *statements of account,* page 167; *credit notes,* page 170.

Complaints, page 126.

● Extension tasks

E18. *Write Hoxted's reply, enclosing a credit note. (Use the appropriate blank document from the selection in* The Forms Bank, *page 359.)*

Help ?

See Section 2: The Information Bank

Complaints, page 126. (You are advised to scan this entry first, to identify which sections are relevant to your task.)

E19. *Make out the credit note.*

Help ?

See Section 2: The Information Bank

Invoices: credit notes, page 170.

E20. *Hoxted Horticulture operate a ledger card system. Enter Eve's transactions for the next month on the blank card below.*

HOXTED HORTICULTURE

CUSTOMER ACCOUNT CARD

NAME: ....

CREDIT LIMIT: ....

Date	Details	Ref number	Debit	Credit	Balance

She bought fertiliser on the 6th (55.50), 8th (15.50) and 26th (15.50). She also bought plants on the 21st (22.00).

Help ?
See Section 2: The Information Bank
Invoices: ledger cards, page 169.

Unit 16 – Eve organises her day

Organising your work.

> Eve finds that life is now getting rather hectic. She has both her gardening work to do, the stall on Saturdays, and also organising the collection or delivery of supplies. She is doing well financially, but she has never worked so hard – she'd thought that being your own boss would mean that you could do as you liked with your time.
>
> She decides that she must in future plan her tasks and timetable more carefully.

● Tasks

30. *Here are Eve's tasks for one Tuesday. Plan out her day.*

    She has two jobs to do. Mr Bridge (who lives in the suburb of Appleton) will take four hours, and Mr Towers two. Mr Towers lives in another suburb, Eastcote. Mr Bridge will be at home all day, but Mr Towers can only be around in the morning. She has to get to Awl and Mallet back in the centre of Codlington for an edging tool before 1pm, as it is early closing day. She will also want to go to the bank near Mr Bridge's house – he is giving her a cheque for materials. She leaves the house at 9.00. Lunch is variable – she often just breaks for half an hour. She likes to get home between 5 and 7. For convenience assume that any journey around Codlington will take half an hour.

Help ?
See Section 2: The Information Bank
Work methods: organising your work, page 293.

● Extension tasks

E21. *Using the following information, plan the morning of Barbara Murray, who works in the offices of a large stationery supplier.*

    £20 worth of first class stamps to be obtained from the post office. A
    petty cash voucher from Beth Wilson to be dealt with. Get out price lists
    to obtain information needed for a quotation. There is a note from Barbara's

boss that she wants the last statement for customer account WES345: Mr J.A.
Wesley. A petty cash voucher authorised by Mrs Sloane to be paid out to Mr
Greenway. Barbara promised yesterday to ring Mrs Field at Western Printshop
at 10.30 today to give a quotation. A petty cash voucher dealt with at the
last moment yesterday to be entered into the petty cash book. The quotation
for Mrs Field needs to come from her colleague, Beth Wilson. There are three
letters waiting on the desk which came in this morning's post. There is a
letter to hand to Beth, who works in the next office.

Unit 17 – Eve takes on an assistant

Wages: fixed wages; hourly rate; commission. Taxation and statutory deductions (overview).

It is clear that, even with her new-found organisation, Eve cannot handle all the work herself. She therefore advertises for someone to help part-time. One of the applicants is a young man called Dean Cuffey. He encloses a testimonial from the Head Teacher of his old school. Eve is interested to find that this was her own old school, and that she remembers the Head, Miss Beale very well. She decides to give him a try. The experiment is a success. Dean is a lively person and gets on well with the customers.

Eve soon finds that she can employ Dean more frequently. There is often a day when she needs help with moving things, or breaking up heavy ground.

Dean takes to the work and one day he comes to Eve with an idea. There is always a problem deciding how many cut flowers to buy in for the Saturday market. Buy too few, and you lose business; buy too many and you lose profit because they will not last until the following week. Dean lives not far from the Codlington General Hospital. There are always a lot of visitors on a Sunday. Dean says that if he sold flowers near the main entrance, he is sure that Saturday's stocks would be cleared. Another successful idea is launched.

● Tasks

31. Eve offers Dean the choice of a fixed wage or an hourly rate for his Saturday work. Because of the weather, and seasonal changes in shopping, the day will vary. Sometimes the stall will open at 9 and they will finish by 4; at other times they will be at work at 8 and not go home until 6. Dean takes an hour for lunch. His fixed wage would be £25, and the hourly rate would be £3.50. *Which arrangement will leave him better off?*

32. Once the work expands, Eve and Dean agree that an hourly payment is the best way to cope with the irregular hours he works. *Total Dean's wages for the week beginning 23 October.* He now earns £3.75 an hour.

23 Oct	4 hours
24 Oct	no work
25 Oct	2 hours
26 Oct	4 hours
27 Oct	1 hour
28 Oct	stall 9 till 5

33. When Dean starts his flower stall by the hospital, Eve at first suggests an hourly rate, but Dean suggests that he should be paid a commission of 25% on sales ('It'll make me work harder at it', he says). They agree that he should be able to sell £50 worth of flowers. Eve thinks he might reach £70, but Dean thinks the figure could reach £100. *Decide which is his best option, by calculating the commission on each of the above sales totals.* The other relevant details are:

| Hours to work: | 11 till 3 |
| Rate if paid by the hour: | £3.75 |

Help ?

*See **Section 2: The Information Bank***

Wages: main methods of calculating pay, page 267.

● **Extension tasks**

E22. At present Dean counts as a casual worker. *What differences would there be (other than the size of his pay packet) for Eve if she took him on as a full-time employee?*

Help ?

*See **Section 2: The Information Bank***

Wages: statutory deductions, page 271; *the PAYE system,* page 272; *basic requirements of Inland Revenue,* page 273.

Unit 18 – Eve opens her flower shop

Receipts; security; methods of payment; retail sales.

Things continue to go well for Eve. She is becoming very well known, and she understands what people wish to buy. As a gardener, she is known for doing a good job, and people like the fact that she will still take on small jobs.

But Eve still wishes to own a shop, and so when a premises in Farriergate falls vacant, she decides to take a chance. She gives up her stall at the market and advertises for someone to work full time, and decides on Shahida Aziz. The new shop will be called Honeysuckle.

cont/...

But the new venture brings new steps into the process of financial record keeping. Receipts have to be issued to customers who pay cash. And there are now many more sales, so that the cash book entries need to be made easier.

But it also becomes clear that Eve is going to need further flexibility in the way that she is paid. Some plants are quite expensive, and people then wish to pay by cheque. Moreover, an increasing number of people ask if she will take a credit card and she approaches the leading companies to find out how to arrange this.

● Tasks

34. *Make out receipts for the following sales*

   ☐   6 roses £3.00, wrapping £1.00, delivery £1.50

   ☐   wedding bouquet £30.00; special delivery charge £4.50

   ☐   various pot plants: African violets £2.50; hyacinths £3.25; spider plant £4.00.

   (Copy the appropriate document given below.)

Tel: 51412	*Honeysuckle* 17 Farriergate Codlington
	– Flowers for all seasons –

Date: ....

Paid in full: Total:

                              No.:

Help ?
See Section 2: The Information Bank
Methods of payment: receipts, page 206.

35. In handling credit card sales it is easy to make mistakes until you know the routine. *Make a check-list of procedures for credit card sales that Eve can keep beside the imprinter.*

Help ?
See Section 2: The Information Bank
Methods of payment: credit cards, page 207.

● **Extension tasks**

E23. After some months. Eve decides that the shop is so busy on a Saturday that it would be worth investing in a till. When she has done so, Mrs Ash buys a pot of African violets and a bunch of chrysanthemums but does not understand the receipt she is given. *Explain the various items to her.*

```
        HONEYSUCKLE
       17 Farriergate
        Codlington



        30-10-91

  PP CODE 46    2.50
  CF CODE 18    2.00
  SBTL          4.50
  CASH          5.00
  CHNG          0.50



    Thank you for
     your custom
```

E24. Opening the shop means that Eve has to think more carefully about security. *What advice would you give her?*

Help ?
See Section 2: The Information Bank
Work methods: security, page 293.

E25. *How should Eve record her sales in her cash book?*

Help ?
See Section 2: The Information Bank
Methods of payment: end of day routine, page 205.

Entering the world of business

Deductions Working Sheet P11   Year to 5 April 19 ____

Employer's name

Tax District and reference

Complete only for occupational pension schemes newly contracted-out since 1 January 1986.
Scheme contracted-out number

S	4						

National Insurance Contributions à

Earnings on which employee's contributions payable 1a	Total of employee's and employer's contributions payable 1b	Employee's contributions payable 1c	Earnings on which employee's contributions at contracted-out rate payable included in column 1a 1d	Employee's contributions at contracted-out rate included in column 1c 1e	Statutory Sick Pay in the week or month included in column 2 1f	Statutory Maternity Pay in the week or month included in column 2 1g	Month no
£	£	£	£	£	£	£	6 April to 5 May **1**
							6 May to 5 June **2**
							6 June to 5 July **3**
							6 July to 5 Aug **4**
							6 Aug to 5 Sept **5**
							6 Sept to 5 Oct **6**
							6 Oct to 5 Nov **7**
Total c/forward	Total c/forward	Total c/forward	Total c/forward	Total c/forward	Total c/forward	Total c/forward	

40

Employee's surname *in CAPITALS*		First two forenames			

National Insurance no.	Date of birth *in figures*			Works no. etc	Date of leaving *in figures*		
	Day	Month	Year		Day	Month	Year

Tax code †	Amended code †							
	Wk/Mth in which applied							

PAYE Income Tax

Week no	Pay in the week or month including Statutory Sick Pay/Statutory Maternity Pay 2	Total pay to date 3	Total free pay to date as shown by Table A 4	Total taxable pay to date Ø 5	Total tax due to date as shown by Taxable Pay Tables 6	Tax deducted or refunded in the week or month *Mark refunds 'R'* 7	For employer's use
1	£	£	£	£	£	£	
2							
3							
4							
5							
6							
7							
8							
9							
10							
11							
12							
13							
14							
15							
16							
17							
18							
19							
20							
21							
22							
23							
24							
25							
26							
27							
28							
29							
30							

* You must enter the NI contribution table letter overleaf beside the NI totals box - *see the note shown there.*

† If amended cross out previous code.

Ø If in any week/month the amount in column 4 is more than the amount in column 3, leave column 5 blank.

Unit 19 – Eve takes on an employee

Wages; PAYE; gross wages; statutory deductions; Form P11; wage slips.

> Shahida Aziz is a full-time employee. She is to be paid on an hourly rate of £3.00 as opposed to a wage for a fixed number of hours each week. This will mean that the shop can respond to seasonal changes and enable Shahida to earn some extra money when it is busy. Lucy advises Eve to contact the Inland Revenue to find out what has to be done about taxing her wages.

● Tasks

36. *Using the details given, work out for the first week of Shahida's employment*

    a) *her gross wages*
    b) *statutory deductions.*

    Complete the Form P11 on the previous pages and the wage slip below.

HONEYSUCKLE			
Pay advice			
Date	Employee	Tax code	Week
Payments		**Deductions**	
Basic Pay:		Income tax:	
Overtime:		Nat Ins.	
Gross pay:		Total:	
Net pay:			
Gross pay to date:		Tax paid this year:	
Taxable pay:		NI paid:	

Details:

worked 9.30 -12.00 and 1.00 to 4.30 Monday to Friday
8.30 – 12.00 and 1.00 to 6.00 on Saturday

Help ?

See Section 2: The Information Bank

Wages and salaries, page 266; *filling in form P11,* page 275; *paying the employee,* page 280.

● Extension tasks

E26. *Using the following details calculate Shahida's gross wages and deductions for her second week of employment, make out the wage slip, and update Form P11 (on pages 40–41). Then calculate Dean's wages for the week.*

E27. *Make a cash analysis of what denomination of coins and notes Eve will need in order to make up the two pay packets.*

Details:

Shahida: Monday to Thursday 9.30 to 12 1 to 4.30
           Friday   9 to 12 1 to 5.30
           Saturday   8.30 to 12 1 to 6.00
Rate: £3.00 per hour.

Dean   Monday   3 hrs
           Tuesday   2 hours
           Wednesday   no work
           Thursday   2 hours
           Friday   1 hour
           Saturday   9 hours
           Sunday   flower sales £64.80
Rates   as before.

Help ?

See Section 2: The Information Bank

Wages: cash analysis, page 283.

Unit 20 – Eve registers for VAT

Value added tax; basic information; taxable turnover; Form VAT 1; VAT invoice.

Eve's affairs are now thriving, though she has to work very hard. One evening Lucy remarks that Eve must be nearing the VAT threshold. Eve is surprised, saying that though she now has the shop, she is not making a very large income herself, once she has paid for her stock and paid out wages. Lucy says that the VAT authorities are not concerned with your profit, but with your turnover. Eve had better contact the Customs and Excise department, and find out what to do.

● **Tasks**

37. *Find out what action Eve will have to take if her turnover for the twelve months ending 30 June will be £36 251.*

38. *Redesign the Honeysuckle receipts (page 38) to be suitable for a VAT registered business.*

39. *Fill in your redesigned receipt according to the following details.*

   ❑ Honeysuckle VAT registration number is 0602 50438 296
   ❑ date: 2 Feb 1992
   ❑ customer name and address not needed for the shop's routine retail transactions
   ❑ goods: 2 bunches roses @ £5.25; bunch of orchids £6.50; hanging basket £1.95
   ❑ rate of VAT $17\frac{1}{2}$%.

Help ?

See Section 2: The Information Bank

Value Added Tax: taxable turnover, page 253; *Form VAT 1,* page 256; *past turnover,* page 255; *VAT invoice – what it is,* page 259; *filling in the VAT invoice,* page 259; *what to do,* page 265.

If you require further help with reading the documentation, consult the summaries (see *VAT: contents,* page 251) and *Texts,* page 248.

Guidance on the calculation of percentages, will be found in *Calculations: percentages,* page 113.

● **Extension tasks**

E28. *Find out from your local VAT office what the VAT status of the following sales and purchases is. What effect will these items have on Eve's record keeping?*

   ❑ Sale of plants; cut flowers; hanging baskets; flower pots; flowers for hospital ward
   ❑ Purchase of stationery; cleaning materials; coffee and biscuits for staff; window cleaning.

Unit 21 – Enter Moira Faraday: Eve takes on a bookkeeper

The accounts of a business; ledgers and journals; structure of the ledger; sales and purchases journal; customer accounts.

Eve finds that the expansion of her business brings new rewards, but new complexities, especially in the matter of financial record keeping. Firstly, Eve has now registered for VAT. Another issue which now arises is the handling of credit. When they next meet, Lucy points out that Eve is not keeping any formal record of her purchases through her customer account with Hoxted Horticulture. She is just filing the invoices and noting her payment by cheque in her cash book.

Eve then mentions that some of her regular customers at the flower shop have asked if they could open an account. It is at this point that Lucy advises Eve to set up a system for dealing with credit transactions. Eve will then both be able to keep track of what money is owed and by whom, as well as being able to include these transactions in her final accounts and tax return at the end of the financial year.

Eve feels that all this would take a lot of time, and more skill than she has, or has time to acquire. Lucy suggests that it is now time to engage a part-time bookkeeper. She knows someone, and will put her in contact.

During the following week Moira Faraday arrives. She is the ideal person. She is quietly efficient, and seems never to become impatient. She really understands the work, and can explain it clearly to Eve.

Moira says that they will need to set up a ledger, with a new cash book. So far Eve has used an analysed cash book to record her receipts and payments, together with columns listing her main types of expenditure. Now she will need a standard cash book of the type which is used as part of a ledger.

Moira also says that they should set up customer accounts for Eve's credit customers. Moira suggests that as the first step the credit affairs of the shop should be registered in a sales journal. Moira will later transfer this information to the ledger.

● **Tasks**

40. *Summarise the main elements and purposes of the accounting system which Moira describes. You will probably find it helpful to create a diagram.*

Help ?

*See **Section 2: The Information Bank***

Accounts: the accounts of a business, page 72.

Ledgers and journals: structure of the ledger, page 182.

Invoices: customer accounts, page 166.

41. *Enter the following transactions in the sales journal.*

   5 Jan   H. Fox, cut flowers £18.50;
   6 Jan   A Edens, pot plant, £12.00;
   7 Jan   L. Anthias cut flowers, £14.20;
   8 Jan   Rookham Estate Agents, tropical plants, £55.00;
   9 Jan   L. Anthias, cut flowers, £22.00;
   10 Jan S. Newton, pot plant, £11.25;
   10 Jan L. Mardon bouquet, £13.00.

Help ?

*See **Section 2: The Information Bank***
Ledgers and journals: journals, page 179.

(Use the journal sheet from The Forms Bank, *page 359.)*

Assign each invoice a number, starting at 1000. The prices are net of VAT. Calculate VAT to be added (rate: $17\frac{1}{2}\%$), *and complete the records appropriately.* The week ends on 10 January.

When you have carried out this task, you should file and save it for use in Task 43.

● Extension tasks

E29. Moira also sets up a purchases journal to record orders for stock. *Make the entries for the period.* (Use the journal sheet from The Forms Bank, *page 359.)*

Data:

5 Jan consignment of pot plants from Boxhill Shrubs, invoice number C954, £65.00;
6 Jan Hoxted Horticulture, various cut flowers, invoice CT112/494, £108.60;
8 Jan J. Fairfax, tropical plant (fatsia japonica), invoice 3312, £33.00.

When you have carried out this task, file and save it for use in Task 44.

Help ?

*See **Section 2: The Information Bank***
Ledgers and journals: journals, page 178.

Unit 22 – Moira starts a new cash book

The cash book; reconciliation with bank statement.

At the same time as she organises the journals, Moira sets up the new cash book, to replace the former single entry document. This will be a two column cash book.

● Tasks

42. *Make the entries in the new cash book and balance it the for the first week. Cash sales are recorded from the till roll daily totals. (Do not attempt to enter folio numbers or to make the double entries, except between Cash and Bank accounts). (Use the cash book sheet from* The Forms Bank, *page 359.)*

    The transactions for the week (Monday to Saturday) were:

    > 5 Jan till roll £14.00, cheque received, S. Cooke £8.00;
    > 6 Jan till roll £20.50;
    > 7 Jan till roll £15.90, cheque received, R.R. Hood £18.00;
    > 8 Jan till roll £23.70, cheque received, B.B. Woolf £11.00;
    > 9 Jan till toll £52.00, Elite Plumbing (burst pipe) paid by cheque £54.00;
    > 10 Jan till roll £108.70, cheques received, H. Wallace £23.00, F. Drake £15.50.

    On Saturday evening Eve pays Shahida and Dean their wages in cash. This week Shahida receives £105.50 and Dean £54.00. If there is sufficient money on the premises, they are paid from the till.

    Because the bank closes before the shop, Honeysuckle deposits its day's takings either by means of the night safe, or at the counter of the bank the next day. The takings for Friday and Saturday are banked at the same time.

    Moira Faraday continues the shop's policy that £30 in cash is always kept at the shop as a float. She also notes that the balance in the Bank Account is £7356 on the morning of Monday, 5 January.

    The next working day after the week described above will be Monday, 12 January.

    You are advised to make a rough copy of the entries before attempting to enter the final version on your Cash Book sheet.

Help ?

*See **Section 2: The Information Bank***
Cash book, page 115.

● Extension tasks

E30. *Reconcile the cash book with the relevant part of the bank statement. (For the purpose of this exercise the reconciliation will only be for the first week, and not for the whole month). Try to explain any discrepancies.*

Help ?

*See **Section 2: The Information Bank***
Cash book: bank reconciliation statement, page 122.

	DATE	PARTICULARS	PAYMENTS	RECEIPTS	BALANCE

IN ACCOUNT WITH

BANK Mercia

TITLE OF ACCOUNT Eve Adams

BRANCH Sheep Market, Codlington

ACCOUNT NUMBER 05400780

STATEMENT NUMBER 22

	DATE	PARTICULARS	PAYMENTS	RECEIPTS	BALANCE
	5 Jan	balance			7356.00 CR
	6 Jan	Credit		14.00	7370.00 CR
		S. Cooke		8.00	7378.00 CR
	7 Jan	Credit		20.50	7398.50 CR
	8 Jan	Credit		15.90	7414.40 CR
		R.R. Hood		18.00	7432.40 CR
		MERCIA ELEC DD	62.00		7370.40 CR
	9 Jan	Credit		23.70	7394.10 CR
		B.B. Woolf		11.00	7405.10 CR
	12 Jan	Credit		31.20	7436.30 CR
		H. Wallace		23.00	7459.30 CR
		F. Drake		15.50	7474.80 CR

Unit 23 – Moira builds up the ledger

The double entry system; posting of journals to the ledger; recording of invoices; updating customer accounts; delivery notes.

Moira's final action in setting up the accounts is to begin to create the ledger, using the double entry system.

● Tasks

43. *In Task 41 you made entries in the sales journal. Working from this, sketch out what entries will be made from the journal to the ledger.*

Help ?

See Section 2: The Information Bank

Ledgers and journals: double entry system, page 184; posting of journals to the ledger, page 187.

44. *You will also have entries in the Purchases journal (Task E29). Sketch out what entries will be made from the journal to the ledger.*

Extension tasks

(For the tasks below, use the appropriate documents from the selection in The Forms Bank, *page 359.)*

E31. *Update the statement of account for Mrs Anthias. She has not yet settled her account of £85.60 for December.*

Help ?

See Section 2: The Information Bank

Invoices: customer accounts, page 166.

E32. *Make out an invoice to record the following transaction. Outline the journal and ledger entries which will be needed to complete the record.*
On 2 June Mrs L. Anthias orders a clematis (price £8.50 before VAT), and 10 bunches of freesias, which are £1.70 per bunch (exclusive of VAT). Her address is: The Old Manor House, Upper Carsholt.

E33. *Also make out the delivery note to accompany the goods, to be delivered on 4 June (am), carriage paid.*

HOXTED HORTICULTURE
LITTLE ACRE, HOXTED

VAT number: 88 6646 23
Customer: Honeysuckle
          Farriergate
          Codlington

Ref: CT112/1789

Date: 14 July 1991

Quantity	Item	Unit cost	Total before VAT	VAT	Total
5	Rose bushes (Napoleon)	£3.10	17.50	3.06	20.56
24	Lilies	£2.10	50.40	8.82	59.22
			67.90	11.88	79.78

49

Entering the world of business

Help ?

See Section 2: The Information Bank

Ledgers and journals: posting of journals to the ledger, page 187.

Orders: delivery notes, page 216.

Unit 24 – Eve takes out a bank loan

Banking facilities: borrowing money; methods of payment: repayment of credit; interest.

Eve's shop and gardening work continue to prosper, and as time passes it becomes clear that there would be a demand in the town for a garden centre. Hoxted Horticulture is too far to be convenient, especially for people who wish to make just one or two relatively small purchases.

Eve has noticed a site which is well placed for access, but it will need buildings as well as a substantial investment in preparing the ground and buying in stock.

Eve therefore goes to the bank, where she is able to obtain a loan to finance her new venture.

● Tasks

45. *What mechanisms for borrowing can the bank offer?*

● Extension tasks

E34. There are a variety of types of loan. For example, mortgages are often offered on a reducing balance basis, that is, interest is calculated on the amount of the debt which is still outstanding. Also, the rate of interest can vary according to the state of the economy.

However, in this case The bank manager offers Eve a fixed interest, fixed instalment loan. This means that she will pay the same rate of interest throughout the period, and that the repayment will be made by equal instalments. Eve borrows £24 000 for 4 years at a rate of 15% per annum. *Calculate her monthly repayments.*

Help ?

See Section 2: The Information Bank

Banking facilities: borrowing money, page 98.

Methods of payment: repayment of credit, page 209.

Calculations: interest, page 107.

Unit 25 – Moira opens the returns journal

Sales and purchases returns journals; credit notes.

> Eve recognises that she will now have a whole range of new situations to deal with. There will be a steady flow of sales and purchases. Also, as she hopes to provide goods and services to large businesses and perhaps the Council, there will be a substantial need to provide and request credit. Moreover, with an increased volume of trading, there are inevitably occasions on which goods are not supplied as requested, or are supplied damaged.

● Tasks

46. Moira Faraday sets up sales returns and purchases returns journals. *Make the entries given below. (Use the journal sheet from* The Forms Bank, *page 359.)*

    11 October, credit note (ref B422) received from Boxhill Shrubs for damaged mahonia (price £40.00); 13 October, credit note ECN243 sent to Mrs Anthias for return of damaged chrysanthemums (value £32.00); 21 Oct, credit note ECN244 to Mr Edens for return of spade (wrong type, cost £21.00); 24 October, credit note CT112/CN22 received from Hoxted Horticulture, wrong order delivered (invoiced for £85.00)

    The prices quoted do not include VAT, which must be added.

Help ?

See Section 2: The Information Bank

Ledgers and journals: returns journals, page 181.

Invoices: credit notes, page 170.

● Extension tasks

E35. *Make the appropriate ledger entries for the above transactions.*

Help ?

See Section 2: The Information Bank

Ledgers and journals: posting journals to the ledger, page 187.

Unit 26 – Moira starts another cash book

Terms of business; discount; recording cash discount; three column cash book.

Another refinement to the system is needed: it is clear that regular customers, who now include large organisations such as Azure Computers and Codlington Council, will require discount, and that EPG, being a prompt payer, can expect a cash discount.

● Tasks

47. Various invoices are received and issued by Moira Faraday, as listed below. *Calculate the cheques which she should forward when entitled to discount at the rate indicated on incoming invoices. On invoices sent out, calculate VAT, total invoice, value of a 5% discount, and what cheque will be expected from a customer entitled to claim discount.*

Incoming invoices

Supplier	Total before VAT	VAT	Total as shown on invoice	Discount rate	Value of discount	Cheque for ?
Boxhill	120.00	21.00	141.00	5%		
Hoxted	85.50	14.96	100.46	$2\frac{1}{2}\%$		
Churchill	22.25	3.89	26.14	2%		

Invoices issued

Customer	Total before VAT	VAT	Total as shown on invoice	Discount rate	Value of discount	Cheque for ?
Azure Computers	567.00					
Codlington Council	896.00					
Mrs Anthias	102.50					

Help ?

See *Section 2: The Information Bank*

Quotations: terms of business, page 232; *discount*, page 233.

● Extension tasks

E36. To deal with the new situation Moira starts a new type of cash book using three column entry. The Garden Centre cash book starts on Monday 27 October with a bank balance of £3975 and £100 on the premises in cash. Moira settles the three supplier invoices by cheque on 30 October, and she receives cheques from Mrs Anthias on the 28th, and from Azure and Codlington on the 31st. She also sends G Oak a cheque for £124 (no discount allowed) on the 27th, and receives a payment (by cheque) from Debora Allen for £42 (no discount) on the 28th. *Make the entries, and total and balance the cash book at the end of the month.*

Ignore the VAT component. Enter total paid and discount. Remember that as a check, the two should be the same as the original price. (Use the appropriate document from The Forms Bank, *page 359.)*

Help ?

See Section 2: The Information Bank

Cash book: recording cash discount, page 120.

Unit 27 – Eve takes stock

Stock control: stock record cards; requisitions; stock valuation.

There is now a large amount of very varied stock on hand. A system of stock control is therefore needed. A new employee, Mary Douglas, is employed to handle the administrative work of the shop and garden centre.

● Tasks

48. Mary's first job is to set up a set of stock record cards. *Make the necessary entries on one of the cards according to the data given. You will need to calculate the re-order level and quantity beforehand. (Use the appropriate document from* The Forms Bank, *page 359.)*

Large plastic plant pots are bought and sold singly. Their catalogue number is PP14L, and their location coding is PS2B.

The minimum level is 50, and the maximum level to be kept in stock is 400. Re-ordering is done on the basis that it takes 5 days from order to delivery, and that an average of 20 are used per day.

Mary takes stock on 2 April, and finds that there are 250 pots in stock. She receives stores requisitions during the month as follows:

❑ from Gardening Services: 4 April SRS81 30; 8 April SRS89 20; 9 April SRS91 30; 10 April SRS92 40

❑ from the Garden Centre: 5 April SRGC24 50; 15 April SRGC26 30

❑ from Honeysuckle: 12 April SRH13 30

At one point stocks fall to the re-order level, and she sends off an order, reference number ERGS1149 for the re-order quantity.

Help ?

See Section 2: The Information Bank

Stock control and valuation, page 238.

● Extension tasks

E37. Lucy Luca advises that there should be a stocktaking and stock valuation. Mary carries out this task. One of her stock records is as shown below. *Calculate the stock valuation (a) according to FIFO and (b) according to AVCO.*

Item: spades, catalogue number GT15

Date	Receipts	Issues	balance (units)	purchase cost	valuation
1 May			5	£16.00	
7 May	5		10	£16.00	
31		(for month) 4	6	£16.00	
1 June	5		11	£18.00	
21 June		4	7		

Help ?

See Section 2: The Information Bank

Stock control and valuation: three common approaches, page 243.

Unit 28 – Eve needs a payroll

Payroll; cash analysis of wages; Form P45.

There are now several employees in the shop and garden centre. It is up to Mary Douglas to arrange the payment of their wages.

● Tasks

49. *Draw up Moira's first payroll sheet, using the following information:*

Number	Name	Basic	Overtime	Total Gross Pay	PAYE	NI	Total De-ductions	Employ-er's NI	Net Pay
100	H Gilbert	115.50	22.50		14.25	9.41		6.01	
101	I Newton	168.00			18.25	12.11		9.21	
102	J Priestly	136.50	12.00		15.75	10.17		6.31	
103	M Faraday	199.50			21.00	14.84		12.13	
104	C Darwin	126.00			12.50	8.33		5.17	

Totals

Check your work by making internal checks (total basic + total overtime = total gross pay; total PAYE + total NI = total deductions; Net pay + deductions = gross pay; total gross pay = total deductions + total net pay).

Help ?

See Section 2: The Information Bank

Wages and salaries: payroll, page 281.

50. *Make out Moira's cash analysis sheet for the above payroll. (Use the payroll and cash analysis sheets from pages 282-283.)*

● Extension tasks

E38. Over a period of time employees leave. Humphrey Gilbert leaves to take up a job at Radionics, a local firm specialising in electronic supplies. *Use Mr Gilbert's P11 to issue his P45. The EPG PAYE reference is 888/E123M.*

Help ?

See Section 2: The Information Bank

Wages and salaries: summary forms, page 286.

Employee's surname *in CAPITALS*			First two forenames				
GILBERT			HUMPHREY				

National Insurance no.	Date of birth *in figures*			Works no. etc		Date of leaving *in figures*	
PG, 12, 34, 89, D	Day 09	Month 10	Year 54	100		Day 10	Month 11 Year 93

Tax code†	Amended code †				
285 L	Wk/Mth in which applied				

PAYE Income Tax

Week no	Pay in the week or month including Statutory Sick Pay/Statutory Maternity Pay 2	Total pay to date 3		Total free pay to date as shown by Table A 4		Total taxable pay to date 5		Total tax due to date as shown by Taxable Pay Tables 6		Tax deducted or refunded in the week or month *Mark refunds 'R'* 7		For employer's use
BF from wk 30	—	Bt fwd 33 45	£ 75	—		—		Bt fwd 424	£ 00	—		
31		3450	75	1704	69	1746	06	436	50	12	50	
32												
33												
52												
§												

	Pay and Tax totals					† If amended cross out previous code.
	◄ Previous employments ►					§ Complete this line if pay day falls on 5 April (in leap years 4 & 5 April). See Wk 53 instructions in the Employer's Guide to PAYE.
3450 75	◄ This employment ► *Mark net refund 'R'*			436	50	
	Employee's Widow's & Orphans/Life insurance contribution in this employment			£		

Part of P11

Unit 29 – Eve monitors her debtors

Credit control: check on creditworthiness, customer accounts, aged debtors list; letter requesting payment of debt.

Credit is now an important part of the pattern of trade. It brings further record keeping to be done. Moira Faraday urges Eve to adopt a system of credit control.

● **Tasks**

51. *What forms of credit control might Eve adopt?*

Help ?

See Section 2: The Information Bank

Orders: check on creditworthiness, page 213.

Invoices: customer accounts, page 166; statement of account, page 167.

Complaints, page 126.

● **Extension tasks**

E39. At the suggestion of Moira Faraday, Eve examines an aged debtors list each month. *Summarise the importance of this extract from the statement produced by Mary.*

EDEN PLANTS AND GARDENS

AGED DEBTORS LIST as at 15-06-91

Account no	Name	Balance	up to 30 days	over 30 days	over 60 days	over 90 days
53	Eastcote Leisure	402.50	397.00	0.00	5.50	0.00
72	L Anthias	307.00	85.00	65.00	101.00	56.00
78	H Fox	193.50	162.50	31.00	0.00	0.00
91	St Martin's	115.00	115.00	0.00	0.00	0.00
105	Bookham and Rookham Travel Agency	124.00	0.00	0.00	0.00	124.00
Totals		1142.00	759.50	96.00	106.50	180.00
percentage			66.51	8.41	9.33	15.75

To make your report, consider the following questions:

1) *Who owes the most? (What percentage of the total debt is this?)*

2) *Who owes the least?*

3) *Do most people pay their debts within the 30 days allowed?*

4) *Are most debtors only a little overdue?*

5) *Which customers' debts have remained unsettled the longest? Can you suggest*

    a) *possible reasons*

    b) *suitable action.*

E40. *Draft appropriate letters to those debtors.*

Help ?
*See **Section 2: The Information Bank***
Complaints, page 126.
Invoices: aged debt analysis, page 167.

Unit 30 – Eve's petty cash system

Petty cash vouchers; petty cash book.

> There is now a regular stream of requests from employees for cash for day-to-day purchases. Mary Douglas therefore organises a petty cash system.

● Tasks

52. *Check the following vouchers for accuracy.*

Petty Cash Voucher	Folio _____ Date 2 Aug 19 91	
For what required	AMOUNT £	p
Postage	1	65
Envelopes	1	25
	2	90
Signature _____		
Passed by _____		

Petty Cash Voucher	Folio _____ Date 4 Aug 19 91	
For what required	AMOUNT £	p
Travel (Eastcote)	1	60
Travel (Appleton)	1	60
	3	50
Signature *H. Gilbert*		
Passed by _____		

53. *Make up the petty cash book for one week, on the basis of the following information. (Use the petty cash sheet from* The Forms Bank, *page 359.)*

Monday, 17 June: imprest received from Moira Faraday (cashier) £40; columns for postage, stationery, travel; postage £3.55; travel £4.50; 18 June stationery £4.40 (including VAT); 19 June stationery £2.52 (£2.15 + VAT 0.37); 20 June postage £5.10; cleaning materials £ 2.11 (£1.80 + VAT 0.31); 21 June stationery £3.64 (including VAT); pens £2.58 (£2.20 + VAT 0.38). On Monday 24 June Mary balanced the petty cash book, and then obtained cash from Moira to restore the imprest.

Help ?

See Section 2: The Information Bank

Petty cash, page 219.

Note: If you have come to this Unit without having studied either *Unit 12* (the analysed cash book) or *Units 21-23* (accounts), you are advised first to read or refresh *Accounts: basic approach to record keeping*, page 74.

● Extension tasks

E41. *The petty cash book was handled by a temp while Mary was on holiday for a week. Check the work and correct it where necessary.*

Debits £	Date	Details	Voucher number	Credit £	Post £	Stat'nry £	Travel £	Sundry £	VAT £
40.00	25 Jul	Postage	61	2.50	2.50				
	26 Jul	Pens	62	2.34		2.34			1.34
	27 Jul	Travel	63	4.00				4.00	
	28 Jul	Stationery	64	3.20					0.48
	29 Jul	Postage	65	1.50	1.50				
		Totals		13.44					

Unit 31 – Eve looks back over a year

Final accounts: trading and profit and loss accounts; balance sheet; depreciation; bad debts.

The end of the business year has come round again, and Lucy Luca, now the official accountant for Eve's business asks Moira Faraday to gather together the information which will be needed to draw up the final accounts for the year.

● Tasks

54. The summary of the various ledger accounts which Moira brings together is given below. *Turn this into the combined Trading and Profit and Loss accounts for Eden Plants and Gardens.*

Accounts	
Sales	91 250
Purchases	19 320
Wages	22 357
Heating and Lighting	2 965
Transport	4 789
Stock valuation	
Opening stock	25 346
Closing stock	5 214

Help ?

See Section 2: The Information Bank

Final accounts, page 147.

55. *Use the following information to produce the Balance Sheet for the same period. Use the two column format.*

Owner's capital	38 455
Owner's drawings	15 200
Net profit as per Profit and Loss account	
Premises	38 000
Fixtures and fittings	4 650
Vehicle	8 000
Bank loan	24 000
Creditor accounts	4 862
Stock as per Profit and Loss Account	
Debtors accounts	6 678
Money in Bank	8 902
Cash on premises	2 160

Help ?

See Section 2: The Information Bank

Final accounts: balance sheet, page 156.

● Extension tasks

E42. Lucy advises Moira that various ledger accounts have been omitted from the reckoning. Moira then provides the following extra information. *Amend the Trading and Profit and Loss accounts accordingly.*

Accounts	
Sales Returns	850
Purchases Returns	182
Rent of shop	3 600
Depreciation	1 150
Bad debts	367

E43. *Rewrite the balance sheet created for Task 55 in the vertical format.*

Help ?

See Section 2: The Information Bank

Final accounts: balance sheet, page 156.

Unit 32 – Eve goes to France

Bank facilities: foreign dealings: Calculations: foreign currency: measurements - Imperial and metric.

Eve has noticed that an increasing number of the more well-off people in Codlington (such as the senior staff at Azure Computers) are buying second homes in France. Often the properties need work doing; this is certainly true of the gardens and grounds. Her first customer, Henry Nicholson, suggests that some people would be glad of someone like Eve to undertake this work, especially if they do not speak French well. Eve decides to go over to France to investigate the possibilities. She will look over a new purchase by the Director of Research and Development at Azure, Claude Shannon, in the lovely village of Plume de Matante.

● Tasks

56. Eve needs to arrange to pay for things. *What are her options?*

Help ?

See Section 2: The Information Bank

Banking facilities: foreign dealings, page 102.

57. Eve decides to take £85 in cash (French francs). *How much will she receive when the exchange rate is 9.92? A friend suggests to Eve that she should take 1000 francs. How much will this cost her?*

Help ?

See Section 2: The Information Bank

Calculations: foreign currency, page 106.

58. On arriving at Plume de Matante, Eve looks into the cost of labour and materials for Mr Shannon's land. Naturally, the French give the information using the metric system. Eve thinks in Imperial measures.

Mr Shannon owns 3.2 hectares of land *(how many acres?)*. He wants an area of grass for tennis courts for his business visitors. The area would be 80 yards by 40 *(how many metres?)*. This area will be covered with turf *(how many square metres?)*. Turfs will cost 40 francs per strip of dimensions 2 metres long and 50 cm wide. *Will these be cheaper than buying them in England (£1.50 for a strip 6ft by 1 foot)?* Eve thinks that the work will need two gardeners for a fortnight (40 hour week. The rate is 45 francs an hour. *What will labour cost in pounds sterling?*

Help ?
See Section 2: The Information Bank
Calculations: measurements, page 109.

● **Extension tasks**

E44. *Find out from your local bank what facilities there would be for Eve to carry out business dealings, and especially to transfer and bring in money.*

Help ?
See Section 2: The Information Bank
Banking facilities: foreign dealings, page 102.

Unit 33 – Eve pays herself expenses

Expenses and expense claims.

Though her stay in France is very pleasant, and Eve spends some happy hours socialising with the residents of Plume de Matante, the trip is nevertheless primarily for business purposes. Eve wishes to explore the possibilities of her business extending in new directions. Also, though she enjoys a great deal of hospitality, Eve still has to make a considerable outlay of money in order to undertake the visit. There is the cost of travel, and hiring a car to visit various local contractors. She has to pay for accommodation at the Hotel Bovary in the Main Square, and there is the cost of those delicious French meals. She also feels that as Mr Shannon is likely to be an important client, she should take him out for a meal to the leading local restaurant, the Restaurant Dauphine. She also goes into the local bookshop and picks up a few volumes of 'Que Sais-je?' – the French equivalent of 'Teach Yourself' books, so that she can find out the terminology of occupations which are important to her work, such as gardeners and builders. As Mr and Mrs Shannon have been so hospitable, on her last evening Eve also buys a small present, a piece of local pottery, which she knows Mrs Shannon is collecting.   *cont/...*

On her return to England the ever watchful Moira Faraday presents Eve with an expenses claim form. She stresses that though Eve has also had a short holiday, she has been in France on business. Her expenses should therefore be reimbursed and entered in the accounts.

● **Tasks**

59. Moira asks Eve to list what she has spent and to produce any receipts. The result is:

Travel:	taxi out £0.70; train return £12.50; boat £20.00; train (France) 62 francs; taxi (into Plume de Matante) 20 francs; taxi (back) 18 francs; taxi Codlington £0.90. Eve only has a record of her boat booking.
Hotel:	(5 nights bed and breakfast) 165 francs per night (receipt kept).
Car hire:	4 days at 205 francs per day; petrol 78 francs.
Two dinners:	65 francs, and 85 francs (receipt of one kept).
Dinner for Mr Shannon:	325 francs.
Books:	215 francs (receipts available).
Present for Mrs Shannon:	178 francs (receipt available).

Decide:

a) *which of these expenses are allowable*

b) *the cost of each allowable expense in pounds sterling (current exchange rate = 10.12).*

Help ?

See **Section 2: The Information Bank**

Expenses, page 140.

Calculations: foreign currency, page 106.

60. *Make out Eve's expense claim form (using the blank form on the next page). The Cost Centre is 'Garden Centre' and the expense codes are:*

Travel	public transport	100
	car hire	101
Hotel		200
Meals		300
Entertaining overseas		800

● **Extension tasks**

E45. Eve had considered extending her break for a further three nights, so as to have a short holiday, and hiring a car for three more days to visit sites of interest in the area. Imagine that she has done so, basing herself at the Hotel Bovary, and spending another 365 francs on meals and snacks. Her petrol costs her 122 francs, and she buys another piece of local pottery (184 francs) for her mother.

a) *What are her total expenses for this further period (in pounds sterling)?*

b) *Which of these can legitimately be paid by EPG?*

c) *What are the options for Eve when she claims her expenses, and what result will each option have on her income?*

Entering the world of business

EXPENSES CLAIM FORM

Claimant's name (block capitals): ....

Cost Centre: ....

Date: ....

Vehicle Reg. No.: ....

to be completed by claimant ◄— to be completed by cashier —►

Details	Expense Code	Total £ p	Expense Amount (Net of VAT) £ p	VAT £ p
Public transport				
Car hire				
Accommodation				
Meals				
Entertaining - O'sea				
Totals				

Claimant's signature:

....

Expense authoriser:

....

64

Unit 34 – Eve brings in the micro

Computerisation of accounts

> On the evening before she returns to England, Mr Shannon and Eve are chatting and enjoying a bottle of robust local wine. Mr Shannon suggests that Eve might well make substantial improvements in the cost and efficiency of her accounting system if she were to computerise it. Eve is interested, and Mr Shannon says he will arrange for a representative from the company, Mr Turing, to visit her.

● **Tasks**

61. *Devise a presentation of the main points which Mr Turing will wish to make about the advantages of a computer accounts package.*

Help ?

See **Section 2: The Information Bank**

Computerisation, page 131.

62. Mr Turing demonstrates by using a sales ledger program. He asks Mary Douglas to provide the basic information given below. She is then to carry out the task manually, as shown in Units 21–23, while he enters it into the computer. *Use the resources of the micro available to you to carry out the same experiment.*

   a) *Set up accounts for J Hobbs, 12 Blueberry Hill, Appleton, credit limit £200; H Larwood, 34 Meadow Lane, Trentbridge, credit limit £1000; H Sutcliffe, 45 Bats Close, The Wickets, Hambledon, credit limit £400.*

   b) *Enter rate of VAT as 17.5%*

   c) *Number invoices in sequence, starting 1930.*

   d) *Enter the following transactions:*

1 May	Hobbs	turf	£510
5 May	Hobbs	lawn roller	£95
8 May	Sutcliffe	edging tool	£25
9 May	Larwood	grass seed	£32.50
15 May	Sutcliffe	willow trees	£89
21 May	Sutcliffe	gloves (catalogue number GC132)	£14
26 May	Hobbs	netting	£43

   e) *Print out (1) balance of each account (2) total sales for the month.*

● **Extension tasks**

E46. *Find out the main advantages of a particular accounts package.*

Final comment

Eve has come a long way since she first went on the bus carrying her fork and spade to Mr Nicholson's. She has now had experience of the financial documents used by a small trader, in retailing and more recently of the more comprehensive systems of costing which are needed in a somewhat larger business. As you go further in this type of work you will find that there are many small differences between the practice of different businesses. For example, a cash and carry grocery wholesaler will have little or no use for delivery notes and a local authority will pay its teachers' salaries by bank giro – there will be no calculation of pay or cash analysis.

However, what you have done, in following Eve's progress, is to meet all the situations which are really crucial. For example, most businesses need invoices and must have a good system of credit control (though an important exception is certain types of retailing, such as a small grocery shop); the pay of all PAYE workers is liable to statutory deductions; VAT must be added by any registered person. By now you should understand these situations, and have a routine for dealing with them.

But the writers also have had another purpose, in addition to giving you those skills you need to be employable. Sometimes information is given which is not strictly needed just to meet the basic requirements of a task. At these points, we have tried to show why something is done, and how it fits into the wider context of the world of work and finance. We have done so because it always helps your efficiency to understand why you are carrying out a task. Such understanding also lays the ground for more advanced study. For example, the monitoring of credit, in the first instance through an aged debtors list, is a crucial part of the information needed by those who are planning for a business at its highest level.

Section 2

THE INFORMATION BANK

Using the information bank

This section of the book contains a series of entries. These deal with the main subject areas of the course in alphabetical sequence. Each entry is divided into topics, each of which is *numbered*. Usually a reference in the scenario gives the *entry title* and *page number*, for example 'see *Calculations*, page 104'. Every topic in this Section is referred to from the Section 1 scenarios and tasks.

At the beginning of each main entry is a *list of contents*. Use this to save yourself time and effort when looking up information.

The list of contents tells you:

❐ **how the information is divided up into shorter units.**
The units are numbered for convenience, using 'decimal numbering'. This means that a unit numbered '2.3' is the third unit in topic 2;

❐ **whether there is information which you should read *the first time* you refer to the entry;**

❐ **whether there is a separate summary.**
In cases where the entry is quite long, a summary is given.

Section 2 contents

Section 2 contents continued

Accounts

Explanation of the meanings of the word, the main types of account, the concept of credit, and the basic principles of recording transactions in an account

Preliminary reading

Before using the section on *Types of accounts* for the first time, you should read *Nature of accounts*, page 70.

1. Types of account

1.1 Nature of accounts

Earlier uses of the word

This word 'acccount' is one which has several uses in business. The word originally came from the French word 'aconter', which came from the Latin word 'accomputare' meaning, not surprisingly, 'count'. Later people began to use the word to mean not just the act of counting, but what you do afterwards. When you have finished counting, you make or give a reckoning, or explain what the counting means – for instance that there is money to spare, or money due. We still use the word today in a similar way. When we say that someone 'must account for their actions', we mean that they are expected to explain what they have done and why.

What an account is

In modern times when we talk about 'an account' we are talking about two things:

1) *an agreement between two parties* (for instance, a bank and a customer) *to handle money in some way*. At any one time, there is always a creditor and a debtor (see *Accounts: Credit and debit*, page 73, for further explanation).

2) *a written record of money dealings*. This will include a note of money received, money paid out, and money left over (if any), at the end of a given time (the accounting period). The difference between the totals of money coming in and going out is called the *balance*.

Statements of account

When the written record is brought up to date (*drawn up*) and shown to the customer (the *account holder*), it is called a *statement of account*. In business, the account holder will then undertake the *reconciliation* of the account. This is a form of checking the account for accuracy against other records or against money held.

1.2 Bank accounts

If you refer to the entries which deal with bank accounts you will find that there are two basic situations: either the customer is the creditor or the debtor. This is true in all three types of account mentioned in *Banking facilities*, page 97 forward.

The savings account

In this case the customer agrees to save money with the bank. From the bank's point of view this means that they borrow money and pay interest for the use of it. The customer is the creditor, and the record shows how much has been lent by the customer, and how much interest has been added (accrued). A statement shows what the bank's debt currently is.

The loan account

In this case the situation is reversed. The bank lends the money, and the customer is the debtor. The record will start with the original sum, any interest charged, and all repayments of the debt by the customer. The statement shows the balance of the account, which is the present difference between what is owed and what has been repaid.

The current account

In this case the customer may be either the creditor or the debtor, according to the state of the account. If the customer has been spending more than has been paid in, and has gone into overdraft, he or she is in debt to the bank. If the customer is in credit, then the bank is the debtor. The record shows what the customer has paid in, and what has been withdrawn, either in cash or by using cheques. It also shows any charges which the bank has made. The statement shows how much the bank would have to pay a customer who asked to withdraw all the money that was in the account.

1.3 Customer accounts

This type of account is a record of dealings between a business and those of its customers who are allowed credit, that is, he or she is not required to pay immediately (see *Accounts: credit and debit*, page 73). The record will show what purchases the customer has made, and what is owed to the supplier of goods or services. It shows what money which has been paid in (*remittances*) as part or full settlement of what is owed; the record also shows what remains to be paid (the *balance owing*). The customer is informed of the state of the account by means of a statement, typically issued monthly. The keeping of customer accounts is dealt with in *Invoices*, page 166.

1.4 The accounts of a business

When we speak of 'the accounts' of a firm, we are referring to the whole series of financial records which are used. The main elements in this set of records are

- the ledger
- ledger accounts
- the journals
- the cash book
- the petty cash book
- the final accounts.

In earlier times the accounts of a business were kept in one large book, called a *ledger*. Very quickly it became common practice to have several such books, for convenience. Today there are no longer accounts clerks, writing in books with quill pens. Instead, much accounting and record keeping is computerised – there are no books, only disks and screen displays. But the principles of keeping accounts remain the same, and therefore the subject is taught as though record keepers were still copying information from one book to another. Also, many people find it helpful to think of what is being done as though books were still used.

The ledger

The ledger is the name given to the main book in which records are kept. It contains the whole range of accounts kept by the business.

Ledger accounts

Within the ledger will be as many accounts (ie records of different aspects of the business) as are necessary. For example, there will be the customer accounts, and also accounts dealing with particular matters – one of these might be 'furniture and fittings'. The keeping of ledger accounts is explained in *Ledgers and journals*, page 177.

The cash book

The ledger is the book containing all the accounts of a business. However, certain records are used so frequently that it has long been customary to put them into a separate book. The transactions for which this happens are the dealings in cash and through the bank (the Cash account and the Bank account). They are recorded in the *cash book*. How to keep a cash book is explained in *Cash book*, page 115.

Journals

The word 'journal' comes from the French word 'jour' meaning 'day'. A journal is a *daily record of financial activity*. These records are therefore also often known as *day books*.

Another name for such records is *books of original* (or *prime*) *entry*, because in earlier times they were the point at which a first, detailed record of transactions was made. This information was later transferred (posted) to the ledger, the main record of a firm's accounts.

The journals are also referred to as *subsidiary books* because they are subsidiary to or back up the ledger. The difference is that the journals keep all the details of a transaction, so that the ledger entries can be kept much simpler. Also, from the accountant's point of view, the journals are not regarded as part of the ledger.

Nowadays the system has been simplified: firms record many transactions directly into the ledger. However, there are five cases in which journals are still used: these are situations in which detailed records are found to be valuable.

Four journals are used to deal with sales and purchases. These are: the sales journal, the purchases journal, the sales returns journal and the purchases returns journal. The two returns journals are the books of prime entry concerned with the return of sales and purchases (for example, faulty goods).

The fifth journal has various titles: *the journal, the journal proper* or *the main journal*. This is used for transactions which are felt to require detailed entry into the accounts, but which are not part of the sales and purchases process. Examples of the type of thing which might be entered are writing off a bad debt, or the purchase of a vehicle for use by the business.

The keeping of journals is described in *Ledgers and journals*, page 177.

Petty cash book

This is a record of small sums paid out in cash for day to day requirements. Examples would be small amounts for postage or stationery. The keeping of the petty cash book is described in *Petty cash*, page 219 forward.

Final accounts

These consist of three records: the *trading account*, the *profit and loss account*, and the *balance sheet*. They are a summary of the finances of the business made at the end of a year. Details are given in *Final accounts*, page 147 forward.

2. Credit and debit

2.1 Summary of uses of the words 'credit' and 'debit'

1)	*Creditworthy*	can be trusted to pay later, can have goods or services 'on credit'.
2)	*Credit* or *on credit*	dealings which are not cash, which are not paid for immediately, which involve a debt
3)	*Creditor*	person who allows credit
4)	*Debtor*	person who owes a debt
5)	In banking	
	Received a credit or *have credited your account*	the amount of money in your account has increased, or your debt (if you have one) is reduced
	Debit your account	reduce the amount of money in your account, or reduces the debt you have to them

6) In business

   Offer credit firm does not require an immediate settlement in cash (usually done through a customer account)

   When an account holder pays some or all of what is owed, the firm offering the account credits the account with that amount (reduces the debt)

7) In bookkeeping

   The **debit** column is the **left** hand column and basically records **incoming** money.

   The **credit** column is the **right** hand column and basically records **outgoing** money.

   The most basic use of the terms 'credit' and 'debit' in bookkeeping is given in *Basic approach to record keeping,* page 76.

   You should note that what is recorded in the debit and credit columns is in reality more complicated. A fuller explanation is given in *Ledgers and journals: double entry bookkeeping,* page 184.

3. Basic approach to record keeping

3.1 Two column entry

Bookkeeping is essentially about money paid out and money received. The books of a business therefore are divided into two columns to record those two actions. These are:

left hand column	**right hand column**
money received	**money paid out**

We can illustrate this by taking an example.

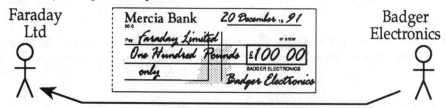

Faraday Ltd's books

MONEY RECEIVED FROM DEBTORS	£	p	MONEY PAID TO CREDITORS	£	p
Badger Electronics	100	00			

Badger Electronic's books

MONEY RECEIVED FROM DEBTORS	£	p	MONEY PAID TO CREDITORS	£	p
			Faraday Limited	100	00

Faraday Ltd supplies electronic parts. Badger Electronics places an order for goods worth £100, which are sent off. Badger Electronics is then £100 in debt to Faraday (that is, Badger is one of Faraday's debtors). Badger settles the debt (by sending money). Faraday then makes an entry in his books, which credits Badger with having paid £100. Since it is money received, Faraday enters it in that column. This is traditionally the left hand column. Put another way, we say that the convention is to use the left hand column for credits (money received).

Badger too will be keeping books. In their case, they will record that money owed has been paid out – their funds have been reduced (debited) the sum of £100. As might be expected, this is entered in the right hand column.

It is worth repeating:

money received = left hand column

money paid out = right hand column.

The following memory aid may help you to remember the above convention:

| R | ight hand side | R | educe your cash |

This is the most basic principle involved in financial record keeping.

3.2 Basic layout of an account

Information about a day's business does not come neatly packaged for the bookkeeper. A list of transactions to be recorded is more likely to look like this:

> *Mr Chaucer sent a cheque for £35*
>
> *Mr Lydgate was sent a cheque for £17.55*
>
> *Mrs Gower spent £13.56 on travel to interview – reimbursed by cheque*
>
> *Miss Dunbar paid her bill for with a cheque for £22.50*
>
> *Mrs Henryson spent £15.75 on stationery (paid by cheque)*
>
> *Cheque received from Wyatt and Surrey (builders) for £8.50 (overpaid)*
>
> *Skelton and Co (pets) sent cheque for £250 for talking parrot for entertainment of office*
>
> *Roy Henry sent cheque for £12*
>
> *Marlowe Borough Council were paid £450.60 (cheque)*
>
> *Beaumont and Fletcher (solicitors) – bill from them for £95 paid by cheque*
>
> *Dekker (Shoemakers) were paid by cheque £42*
>
> *Ben Jonson (Theatrical) sent cheque for £344*

The bookkeeper has first to select the appropriate account (this would actually be the Bank Account, explained in *Cash book*, page 115). The bookkeeper must then enter the information about the day's business in the appropriate columns, and often will total up receipts and payments. The result of entering the above in its simplest form would be:

(Receipts) Debit		(Payments) Credit	
Chaucer	35.00	Lydgate (expenses)	17.55
Dunbar	22.50	Gower (postage)	3.56
Wyatt and Surrey	8.50	Henryson (stationery)	15.75
Skelton	250.00	Marlowe Boro' Council	450.60
Roy Henry	12.00	Beaumont and Fletcher	95.00
Ben Jonson	344.00	Dekker	42.00
TOTAL	£672.00		£624.46

The bookkeeper has now drawn up a basic two column entry account for one day of business. This is the basic pattern of all such work. There are however more complicated systems, in which other columns are added. These are explained in the entries on *Cash book*, page 115, *Ledgers and journals*. page 177, and *Petty cash*, page 219. Also this day's accounts are not *balanced*. This is explained on page 77.

3.3 Headings of the columns

One aspect of the above entry may well be puzzling – the titles of the columns. These are given their professional names: the right hand side is the Credit side, and the left hand side is the Debit side. How can the receipt of money be a debit? When you receive a credit, you are receiving money. But in keeping your books the Credit side records money you pay out!

The first way to explain this difficulty is to remember that it was said in the case of Faraday and Badger that the right hand side was used for money paid to creditors and the left for money received from debtors. This has been done.

A further explanation is that here we have two related but different uses of the same word. Perhaps it does not seem so strange, if you bear in mind that when you get something *on* credit, you owe money.

The way to remember what to do is to ask yourself who is receiving or paying money:

left hand side   **right hand side**

money received (by me/us) from   **money paid (by me/us) to**

DEB(I)Tors   **CREDITors**

3.4 Summary

The basic principle of bookkeeping is to record money coming in and going out.

For these two situations two columns are used.

They are filled and labelled according to the rule:

> Payments MADE   go on the RIGHT which is the CREDIT side

and

> Payments RECEIVED   on the LEFT which is the DEBIT side.

The following poem by the anonymous Bard of Camden, written after a desperate hour with his accounts, may also help you to clarify and remember this somewhat confusing area:

THE BOOKKEEPER'S DITTY

If from the bank you receive a strong letter,
You can be certain that you are the DEBTOR.
But if a young writer's not paid by an editor,
Then to be sure that young person's a CREDITOR.

But keeping of books is a different affair;
You're likely to end up by tearing your hair!
For it's all back to front how they put it down there.

At the bank you're in credit,
You record it as DEBIT,
And you put under CREDIT
Every bank account debit!

So this is the way that you keep yourself sane:
Just let all the letters of CREDIT explain:

C redit side is

R ight hand side.

E nter

D ebts as paid

I n cash or cheques

T o others.

3.5 Balancing the account

The first task of the bookkeeper is to enter all payments and receipts into the accounts, as explained in the previous section.

At the end of the day (or whatever other accounting period is used, such as a week) the bookkeeper has then to calculate the totals for the columns.

At the same point there is one more process to be added: this is the calculation and recording of the *balance*. This is best explained by an example.

Assume that you have a set of entries and the totals are as follows:

Debit	**Credit**
£1356.00	£1120.00

1) subtract the smaller total from the larger:

$$
\begin{array}{r}
£ \\
1356.00 \ - \\
1120.00 \\
\hline
236.00 \\
\hline
\end{array}
$$

2) The debit side is £236.00 greater than the credit side, so we say that you have a *debit balance*.

3) You add *(carry)* this amount to the *other side* (in this case the credit side) to make the totals equal. This entry comes immediately after the last transaction which you recorded, and before the totals, so that the last lines of your account will look like this:

Debit			Credit		
Dec 12	Sales L6	125.00	Dec 12	postage L3	12.00
			Dec 13	balance c/d	236.00
		£1356.00			£1356.00

'Balance c/d' means 'balance carried down'

4) Finally you must *bring down* the balance. This means that you record its existence on the appropriate side (in this case it is a debit balance). You do this after the totals so that it is the first entry of the next accounting period. The final result is as follows:

Debit			Credit		
Dec 12	Sales L6	125.00	Dec 12	postage L3	12.00
			Dec 13	balance c/d	236.00
		£1356.00			£1356.00
Dec 15	Balance b/d	236.00			

'Balance b/d' means 'balance brought down'

You have now balanced off the account.

Bank documents

The function and handling of common bank documents

Contents

1. Bank giro

The banks have made it possible to avoid the need for making large numbers of payments which each have to be posted individually to the various recipients or their banks. Instead, a single payment can be made through the ***bank giro credit transfer system***. The process is often simply referred to as 'paying by Giro' or 'credit transfer'.

The bank giro system avoids the security risk of having to move around large sums in cash, or large numbers of cheques. The system also has the advantage to anyone paying bills by cheque that there is no need to post them, with the risk of loss or theft. The money is credited directly between the relevant bank accounts, hence the name 'credit transfer'.

The system can work in several ways:

1) The person paying gives to his or her own bank a slip detailing the payment to be made, and cash or a cheque to cover the total amount. The bank then transfers money to the relevant account.

2) The person paying can fill in slips to settle many bills, covering these with a single payment (cash or cheque) for the total amount; for this reason the system is known as multiple credit transfer. It is a system often used by employers to deal with wages.

3) The system can be used by customers who cannot reach their own branch (for instance while away on business) to deposit cash or cheques into their own account. They simply fill in a slip and hand in both it and the money (cash or cheques) to be transferred at any bank.

4) The system can also be used to deposit cash or cheques into *another* person's account, as long as the depositor knows the bank, branch, account name and number of the recipient.

For the convenience of regular users of the system, the banks provide books of bank giro slips. Whether used singly or from a book, the bank giro form is in two parts. The larger part is torn off, leaving a stub, known as the **counterfoil**. This contains a summary of the payment made. It is important to keep the counterfoil as a record of the transaction.

The information given below must be included on the slip.

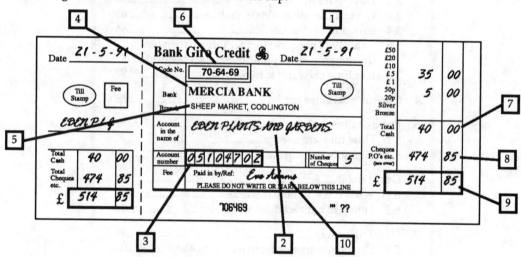

The following information is included on the form:

1 The date on which paying-in took place.

2 The name of the account (eg Eastcote Printers) or account holder (Debora Allen) to be credited with the money (known as the 'beneficiary'). Note: Eden Plants and Gardens in the example above.

3 The account number of that account.

4 The name of the bank with which that account exists.

5 The name of the branch at which that account is held.

6 The sort code of that branch. (This is a code number, different for each branch, to help in the computerised processing of the transfer).

7 Total cash paid in.

8 The total of the cheques paid in.

9. The total amount paid in.

10. Signature of the person who pays in the money.

11. On the back of the slip there is usually a space to itemise a batch of payments.

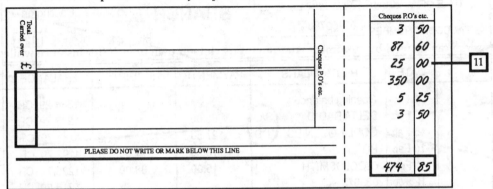

In the case of large organisations with regular customers (eg Electricity) there will often also be:

12. The reference number or account number which is allotted by the person or company receiving payment to the person who is paying in the money.

Large organisations often make special arrangements with the banks. The data, for instance for a large payroll, is sent on a computer tape to be dealt with by the Clearing House system (BACS) (see *Banking facilities: clearance of cheques*, page 100). In order to facilitate incoming payments, large organisations often also issue their customers with forms on which certain of the information is already printed.

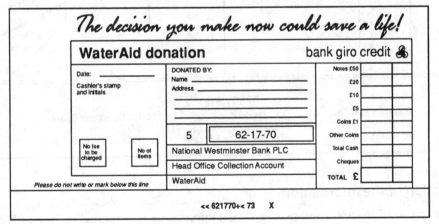

Preprinted form – WaterAid

2. Bank statements

2.1 The basic information and how it is organised

All businesses, and all individuals who have a bank account receive regular bank statements. These are summaries of what money has been received on behalf of the customer ('credited to the account'), what money has been paid out on behalf of the customer ('debited from the account') and what money ('balance') is left over at the time when the statement is drawn up.

Bank documents

A typical bank statement would look like this.

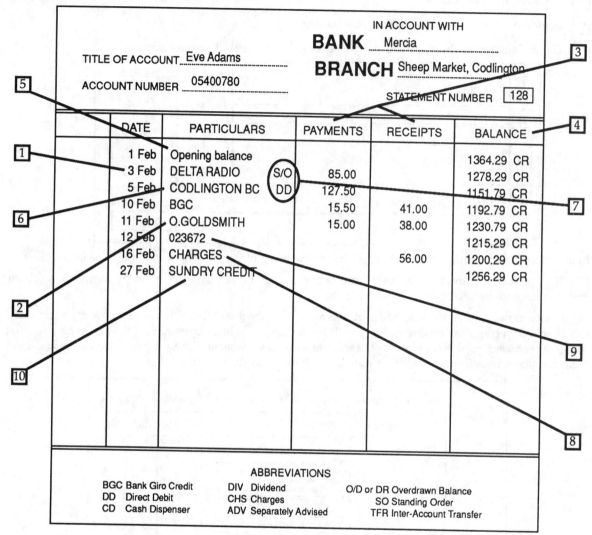

2.2 Presentation of the information

The conventions (rules of the organisation) of how the information is presented differ a little from bank to bank, but the principles are the same. The conventions used in this example are taken from Lloyds' current accounts.

1   Each entry must be dated

2   It must have suitable particulars

3   The amount is entered in one of two columns: 'Payment' (*by* the bank on behalf of account holder) and 'Receipts' (paid *to* the bank in favour of the account holder).

4   There is also a column for the balance and this is *calculated at the end of each day's business.*

⑤ The sheet first lists (as the *opening balance*) the balance shown at the end of the previous sheet of the statement. There is an indication of whether the account is in credit or overdrawn (usually by the letters OD in the latter case).

⑥ In the case of standing orders and direct debits the name of the payee is given.

⑦ The particulars column is filled in as follows by Lloyds:

BGC   Bank Giro Credit

SO   Standing Order

DD   Direct Debit

⑧ The word 'charges' refers to charges made by the bank for their services (for details see *Banking facilities: bank charges*, page 101).

⑨ Cheques drawn on the bank are designated by their serial number.

⑩ When several cheques are paid in at the branch by the account holder, this is indicated by the entry 'Sundry Credit', but a detailed breakdown is not given. This is one reason why the counterfoil of deposit slips are important to the person keeping business records. The same applies to Bank Giro credits.

3. Cheques

3.1 Drawing a cheque; the basic process

When you open a current account, you put money into the account. You are then issued with a cheque book and often a *cheque card*. The use of cheques enables you to pay bills where the use of cash might be inconvenient, unsafe or impossible. Cheques are also valuable to businesses, because the way in which they are processed involves the creation of various types of written record, such as counterfoils (see *Cheques*, page 85) and bank statements (see *Bank statements*, page 81). Such records make it easier to keep and check a firm's accounts.

Who is involved?

In order to pay by cheque there has to be a person who writes the cheque, known as the *drawer*. The money which the cheque transfers is deducted (*debited*) from the drawer's account. Second, there is the person who receives the cheque, who is known as the *payee* (French for 'person who is paid'). Money is added (*credited*) to the payee's account. Finally, there is the source of the money, the bank, which is holding money for the drawer, and which transfers money from the drawer's account to that of the payee. The bank is known as the *drawee* (person drawn upon) and we say that the cheque is *drawn upon* that bank.

Clearance of cheques

In order for the payee to be paid, the cheque must be cleared. This means that it must be passed through the banking system, and the money must be transferred. For a full account of clearance see *Banking facilities*, page 100.

The important thing to remember is that the process normally takes *three working days*.

Bank documents

3.2 How to fill in a cheque correctly

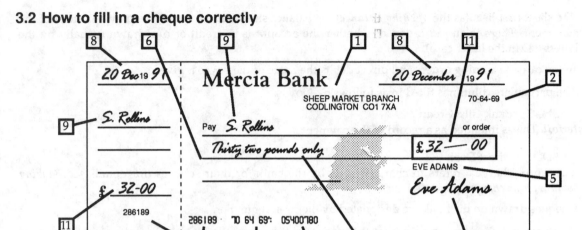

For a cheque to be acceptable to the payee and drawee, it must be correct in various ways.

Printed information

A cheque contains information which is printed on it before it is ever used.

1. The name and address of the branch upon which the cheque will be drawn.
2. The bank sort code (the branch reference number – included to assist the computerised processing of the cheque). Note that this appears in two places.
3. The drawer's account number
4. The cheque number
5. The name or names of those entitled to use the cheque. Note that this may differ from the signature: Mr J.P Smith could sign 'Jack Smith'.
6. Space and lines upon which to write the amount to be drawn.
7. Some cheques will also have a printed crossing (see *Cheques 3.4*, page 86)

Added information

To the printed cheque is added various other information. Some of this is extremely important. This information is normally written by hand, but can be added (except for the signature) by a typewriter or by a computerised system, such as you now find at many supermarket checkouts.

8. The date. From the payee's point of view this must not exceed six months before the date on which the cheque is paid in. Otherwise the cheque is known as 'stale' and is not paid (*honoured*) by the bank. A date in the future can be inserted (known as a post-dated cheque) if the payee will accept it. If you are offered a post-dated cheque, remember that (a) the bank is not obliged to pay you until that date and (b) the lapse of time means that the drawer could then 'stop' the cheque, ie instruct the bank not to honour it.
9. Name of payee. This will need to be in a form which the bank will accept, and which clearly indicates the payee (for example, 'A.J. White' and not just 'White').
10. Amount in words. This must be the same as (11).
11. Amount in figures.

| 12 | Signature of drawer. This must be the usual signature of the drawer. When the account is opened, the bank takes a specimen signature. The drawer should not then sign in a very different style (eg italic writing, capitals). |

| 13 | There may be a crossing (see *Cheques 3.4*, page 86). |

| 14 | There may be an endorsement (see *Cheques 3.5*, page 87) |

Note that the cheque is in two parts. The larger part is torn off, leaving a stub, technically known as the *counterfoil*. This is intended as a record of the payment.

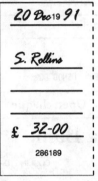

Cheque counterfoil

3.3 Using a cheque to obtain cash

Drawing cash at one's own branch

❒ At his or her own branch the current account holder may use an open cheque by writing 'cash' (instead of a name) on the top line, followed by the amount.

❒ A crossed cheque may be used (see *Cheques 3.4*, page 86) , but it is supposed to be opened by writing 'pay cash' and the drawer's signature between the crossings. In practice, with a well known customer, this is not always required.

Drawing cash at another branch or bank

❒ Money may be withdrawn from another branch of the customer's bank, or even from a different bank altogether. This is done by using a cheque as above, supported by a cheque card (see *Bank documents: cheque guarantee cards*, page 89). Up to £50 (increasingly, £100) may be drawn out in any one day. The cheque book must be stamped and initialled (or marked in some other approved way) by the cashier. This is to ensure that the customer does not draw out money beyond the limit.

❒ Money may be withdrawn at another bank if an arrangement has been made between it and the drawer's bank in advance. This facility is useful when sums above the cheque card limit are required.

❒ A person well known to you, such as a local trader, will sometimes be willing to give you cash in exchange for a cheque which is made out to you, if you *endorse* it, that is, sign it on the back. Another option is to give the drawer of the cheque change in cash for a cheque which is made out for more than the sum due when buying goods. Note, however, that many traders are unwilling to allow this (or any other form of credit) because of their fear of losing money through fraud or inability to pay. Even if a trader is willing or able to allow a customer this facility, the bank can refuse to honour the cheque in two circumstances:

a) the original drawer's cheque is not supported by a valid cheque card

b) a crossed cheque bears the words 'not negotiable' – this means that the cheque cannot be passed on to anyone else.

3.4 Crossing of cheques

Open and crossed cheques

Open cheque

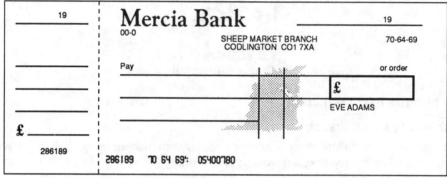

Crossed cheque

Compare these two cheques. The first one is known as an *open* cheque. This means that the payee can obtain cash to the amount stated by presenting the cheque at the drawer's bank. The danger of using an open cheque is that, if it is stolen, the thief can use the cheque to obtain cash.

The lines on the second example indicate that it is a *crossed* cheque. A cheque which is crossed has to be paid into a bank account. Crossing is therefore used to ensure greater security; with a crossed cheque it is much harder to obtain money to which one is not entitled.

There are two types of crossing: *general* and *special*.

a) *General crossings:*
    Two lines, often with the words 'and Co' between, is just a way of indicating that the cheque is crossed, and must not be honoured in cash. By adding 'a/c payee only' in the crossing, the writer of a cheque can specify that only the person named can receive payment.

    The writer of the cheque can also specify a limit to how much may be paid (eg 'under £50'); this device is often used by public bodies to ensure that, in the event of error or fraud, only a small sum will be lost. All the above additions are known as 'general crossings'.

b) *Special crossings:*
    If the drawer names a particular bank where the cheque must be presented, this is known as a 'special crossing'.

3.5 Validity of cheques: further information

Endorsement of cheques

You can 'hand on' a cheque to someone else by signing it on the back. This is called an *endorsement*. Technically, the cheque is a *bill of exchange*. This means that the payee can transfer ownership to another person, for instance, in payment of a debt, if the third party will accept it.

Alterations

Banks do not like alterations to the added written instructions, because of the danger of forgery. If a change is really necessary, it has to be initialled by the drawer.

Bouncing cheques

When we say that a cheque 'has bounced' we mean that the bank has refused to pay it. In technical language we say that the bank has 'refused to honour' or has 'dishonoured' the cheque. If this happens, the bank usually writes 'R/D' (return to drawer) on the cheque and returns it to the person who wrote it.

The bank may do this for various reasons:

1) The cheque has not been correctly filled in.

2) The drawer has instructed the bank to 'stop payment', for example, because goods paid for have not been received.

3) The drawer does not have sufficient money in the account to cover the payment.

3.6 Handling cheques – summary

Who is involved?

1) person who writes the cheque: the *drawer*
   money is debited from the drawer's account.

2) person who receives the cheque: the *payee*
   money is credited to the payee's account

3) bank holds money for the drawer, and transfers money to account of the payee
   bank is the *drawee*; cheque is drawn upon the bank

Clearance

1) The payee puts the cheque into the bank, which records its receipt on a computer. The payee's account is credited at that time with the relevant amount.

2) When the cheque is returned to the drawer's branch, the relevant sum is debited from the drawer's account. This is the last stage of the process, which normally takes three working days. (For a full description of the process of clearance, see *Banking facilities: clearance of cheques*, page 100.)

To obtain cash

1) at drawer's own bank
   - open cheque: write 'cash' (instead of a name) on the top line, followed by the amount.
   - crossed cheque: opened by writing 'pay cash' and the drawer's signature between the crossings.

2) at another bank
   - use cheque as above, supported by a cheque card.

❏   if an arrangement has been made.

3) from another person

❏   cash in exchange for a cheque which is made out to the person seeking cash, if that person endorses it (signs it on the back).

❏   change in cash for a cheque which is made out for more than the sum due when buying goods.

Format and validity of a cheque

If a cheque is not valid, a bank will not honour it. For it to be valid it must contain the following information:

Printed

1) name and address of the branch.

2) bank sort code (the branch reference number).

3) drawer's account number.

4) cheque number.

5) name or names of those entitled to use the cheque.

6) space and lines upon which to write the amount to be drawn.

7) possibly a printed crossing.

Added information

8) date must not exceed six months before the date on which the cheque is paid in.

9) name of payee.

10) amount in words. This must be the same as (11).

11) amount in figures.

12) usual signature of drawer.

13) possibly a crossing (see below).

14) possibly an endorsement.

Alterations have to be initialled by the drawer.

Cashier's basic checklist

Check:
- ❏   date (today's date)
- ❏   name of payee
- ❏   signature (same as name)
- ❏   amount in words (same as amount in figures)
- ❏   the amount in figures

(This assumes that the printed document is genuine.)

Refusal to honour a cheque

(Cheque 'has bounced', the bank has 'refused to honour' or has 'dishonoured' the cheque). Bank usually writes 'R/D' (return to drawer) on the cheque and returns it to the person who wrote it.

Banks can refuse to honour cheques when:

1) The cheque has not been correctly filled in.

2) The drawer's cheque is not supported by a valid cheque card.

3) The drawer has instructed the bank to 'stop payment'.

4) The drawer does not have sufficient money in the account to cover the payment, or has exceeded his or her credit limit.

Crossings

Open cheque: payee can obtain cash by presenting cheque at drawer's bank; crossed cheque has to be paid into a bank account

General crossings: two lines, often with *'and Co'*
can add: *'a/c payee only'* – only the person named can receive payment.
limit to how much may be paid
'not negotiable' – cannot be passed on to anyone else.

Special crossing: drawer names a particular bank where the cheque must be presented.

4. Cheque guarantee cards

When a customer who has a current account is felt by the bank to have a responsible attitude towards the management of that account, the bank can issue a cheque guarantee card (also known as a banker's card, or most commonly as a cheque card). An example is given below.

As with a cheque, there is various printed and added information which must be in order, if the card is to be accepted by the payee and drawee (bank).

Printed information

1) The name of the bank upon which cheques will be drawn.

2) The bank sort code (the branch reference number – included to assist the computerised processing).

3) The drawer's account number.

4) The card number.

5) The name the person entitled to use the card. Note that this may differ from the signature: Mr J.P Smith could sign 'Jack Smith'.

6) The expiry date of the card.

7) The limit to which the guarantee operates. This has normally been £50, but many banks now allow a limit of £100.

8) Some cards will also have other information to enable them to have multiple uses, notably as a card for use in a cash dispenser, and as a Visa card, which can be used in many places instead of a cheque.

Added information

The card contains a space for the signature of the holder, which must be written by hand.

Use of a cheque card

The card can be used as follows:

1) When offering a cheque, as a guarantee to the payee. The latter must ensure that

   a)   the expiry date is not past,

   b)   the account numbers on the cheque and on the card are the same, and

   c)   the signatures on the two are the same.

   When this has been done, the payee must write the card number on the back of the cheque.

   If this is not done, or if it is not written by the payee, the bank can refuse payment. But if everything is in order, the bank then guarantees to pay any sum up to the limit. Even if the drawer does not have sufficient funds, the payee will still receive payment.

2) By using the card with a cheque, the drawer can go to any bank which operates the scheme and obtain up to £50 cash on any one day.

3) By using the card with a cheque, the drawer can go to any bank in Europe which operates the scheme and cash two cheques for up to £50 on any one day.

The above facts raise various questions of security.

The *bank* will be very insistent that every aspect of the process is correctly carried out. Also, if the drawer uses the card without having sufficient funds in his or her account, the bank is likely to call in the card.

The *payee* needs to be very careful to check all the details, since the card only guarantees the money when these are in order. However, when a correctly guaranteed cheque is accepted, it cannot be stopped by the drawer.

The *drawer* must be certain that satisfactory service has been given, since a properly guaranteed cheque cannot be stopped. Consequently, it would unwise to pay for something one has not seen. It is also important to keep the card and cheque book separately, as a precaution against theft or loss. The card is no use without a cheque book, and increasingly, payees require the support of a card. But if a thief can get hold of both cheque and card, he has a specimen signature, which he can learn to counterfeit. If he can do this, he can then use all the cheques in the book – which become worth several hundred pounds. Banks lose millions of pounds a year through fraud of this type. They therefore agree to meet the cost after a loss or theft only from the time at which they are notified. It is thus in the drawer's interest to do so at once, even in the middle of the night (there is a 24 hour emergency service).

5. Deposit slips

5.1 How they are used

Money may be paid into a bank in the form of cheques or cash, at the customer's own branch or at another branch, or even at a different bank. To pay in money, the account holder fills in a deposit slip (also known as a *credit slip* or *paying-in slip*).

Several further points need to be made.

1) When paying in money to your own account at your own branch, you use an 'in-house' credit slip like the one shown below. This is designed for use only in that branch.

2) When paying money to your own account at any other bank, you need to use the Bank Giro system (see *Bank documents: bank giro*, page 79).

3) When paying money to someone else's account, you need to use the Bank Giro system.

4) From the point of view of keeping financial records it is important that the form is filled in correctly, and the counterfoil kept safely. In the event of error (accidental or fraud) the slip is proof of what was paid, when, and by whom. The slip also itemises the transaction (ie it gives full details), whereas the entry in a bank statement (see *Bank documents: bank statements*, page 81) will only give the total payment. This is important when records have to be inspected by a chief cashier, accountant or tax officer.

5) People who deposit money frequently at their own branch can ask for a paying-in book, which has the advantage of providing many slips at one time, and of keeping the counterfoils together, so reducing the risk of losing them.

5.2 Filling in the slip

The front of a filled-in slip looks like this:

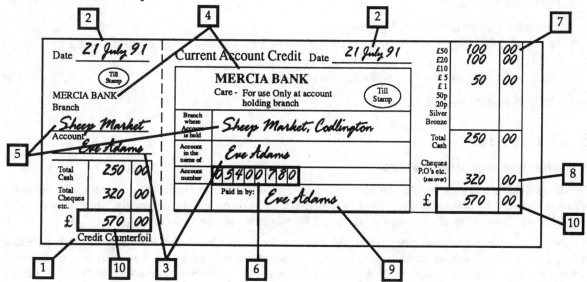

91

Normally, the back of the slip looks like this:

Cheques PO's etc.			Brought Forward				Cheques PO's etc.		
Martin	100	00					100	00	
Donahue	150	00					150	00	
Smithson	70	00					70	00	
Carried Forward	320	00	Total Cheques PO's etc. £	320	00		320	00	Total Carried Over

Notes:

1. The form has two parts. The smaller part is called the counterfoil. It is torn off by the cashier, stamped and handed back to the customer. It is intended as a record that the money has actually been paid in.

2. The date on which paying-in took place.

3. The name of the account (eg Luxury Curtains Ltd Business Account) or account holder (R.S Peters) to be credited with the money.

4. The name of the bank with which the account exists.

5. The name of the branch at which the account is held.

6. The account number.

7. A detailed statement of the cash paid in.

8. The total of the cheques paid in. (Space for a detailed listing of the cheques is given on the back of the form).

9. Signature of the person who actually paid in the money.

10. The total amount paid in.

6. Direct debit

6.1 What it is and how it works

The direct debit is a system used by banks to pay bills on behalf of a customer automatically. The customer is saved the need to make a special effort to remember and pay each debt separately. This is very useful with bills which arrive regularly, such as payments for gas or telephone service.

A direct debit fulfils the same purpose as the use of a Standing Order (see *Bank documents: 7. Standing orders*, page 94), but reduces complications in the administration of accounts. The money is transferred directly from the customer's account to the account of the person or organisation who is to be paid, instead of through a bank payment which is then claimed back from the customer.

INSTRUCTIONS TO YOUR BANK TO PAY DIRECT DEBITS

Please complete parts 1 to 5 to instruct your bank to make payments directly from your account. Then send the form to your bank.

Originator's Identification Number

9	7	1	4	7	7

To The Manager,

MERCIA Bank,

SHEEP MARKET,

CODLINGTON CO1 7XA

1   Please write the full postal address of your bank branch in the box above.

2   Name of Account Holder

EDEN PLANTS AND GARDENS

3   Bank account number

0	5	1	0	4	7	0	2

4   Please write Customer Account No. in box below

m	E	V	g	-	1	0	3	-	1

5   Your instructions to the bank, and signature

*   I instruct you to pay direct debits from my account at the request of the Borough of Codlington

*   The amounts are variable and may be debited on various dates

*   I understand that the Borough of Codlington may change the amounts and dates only after giving me prior notice.

*   I will inform the bank in writing if I wish to cancel this instruction.

*   I understand that if any direct debit is paid which breaks the terms of this Instruction, the bank will make a refund.

Signature(s)   *Eve Adams*

Date   *11 Oct 1991*

Banks may refuse to accept instructions to pay direct debits from some types of account.

Customer Account No.   *mEVg 103 1*

Name   *EDEN PLANTS AND GARDENS*

Address   *67 PEARMAIN DRIVE*

CODLINGTON CO4 9BR

To   The Director of Finance
Borough of Codlington
Town Hall
Codlington
CO1 4AB

After completion the bank branch should detach the lower part of the form and return it to Codlington Council.

FOR BANK USE ONLY

Branch title ....

Sort Code   ☐☐ - ☐☐ - ☐☐

A/c no.   ☐☐☐☐☐☐☐☐

A/c name
....

(Maximum 18 characters)

Direct debits in respect of our customer's Instruction under the reference number quoted should be made out as above.

For .... Bank

Manager .... Date ....

A further advantage of this system is that a fixed sum need not be named, if the customer is willing to sign a variable direct debit mandate. This is clearly an advantage when the amount of money to be paid is likely to change frequently. For example, when mortgage rates are changing every few months, a great deal of trouble and cost to both mortgage company and customer is saved in cases where a variable direct debit mandate permits a simple adjustment. The payee simply claims from the bank whatever the new amount is to be. There are of course safeguards against improper use of the system.

6.2 Filling in a Direct Debit mandate

Large organisations normally provide their own mandates for their customers. As a consequence much of the information which has to be filled in on a standing order mandate is already provided. The example overleaf indicates the points at which the person making the payment must complete the form.

7. Standing orders

7.1 Paying out money from a current account

The customer of a bank can use a current account to settle debts by withdrawing money and then making payments in cash, or by signing a cheque. In cases where there is a need to make regular payments (for instance, electricity bills), there are other options. One is the direct debit (see *Bank documents: direct debit*, page 92). Another is the standing order.

7.2 How standing orders operate

The account holder gives a written instruction (known as a standing order mandate) to the bank to pay a particular sum to a named person or organisation (eg the Electricity Board) on a particular date. The bank does so and then debits the customer's account. This saves the cost and trouble of writing out a cheque each time and avoids the danger of forgetting to pay an important bill. From the point of view of business, reminders and requests for payment are not needed.

7.3 How to fill in a standing order mandate

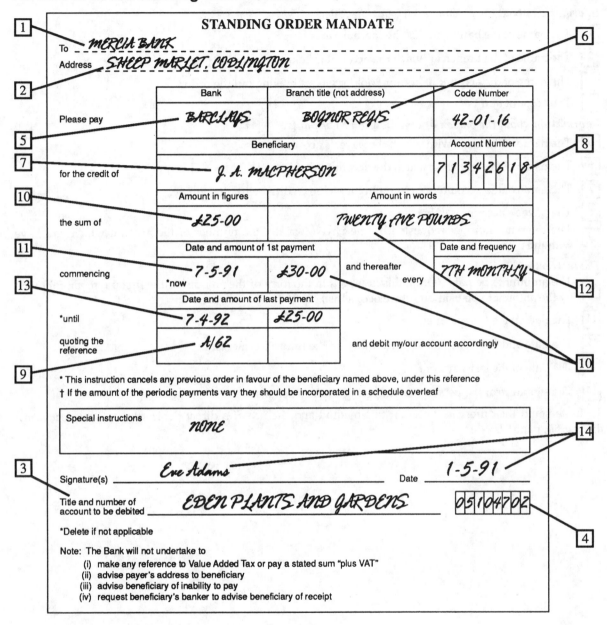

1

STANDING ORDER MANDATE

To MERCIA BANK

6

Address SHEEP MARKET, CODLINGTON

2

	Bank	Branch title (not address)	Code Number
Please pay	BARCLAYS	BOGNOR REGIS	42-01-16

5

	Beneficiary	Account Number
for the credit of	J. A. MACPHERSON	7 1 3 4 2 6 1 8

7

8

	Amount in figures	Amount in words
the sum of	£25-00	TWENTY FIVE POUNDS

10

	Date and amount of 1st payment			Date and frequency
commencing	7-5-91	£30-00	and thereafter every	7TH MONTHLY
	*now			

11

13

12

	Date and amount of last payment	
*until	7-4-92	£25-00
quoting the reference	A/62	and debit my/our account accordingly

9

10

* This instruction cancels any previous order in favour of the beneficiary named above, under this reference
† If the amount of the periodic payments vary they should be incorporated in a schedule overleaf

Special instructions   NONE

14

Signature(s) _Eve Adams_   Date 1-5-91

3

Title and number of account to be debited   EDEN PLANTS AND GARDENS   0 5 1 0 4 7 0 2

4

*Delete if not applicable

Note: The Bank will not undertake to
   (i) make any reference to Value Added Tax or pay a stated sum "plus VAT"
   (ii) advise payer's address to beneficiary
   (iii) advise beneficiary of inability to pay
   (iv) request beneficiary's banker to advise beneficiary of receipt

A standing order mandate contains the following information:

Information about the person making out the order:

1. The name of the bank with his/her account exists.

2. The name of the branch at which the account is held.

3. The name of the account or account holder who is making out the order.

4. The account number.

Information about the person or organisation to be paid:

5. The name of the bank with which the payee's account exists.

6. The name of the branch at which the account is held.

7. The name of the account or account holder to be credited with the money.

8. The payee's account number.

9. The reference number requested by the payee (usually the number of the account which you have with the payee).

The instructions

10. The amount to be paid. (Often this is set out in the form of the amount of the first payment, followed by the amount to be paid on future occasions.)

11. The date of the first payment.

12. The date and frequency (usually monthly) of the future payments.

13. The date of the last payment.

14. The signature of the person (dated) giving the instructions.

To understand the difference between this method and the use of a direct debit, turn to *Bank documents: direct debit*, page 92.

Banking facilities

Information about the basic working of banking facilities

Preliminary reading

The first time you use this section you should begin by reading *Structure and functions*, below.

Contents

Note: Guidance on how to calculate currency conversions will be found in *Calculations: foreign currency*, page 106.

1. Structure and functions

1.1 The commercial banks

There are four main *commercial banks*: Barclays, Lloyds, Midland and National Westminster. Both Williams and Glyn and Coutts are also commercial banks, though much smaller. All these banks are concerned with offering the public *a system of depositing and transferring money* (ie saving money, and making payments).

These banks are also known as *clearing banks* because they belong to the Bankers' Clearing House. It is so named because it is concerned with the handling of cheques, a process referred to by bankers as 'clearing'. The Clearing House system eases the problem of moving millions of cheques daily around the country. The process of clearing cheques is handled by the computerised Bankers' Automated Clearing Services (BACS). At the end of each day's business, the banks settle up what they owe each other through accounts held at the Bank of England. The clearing process is described in more detail in *Banking facilities: clearance of cheques*, page 100.

1.2 Uses of banks to individuals and businesses

Banks offer a range of services which are useful to the individual. There are accounts to assist saving, borrowing, and the transfer of money. There are also procedures to ease the payment of money, notably by means of cheques, credit transfer, standing orders and direct debits. The bank can provide loans, and give assistance in dealing with foreign currencies. Other useful services include cash dispensers and safe deposits (for valuable documents).

The facilities offered by banks are also helpful to the business world. It is possible to save capital and profits, and to borrow for investment. The use of cheques and credit facilities makes it easier for the customer to pay; bank statements make it easier to keep a check on the flow of money within a business. The banks can make dealings with foreign customers easier. Safe deposits and night safes mean that valuable documents or cash are are kept more securely.

2. Types of account

If you have money to save, the bank will encourage you to use some form of *savings account*. Two factors are important in such accounts.

First, the bank wishes not only to know how much you will save (known as the *principal* or *capital sum*), but for how long. In order to use the money, say to invest in a construction project which will take five years to complete, they need to know that they will have a sufficient amount of money for that period. Savings accounts therefore state the length of time which must elapse before the lender (known as the *investor*) can withdraw any of the money.

Second, the bank needs to make it worth your while to save with them. They do this by offering *interest*, ie a payment for borrowing. To encourage the customer to lend large sums for a long period, the amount of interest is related to the size and length of the savings. Interest is calculated as a percentage of the sum borrowed. (For further detail on interest and its calculation see *Calculations: interest*, page 107).

3. Borrowing money

3.1 General principles

Both individuals and businesses often have to borrow money. What we wish or need to spend may be in excess of the money which we have saved, or can raise in the immediate future. Similarly a business may wish to acquire machinery, premises or transport and not have the money available. In such a case they may well apply for a bank loan.

The lenders naturally wish to ensure that the money will be repaid. They therefore look for an indication that the borrower will have enough money to do so. The bank will want a detailed indication of what the borrower's business is likely to earn in the future. An important source of information about the prospects for the business will be the Final Accounts (see *Final accounts*, page 147).

The lenders also seek some guarantee that they will still get their money back, even if the borrower is no longer able to meet the payments. A bank will usually ask for some sort of guarantee (known as a *security*). For example, they may reserve the right to sell off valuable assets, which will mean that the bank does not lose money, if the borrower cannot repay the debt.

The lenders have a further requirement. They are not a free public service; instead they are in the business of making money by handling money – in this case by lending it. Banks therefore charge *interest* – a payment for borrowing (see *Calculations: interest*, page 107).

3.2 Individual borrowing

Banks can help the individual who wishes to borrow money in four main ways.

First, they can give a *personal loan*. At present the banks favour *fixed loans*, that is, the borrower is given a set period of time in which to repay. There is a fixed rate of interest on the total sum borrowed which is included in the repayments. The whole sum and the interest must be repaid, even if the borrower is able to repay more quickly than anticipated.

A second way of borrowing money is by means of an *overdraft*. This means that holders of a current account are allowed to spend more money than is coming into their account. For this service they pay interest at the current rate. This may change very quickly, because of changes in the national economic situation. Interest is paid on whatever debt is outstanding – so it is best for the borrower to pay back the money as quickly as possible.

The *budget account* is another way of borrowing money for short periods, which some people find useful. This type of account is helpful in dealing with fairly large bills which occur at intervals (eg electricity, mortgage). The customer with a budget account names what payments are to be made over the year, and allots sufficient of his/her income in equal instalments to cover the annual bill. The bank then guarantees to find the necessary payments, even when this means that, for a period, the payments total more than the income so far received. For this service a charge is made.

A fourth way of borrowing money is by means of *credit cards*. These are covered in the entry *Methods of payment: credit cards*, page 207.

4. Transfer of money

4.1 General points

Both individuals and businesses find that the banks provide a vital, convenient and secure way of transferring money from one person or organisation to another. If we buy something in a shop, or if we provide a customer with goods or services, money has to be *transferred* in some way to pay for what is received. Often this transfer involves only the handing of cash from one person to another (for example in paying a bus fare). But on other occasions it may not be desirable or possible to carry around the sum involved. It may also be necessary to commit oneself to a payment which is not made for some days, weeks or months.

4.2 Current accounts

The bank enables you to transfer money easily by means of a *current account*. In this type of account, in return for putting in money regularly, the bank gives you facilities for transferring that money to those whom you have to pay. The commonest way of doing this is by means of a cheque. The use of cheques is described in *Bank documents: cheques*, page 83.

The bank agrees to pay all cheques at once, up to an agreed limit. To reassure the person who accepts the cheque, the customer may well have a *cheque guarantee card*. The card guarantees that the bank will pay the agreed sum (for details see *Bank documents: cheque guarantee cards*, page 89). Provided that you are likely to have money coming in, you can even borrow (overdraw) for a short period.

However, because the money is moving in and out of the bank so quickly, the bank has far less scope for using the money for investment than it does when we use a savings account. They therefore make *charges* for the use of the account, and they charge interest on overdrafts (see *Banking facilities: bank charges*, page 101). Until very recently they also paid no interest on current accounts because the money could not really be used to make money. This situation is now changing because of the intense competition between the banks, and also between the banks and the building societies.

4.3 Paying in and withdrawing money

In current accounts we need to pay in and withdraw money frequently. There are a variety of options for the current account holder. Money may be paid or withdrawn in in the form of cheques or in cash at the customer's own branch. Money may be paid in or withdrawn at another branch or bank, through the bank giro system (see *Bank documents: bank giro*, page 79).

4.4 Paying out money

There are several ways in which you can use a current account to settle debts. You can withdraw cash, at the counter of the bank or at a cash dispenser or you can go to another bank. The other common means of payment is to sign a cheque. For regular payments you can use the standing order and direct debit facilities, in which the bank arranges for payment automatically.

4.5 Credit transfers

The banks have made it possible to avoid the need for making payments, which have to be posted to the various recipients or their banks. This is done by the bank giro credit transfer system. For details see *Banking documents: bank giro*, page 79.

5. Clearance of cheques

The basic process of drawing a cheque is described in *Banking documents: cheques*, page 83. This entry describes what happens once the cheque has been written, handed over, and accepted, often after a cheque guarantee card has also been presented in support of the cheque.

In order for the payee to be paid, several things have to happen.

1) *The drawer* (who, for example, banks at Barclay's) makes out the cheque, and *gives or sends it to the payee*.

2) The payee checks that the cheque is in order (for details see *Banking documents: cheques*, page 83) and if so, *puts the cheque into his or her bank* (which for this example can be the Midland Bank).

3) The *Midland bank* checks that the cheque is in order, and if so, records its receipt on their computer. *The payee's account is credited with the relevant amount.*

cont...

4) The *cheque is then placed in a batch* along with other cheques which are being *drawn on the same bank* (which is Barclay's – why? If in doubt, reread point 1).

5) The Midland bank then sends the cheque to the *clearing department of its head office in London*. The cheque is then added to boxes of other cheques from the same bank (Barclay's), ready for return to that bank.

6) The boxes of cheques are *exchanged at the Banker's Clearing House*. It is so named because it is concerned with the handling of cheques, a process referred to by bankers as 'clearing'. The Clearing House system eases the problem of moving millions of cheques daily around the country. The process of clearing cheques is handled by the computerised Bankers' Automated Clearing Services (BACS). At the end of each day's business, the banks settle up what they owe each other through accounts held at the Bank of England.

7) The Barclay's *clearing department* then processes the cheque and sends it back to the branch from which it originally came.

(8) *At the drawer's branch* the cheque is checked once again, and if in order, *the relevant sum is deducted (debited) from the drawer's account*. The process will normally have taken three working days. (The Clearing House does not carry on business on Saturdays or Sundays.)

6. Bank charges

At intervals the accounts department of a business will check their records against their bank statements (this is known as *reconciling* the two records). This process is described in detail in *Cash book: bank reconciliation statement*, page 122). The person undertaking the task often finds that the totals do not agree. In particular outgoings may be higher than expected. This situation often arises because of a failure to anticipate bank charges.

Such charges are a way in which the bank deals with the cost of administrating an account. They can also be used as a deterrent to customers who are inclined to overspend.

The common charges are:

1) *A basic arrangement fee* for undertaking the work. This will be a set figure. Its importance therefore decreases, the larger the volume of business.

2) *Service charges* calculated according to the number of transactions. It costs money to write a cheque!

3) *Interest charges* (often listed separately) made on overdrafts.

The above charges normally apply to business accounts. Personal accounts tend to bear charges only when overdrawn.

With regard to the latter situation, it is worth bearing in mind that, if a cheque, standing order or direct debit is not honoured (for details of these see *Bank documents*, page 87), a charge of some £40 is made. A quotation from a recent letter illustrates the reasoning behind the principle that those who cannot pay should be charged more:

'The need to advise you of this action has of course involved us in unnecessary administration for which we propose to debit your account £15, in addition to our charges for returning direct debits, of a further £25'.

You may like to consider this advice and its wording in the light of the entry *Complaints*, page 126 forward.

7. Foreign dealings

7.1 Some problems

Banks provide very useful services to individuals who wish to go abroad, and to businesses with foreign customers or suppliers. When you are dealing with overseas colleagues, difficulties are likely to arise because of distance and differences of language. But there are also differences between countries with regard to procedure, institutions and currency. All of these could create problems without the specialist services which banks can offer.

Institutions and the laws governing trading may differ greatly from country to country. Furthermore, different countries have different laws about the import and export of goods; it is illegal, for instance, to export certain types of computer product from the USA to the Soviet Union. In many countries certain types of goods must be accompanied by a permit or customs document (eg perfumes coming into Britain).

7.2 Methods of taking money abroad

There are various ways in which someone who is going abroad can obtain the foreign money he or she needs. The bank can supply *bank notes and coins* in exchange for sterling. It can provide a *cheque book and a cheque guarantee card* which is acceptable in many foreign banks. The bank can provide a *credit card* which is acceptable in the country being visited. It can issue travellers' cheques, which can be changed for foreign currency when abroad. The bank can also make *arrangements with a particular bank* in the place being visited to allow withdrawals of cash up to a named limit.

7.3 Making payments in international trade

Banks can be invaluable in arranging payments to and from foreign customers. The process is now aided by the computerised SWIFT system. (Society for Worldwide Interbank Telecommunications), which allows a trader to make a credit transfer.

A system of payment which is still used, though, is the *bill of exchange*. In this case, the exporter sends a draft bill, which is checked and signed and returned as an accepted bill by the importer. Usually, a period is agreed on, for example 30 days, until the end of which the importer is allowed credit.

If there is some doubt about the reliability of the foreign importer, the exporter may prefer to use a *documentary letter of credit*. With this method the exporter asks the importer to open a letter of credit to cover the value of the goods. The importer gets his bank to arrange a credit in favour of the exporter. When relevant documents have been received the importer's bank guarantees that the exporter will be paid at the end of an agreed time. There are various types of credit available. The most secure is a *confirmed credit* in which both banks agree to guarantee that the exporter will receive payment.

8. Exchange Rates

8.1 What is an exchange rate?

Most people know that different countries use different types of money (currency), eg Spain – *peseta*; France – *franc*. These do not have the same value as an English pound. Dependent on international conditions, the number of, say, pesetas you get for a pound may very considerably. This is important to the holiday maker, as it can substantially reduce or increase the amount of money he or she has available to spend. For businesses a change in the exchange rate is also very important. It can make a crucial difference to the price or profitability of what is being bought or sold.

The amount of one currency which you receive for one unit of another is called the *exchange rate*. For example, if you get 10 francs for one pound, the exchange rate for pounds into francs is 10. This will be the rate at any one time. It tends to change daily. The reason is that the demand for currency by the money markets may increase or decrease. This will depend on what dealers in international markets think of a country's economic state – whether prospects for trade and profit are good. You can find today's exchange rates by looking in the financial sections of the newspapers.

As an example, suppose that the American dollar is much in demand. Dealers in foreign money will then make you pay more for each dollar (ie you get fewer per pound). If you are selling dollars, though, they will pay more for them (ie you will get more pounds to the dollar). In recent years this factor has often helped British holiday makers going to countries such as Italy or Portugal. The pound has been 'strong' (eg in demand in Portugal), so holidaymakers have tended to get more *escudos* than previously for each pound they change. However, good news for some people is often bad news for others. For example, what do you think the effect would have been on exporters of refrigerators?

8.2 Converting currencies at the bank

A business dealing in large sums can arrange this through the system of international credit transfer. However, an individual wanting cash to go abroad will have to make the arrangements in person.

On arriving at the bank the person who is intending to travel will see a notice which states both the price at which the bank will buy in foreign currency, and the amount you will receive if you change pounds into another currency.

These prices are not the exchange rate, though they will be something close to it. They are the prices at which the bank is prepared to buy and sell currency. The difference between the two prices is part of the bank's profit on the transaction (making a profit is the reason for offering the service).

When a person or business wishes to change sterling into a foreign currency, or to change money received from abroad into pounds, they are said to *convert* the currency which they start with into the new currency.

The bank takes the money which is being brought in (or which is being debited from an account) and works out how much of the desired currency can be obtained. There is then a deduction for the bank's adminstrative charge. The bank makes a profit partly by this means but mostly through the difference between the prices at which a given currency is bought or sold.

The details of the method for calculating the conversion of one currency into another are given in *Calculations: foreign currency*, page 106.

Some common currencies

Australia	dollar	Ireland	punt
Austria	schilling	Italy	lira
Belgium	franc	Japan	yen
Brazil	cruzeiro	Netherlands	guilder
Canada	dollar	Norway	kroner
Denmark	ore	Portugal	escudo
Finland	markka	Spain	peseta
France	franc	Sweden	kronor
Germany	deutschmark	Switzerland	franc
Greece	drachma	USA	dollar
Hong Kong	dollar	USSR	rouble

Calculations

How to carry out the calculations needed in financial record keeping

Preliminary reading

The first time you use this entry in order to find out about percentages, you should begin by reading the section on *Decimal division*.

Contents

1. Decimal division

1.1 Self-check

The purpose of this check is to find out if you really do need guidance about decimal division. Test yourself by working out the following problems. Do not use a calculator: the purpose is to see if you know how to work the problem out for yourself.

Calculate the following to three decimal places, then round to two places of decimals.

1) 973 ÷
    11
    ___

2) 4265 ÷
    100
    ___

When you've tried them, check your answers with a calculator.

If your answers are correct, you are clear about how to solve problems using decimal division. If you are reading this before looking for information about percentages, go on to *Calculations: percentages*, page 113.

If your answer is wrong, go on to section 1.2 below.

1.2 Decimal division – method and checklist

Go over your working from the start, and ask yourself each of the following questions. Get into the habit of 'being your own doctor' and diagnosing your own problems.

Points to check if your answer is wrong

☐ Is there a problem of *layout*? If your work isn't neatly and clearly laid out you are very likely to make silly errors, such as adding the wrong columns.

☐ Is the *decimal point* in the right place? Very important – would you prefer £10.00 or £100.00?

☐ Are you clear what is meant by working to so many *'places of decimals'*? (It means the number of figures after the decimal point).

☐ Did you *insert a 0* to the required number of places? Though it does not alter the problem in this case, doing this helps to keep your thinking clear.

☐ Do you know how to tackle a *long division* problem?

☐ Do you understand what is meant by 'rounding'? Can you do it?

If you now feel confident about decimal division and rounding, and you are reading this before looking for information about percentages, go on to *Calculations: percentages*, page 113.

If you are not certain about rounding go on to section 3 of this entry.

If you are still uncertain about decimal division, or long division, you should consult your tutor so as to solve this problem quickly, as it is a skill you are going to need a great deal in this field of study and work.

1.3 Rounding – method

'Rounding' means that you simplify a figure; for example, 12.3556, rounded to one place of decimals, becomes 12.4.

To round a number, follow this method.

1) Look at the last figure.

2) If it is 6 or above increase the column before by 1 (eg 88.456 would be 88.46 to two places of decimals). Otherwise leave that column as it is.

105

3) Cross off the last figure.

4) Move back (to the left) one column.

5) Repeat the process until you have the desired number of decimal places.

Try this on 12.3556 to see why we round it to 12.4 and not 12.3.

If you are still uncertain, you should consult your tutor before going any further.

2. Foreign currency

2.1 Converting pounds into another currency – method

1) Write down the sum to be changed in decimal form.

2) Find the *exchange rate* for that currency.

3) Write the rate down in decimal form, so that you have set out a multiplication problem.

4) Multiply SUM TO CHANGE x RATE. The answer is the amount of currency you will receive, before any bank charge is deducted.

Example

£111 is to be changed into US dollars. The exchange rate is $1.87 to the pound.

$$
\begin{array}{r}
111.00 \div \\
1.87 \\
\hline
7.77 \\
88.80 \\
111.00 \\
\hline
\text{total} \quad 207.57 \\
\hline
\end{array}
$$

So the customer will receive $207.57 before charges.

2.2 Converting into pounds from another currency – method

1) Write down the amount to be changed

2) Find the rate of exchange.

3) Set this out as a division problem.

4) Make the calculation. The answer is the number of pounds which will be received before any charge is deducted.

Example

How many pounds will be received for 234 Austrian schillings, when the exchange rate is 22.12?

$$
\text{Answer} = \frac{234}{22.12} = \frac{23400}{2212}
$$

(making the decimals into whole numbers)

then normal division:

```
              10.57
     2212 ) 23400.000
            2212
            12800
            11070
            17300
            15484
             1816
```

So the customer will receive £10.57 before deductions.

If you do not understand how the above calculations are worked out, you should ask your tutor for guidance.

3. Interest

3.1 What it Is

Various organisations exist to handle money, and in doing so offer or charge interest. Interest is a sum of money charged or paid for the provision of a loan. It is calculated as a percentage of the sum loaned. For details see *Banking facilities*, page 98.

An agreement to pay interest is stated in terms of:

1) the *sum* of money to be loaned or borrowed

2) the *period of time* over which the money is available

3) the *type* of interest (simple or compound)

4) the *rate* of interest, as stated as a percentage.

3.2 Type of Interest

Interest may take two forms:

SIMPLE   The same sum is paid throughout the period of time.

For example on a loan of £1000 with an interest rate of 10% the investor receives £100 every year for the period of the loan.

| Year 1 | Year 2 | Year 3 |

COMPOUND   The interest paid to an investor is added to the capital sum. In the next year of the loan, it is this sum on which the amount due is calculated.

Note that the rate of interest does not change; the amount paid does, as the capital grows. In this case the loan of £1000 earns £100 in the first year. This is added to the capital sum, so that interest is paid on £1100 in the second year – that is, the investor receives £110.

Year 1	**Year 2**	**Year 3**

To summarise:

☐ Simple interest is calculated on the original sum (principal) only

☐ Compound interest is calculated on the original sum plus all interest earned so far.

Note

1) The above examples refer to the situation in which the amount of money loaned remains constant. There are many loans in which this is not the case. One well known example is the capital repayment mortgage, in which the borrower pays off part of the sum borrowed each year. The interest due will thus fall in amount, as the sum owed falls.

3.3 Calculation of simple interest

Original sum (the principal): £500

Interest is calculated as a percentage of the original sum

Interest: 10 per cent

earns

Year 1   £50

Year 2   £50

Year 3   £50 etc

So £500 earning 10 per cent simple interest for 3 years will earn 3 x £50 = £150

and sum paid back at end of time = £500 + £150 = £650.

Formulae

1) Amount earned per year $= \dfrac{\text{PRINCIPAL}}{100} \times \text{RATE}$

2) Amount earned in N years   = (Amount earned per year) x N

$$\left[\frac{P}{100} \times N \right]$$

3) Amount repaid after N years   = PRINCIPAL + AMOUNT EARNED IN N YEARS

$$\left[P + \frac{P}{100} \times N \right]$$

3.4 Calculation of compound interest

Principal: £500

Borrowed at 10 per cent compound interest for 3 years.

Year 1:	Principal	=	£500.00
	end of Year 1, 10% interest	=	£50.00
Year 2:	new investment	=	£550.00
	end of Year 2, 10% interest	=	£55.00
Year 3:	new investment	=	£605.00
	end of Year 3, 10% interest	=	£60.55
	Paid back at end of period:		£665.50
	interest	=	£165.50

Formula

For amount (A) received on principal (P) at a rate R over N years

$$A = P (1.0R)^N$$

In the above example:

$$\text{Amount} = 500 (1.010)^3$$

(If you do not understand this formula, you should ask your lecturer for help.)

4. Measurements

Dealings between British and overseas firms are made slightly more complicated by the fact that there are different systems for measuring weight, length, area and volume.

4.1 The Imperial system

Until recently Britain used the Imperial system of weights and measures. The most well-known of these are:

LENGTH:	
	12 inches = 1 foot
	3 feet = 1 yard
	1760 yards = 1 mile

Fortunately children in schools and most adults no longer have to memorise such quaint formulae as $5\frac{1}{2}$ yards = 1 rod, pole or perch. Cricket lovers will be aware that the wicket is 22 yards long. Whether they would know that 22 yards is 1 chain, which equals 4 rods, poles or perches is less certain!

The other measures which are in common use are:

AREA:	
	9 square feet = 1 square yard
	4840 square yards = 1 acre (an area equivalent to a piece of land about 70 yards square)

VOLUME:	
	27 cubic feet = 1 cubic yard (ie a cube with sides 3 feet long)

LIQUIDS:	
	4 gills = 1 pint
	2 pints = 1 quart
	4 quarts = 8 pints = 1 gallon

```
WEIGHT:           16 ounces  =  1 pound
                  14 pounds  =  1 stone
                   8 stones  =  1 hundredweight (= 112 pounds)
         20 hundredweights   =  1 ton (= 2240 pounds)
```

The abbreviations are:

```
        foot  – ft              gallon  – gall
        yard  – yd              ounce   – oz
       metre  – m               pound   – lb
        pint  – pt              stone   – st
       quart  – qt       hundredweight  – cwt
```
Note the following alternatives:
```
   4840 sq yd  or  4840yd²           27 cub ft or 27ft³
```

4.2 The metric system

The metric system was first devised in France at the time of the French Revolution. It is much simpler because measurements are made in units of ten, and calculations can be worked out in decimals. The system is of importance for three reasons.

1) It is the system internationally used by scientists.

2) It is the legal system in many countries, and in particular those of the European Community.

3) For the latter reason it is the system increasingly used by British industry and commerce instead of or alongside the Imperial system.

To illustrate that the system does work in tens, the whole system for length is given here.

```
LENGTH:     10 millimetres  =  1 centimetre
            10 centimetres  =  1 decimetre
            10 decimetres   =  1 metre
            10 metres       =  1 decametre
            10 decametres   =  1 hectometre
            10 hectometres  =  1 kilometre
```

The units you will meet most commonly are:

```
      10 millimetres  =  1 centimetre
     100 centimetres  =  1 metre
    1000 metres       =  1 kilometre
```

```
AREA:     10 000 square millimetres  =  1 square metre (a square with sides 100 cm long).
```

When dealing with land measurements the unit used is the hectare.

```
         1 are  =  100 square metres
     1 hectare  =  100 ares
                =  10 000 square metres (an area equivlent to a piece of
                   land 100 metres square)
```

| VOLUME: | 1 000 000 cubic centrimetres = 1 cubic metre (a cube with sides 100 cm long) |

| LIQUIDS: | 10 millilitres = 1 centilitre |
| | 100 centiletres = 1 litre (= 1000 millilitres) |

| WEIGHT: | 1000 grams = 1 kilogram |
| | 1000 kilograms = 1 tonne (note spelling) |

The abbreviations are:

millimetre – mm	millilitre – ml
centimetre – cm	litre – l (or lr)
metre – m	gram – g (or gm)
kilometre – km	kilogram – kg

4.3 Conversion factors

Below are given the conversion factors between the various units. The conversion factor gives the measurement in the second system which corresponds to one unit of the first system (eg number of pints which you get when you buy one litre).

1 inch	=	2.54	centimetres	
1 foot	=	30.48	centimetres or 0.3048 metres	
1 yard	=	91.44	centimetres or 0.9144 metres	
1 mile	=	1.60934	kilometres	
1 gill	=	0.142061	litres or 14.0 centilitres	
1 pint	=	0.568245	litres	(rounded 0.57 litres)
1 quart	=	1.13649	litres	(rounded 1.14 litres)
1 gallon	=	4.54596	litres	(rounded 4.55 litres)
1 ounce	=	28.37	grams	
1 pound	=	0.453592	kilograms or 454 grams	
1 stone	=	6.350288	kilograms	(rounded 6.35 kilograms)
1 hundredweight	=	50.8023	kilograms	(rounded 50.8 kilograms)
1 ton	=	1016.05	kilograms	
1 acre	=	0.4047	hectares	
1 millimetre	=	0.03937	inches	(rounded 0.03 inches)
1 centimetre	=	0.39:3701	inches	(rounded 0.39 inches)
1 metre	=	39.3701	inches	(rounded 39.37 inches)
	or	3.28084	feet	(rounded 3.28 feet)
	or	1.09361	yards	(rounded 1.09 yards)
1 kilometre	=	0.621371	miles	(rounded 0.62 miles
1 millilitre	=	0.00022	gallons or 0.00176 pints	
1 centilitre	=	0.0022	gallons or 0.0176 pints	
1 litre	=	0.219975	gallons or 1.7598 pints	

Calculations

1 gram	=	0.0022046	pounds or 0.02834 ounces	
1 kilogram	=	2.20462	pounds	(rounded 2.2 pounds)
1 tonne	=	2204.62	pounds	
1 hectare	=	2.471	acres	(rounded 2.5 acres)

For everyday (rather than accurate commercial) purposes and dealing with small quantities, it may help to think of the commonest units as being very approximately as follows:

$$1 \text{ metre} = 1 \text{ yard } 3 \text{ inches}$$
$$10 \text{ kilometres} = 6 \text{ miles}$$
$$1 \text{ pint} = \text{half litre}$$
$$25 \text{ grams} = 1 \text{ ounce}$$
$$100 \text{ grams} = \text{quarter pound}$$
$$1 \text{ pound} = \text{half kilogram}$$
$$1 \text{ hectare} = 2\tfrac{1}{2} \text{ acres}$$

4.4 Method of conversion

If you need to calculate the metric equivalent of a measurement expressed in Imperial measure, or vice versa you set about it as follows:

	Example	**Example**	**Example**
❑ Write down the measurement you have	half pound (= 0.5 pounds)	15 litres	9 acres
❑ Look up the conversion factor needed	0.454 (kilograms)	1.76 (pints)	0.405 (hectares)
❑ Multiply the two	0.227kg	26.4 pints	3.645 hectares

4.5 Temperature

Though the temperature is not entered in our financial records, it is often relevant to our work (for example, temperature at which goods should be kept). Again, Britain has a different system from science and from many countries. The UK uses the Fahrenheit scale, but is moving over to the Centigrade scale (also known as the Celsius scale) used by the rest of Europe. Both are measured in degrees. For practical purposes, both are related to permanent characteristics of pure water.

Freezing point of water = 32° Fahrenheit = 0° Centigrade
Boiling point of water = 212° Fahrenheit = 100° Centigrade

Conversion between the two scales
❑ Fahrenheit to Centigrade:

	Example
Write down Fahrenheit temperature	68°F
Subtract 32°	36
Multiply result by 5	180
Divide this result by 9	20°C

❑ Centigrade to Fahrenheit

	Example
Write down Centigrade temperature	10°C
Multiply by 9	90
Divide this result by 5	18
Add 32	50°F

5. Percentages

5.1 Calculating percentages – self-check

First see if you need guidance. Test yourself by working out the following problems. Do not use a calculator.

❑ What is 8% of £496 000?

❑ How much is a service charge of 10% on a bill for £23.40?

(In a restaurant where there is a service charge of 10 percent, the cost of the meal is totalled up, and 10% of that figure is added on to the bill.)

When you've tried the problems above, check your answers with a calculator.

❑ If your answers are correct, go on to 5.3 *Fractions of a percent*.

❑ If your answer is wrong, go on to 5.2 *Calculating percentages*.

5.2 Calculating percentages – method

1) The word 'percentage' comes from two Latin words *per* (meaning 'for' or 'out of') and *centum* ('a hundred'). When dealing with money, it is an amount which is added to or taken away from each pound. When we pay interest or a service charge, a certain amount for every pound owed is added to our debt. When we receive a discount, a certain amount for every pound owed is deducted from our bill.

Example

Eve Adams buys supplies worth £100. She is given a 5 percent discount. How much does she pay?

Original bill	£100
Discount 5%	£5
Amount to pay	£95

Because a pound has 100 pence, calculating percentages of money is often fairly easy: 12 percent of one pound is 12 pence. But you can have a percentage of any sum; you therefore need a method for calculating percentages.

2) **To calculate a percentage of a given sum of money**   **Example:**

   a) First, name sum of money for which percentage is to be calculated.   — 13% of £330

       Write it down in decimal form   — 330.00

   b) Find one percent   — Result: £3.300

       (This is straightforward. One percent is one unit per hundred, so divide by 100. You will find that all you need to do is move the decimal point two places to the left.)

   c) Multiply this figure by the required number   — £3.300 x 13 = £42.90

3) To calculate ten percent is always straightforward: just move the decimal point one place to the left.

   Example: 10% of £178.50 = £17.85

5.3 Calculation of fractions of a percent

Bank rates and similar money lending devices often move in fractions of a percent. Service charges are sometimes $12\frac{1}{2}$%. In 1991 the Government changed the rate of VAT to $17\frac{1}{2}$%.

A simple way to build on what you have done so far is:

a) $\frac{1}{2}$ percent:
    find one percent and divide by 2

Example

$12\frac{1}{2}\%$ service charge on a bill for £49.50

$$1\% = £.495$$
$$\frac{1}{2}\% = £.495 \div 2 \quad = £.247$$
$$12\% = £.495 \times 12 \quad = £5.840$$

total £5.84 = £0.25   = £6.09

b) **Procedure for calculating $\frac{1}{4}\%$**

    Find one percent and divide by 4.

c) **Procedure for calculating $\frac{3}{4}\%$**

    Find one percent and divide by 4, to get one quarter percent. Then multiply the result by 3.

5.4 Summary

How to work out percentages

☐ **Name sum**

☐ **Find *one* percent**

☐ **Multiply by number of percent to be found**

In detail:

1) First name sum of money for which the percentage is to be calculated.
    Write it down in decimal form.

2) **One percent (1%)** = decimal point **two places to left**

3) For **ten percent** just move decimal point **one place to left**

4) **Fractions of a percent**

    a) to find $\frac{1}{2}$ percent
        ☐ find one percent and divide by 2.

    b) to find $\frac{1}{4}\%$
        ☐ find one percent and divide by 4.

    c) to find $\frac{3}{4}\%$
        ☐ find one percent and divide by 4
        ☐ multiply result by 3.

Cash book

Information about the structure and purpose of the cash book, together with the procedures needed for maintaining it

Preliminary reading

You should not study this section unless you have read *Accounts: basic approach to record keeping*, page 74. It is also desirable, but not vital, to have studied *Ledgers and journals*, page 177.

1. Nature and purpose of the cash book

1.1 Relation to the ledger

A large and important part of the activity of any business is the payment and receipt of money. It was therefore felt at an early period in business history that it would be useful to have a special part of the ledger devoted solely to the recording of those activities. This section of the ledger is known as the cash book.

In fact the cash book is unique among accounts in two ways:

1) **It is both a ledger account and a book of original entry**

   For the latter reason, as in the case of journals, receipts and payments are first entered in the cash book. However, because the cash book is part of the ledger, transactions are recorded by double entry. The second entry will be made in an appropriate ledger account. For example, if customer Mr A. Edens settles his account, the receipt of the payment will be entered in a debit column of the cash book, and in the credit column of Mr Edens' personal account.

2) **The cash book in fact contains two accounts – Bank and Cash**

   This is explained in *The two column cash book*, below.

   If you do not understand about making ledger entries, you should look up the relevant topic in the entry *Ledgers and journals*, page 177.

1.2 The cashier

The record keeper who is in charge of the cash book is known as the *cashier*. The cashier has duties with regard to payments both in cash and by cheque as follows:

cash

☐ records receipts of and payment in cash

☐ makes cash payments when authorised

☐ is responsible for cash kept on the premises (whether kept in a till, petty cash box or safe)

☐ issues cash to the petty cashier (see *Petty cash*, page 219).

cheques

☐ records receipts of and payments by cheque

☐ prepares cheques for signature by authorised persons

(For details of how to carry out the latter see *Bank documents: cheques*, page 83.)

The cashier will also be responsible for **reconciling the cash book entries with bank statements** (see *Bank reconciliation*, page 122).

Note that in the case of both cash and cheque payments, authorisation is mentioned. There is no reason why the cashier should not be the authorised person, but often this is not so for the following reasons.

☐ To have at least one other person involved in the making of payments offers some safeguard against error and fraud.

☐ The payment may need to be approved. For example, in a payment of a fee or wages, a manager will need evidence that the work has been done.

☐ Bank accounts for businesses and organisations will require that there is a named person or persons who will sign cheques. The bank will not honour a cheque drawn on such an account, unless the cheque is signed by an approved *signatory*.

2. Two-column cash book

2.1 Layout

The layout of the cash book differs from that of the typical ledger account. It looks as follows:

Debit   Credit

Date	Details	Folio	Cash	Bank	Date	Details	Folio	Cash	Bank
			£ p	£ p				£ p	£ p
1 Sep	Balance b/d		210.00	1500.00	1 Sep	G Oak 110691	S1		75.00
2 Sep	Sales		156.00		2 Sep	Stationery 110692	A4		35.00
2 Sep	E. Heath	C71	65.00		3 Sep	Cleaner	W1	15.00	
3 Sep	Bank	C		100.00	3 Sep	Cash	C	100.00	
4 Sep	T Hardy	C23		72.00	5 Sep	Cash	C		30.00
5 Sep	Bank	C	30.00		5 Sep	balances c/d		346.00	1532.00
			461.00	1672.00				461.00	1672.00
8 Sep	Balances b/d		346.00	1532.00					

Explanation

1) There are debit and credit columns, as in other ledger accounts
2) There are two columns on each side – one for the Cash Account, and one for the Bank account. It is traditional to use the left hand column for the Cash Account.

As with other ledger accounts there are

3) The date
4) The details of the transaction
5) The folio number
6) The balance entered at the beginning of the accounting period
7) The balances calculated and entered according to standard procedure at the end of the accounting period

The entries in the above cash book page are as follows:

Debit column

❏ **Cash account**

Sales	£156 taken in the retail side of the business; this will be entered in the sales account
Egdon Heath	This customer settled his account by paying cash at the counter; the folio number refers to his account in the Customer Personal accounts.
'Bank'	This means that £30.00 has been drawn from the Bank account (for example for petty cash use).
C	The letter 'C' stands for contra entry. Contra is the Latin word for against or opposite. It indicates that the double entry is on the same page. A contra entry records a transfer between accounts, and some bookkeepers add the words 'Transfer to' or 'transfer from' (eg Transfer to Bank)

117

❑ **Bank account**

'Bank'   means that £100 cash was deposited in the Bank account. This is another contra entry.

T Hardy C23   Thomas Hardy who has a customer account folio number C23, settled his debt with a cheque for £72.

Credit columns

❑ **Cash account**

'Cash'   This is the contra entry recording the moving of cash into the Bank Account.

Cleaner   A cleaner employed on a casual basis was paid £15 in cash. This is recorded also in the Wages account, folio number W1.

Cash £100   This is the double entry for the money deposited at the bank.

❑ **Bank account**

G Oak 110691   This records a payment to a supplier. The number is the serial number of the cheque which was issued.

Stationery 110692 This is another payment for supplies. Details are not given, but there is a double entry to the Stationery Account.

'Cash'   records the contra entry of the withdrawal of £30 in cash.

2.2 Balancing the cash book

This follows exactly the procedure described in *Ledgers and journals: balances*, page 189, and so will not be repeated here. Two points should however be made:

1) Remember that though the accounts are kept in the same book and are recorded in adjacent columns, this is only a matter of tradition and convenience. You are in fact dealing with *two separate accounts*. There will always therefore be *two* sets of totals, and *two* balances.

2) If, as often happens. there are more entries in one column than in the other, many bookkeepers draw a diagonal line through the empty space. This is to prevent entries from being made in the space, after the accounts have been balanced.

3. Analysed cash book

In a small business the volume of trade and amount of time available for book keeping may mean that it is not worthwhile having the labour of keeping separate accounts, maintained by double entry. Such businesses may decide to record all transactions in a single volume. This will basically take the form of a cash book, and have Cash and Bank columns. But it will also have additional columns as shown in the diagram below.

Example

When Eve Adams first sets up her business, she keeps her own records. A possible layout of her analysed cash book might usefully be:

Date	Details	Cash		Bank		Lawns & hedges		Replanting		Landscaping	
1 Jun	Fee	10	00			10	00				
2 Jun	Fee			45	00			45	00		
3 Jun				200	00					200	00

Debit side of cash book

Date	Details	Cash		Bank		Plants		Fertiliser		Equip-ment		Expenses	
1 Jun	Travel	3	20									3	20
2 Jun	Boxhill			15	00	15	00						
2 Jun	Meadowside	6	50					6	50				
3 Jun	Hoxted			22	50					22	50		

Credit side of cash book

The debit records record a cash payment for mowing a lawn and cutting hedges; a payment by cheque for replanting a flower bed; and a cheque for a major landscaping of a large domestic garden the week before.

The credit entries reflect the following transactions: travel to lawn and hedge job on June 1; plants bought by cheque from Boxhill Shrubs on June 2nd; compost paid for in cash from Meadowside Garden Centre on the same day; and purchase by cheque of a spade from Hoxted Garden Equipment on June 3rd.

This type of record is known as an *analysed cash book,* because the various entries are broken down and grouped *(analysed)* into basic types of transaction. There is no set number of columns or type of classification of entry; the choice depends on what the record keeper feels to be most relevant.

The columns are totalled at suitable intervals. Balances are calculated for the Cash and Bank accounts, but not on the analysis columns.

Because each transaction is recorded only once, this type of cash book is referred to by some people as a *single entry cash book,* to distinguish it from record keeping by double entry.

If you are the cashier responsible for such a cash book, attention to keeping the book safe and secure is especially important, as it will be the only copy of the financial records of the business.

4. Recording cash discount

4.1 Cash and trade discount

Trade discount is a reduction in the original price, at the point of sale. This reduction is important in calculating the sale price of goods bought in, and will be closely related to the making and calculation of profit. But from the accounting point of view, there is nothing special to record. Purchases are entered at the *price actually paid*. The fact that this price is lower as a result of trade discount than it might have been is of no importance to the record keeper.

Cash discount, whether offered to a business by a supplier, or by a business to its customers, is a different matter. First, at the point when the record of a credit sale (or purchase) is made, the discount has only been offered. It is not taken off the amount due until and unless payment is made according to the terms of business. Until then, the records need a reminder (known as a *memorandum*) that the discount is offered. When the payment is made, the remittance can be reduced by the allowed percentage. Also important to the records is that discount can then be entered as part of the accounts. This is because the discount give is counted as an expense, and discount received is counted as income, both of which are entered in the ledger (see *Ledger and accounts*, page 177).

4.2 Three-column record of discount

If you need further information about the nature and calculation of cash discount, you should first read *Quotations: terms of business*, page 232.

In order to record discount, the cash book is amended to a three column format, as follows:

Debit   Credit

Date	Details	Discount	Cash	Bank	Date	Details	Discount	Cash	Bank
2 Jun	A Edens	5.00		95.00	3 Jun	G Oak	20.00	200.00	

These entries mean that:

On June 2 A Edens settled an invoice for £100, subtracting first a discount allowed of 5%.

On June 3 G Oak settled a debt of £200. He handed over £180 in cash, because he was claiming a discount of 10%.

4.3 Method of dealing with discount

1) Check with invoice
   - ❏ whether a cash discount is allowed
   - ❏ that the payment will be made within the time allowed
   - ❏ if it will, what percentage discount is offered.

2) Calculate the discount.

3) Calculate   Invoice full amount

                                  − Discount

        to find   Balance owed or owing.

4) If paying a supplier:
   - ❏ prepare a cheque for the balance owing

OR if receiving payment from a customer

- ❑ check that the remittance is for the balance owed.

5) Record the transaction.

- ❑ Record the incoming or outgoing payment as indicated on page 116.
- ❑ Enter the discount in the adjacent column.

6) At the end of the accounting period

- ❑ total and balance the cash book as indicated on page 118.

7) Total but do not balance the discount columns.

4.4 Transfer to the ledger

Discount allowed or received is recorded elsewhere in the ledger. One record will be in the appropriate column of a customer or supplier account. The other may be in a special account which records discount. Some accountants dispense with this record, if there is a three-column cash book, and transfer (post) the totals of the discount column directly to the profit and loss account (see *Final accounts*, page 147).

5. Method for making entries in the cash book

1) Decide whether the entry is a *debit* or a *credit*

2) Enter the *date*

3) Decide whether the entry is *Cash* or *Bank*

4) Enter the *amount* in the correct column (left – Cash, right – Bank)

5) Enter *details*. This may take the form of:

- ❑ *account name*
- ❑ *name of person* or firm paid or paying
- ❑ *cheque serial number* (noted in the case of payments outward)

6) Enter *folio number*

- ❑ either: folio number as in all ledger entries
- ❑ or: 'C' if transaction is a transfer between Cash and Bank Accounts

In the case of an analysed cash book, there will be no folio numbers. Instead, at this point, enter the transaction under the relevant analysis columns.

7) Enter *discount* if relevant

- ❑ Check first that
  - a) the remittance is the correct sum owed
  - b) what the amount of discount is

8) Look over the entry to check that you have not recorded the transaction in the wrong account.

9) *At the end of the accounting period, calculate and enter balances.* Remember that there will be two separate balances.

10) If there is empty space in one of the columns, draw a diagonal line to prevent further entries from being made.

6. Bank reconciliation

Before reading this entry you should have studied:

1)   The earlier entries in this section

2)   *Bank documents: bank statements,* page 81.

The cash book contains both Cash and Bank Accounts. At intervals the bank sends its customers its own record of the transactions which have occurred in a given period. If both sides have kept their records accurately, you might expect to find that the two records would be exactly the same. In practice this is mostly not the case for the reasons given below.

6.1 Finding the differences

In Eve Adams' cash book the version of the Bank Account for the month of May was as follows (the Cash columns are left blank for the sake of clarity):

Cash book

Debit   Credit

Date	Details		Cash	Bank	Date	Details		Cash	Bank
1 May	Balance b/d			8017.00					
2 May	A Edens			143.00					
					6 May	Boxhill 110634			64.90
					12 May	G Oak 110635			58.00
23 May	D. Allen			55.00	31 May	balance c/d			8211.10
31 May	C. Woodcroft			119.00					
				8334.00					8334.00
1 Jun	Balance b/d			8211.10					

The bank's statement for the same period was as follows:

	DATE	PARTICULARS	PAYMENTS	RECEIPTS	BALANCE
		IN ACCOUNT WITH			
		BANK Mercia			
		BRANCH Sheep Market, Codlington			
		TITLE OF ACCOUNT Eve Adams			
		ACCOUNT NUMBER 05400780		STATEMENT NUMBER	227

	DATE	PARTICULARS	PAYMENTS	RECEIPTS	BALANCE
	1 May	Balance brought forward			8017.00 CR
	3 May	MEB SO	120.00		7897.00 CR
	4 May	Sundry Credit		143.00	8040.00 CR
	10 May	Mercia Gas DD	42.00		7998.00 CR
	12 May	110634	649.00		7349.00 CR
	15 May	110636	72.00		7277.00 CR
	19 May	BGC Azure		252.00	7529.00 CR
	25 May	Sundry Credit		55.00	7584.00 CR
	31 May	Charges	45.00		7539.00 CR

The cashier's first actions should be:

1) Go through the two records. Whenever they agree, tick the two entries.

2) Where there are differences or omissions in one of the records, make a note of these.

Types of problem

The example given above illustrates the main types of reason why there can be a difference between the accounts as shown by the cash book and the bank statement. The first stage of checking (*reconciliation*) showed that there was the opening balance and two cheques (debit column for £143 and £55 for which the records did agree, but that the following differences remained:

```
Cheque 110634: Bank clerk mistyping (£649.00 for £64.90!)
```
```
Cheque 110636 (£72, Hoxted Garden Equipment): Not entered in cash book
```
```
Cheque 110635 (£58, G Oak): Not in bank statement. A phone call
revealed that, owing to illness, the creditor had not yet presented the
cheque.
```
```
Cheque (Woodcroft, £119): This was received, and entered in the cash
book on 31 May. Owing to the oversight of an employee, it was deposited
at the bank on the next day (June 1st) and so would appear in the June
statement.
```
```
BGC: This was a bank giro credit from Azure Computers. There was thus a
credit transfer directly to the EPG's bank account, rather than a
```

Cash book

```
      payment which was received, recorded in the cash book and banked by the
      cashier.SO: This is a standing order to Mercia Electricity. It is made
      by the bank, not the cashier and so does not appear in the cash book
      record.DD: This is a direct debit in favour of Mercia Gas. Again the
      payment is not made by the cashier.Charges: These are the charges made
      by the bank for its services.
```

As might be expected, the final balances are completely different.

You will be glad to hear that you are unlikely ever to have so many sources of difficulty in one set of records!

Summary

The main causes of differences between the Bank Account and a bank statement are likely to be:

1) Clerical errors   wrong figures entered
                     entry omitted

2) Cheques   not yet presented
               not yet cleared

3) Payments not made by the cashier   bank giro payments check
                                         standing orders
                                         direct debits
                                         interest payments
                                         bank charges

6.2 Updating the cash book

When the cashier has identified the sources of any discrepancy between the accounts, there are three stages of action to be taken:

1) Follow up errors or entries which remain unexplained.

2) Update the cash book (Bank Account) to make the records agree (reconcile them).

3) Draw up a *bank reconciliation statement*.

In the above case, the cash book would be updated as follows:

Debit   Credit

Date	Details	Cash	Bank	Date	Details	Cash	Bank
	Balance b/d		8211.10	3 May	Electricity		120.00
19 May	Azure		252.00	10 May	Gas		42.00
				15 May	Hoxted 110636		72.00
				31 May	Bank Charges		45.00
				31 May	Balance c/d		8184.10
			8463.10				8463.10

To update the cash book the cashier will need to add

1)   clerical errors entry omitted

2)   payments not made by the cashier   bank giro payments check
                                          standing orders
                                          direct debits
                                          interest payments
                                          bank charges

6.3 Format of bank reconciliation statement

Though there are slight differences in the practices adopted by some record keepers, the format of the bank reconciliation statement is as follows:

```
EDEN PLANTS AND GARDENS
Bank reconciliation statement as at 31 May, 1991
Balance at bank as per cash book                    8184.10
Add:   cheque issued, not yet debited                 58.00
                                                    _____
                                                    8242.10

Less:  Cheque paid in, not yet credited              119.00
                                                    _____
                                                    8123.10
cheque overpaid by bank                              584.10
                                                    _____
Balance at bank as per statement                    7539.00
                                                    _____
```

To produce the reconciliation statement the cashier will need to include items not recorded in the cash book, namely cheques which, whether issued or paid in, have not yet been cleared. Sometimes there will be cases in which a cheque has not yet been presented.

Errors such as the mistyping will also need to be mentioned. This situation will be remedied in two stages. First the bank will make a contrapayment of the same amount. This will wipe out the effect of the transaction. They will then re-enter the correct amount and process it in the normal way.

Complaints

How to make or deal with written complaints about financial matters

Preliminary reading

The first time you use this entry, you should read the entry *Types of situation*, below. Before first using the entry *Useful phrases*, page 129, read *Importance of language used*, page 128.

1. Types of situation involving complaints

Both as a member of the public, and as an employee, you are almost certain at some time to be involved in the process of making a complaint. This can be especially difficult when money is involved. People can become very suspicious or aggressive, and many people still feel some embarrassment about discussing money.

People who deal with business record keeping need to identify approaches and phrases which they can use in dealing with a complaint.

Some of the commonest sorts of situation (in financial record keeping) which give rise to complaints are:

a) problems of *quality of goods* (not the concern of financial record keeping);

b) problems of *service* (delays, rudeness) – the concern of the customer services department;

c) problems with *money* – very commonly that customer believes him/herself to have been overcharged.

Among the commonest types of money problem are:

a) actual error on part of firm (eg sending out the wrong invoice);

b) apparent error, when the customer is mistaken (eg customer's records are faulty, or the charge is correct, though perhaps unjust);

c) the service or goods are not as expected or advertised and the customer suspects the integrity of the firm (eg there may be misleading advertising, shoddy workmanship or dubious business practice);

d) requests for payment of an overdue debt.

126

The most difficult part of the task of receiving or making a complaint is the handling of awkward situations, such as:

a)   telling the other person that he/she is wrong;

b)   requesting action;

c)   refusing action;

d)   apologising.

There will, of course, often be situations in which your employer has already decided on a course of action, but when it is up to you, the first step should be to decide what you really want to be done (for instance, should there be a refund, a credit note, or an apology). *Think out the situation* – talk it over with someone if it helps – and *plan what you are going to say*. Try to state in a sentence or so, in simple language, and without either abuse or apology, what it is that has happened and what you want.

2. Basic pattern of letters

2.1 General approach

a)   There is always a need for planning.

b)   Give a simple statement of the facts.

c)   Be sure that there is a polite handling of difficult points.

d)   Follow the *KISS* principle – 'Keep It Short and Simple'.

2.2 Language and format

Except for the handling of difficult points (see *Complaints: 3. importance of language used*, page 128), the language and format will be like those of all business letters. (How to write a standard business letter is explained in *Letters*, page 195.)

2.3 Basic framework

In the letter there will be:

a)   various routine material;

b)   the more difficult part, which handles the complaint.

A useful pattern is given below. Often you can use standard phrases, as indicated.

a)   **Thanks for letter received**

```
Thank you for your letter dated June 20th, reference BC/456.
```

b)   **Statement of purpose of letter**

Customer:

```
I am writing in connection with... [details]
```

Firm:

> With reference to your complaint about..., we have now looked into
> the matter and can advise you as follows/wish to make the following
> comments:...

c) Statement of facts

There will normally be a set of facts to be conveyed (eg that an invoice is wrong in various places, etc). There are two common ways in which such information can be conveyed:

1) a numbered list of points:

> the details are as follows:
> (1) Invoice no. 1234 is in error...
> (2) The date of delivery of...

2) as an account of events:

> On 14th July last we wrote to you explaining... On 30th July we
> received your reply, to the effect that...

Which pattern is best will depend on the nature of the situation you are dealing with. There is no easy answer.

What remains will be the difficult part of the task. This is the handling of awkward situations. These are dealt with below.

3. Importance of language used

Most adults have received a letter (often in connection with money) which has caused them offence. Here is a genuine example, which irritated the customer, causing him to close his account. The letter was sent on 24th September; the customer had sent a cheque for that amount on 23rd September.

> Dear Sir or Madam,
>
> According to our records your bill as of 24th September was £82.50
> in arrears. We request that you forward a remittance by return of
> post to clear this debt. Failure to do so may result in legal
> action for recovery of the sum owed and legal expenses incurred.

Consider now which words or phrases sound harsh, and how they could be changed.

a) *'According to our records...'.* – a gentler start might be 'Dear Mr Smith, We find that...'.

b) *'in arrears'* is correct but very formal – how about 'there was £82.50 outstanding'?

c) *'We request that you...'* – 'please' or 'we would appreciate'.

d) *'to clear this debt'* – debt is correct technically but sounds very serious to many people. The customer is a bit behind in payments – so why not just 'settle this bill'?

e) *Legal action* – surely unnecessarily menacing at this stage?

f)   Most important – it would have helped to put in a sentence along the lines:

'Please ignore this letter if you have posted a remittance within the past seven days.'

This would take much of the irritation out of the situation for a customer who has in fact paid, but whose payment has not yet been received because of delays in the postal and accounting systems.

You may still feel that the customer was behind in payments and in the wrong. But the company's aim is to get him/her to pay, rather than to alienate people who are basically good customers. And the letter wouldn't deter those who set out to defraud the company.

The amended version would read:

```
Dear Mr Smith,

We find that according to our records, there is £82.50 outstanding
on your account. We would be grateful if you would settle this bill
as soon as possible. Please ignore this letter if you have posted a
remittance within the past seven days.
```

4. Useful phrases for dealing with complaints

Here are some common points of difficulty, and some phrases which you could use to cope with them.

❏   **Telling the other person that they are wrong**
We regret that there has been/is an error in your invoice...
We believe/note/would point out/would remind you that...
You will note that clause 14 says...
We believe that there are errors...

❏   **Requesting action**
We are writing in response to [details] to draw your attention to/enquire/make a complaint about
We regret to say that we are very unhappy about/disturbed by/
We therefore suggest/request/require/demand that...

❏   **Refusing action**
We are unable to guarantee supplies...
It is not company policy to...
We regret that we are unable to be of further assistance in this matter...
We very much appreciate your difficulties. However, we have to inform you that...

❏   **Making apologies**
We regret that there has been an error on our part/a misentry in our accounts...

❏   **Final paragraph**
Often a problem is how to round off the letter. In most letters all that is needed is an appropriate expression of goodwill. But in this case we are seeking action and need to emphasise that point. Some possible lines are:

Customer:

We trust that the matter will receive your prompt/urgent/immediate attention...

We hope/expect to hear by return of post

We have therefore to inform you that unless you rectify the situation... we shall be obliged to withhold payment/withdraw our custom/take legal advice/take legal action...

Firm:

We hope that this clarifies/explains the matter to your satisfaction...

We will adjust/amend your account immediately...

We have therefore adjusted your account by that amount...

We are happy to enclose a refund/credit note...

We apologise (once again) for any inconvenience which you have suffered...

You are not expected to achieve results of this quality in the letters which you write during your course. But if you take note of these and any other models of good practice which you may meet, you will develop a feel for a polished and effective style in this type of writing.

Remember, finally, that it is both possible and necessary to show understanding of the customer's problem and also to be quick to apologise when you are in the wrong. Being responsive to the customer's feelings is always good business practice.

Computerisation

An overview of the use of computers in financial record keeping

Preliminary reading

Before studying this section for the first time you should read *Purpose of this section*, below.

If you have not studied computers before at all, you will find it valuable to read *Computers – the basic principles*, page 132, before you first use this section.

Contents

1. Purpose of this section

This section aims to give an overview of the use of computers in financial record keeping. Once you have read it, the information can then be a reference source, for occasions when you wish to refresh your knowledge. For your convenience a glossary of the terms used in this section is given on page 139.

This entry cannot begin to give the detail which is needed to handle a particular computer system. You will only acquire this in the best possible way, that is by 'hands-on' experience, supported by tuition and manuals.

This section also makes no attempt to explain the way in which the computer actually handles the process of record keeping. How things are done once information is entered into the computer is an area for computer specialists. Other than that, the computer is only a tool which makes the work of record keeping less laborious and more efficient.

All the references made to record keeping draw upon material which is given elsewhere in this Information Bank. If therefore an example is given which you do not understand, you will need to decide whether to ignore it, or to use the index to find the full explanation of the topic.

2. Computers – the basic principles

A computer is, quite simply, an electronic machine, which is in some ways no different from a television set or a hi-fi. Where it does differ is that it is able to process information.

Originally computers were simply very powerful adding machines, hence their name. But it was then realised that they could be used to process other types of information, eg language.

To understand how this became possible, consider first the fact that you think in and speak language. As a child you learn that you can represent language (that is, what you say) by writing (letters and numbers). The important recognition in the early days of computing was that the letters themselves can be given numbers (eg A = 1, B = 2 etc). This means that all the information we wish to process can be expressed as a stream of numbers. To have to read numbers instead of letters would be heavy work for us, but doesn't worry a machine. The process of turning one sort of information into another is called *encoding*. The encoded information is processed by a block of electronic circuitry called the *Central Processing Unit* (for short, the CPU).

To the specialist, it is the CPU (together with related electronics) which is the computer. To the general public, though, the computer is what they can see, namely a television screen (for which the proper name is a VDU – *visual display unit*) and a typewriter-style *keyboard*. Somewhere connected to these will be a *disk drive* (more rarely a tape recorder) and usually a *printer*. There are various types of printer. The most familiar is the *dot matrix* printer. The name derives from the fact that every character (letter, number or symbol) is built up by filling spaces on a tiny grid (the matrix) with dots. It gives a simple but effective print. A higher quality of print is given by a *daisy wheel* printer. For print of an even higher quality, for example, for the production of books, a *laser* printer is used.

The purpose of the VDU, keyboard and printer (known technically as *peripherals*) are clear enough. You type things into the computer, you can see what is happening, and you can get things printed onto paper (referred to as hard copy). But what about the disk drives? As the name suggests, they are there to take disks. The nature and purpose of the disks is similar to that of the audio or video tapes with which we are all familiar. Information (music, tv pictures, typing) is encoded electronically (turned into electrical form). This encoding can be recorded on suitable materials (dor instance the brown surface of the audiocassette), and can be played back whenever we wish. In the case of disks it means that information created for or by the computer can be recalled *(retrieved)* for future use.

Disks don't seem to be round when you look at them; this is because of their protective covering. They vary in size. *Floppy disks* (which usually aren't floppy at all!), which most people have now seen, come as 3, $3\frac{1}{2}$ and $5\frac{1}{4}$ inches. Businesses tend to use *hard disks*. These are larger, can hold vastly more information, and also are far more safe and reliable than floppy disks.

All computers operate on the same basic principles, no matter how different they look, nor how they may be named. Many people are familiar with the *microcomputer*, which is portable enough for us to use in our home. There are even smaller ones (*laptops* and *portables*) which can be carried around on business. And there are large machines such as those owned by the utilities such as gas and electricity – these are known as *mainframe* computers.

3. Computers in the world of work

3.1 Putting in data

It may truly be said that computers take the work out of working! More precisely they take away the mechanical labour of routine actions and copying, while at the same time as ensuring speed and accuracy. As a general rule, you only need to type in (key in), the information once. Then, provided that the initial data entry is accurate, it will, short of a major malfunction in the system, remain accurate.

This is true of all computing, but the way in which people use computers in their workplaces is often rather different from the patterns which apply to domestic machines.

First, the volume of work is such that it is worth employing people with a high keyboard skill to type in the information. The information itself is usually referred to as *data*, and often need to be prepared in some way, for instance by *data processing* personnel. Essentially, data processing compresses the information (rather like writing something in note form); an important part of this operation is the use of *codes*. For example, it is quicker and more economic of the storage space available in the computer to type in 17:27 than the words 'Expense account – office supplies: envelopes'. The data processing staff will also be concerned with how information is to be stored. In particular items of information *(fields)* will make up information about one person (a *record*); this will in turn be part of a *file* (group of records on one topic). (A record need not deal with a person; it can equally hold information about an organisation, or a type of object, such as a chair.)

This may be made clearer by an example. A file might deal with OFFICE STATIONERY. One record might be PHOTOCOPY PAPER. Some of the fields might be

1:    size (A4)

2:    weight (80 gram)

3:    colour (white)

4:0   number of sheets per pack (500).

In the world of work, it is often found to be more efficient to handle transactions in bulk. Such blocks of entries are known as *batches*. For example, the handling of payroll through BACS is carried out in batches.

3.2 The mouse

There are many people who are not concerned with the main body of data entry. These people use computers less often, and so do not need to type so well. Indeed, they may well have little or no keyboard skill. This is often true of management. To help such people, the computer industry invented the *mouse*. The device is so called because it is small and moves around in short movements, like the cheese-eating variety. But its purpose is to act as an electronic pointer. It controls a symbol on the screen (typically an arrow), and permits the user to 'point at' the screen. You make things happen by pressing a switch which is part of the mouse. For example, to give the answer 'yes' to a question put by the computer, you can point at the word 'yes' which is shown on the screen, and press the switch. This will have the same effect on the computer, as would typing in the word on the keyboard.

3.3 Menus, commands and data

Why might anyone wish to answer 'yes' at all? To understand this, you need to consider the ways in which you can use a computer.

It is possible to use it in much the same way as you would a video cassette player. You put in your disk, press 'go', and sit back and enjoy the show. But the distinctive value of a computer is that it can be organised *(programmed)* to do many other things – such as keep your ledger. However, the computer has no mind of its own – nothing is more dumb than a computer, especially when it's switched off! It needs humans to tell it what to do. What it asks for are *choices, commands* and *data*. Unlike the video recorder, which either plays or does nothing, the computer is capable of being *interactive*.

To make the computer respond, in many cases, including accountancy, the user is offered a *menu*. Like the sort you get in a restaurant, it offers you choices. For example, suppose you wish to change the layout of a worksheet. Here is an example of what would happen if you were using the *Lotus 1-2-3* package.

You first arrive at the Main Menu, which offers:

| **Worksheet** | Range | Copy | Move | File | Print | Graph | Data | Quit |

You move the pointer to select 'Worksheet'. Having done so, you are offered the Worksheet sub-menu:

| Global | Insert | Delete | **Column-width** | Erase | Titles | Window | Status |

Choosing again, you are taken to the Column-width sub-menu, where you are offered:

| **Set** | Reset |

To make your choice you will either type in or signal with the mouse what you want.

A menu is a means of asking you for a *command,* an instruction for the computer to take a certain type of action.

The other main need of the computer is for *data* – information on which it will operate. Continuing with the *Lotus 1-2-3* example, suppose you choose Set (column width), and the computer replies with an instruction (known as a prompt) to you as follows:

Enter column width (1...72).

You choose the number you want, say 12, and type it in. Usually you will press a key (Return or Enter) on such occasions, so that the computer knows that you have finished your entry. The column width of the worksheet it produces will then remain 12 until changed again by the same procedure.

3.4 Communication with others

If you have ever operated a home computer system, you will have done so by yourself, or perhaps with a friend at the same machine. In the world of work this would soon be quite restricting. The computer industry has therefore made it possible for users to communicate with each other in two main ways.

Terminals

The home computer is a self-contained system, that is, it has everything which you need to operate it. By contrast, in many places of work, the employees only have a *work station* or *terminal*. This means they have a VDU and keyboard, but little or no computing power (that is, no CPU). (Devices which have a restricted amount of computing power are said to be 'smart'). Typically, too, the work station has no printer. Instead, the terminals are linked to a *host computer* (often a mainframe) which serves all the users. This means that one record keeper can type in data which the computer saves and which can be accessed by another employee (that is they can call up the information on their terminal). Because large volumes of information are stored, the computer does not use floppy disks, but either hard disks, or large reels of magnetic tape on special tape recorders.

Networks

Because computer information is encoded and stored in electronic form it is possible to send it along wires, and in particular those of the telephone system. To do this a special device is used, which is called a *modem*. This turns the data which your computer sends (output) into a suitable form, and also turns messages from other people's computers (your *input*) into a form which your computer can understand. In principle this process may occur between any two computers: you can thus communicate with someone miles away. For business purposes the system has been developed and systematised to make it more efficient and convenient. The links between, say, branches of a given company, are known as *networks*. You can have a LAN (*local area network* – the same building or site) or a WAN (*wide area network* – across some distance).

4. Some important advice for computer users

Here is some important guidance on using a computer. It is vital for beginners – but it is surprising how often experts make the same mistakes!

Only humans think

❏ *Computers don't have any common sense!*
The great value of a computer, especially in financial record keeping, is that you only need to key in data once. Once data has been entered, the computer can copy it easily: you don't need to key in data twice to make a double entry.

BUT

It is therefore doubly important to be accurate. Certain types of check are often built in, but the computer will quite happily reproduce the fact that Mr Smith's claim for a bus fare was £110.00 rather than £1.10.

❏ *Computers can't make judgements*
Though there are computer programs to help management, and the computer can even prepare company reports, basically the computer is a machine which is good at carrying out boring and repetitive tasks. For example, it can record that an expense is paid; it can even query expenses which it is not programmed to accept. But it can't decide if a new expense is allowable. For instance, suppose that sales rep Simon Page visits Skegness on business. Instead of staying in a hotel (cost £50) he stays with a friend and pays him £30. The computer can query that there is no hotel name, but only a manager can decide if Simon will be allowed to do this.

Computers run on electricity – so don't cut off the power!

This point has an important practical consequence (which even the best of us can forget).

When you are working on a computer, what you have done is stored in its memory (the CPU and related electronic parts). This only works while the power is *on. So you must not switch off until you have recorded (saved) your work on a disk (or tape).*

Disks are vulnerable too!

Regular users of computers are convinced that, *if a disk contains the only copy of a piece of work, that disk will be struck with misfortune.* (That is, it will be destroyed by fire, lost, become faulty, or someone will wipe out (erase) its contents). So the rule is – *always make a second (backup) copy of important work.*

5. Security

5.1 Some risks

Security is at least as important in a computerised system as in any other area of financial record keeping. There are various considerations.

❏ Data which is encoded and stored electronically is very vulnerable (see last section). Procedures to protect data must be strictly followed, and disks and tapes must be carefully handled and stored to protect them from physical damage.

❑ The Data Protection Act of 1984 requires that

 a) people have a right of access to information which is kept about them on computers, but

 b) they also have a right to privacy – the information is confidential, and must be kept from general public access.

Means therefore have to be devised to prevent unauthorised staff from having access to confidential material.

The latter point also applies to material which may not be covered by the Act but which is sensitive from the company's point of view. Most readers will have heard of *hackers*, who have gained access to secret material, by discovering how to enter the memory of a computer through telephone lines (ie via a modem link).

❑ Unlimited access to accounts presents tempting opportunities for fraud. The story is by now well known of the bank employee who realised that currency transactions use several places of decimals. He arranged for the last place to be deposited in his account. .0001 pence won't buy much in a supermarket, but multiplied by millions it yields a very healthy bank balance!

5.2 Some protective measures

1) There are various ways in which a keyboard can be *disabled*, so that it cannot be used by an unauthorised person.

2) A system of *passwords* can be used. In order for the computer to disclose, say, an aged debtors list, the employee must type in a particular word or code.

3) Sensitive files which are no longer in use can be *erased*, rather than *deleted*. When a file is created, it is given an identification code (rather like a reference number) which enables the file to be retrieved. When the file is no longer wanted, the normal process is to use a DELETE command. This deletes the 'reference number', so the file cannot be found. This is rather like losing someone's name and address. But just as in the latter case the person still exists, the computer file still remains recorded on the disk or tape. It is possible (though difficult) to retrieve this information – this was done to provide evidence in a drug smuggling trial in 1987. This could not have happened if the file had been erased, in the way that you can erase an audiocassette recording by recording over it (this is known as *overwriting*).

4) A security software package such as *PS3* or *Fortress Plus* can be used. These ensure the use of passwords and deletion. They also include *encryption* (files turned into a code to make them unreadable if stolen) and blocks to prevent the use of floppy disks so as to access files on a hard disk.

5) An important way of preventing or detecting computer fraud is by the use of internal checks and various other controls. Checks are built in to check entries, and reconcile various types of record. The description of these in any detail is beyond the scope of this book.

6. Financial packages

6.1 What is software?

The parts of the computer system which you can see, together with the components inside it (eg the CPU) are known as the *hardware*. What makes it able to work for us, and appear to be intelligent, is the *software*.

Software is the name for the *programs* (sets of instructions) which specialists devise to guide the CPU how to handle and process commands and data.

Programs can be linked together to create *packages*, which will handle a range of needs. These have become very popular in financial record keeping as they not only relieve the worker of much mechanical and repetitive work – they yield substantial gains in productivity.

Programs are grouped into two broad areas. *Systems software* consists of programs which deal with the basic operations of the computer system. There will, for example, be a program to handle the control of the printer. Such software can be dauntingly complex, so the computer companies try to ensure that the average user does not have to deal with it. Where this is impossible, they try to make it *user-friendly* by reducing the number of operations to the minimum and by using everyday (rather than specialist) language.

6.2 Applications software

The other broad area of computer software is applications software. This consists of programs designed to carry out a particular practical activity, for example stock control.

6.3 Three common types of package

There are three types of applications software for financial record keeping in common use.

1) **Spreadsheets**
   This is a basic type of package, which is also frequently used by people who do not work professionally with financial records. The name comes from the time when accountants used to draw up financial plans for businesses by using columns on a large sheet of accounting paper, which was spread wide open. A spreadsheet enables you to input data, make calculations and move these around so as to put them under different sorts of heading. Spreadsheets do have more complex applications for accountants, but these are beyond the scope of this book.

2) **Cash trader packages**
   Such packages basically create an analysed cash book (see *Cash book*, page 118). They handle day to day trading, the record of sales and purchases, invoices and similar cash transactions. They are thus very suitable for small businesses.

3) **Complete ledger packages**
   These meet the whole range of ledger needs, including double entry and production of final accounts.

7. Accounts packages

The computer can be used for:

Stock control

Receipts and issues of stock can be entered as they happen. In large stores, the sales made at the check out can be fed at once into the stock control system. Stock cards can be produced as hard copy where they are useful. However, since they are only a convenient means of monitoring stock movements, the information can be kept on computer files, and accessed as needed. Electronic stock control enables the list (inventory) of stock to be updated at once. Management can know immediately what stock levels are and how they are moving. For instance, the W H Smith headquarters at Swindon can at once see the results of thousands of sales daily. Supplies of lines which are in demand can be sent out immediately, and only to the branches where they are needed. Such quick and targeted response is crucial, especially where, as in large enterprises, sales may be on a massive scale, and have a small profit margin.

Journals

It is a simple matter for the computer to record at the same time the operations which are covered by keeping the sales, purchases and returns journals. However, data, once entered, is immediately accessible for the whole range of options offered by a package. Potentially, this eliminates the need for journals, because they were devised at first to cope with the fact that information had to be written down by one person and then later copied by another. With a computer system, the information can at once be transferred to the ledger with minimum expense of time and effort.

VAT account

The noting, calculating or abstraction of VAT can be carried out by even an elementary computer program. The VAT component in a transaction can be marked off *(flagged)* for the special treatment which it needs in the accounting process.

Invoices

Since the data involved in a transaction (whether purchasing or selling) is entered at the first stage, there is no problem in transferring this onto an invoice. The computer can be instructed to draw upon particular files, and any new data can be entered. The invoice can then be printed out.

Customer accounts

The same principle of abstracting information from data which has been entered enables the computer to set up or update almost instantaneously a customer account, whenever an invoice is sent or received.

Aged debtors list

Since the computer is first and foremost an adding machine, there is no problem in adding up the entries in an account, and finding a balance. The computer can thus produce a listing of the balances on the customer accounts. But data can be be given reference codes at the time of entry, which means that you can, for example, link amounts and dates. The computer can therefore search through accounts whenever required, and print out debts and the length of time for which they have been outstanding, thus giving an aged debt analysis. The computer thus offers a quick and useful way of controlling the level of debt in a business.

Ledger accounts

The whole process of double entry can be carried out by the computer. All that is needed is that the person making the first entry is given a prompt, to ascertain the destination of the double entry. In fact, in many cases, even this entry is not needed – the process can be made automatic. For example, a sales invoice sent out automatically requires a credit entry in the sales ledger and a debit entry in the customer's personal account.

Such software is called an *integrated package*. Perhaps the best known package of this type is *Pegasus*.

Final accounts

As might be expected, the ability to the computer to total or abstract figures can be taken further. This is what is needed to create a trial balance, trading and profit and loss accounts, and a balance sheet. Whatever is in the ledger can be readily accessed.

However, modern accountancy programs can go further. The format of a company report (which accompanies the final accounts for a year) is to a great extent standardised. Consequently, the computer can 'stitch together' a standard report, and insert the appropriate accountancy data. Because no standard report will meet every possible situation, the computer's word processing facility can be used to customise the draft.

The production of reports and other hard copy for public consumption can be made more effective by the computer's ability to produce graphics. For many years, it has been possible to make the computer create mathematical aids such as graphs, pie charts and bar charts on the screen and on its print outs. These do not even have to be specially drawn. The computer uses the data which you instruct it to find, as the measurements for its graphic work.

Payroll

Another labour saving facility which is available is the handling of the payroll. In this case the computer user has to input the data regarding the time and rate of pay which is on the attendance record (unless it is a computer card system). Thereafter the computer can total up the wage, calculate deductions, (which can be keyed in once, and then left until a change is needed), find net pay, and print out a wage slip. In cases where payment is by cheque or bank giro, the computer can print the necessary data onto the document. The use of bulk processing through BACS is also an option.

Nevertheless, expert opinion is that payroll may not be a cost-effective activity for computers in small businesses. This is because payroll is an important area for fraud, and taking suitable security measures may be cumbersome. Also payroll involves information which is covered by the Data Protection Act. Ensuring that the rights of employees are not infringed may not be worth the trouble where a small number of employees are involved.

8. Glossary

applications software	computer programs designed to perform a specific type of work
batch	a block of files or data which to be processed at the same time
bulk processing	handling of many records or files at the same time
cash trader package	accounting package that performs the functions of an analysed cash book
central processing unit (CPU)	that part of the hardware which controls and handles the most important operations of the computer (the 'brain' of the computer)
command	instruction given by a user to the computer to perform some action
data	any information which is to be processed by the CPU
data processing	the turning of data into a suitable form for filing and handling
DELETE	a command as a result of which the computer erases the information which enables it to identify a file (the address)
disk storage	device for computer data
disk drive	device for reading from and writing to disks
dot matrix printer	printer on which the characters are formed by inserting dots into a grid
encoding	process of turning one sort of information into another
encryption	the coding of files in a form which makes them unreadable by anyone but the user
erase	permanent destruction of a file by writing new data into the place where it was stored on a disk
field	one data item in a record
file	set of records of the same format concerned with one topic
hardware	the physical equipment in a computer system
integrated package	set of programs meeting all the requirements of a particular type of work
local area network (LAN)	set of microcomputers connected over a short distance
mainframe computer	computer capable of handling many users and much information simultaneously
menu	range of options offered to a user by a program
modem	device used to connect computers through the telephone network
mouse	movable device for controlling a pointer on the VDU
systems software	programs which deal with the basic operations of the computer
terminal device	(typically a VDU and keyboard) with little or no computing power of its own, which is connected to a computer permitting the user of the terminal to access the computers
visual display unit (VDU)	a cathode ray (television) screen which enables the computer to display information so that the user can see it
word processing	software which enables the user to input, edit and print out text

Expenses

The types of expense claims, and the documents and procedures for making such claims

Contents

1. What expenses are

It often happens that employees of a firm have to pay out their own money in order to obtain goods and services which are necessary for carrying out their employer's business. A well-known example is the travelling sales representative, who in the course of a sales trip will typically have to pay for travel (cost of public transport, or fuel for a car), meals, and hotel accommodation.

Since it is his or her own money which is paid out, the representative will naturally wish to claim these *expenses* back. The employer will accept his claim, realising that the employee has laid out personal money in the interests of the business. Acceptance of the claim will be subject to seeing evidence of payment, say in the form of a receipt.

However, the employer will wish to ensure that the money spent is in turn seen as one of the *expenses* of running the business. It can then be presented as such in the final accounts and when dealing with the tax authorities.

Note, though, that not all the expenses that a business may agree to repay to its employees are seen as allowable by the Inland Revenue or Customs and Excise.

(For a further explanation of how expenses are seen when drawing up accounts, see *Final Accounts*, page 147.)

2. Basic expense claims procedure

Because expense claims are made frequently in many businesses, and because they are included in the firm's accounts, there has to be a procedure to ensure that claims are *allowable* (*valid*) and are properly recorded. The typical procedure is as follows.

1) The employee *makes the payment*, and collects a *receipt* or similar document as proof that the money has been laid out (ie that it is a **verifiable** expense).

2) The employee fills in an *expenses claim form* (see below).

3) The form is then *processed* by a member of the accounts department. The aim is to see that the claim is fully in order, and that the repayment (reimbursement) of expenses can be *authorised*. Details of what has to be done are given below.

4) In a large firm the claim will then be passed to the Cashier for payment; in a smaller organisation the Cashier will probably both check the form, and then authorise and make the payment.

5) The details of the transaction are then recorded in the accounts (see page 147).

The whole process of claiming and reimbursing expense claims is usually made under two separate headings. Small items of cash expenditure are met from petty cash (see *Petty Cash*, page 219); they are therefore not described further here. The other, larger items are the subject of this entry.

3. Authorisation

There is no rigid rule about what expenses are allowed; the rules laid down vary from firm to firm. Certain types of claim (eg transport, accommodation) are, however, almost universally accepted. Management also decides what the upper limit of petty cash claims is to be, as well as what items are to be paid for out of petty cash. Authorisation of routine claims will be made by the Cashier or an accounts clerk. Unusual expenses will be referred to a manager.

4. Differences of procedure between small and large organisations

The handling of expenses is a good example of a general pattern in the world of work; that the larger the organisation, the more formal and complex the process of handling transactions. But in fact the same type of activities take place at all levels of business life.

When Eve Adams starts out, she has expenses, such as going on the bus to a job. This is a travel expense for the purpose of her business, just as much as the fare on Concorde paid out by (or for) the Head of a multinational industry. But all Eve needs to do is to keep her receipts as evidence, and enter the expense in her analysed cash book.

By the time that she opens her garden centre, she needs a means of handling small items of expenditure made by her staff (for instance, postage of certain types); this is done through petty cash. But larger expenses, for example an occasional hotel bill on a business trip, are still on a small enough scale to be logged by the cashier, and repaid as they arise.

However, in a large company, such as Azure Computers, there will be many employees who are running up considerable sums in expenses; the petrol bill of, say, ten sales representatives for a week is quite considerable. And with the loss of the close personal contact to be found at Eve's garden centre, there are greater opportunities for error and fraud. It therefore becomes necessary to have an organised and secure system for submitting claims, and a suitable form for doing so. The procedure is explained below.

5. Cost centres and expense codes

The accounts of a large firm will often be broken down for convenience and for more effective management into smaller accounts relating to the main divisions of a company. In Eve's case, for example, it will be convenient for Honeysuckle (the flower shop) and the Garden Centre to handle a lot of their financial affairs separately during the year. These will then be brought together at points of review, most notably when the final accounts are drawn up.

In Azure Computers, the division of accounts is typical of many companies:

- Purchases
- Sales
- Personnel
- Research
- Administration.

Each of these divisions has to pay back the expenses laid out on its behalf. A part of a business which is accountable for costs is known as a *cost centre*.

To save labour, and especially when using a computerised accounts system, expenses are grouped together and *coded*. Thus bus, rail and air fares, and the cost of petrol and oil bought by employees while using a motor vehicle on company business might all be grouped together as 'Travel', and be given a code such as 412.

6. Filling in an expenses claim form

On the next page is a typical expenses claim form. There are three types of entry to be made.

- First, there will always be a need for
    1) the name of the person making the claim (the claimant)
    2) the cost centre (if this system is used)
    3) the date when the claim was made
    4) the signature of the claimant
    5) the signature of the person authorising the expense.
- Next the form will have two sections. One of these will be completed by the claimant, and will contain:
    6) details of the claim
    7) the expense code (if this system is used)
    8) the various sums laid out
    9) the total sum which is claimed.
- The second section will normally be filled in by the employee who first processes the form, and contains:
    10) the sum paid, net of VAT
    11) the VAT paid on the expense (if any),
    12) totals for 10) and 11).

EXPENSES CLAIM FORM

Claimant's name (block capitals): D. CUFFEY   Cost Centre:

Date: 7 July 1991   Vehicle Reg. No.: AOT 758 T

to be completed by claimant ←— to be completed by cashier —→

Details	Expense Code			Total £ p			Expense Amount (Net of VAT) £ p			VAT £ p		
Public transport	1	0	0									
Car hire	1	0	1	4	4	0 6	3	7	5 0		6	5 6
Accommodation	2	0	0									
Meals	3	0	0		7	6 3		6	5 0		1	1 3
Entertaining - O'sea	4	0	1									
Totals				5	1	6 9	4	4	0 0	7	6	9

Claimant's signature: *D. Cuffey*

Expense authoriser: *M. Faraday*

143

7. Duties of the accounts clerk or cashier

1) Check that the member of staff is authorised to claim expenses.

2) Check that the expense claimed is one authorised by the firm.

3) Check that the receipts or invoices and the claim form reconcile.

4) Check the calculations for accuracy.

5) Calculate VAT and enter it on the claim form.

6) Allocate the relevant expense code.

7) Enter the relevant cost centre.

8) Sign the form to authorise the claim.

9) Pass the claim for payment.

Notes:

a) Stages 1) and 2) above will be achieved by checking against a list or memorandum from management. Such guidance will also usually be given to employees who are likely to make claims. For example, a typical extract reads:

> VEHICLE: claims made under this heading may include charges for petrol, oil, parking and garaging. Receipts or invoices showing the payment made and VAT paid must be attached to the claim form. Charges for servicing when this is essential to enable the vehicle to return to Azure House must first be cleared with the Cashier by telephone.

b) With regard to Stage 9, the claimant will receive the full amount laid out (that is including VAT paid). The firm will reclaim the tax paid through the VAT account (see page 261).

10) At appropriate points (weekly or monthly) it will often be necessary to complete summaries of the types of expense claimed, according to code, and according to cost centre. A typical summary document looks as follows.

EXPENSES RECORD

Claimant's name: E. ADAMS

Month: May 1991

Total mileage: 108

Cost Centre: Admin

Date	Details	Miles	Public Transport 100	Car hire 101	Accom- modation 200	Meals 300	Entertaining O'seas 401	Entertaining Other 402	Other	Total
7 May	Hoxted	46		25.50		3.50				29.00
15 May	Longmeadow	16		15.50						15.50
21 May	Hoxted	46		25.50		2.90				28.40
Totals				66.50		6.40				72.90

Advance (if any)		
Amount due	£	72.90

8. Payment of expenses

The employee will normally be reimbursed by cheque at the end of a named period, which varies according to company policy. The relevant part of a typcial expenses memorandum is:

> Expenses for a given month must be completed for that month only, on the last working day of the month. Claim forms must be submitted by the 7th of the next month. Repayment of claims is made on the 21st of that month. Claims not received by the 7th of the month will be held over until the repayment date in the following month.
>
> **Example**
> Suppose expenses were laid out on 26 May and 2 June. Your claim can only be made for the May expenses. Your claim form must be received by 7 June for payment on 21 June. Claims received after 7 June will be reimbursed on 21 July.

The repayment of expenses is normally kept apart from the payment of wages and salaries, so as to avoid complications in calculating tax and National Insurance deductions (see *Wages and salaries*, page 271).

9. Taxable and non-taxable expenses

Two forms of tax apply to expenses.

1) *VAT*

   Suppliers of goods and services who are registered for VAT will add that tax to the amount which the claimant pays. The claimant will be repaid both the basic cost and the VAT by the employer. The employer in turn will record the payment of input tax on goods and services supplied in the VAT account with a view to reclaiming this money at the end of the VAT year. (For further detail see *Value added tax*, page 253.)

2) *Income tax*

   The money paid out by the employee is in pursuit of his or her employer's business, and is therefore reclaimed. The money is not a part of the employee's salary, since it is only a repayment of money spent on goods or services which were not for the employee's personal use. It is not therefore subject to tax.

The rule of the Inland Revenue is basically quite simple: that expenses laid out wholly in the pursuit of one's business are to be distinguished from money laid out for personal use. (They distinguish the *business entity* from the person – see Section 1, page 25).

But if the employee is paid by the employer for something which is only partly used for business, that part which is not used for business counts as a personal benefit and is regarded as a part of the employee's income. For example, suppose the employer pays for the purchase, fuel and running costs of a car which the employee also uses to go on holiday. The holiday use in not a business use. It is a personal benefit (known as a perquisite, or popularly a 'perk') and the money claimed or received for fuel etc for that period would be liable to be included in the calculation of PAYE.

10. Where expenses are recorded in the accounts – summary

- The repayment made will be recorded in the Cash Book (because it is paid by cheque).
- The Cash Book repayment will be given a double entry in the ledger.
- The expense goes into the relevant expense account.
- VAT goes into the VAT account.

Final accounts

Information about the purpose of the balance sheet, the trading and profit and loss accounts and how to draw them up

Preliminary reading

Before reading this section you should have read *Accounts: basic approach to record keeping*, page 74.

1. Final accounts – what they are

1.1 Definition

Final accounts are accounts which are drawn up at the end of the accounting period (which is normally one year). The final accounts consist of:

☐   the trading account

☐   the profit and loss account

☐   the balance sheet

(These are explained later in this section.)

1.2 Definition of 'year' in business

There are several senses in which the word 'year' is used in business.

a)   **The calendar year**
    This is the year which we all use in everyday life to reckon our time. It begins on 1 January and ends on 31 December.

b)   **The financial year**
    People who deal with money find it useful to have an agreed start and finish to their year. You might expect this to be the calendar year, but in fact it begins on 6 April of one calendar year, and finishes on 5 April of the next. Of particular importance is the fact that the Inland Revenue and the Treasury (which handles the Government's finances) both use 6 April as the starting date for their year. The reason for the choice of date is that in earlier times it was customary to settle accounts on Lady Day, 25 March. In the eighteenth century the calendar was altered, and the numbering of the days was shifted. At that point, the old 25 March became April 5.

c)   **The financial year of a business**
    Businesses need to draw up their accounts periodically. Normally this is done at the end of a year, and this is referred to as the accounting period. At this point the accountant draws up the final accounts. But the business year can begin at any point in the calendar year, because businesses do not all begin trading on the same day of the year.

d)   **The VAT year**
    This may well be different again from the above. For details see *Value added tax: registration*, page 255.

2. The trading account

The trading account is a statement of the gross profit which has arisen from the normal trading operations of a business.

2.1 Gross profit

The gross profit of a business is calculated as being

> **sales − cost of sales = gross profit**

Example

In its first month of trading Eden Plants and Gardens (EPG) bought plants and garden supplies for £1037. All the goods were sold, for a total of £1588.

    Gross profit = £1588 − £1037 = £551

These figures were obtained by totalling the Sales Account and the Purchases Account (see *Ledgers and journals*, page 186).

2.2 Stock in hand

In reality, firms rarely sell off all their stock in a way which fits neatly with the accounting period. At the start of the period, there will be goods not yet sold which are left over from the previous business year. This is called the *opening stock*. At the end of the year there will be goods which have not yet been sold – this is the *closing stock*. The total amount of stock in hand may have risen or fallen over the year. But in in order to calculate the gross profit the accountant only wishes to know the cost of goods which have been sold.

To calculate this the business checks the stock, and then calculates its value. This is done by using the formula

> **number of units x value per unit**

for each type of item. The various totals are then added together. For a fuller account of the valuation of stock, see *Stock control and valuation*, page 238.

To calculate the cost of goods you then use the formula given below. As an example assume that EPG's total sales were £13 956, total purchases were £6215, opening stock was worth £1432, and closing stock £888.

Value of opening stock		1432
Add	cost of new purchases	6215
		7647
Subtract Value of closing stock		888
The result is the *Cost of Goods*		6759

The gross profit will then be £13 956 – 6759 = £7197.

2.3 The trading account – what it is

Gross profit may be calculated at any time, in order to check the profitability of a business. The *trading account* is the annual statement of gross profit. An important benefit of drawing up the account is that the figure for gross profit can be compared with other years, so giving an indication of the progress of the business.

2.4 Layout

The trading account looks as follows:

Trading account of Eden Plants and Gardens for the year ended May 1, 1991		
	£	£
Sales		13 956
Opening stock	1432	
Purchases	6215	
	7647	
Less closing stock	888	
Cost of goods sold		6 759
Gross profit		7 197

2.5 Method for creating the account

1) In *right hand column* write down *total sales* as shown in Sales Account.

2) Move to *left hand column*. Write down *value of stock in hand at start of period*.

    (value = cost price x number of units)

3) In *same column* write down *total purchases* as shown in Purchases Account.

4) Write underneath the figure given when you *add Opening stock and Purchases*.

5) *In left hand column* write down *value of stock in hand at close of period*.

    (value = cost price x number of units)

6) *Subtract this figure from that found in 4.*

7) Write the result in the *right hand column*. This is the *cost of goods*.

8) *Subtract 7) from 1)* (ie Sales – Cost of Goods). Write the result in the *right hand column*. This is the *gross profit*.

Notes:

1) If the cost of goods is greater than the sales, the business has made a gross loss.

2) When management compares the trading accounts and gross profit for different years, it is often found to be particularly helpful to compare the gross profit margins. The gross profit margin is calculated according to the formula

$$\frac{\text{gross profit}}{\text{sales}} \times 100$$

In the example just given this gives $\dfrac{7197}{13\,956} \times 100 = 51.56$

The gross profit margin is thus said to be 51.56%.

3. The profit and loss account

3.1 Expenses

In reality a business does not only spend money on the cost of goods. It must also lay out money which is not part of the immediate cost of goods, but which is nevertheless essential if the business is to produce goods and provide services. Examples are the cost of transport, rent of premises, services (eg electricity) and the wages of employees. Since this money has to be spent, it must be included in any statement of accounts, if the performance of the business is to be accurately measured.

For example, in early December, a hotel may well seem to be making a profit, if you only consider the difference between receipts from visitors, and the cost of their meals and heating their rooms. But if December is a slack period (as it tends to be at the seaside) the cost of keeping on essential staff, heating the empty parts of the building, and so forth, may well mean that the hotel is actually running at a loss. Such costs are usually referred to as *expenses*; more precisely, they are *revenue* expenses (see below).

Accountants normally divide expenses into two categories. *Capital expenses* are those which are laid out on the acquisition of assets or which result in an improvement in the earning capacity of the business. An *asset* is something which a business acquires from which there is expected to be a future benefit. For example, if our hotel extends its accommodation by building an annexe, it acquires an asset. More people

More people will be able to stay in future, generating more income. Capital expenses of this type are included in the balance sheet.

Suppose, though, that the hotel does not build a new annexe but uses the same contractors to re-paint existent accommodation, and to repair a bathroom. This work is carried out as part of current trading (it is meant to improve the situation for current visitors). The work is also designed to maintain the current earning capacity of the hotel (a bathroom out of order may mean that some rooms cannot be used). Such expenses as these are known as *revenue expenses,* and are included in the summary of trading, which is the profit and loss account.

3.2 Net profit

A further means of calculating the profit which is left at the end of an accounting period, is to use the formula:

> **Gross Profit (Sales – Cost of Goods)**
> *less* **Expenses**

The result is known as the *net profit*. If the expenses are greater than the gross profit, the result is a *net loss*.

This calculation gives a fuller picture of the state of the business because it includes the expenses of running the business, and not only the cost of sales.

3.3 Layout

The profit and loss account looks as follows:

Profit and loss account of Eden Plants and Gardens for the year ended May 1, 1991

	£	£
Gross profit		7197
Less		
Premises	2500	
Wages	2600	
		5100
Net Profit		2097

3.4 Method for creating the account

1) In *right hand column* write down *Gross Profit* (from Trading Account).

2) Move to *left hand column*.

3) Write down *totals for expenses* from each of the expense accounts.

4) *Add* these together.

5) Write the result in the *right hand column*. This is the *total expenses*.

6) *Subtract 5) from 1)* (ie *Gross Profit – Expenses*). Write the result in the *right hand column*. This is the *Net Profit*.

151

Notes:

1) If the expenses are greater than the gross profit, the business has made a net loss.

2) It can be of help in assessing progress to measure the net profit margin, which is defined as

$$\frac{\text{net profit}}{\text{sales}} \times 100$$

In the example so far used, this gives $\frac{2097}{13\ 956} \times 100 = 51.56$

The net profit margin is therefore 15.02%.

4. Combined trading and profit and loss account

It is regular practice to combine both trading and profit and loss accounts as follows:

Trading and Profit and loss account of Eden Plants and Gardens for the year ended May 1, 1991	£	£
Sales		13 956
Opening stock	1432	
Purchases	6215	
	7647	
Less closing stock	888	
Cost of goods sold		6 759
Gross profit		7 197
Less		
Premises	2500	
Wages	2600	
		5 100
Net Profit		2 097

The final figure belongs to the owner or owners of business, and is the figure upon which any taxation is paid.

5. Other factors

In the calculation of a set of final accounts, various other factors are included. These are:

☐ prepayments
☐ accruals
☐ bad debts
☐ depreciation.

152

5.1 Prepayments

A prepayment is simply a *payment made in advance for goods or services*. A good example is an insurance premium which is paid annually. A payment made, say, on 1 August ensures insurance cover until 31 July of the following year. This type of payment is clearly an expense of the business.

Suppose that the accounting period runs from 1 October. This means that a year's premium (say £120) is actually paid during the accounting period, but cover has only been enjoyed for August and September. Does the accountant include the sum actually paid in the profit and loss account?

In fact, the practice adopted is to include in the accounts *only that proportion of the money which applies to the current accounting period*. In the case just given, the profit and loss account will therefore include $\frac{1}{12}$ of the premium, that is £20.

This may not seem quite fair, as the whole sum has actually had to be found. But in fact things balance out. The allowance is recorded in the relevant expense account, and the remainder of the sum actually paid is carried over as part of the opening balance of the next year's accounts. It is thus an asset, since there is a future benefit for the business. When that year's profit and loss account is drawn up, £100 of expenses will be included for which money did not actually have to be laid out.

The relevant entries in the accounts will be

Insurance account

DEBIT						CREDIT
Date			£	Date		£
1990 1 Aug	Bank		120	1 Oct	Profit and Loss a/c balance prepaid	20 100
1991 1 Aug	Bank		120	1 Oct	Profit and Loss a/c balance prepaid	120 100

Profit and Loss account

(includes)

		£
1990	Insurance	20
1991	Insurance	120

Note:

The prepayment is included on the balance sheet (see below), as it is one of the assets of the business.

The profit and loss account is treated as another ledger account.

5.2 Accruals

An accrual is an *expense which,* unlike a prepayment, *has not yet actually been paid for*. It is still a *debt owed*. In this case the accountant's principle is that such debts are included in the records at the date on which they are incurred (taken on), and not at the time at which they are paid. Again, as with prepayments, the situation balances itself out. In the case of an accrual, traders get the benefit at the time when they incur a debt, but do not have any benefit in the accounting period in which the debt is actually settled.

The entries which are required in the records for an accrued expense can be illustrated as follows:

Suppose a business rents premises for £8 000 a year, and this is paid quarterly. The rent is actually paid in arrears on the first day of the new quarter. For the last quarter of the calendar year, the rent up to 31 December is paid on 1 January. But in this company the accounting period ends on 31 December.

In the accounting period £6 000 (three payments) have actually been made. But the rent owed was £8 000. Following the principle described above, the entries in the accounts will be as follows:

The Rent account contains the actual payments, plus the balance accrued. The total, which is the full amount owed, is transferred to the profit and loss account, and a balance brought down into the next accounting period. The latter will cancel out the effect of the payment, when it is actually made on 1 January. The relevant part of the accounts will look as follows:

Rent account

		£			£
1990			31 Dec	Profit and Loss a/c	8 000
1 Jan	Bank	2 000			
1 Apr	Bank	2 000			
1 Sep	Bank	2 000			
31 Dec	Balance accrued c/d	2 000			
		8 000			8 000
			1991		
			1 Jan	Balance accrued b/d	2 000

The Profit and Loss account entries will contain the Expense; 'Rent £8 000'.

Note that the balance sheet will also include the accrual as a liability. Though the records have taken account of the accrual, the money has in reality still to be paid, and therefore remains a debt of the company.

5.3 Bad debts

Credit sales are first recorded in the sales journal and then posted to the Sales Account, and to the Customer's Personal Account. Such debts will normally be settled at the end of the period of credit (see *Invoices: customer accounts*, page 166. Some will not. These will be recorded as outstanding debts, and will continue to affect the balance on the customer's accounts. But sometimes it will become clear that the debt either will never be paid, or is highly unlikely to be cleared. For example, a business can become insolvent, that is, unable to pay its debts. When its affairs are wound up, there will be some attempt to pay creditors. But there are likely to be those whose invoices remain unpaid. They will continue to be in that situation, because there is no more money left.

At this point the debt is *written off*, and is described as a *bad debt*. The keeping of accounts must reflect this situation. The process can be illustrated by the following example:

Eden Plants and Gardens (EPG) has been supplying Antonio Venezia, a jobbing gardener, with garden supplies on credit. Mr Venezia dies, and when his affairs are sorted out it becomes clear that nothing is left to pay the outstanding sum of £85.60 which he owes to EPG. They then accept that this is a bad debt and the records are altered as follows:

A. Venezia Customer account

DEBIT		£	CREDIT		£
23 Aug	Balance	85.60	23 Aug	Bad debts	85.60
		85.60			85.60

Account closed

The bad debt is debited under Mr Venezia's name to the Bad Debts account. At the end of the accounting period this account is totalled and the total of bad debts accrued is added to the expenses in the Profit and Loss account. It is said to be written off from the profits as a loss.

5.4 Depreciation

The cost of fixed assets are not included in the profit and loss account. There is however one expense relating to fixed assets which will normally appear in the profit and loss account: this is *depreciation*.

What it is

Depreciation is a fall in value of a fixed asset. For example, a company buys a computer system to handle its accounts and administration, costing £3000. As soon as it is purchased, the system loses value, because it is now second-hand. Over the years, with changing market conditions, and as the computer ages, its value will tend to fall steadily. At a certain point it will be replaced. In the case of high technology or irreparable damage, say by fire, it may have no resale value whatsoever. The original asset which was worth £3000 is now worth £0. The asset has depreciated 100% in value. In some respects, therefore, the business is worse off. (Of course, the asset may have made it possible to make large profits, as has happened, for example, in the robot assembly of cars). The depreciation is in part a current factor in the firm's situation and is accounted for in the records.

Entry in accounts

A figure is decided upon for the amount of depreciation. (How this is done is explained below). This is first entered into the relevant account, for example:

Computers

DEBIT		£	CREDIT		£
1 Jan	Bank	3000	31 Dec	depreciation	600

(The depreciation is a credit entry, being the reduction in value of an asset).

This entry may also be recorded in a Depreciation account. It will certainly appear as another expense in the Profit and Loss Account.

The depreciation will also be recorded as a reduction in assets on the balance sheet.

Calculation of depreciation

There are two well-known ways for estimating the figure to be allowed for depreciation. The figure has to be an estimate, since no one can foresee what will happen in the future.

☐ *'Straight line' method* (also known as the *equal instalment method*)
The length of time for which the asset will be in use is noted or estimated. The cost is divided by this figure. For example in the case of the computer mentioned above, suppose that the machine is expected to be in use for 5 years, then the depreciation is calculated as 3000/5 = £600 a year.

It is possible to modify this formula to allow for resale or scrap value at the end of the period. Suppose that the company believes that they will get £500 from a technology museum after 5 years. The calculation will then be

$$\frac{\text{cost} - \text{estimated scrap value}}{\text{estimated life (years)}} = \frac{3000 - 500}{5} = £500 \text{ pa}$$

❑ *Reducing instalment method*

With this method the figure is arrived at by assuming depreciation to proceed by the same percentage each year. In these circumstances, the amount of depreciation allowed on the asset will fall steadily over the years, as the following calculation shows:

Rate of depreciation 50% yearly

Year 1	Computer cost	£3000
Year 2	worth	£1500
Year 3		£750
4		£375
5		£187.50
etc		

Which method is used will depend on decisions as to what most suits the financial interests of the business. This case thus illustrates well the fact that though the techniques of accountancy are logical and mathematical, there will remain many situations which are not clear-cut and mechanical, but which involve decisions. These will be matters of judgement. The popular idea that accountancy is entirely down-to-earth and does not have at least some of the uncertainty to be found in other areas of life, such as art or politics, is very mistaken.

6. The balance sheet

6.1 What it is

The balance sheet *is a statement of the assets and liabilities of a business at a particular point in time*. In practice it will tend to be produced annually, along with the trading and profit and loss accounts. It has a different purpose from the latter, because it is designed not to show how trading is progressing, but the total state and value of a business. It shows the balance between assets and liabilities.

The balance sheet is a financial record which is a summary of information extracted from the ledger, but it is not a part of the ledger. Therefore there are no double entries to it.

The following table compares the three types of record described in this section.

Topic	Trading account	Profit and Loss a/c	Balance Sheet
Time involved	the accounting period		one date
Type of record	ledger account		statement
Purpose (to show...)	gross profit (sales purchase)	net profit (sales – cost of goods and expenses)	assets and liabilities
	progress of trading		overall state

Further explanation of the wider financial significance of the balance sheet is given below in *Assets and liabilities*, page 159, and *Balances and the accountancy equation*, page 160.

6.2 Layout

The balance sheet can be presented in one of two ways.

Conventional layout.

This takes the form of two columns. Note that, unlike in all the other accounts discussed in this book, the liabilities (accounts with credit balances) are shown on the *left*, and the assets (accounts with debit balances) on the *right* – the opposite of the procedure otherwise adopted.

At the head of the columns are given the longer-term factors – the fixed assets, and the long-term liabilities. Lower down are the current assets and liabilities. As far as possible, the entries are arranged so that the lower you look down the column, the greater the liquidity.

Example

Balance sheet of Badger Electronics as at 31 December 1992

	£		£	£
Capital 20 000	*Fixed assets*			
Less drawings	1 000	Premises	8 000	
	19 000	Vehicle	5 000	
		Equipment	2 000	
Bank loan	5 000			15 000
	24 000			
Add Net profit	2 500			
	26 500			
Current liabilities		*Current assets*		
Creditors	800	Stock	10 400	
		Debtors	1 200	
		Cash	700	
				12 300
	27 300			27 300

Method:

Follow the basic format:

Capital	*Fixed assets*
less drawings	
add net profit	
subtotal	subtotal (may differ)
add: *Current liabilities*	add: *Current assets*
Total	*Total* (which should balance)

List the entries in order of liquidity, starting with the least liquid.

Note: This format reflects the accountancy equation that

assets (fixed + current) = capital + current liabilities

(see below, page 160, for further comment on this).

Final accounts

Vertical layout
Example

Fixed assets		
Premises		8 000
Vehicles		5 000
Equipment		2 000
		15 000
Current assets		
Stock	10 400	
Debtors	1 200	
Cash	700	
	12 300	
Less Current liabilities		
Creditors	800	
Working capital		11 500
Net assets		26 500
Financed by		
Capital		20 000
Add net profit		2 500
		22 500
Less drawings		1 000
		21 500
Long term liabilities		
Bank loan		5 000
		26 500

Method

The same information is given, but in the following format:

Format:	Notes
Fixed assets	listed and totalled (**Total 1**)
Current assets	listed
Current liabilities	listed (usually total owed by creditors The result of subtracting current assets from current liabilities is totalled and entered. (**Total 2**). This difference is known as *working capital*.
	Totals **1** and **2** are added. This total gives the Net assets of the business. It is also called the *Net worth*.
Financed by capital	
add: net profit	net profit (see *Profit and loss account*, page 151), is added to the capital.
less: drawings	If the owner of the business has taken out money for personal use during the accounting period, this is itemised as 'drawings'.
	Note that these are personal expenses and not for the business, and therefore are not entered into the business expense accounts.
add: long term liabilities	bank loans etc
total	This is the result of totalling the factors listed after 'financed by'. It will equal the Net Assets.

This layout is derived from changing the accountancy equation (see below) into the form:

Fixed assets + (Current assets – Current liabilities) = Capital (+ long term liabilities)

Net profit is also added to the right hand side, as it represents an increase in capital. Many accountants prefer this format because it makes explicit the working capital and net assets.

Note that the examples given above relate to a sole trader; the balance sheet of a limited company would have a few differences, to allow for such factors as the payment of dividends to shareholders. Also, there would not be 'drawings'.

7. Assets and liabilities

7.1 Assets

Assets are the possessions or advantages of a business on which a money value can be placed. Assets may be physical (vehicles, office equipment, stocks of goods) or they may take the form of money at the bank. Debts owed by customers are also regarded as assets, because it is assumed that they represent money which will be paid at a later date.

Assets are classified as being *fixed* or *current*.

Fixed assets
- are relatively permanent
- are needed in order to make a profit in the business as a whole but are not acquired with the sole purpose of generating a profit *themselves*
- tend not to change in value, or only to change slowly.

Current assets
- are owned for a short time
- are acquired in order to generate a profit themselves
- change value quickly (at least when taken as a block)
  (for example, a supermarket may have assets in the form of £1000 worth of butter in stock on Monday, and have sold all but £50 of this by Saturday).

Assets are often spoken of as being more or less *liquid*. The liquidity of an asset is said to be the greater the more easily it can be turned into cash. Cash is the most liquid form of asset. By contrast the ingredients for toothpaste, which are also part of the assets of a company such as Colgate are less liquid. It takes time to manufacture and market the toothpaste, and so turn the investment in ingredients into money.

7.2 Liabilities

Liabilities will normally represent *sources of finance*. In order to start up and to operate, a business will need to obtain cash. It will, for instance, borrow money. This may come from various sources – perhaps the most obvious is a bank loan.

Another major source is *capital*. The accountant's rule is that the capital put into a business is entered on its balance sheet as a liability. The reason is that capital is seen as being loaned (even if permanently) to the business by the owner or owners. It is money which the business could be required to pay back. This is even true of a one person business. For accountancy and legal purposes the real person whom you can meet socially is distinguished from the person who is actually carrying on the business. The business is said to be a *separate entity*. The reasoning is that though it happens that one person owns the capital and runs the business, this need not be so.

Another type of liability which most businesses rapidly acquire is the debts which they owe to creditors. The existence of the latter type of debt leads accountants to divide liabilities into two sorts: long term and current. The normal way of distinguishing the two types is to say that liabilities which are expected to be repaid in under a year are *current* (eg debts to suppliers). A well-known form of *long-term liability* is a mortgage, on which repayment may be extended over 20 or 30 years.

Students are sometimes confused about how to classify bank overdrafts. These are defined as current liabilities, because, unlike with a mortgage or a loan, there is no agreed period for repayment. The bank could request repayment immediately. They do not do so very often, but they certainly use pressures such as raising the interest rate, when they wish to reduce the amount of customer borrowing.

8. Balances and the accountancy equation

'Balance' – some different meanings

At many points in this book you will come across the word 'balance'. Important uses of the word are:

☐ *balance the account/cash book/ petty cash book*
When we use the term in this way we mean that we total the two columns (debit and credit) and then record the difference between them. In one column the figure *(balance carried down)* is the amount needed to make that column equal to the other. In the other column, the figure is copied (the *balance brought down*) so as to start the next accounting period with a record of the amount by which the column total was in surplus.

In these accounts the debit column records incoming money (either as cash or debts owed). It also records any other increase in assets or reduction in liabilities. The credit column does the opposite, recording outgoing money, debts owed, falling assets and increasing liabilities.

☐ *trial balance*
In this case the balance is used as a *test of the accuracy of the accounts*. If double entry has been carried out properly, the amount arising from totalling the debit columns will equal that to be found from the credit columns. Because the accounts are being considered as a whole, the different totals which go into the trial balance sometimes represent money coming in or going out, sometimes debts owing and owed, and sometimes changing situations in expense accounts. The latter will include matters outside of the purchases, expenses and sales of day-to-day trading, such as the purchase or disposal of fixed assets (such as machinery) or the taking on of a loan. The trial balance thus weighs up the situation between assets and liabilities.

☐ *balance the profit and loss account*
Again there are debit and credit columns, and assets and liabilities are being measured. But because the account is summarising the trading activities of the business, it does not include fixed assets and long term liabilities. It is only concerned with short term movements (within one year).

☐ *the balance sheet*
As has already been stated, the balance sheet sums up the *state of the finances of a business at a given point*. To do so it lists the assets and liabilities. As might be expected, these too have to balance. This fact can be summarised in what is known as the accountancy equation, which is:

$$\text{assets} = \text{liabilities}$$

This is often expanded to mention capital, as follows:

$$\text{assets} = \text{capital} + \text{liabilities}$$

An equation is a formula in which each side is equivalent to the other. So in words the accountancy equation means that *the total assets (fixed and current) of a business are always equal in value to its total liabilities (current and long term) including its capital.*

Invoices

Explanation of the process of payment of invoices

Preliminary reading

It is assumed that you have studied *Orders*, page 211.

Contents

1. Types of invoice

1.1 Format and contents

The scenario takes you through the process of purchasing goods by obtaining a quotation, placing an order, and accepting delivery. The final stage is a request for payment by the supplier, and the making of that payment by the customer.

In order to notify the customer what payment is due, and when it is required, the supplier sends an *invoice*. In the example used so far, it will look like this:

KUTKASH

HIGHWORTH WAY CODLINGTON C02 1ZZ
TEL: 0201 82641   FAX: 0201 01210

INVOICE

26 March 1991   ORDER NO.: C742

Star Minimarket
Middle Lane
Huxted

Quantity	Item	Unit	Price	Total
28	streaky bacon	(4)	2.06	14.42
24	(80) tea bags	(6)	3.42	13.68
80	cornflakes	(10)	5.99	47.92
24	tomato sauce	(12)	4.05	8.10
36	1 ltr washing up liquid	(12)	3.15	9.45
36	(250ml) cola	(12)	1.45	4.35
36	(250ml) lemonade	(12)	1.45	4.35
20	steak and kidney pies	(5)	3.60	14.40
20	tomato and cheese pizza	(4)	0.75	3.75
108	(4) beefburgers	(12)	6.30	56.70
72	(10) cod fish fingers	(12)	6.48	38.88

TOTAL excl. VAT		216.00
VAT		
TOTAL		216.00

VAT Reg. No. 130 774106

The invoice will contain the following information. Some will be printed on the invoice, some will be filled in at the time of issue:

❏   name and address of firm

❏   name and address of customer

❏   (phone/ telex /fax numbers)

❏   document number

❏   account reference number (if any)

❏   date

❐ quantity of goods

❐ type of item

❐ (sometimes) catalogue reference number

❐ price per unit

❐ subtotals for individual items

❐ final total

❐ Vat due (if applicable – it is not on these items)

❐ tax point for VAT (see *Value added tax*, page 259)

❐ discount

❐ other terms of business

1.2 Nature and purpose

The invoice has been described as the most central business document. As can be seen from the above example, the invoice sets out details of the goods (quantity, type etc), and the charge (price per unit, subtotals and final total). The invoice will also include a statement of taxation (eg VAT) and discount if any. Where applicable it also sets out the terms of delivery (for example, COD). It is the first request for payment.

An invoice is therefore what the ordinary person would refer to it as a 'bill'. The term 'invoice' is preferred for various reasons:

1) The term bill also refers to documents which stand in place of cash, and may be transferred to a third party. There are various official types of bill, such as the treasury bills issued by the government and the bills used in international trade (see *Banking facilities: foreign dealings*, page 102).

2) In legal and commercial affairs, a bill is a written order by the writer (drawer) to another person (drawee) to pay a sum on a given date to the drawer or to a third party. A cheque is thus a bill, and can be transferred by endorsing it (see *Bank documents: cheques*, page 83).

3) Over the years, the term 'bill' came to be associated in everyday life with a demand for immediate payment by one person to another, as for example, in a restaurant.

4) Though a bill usually does give details of what has been supplied, in the mind of the ordinary person a bill is primarily a demand for payment. A bill which was not set out in detail (itemised) still serves this purpose, and is often quite acceptable, when we know and are satisfied with what we have received (as for example with a dentist's bill).

5) By contrast, an invoice must contain all the details mentioned earlier. This is important to those engaged in financial record keeping, because it allows them to check also that the costing of the goods is as expected, and that the payments requested are correct. The details are also essential for entering the transaction into the appropriate journals and ledger accounts (see *Ledgers and journals*, page 177).

1.3 The pro forma invoice

This term is used to refer to an invoice which is issued before the despatch of the goods, it gives details of goods and payments required. In foreign dealings it is used to indicate to the purchaser what the final invoice will be like. In home dealings it is used in three sorts of situation, both of which tend to apply to single or occasional purchases and small amounts of money. These are as follows:

1) Customers who do not have or are not allowed a customer account, and so must settle their debts at once.

2) Customers who work on a sale or return basis.

The invoice records what has been sent and must be returned if there is no sale, and what must be paid if the goods are not returned.

3) Customers who are sent goods on approval.

The customer then returns the goods, or sends payment. This is the situation with much mail order dealing.

1.4 VAT invoice

This is a requirement of transactions subject to VAT, and so is dealt with under *Value added tax*, page 259.

1.5 Action needed

A pro forma invoice requires payment as described above.

In the case of invoices issued to holders of a customer account the action needed is more complex. Incoming invoices relate to purchases. They are first recorded in the *purchases journal* and later in the relevant ledger accounts. Outgoing invoices relate to sales. The fact that they are being sent is therefore recorded in the *sales journal*, and, once again, appropriate entries are later made in the relevant ledger accounts. The accounts are settled at a later date, which depends on the conditions applicable to the holding of a customer account (see page 166). The processes of entry in the above mentioned journals and ledgers are described in *Ledgers and journals*, page 187.

The accounts department will often reconcile an incoming invoice with the delivery note.

2. Similarities between documents

2.1 Repetition of information

You will see from the various entries in this section that in the various documents used in the process of purchasing goods you are largely repeating the same information. The example of the transaction between Kutkash and the Star Minimarket has been used throughout to make this point stand out.

In all cases you will include some items on the list given in section 2.3 below. The information has been repeated in the various sections for the convenience of the reader who only needs to look up one entry.

This repetition of information makes life easy in one respect. Once you are clear about the first document, the rest is largely a matter of copying. A machine could do it, and increasingly these days does so. But it is important to remember that what is mechanical rapidly becomes boring to human beings. It is then very easy to make errors or omissions. It is therefore important to get into the habit of checking systematically what you have done.

2.2 Function of documents

Since there is so much repetition, why have different documents? The reason is that though many of the details are the same, the function of the documents is not.

❒ The *quotation* only sets out what the supplier can offer;

❒ the *order form* makes a firm commitment to buy;

❒ the *acknowledgement of order* confirms the sale;

❒ the *advice note* alerts the customer to the planned delivery;

❒ the *delivery note* assists checking that the goods are as promised or expected;

❐   the *invoice* is a request for payment.

2.3 Content of the various documents used in a sale

The details which will be included are:

1)   **Parties involved in the transaction**
   ❐   name and address (including telephone/telex/fax numbers) of supplier
   ❐   name and address (including telephone/telex/fax numbers) of purchaser

   Note: The partysending the document will have their own details printed on their stationery.

2)   **Circumstances of transaction**
   ❐   document number
   ❐   account reference number (if any)
   ❐   date

   Note: These will also need to be inserted by the supplier. It is important (a) not to omit them and (b) that they are correct. This is because in a firm of any size there will be many transactions, and the reference numbers are crucial to the filing of documents. Much time can be wasted if a reference is incorrect. The date is often necessary for legal reasons.

3)   **The goods and cost**
   ❐   quantity
   ❐   type of item
   ❐   (sometimes) catalogue reference number
   ❐   price per unit
   ❐   subtotals for individual items
   ❐   final total
   ❐   discount (terms)

   Note: Details of price are often omitted on delivery documents. Discounts are often omitted , after the quotation, until the invoicing stage.

4)   Terms of business

VAT	(this will be mentioned in the quotation, but may be omitted until invoicing if not included in the price of the goods)
discount	(see above)
terms of delivery	(sometimes omitted after acknowledgement of order, until invoicing)
despatch details (transport, number of packages)	(on despatch documents only)

2.4 Checklist – main data to be entered

You will see that some of the details are not always included. Practices vary between firms. What is important to remember is what will definitely be required, namely:

```
┌─────────────────────────────────────────────┐
│                 All documents                 │
│                  addresses                     │
│              reference numbers                 │
│                 list of items                  │
└─────────────────────────────────────────────┘
```

```
┌──────────────────────────────────────┐   ┌──────────────────────────────────┐
│ quotation, order, acknowledgement,     │   │      despatch documents            │
│              invoice                    │   │      details of delivery           │
│           prices of items               │   │                                    │
│     discount and VAT if applicable      │   │                                    │
│           terms of delivery             │   │                                    │
└──────────────────────────────────────┘   └──────────────────────────────────┘
```

3. Customer accounts

3.1 Nature and purpose of customer accounts

Where only a single purchase is involved, the supplier will usually require prompt payment. But often there is regular trading between two firms; in such cases it is not always convenient to settle up debts immediately. In these circumstances the supplier will often set up a *customer account*. The customer is allowed credit, rather than being required to pay cash (see *Accounts: credit and debit*, page 73).

The handling of customer accounts follows the same basic principle as other accounts (see *Accounts: basic approach to record keeping*, page 74). There are debit and credit columns, some details, and the account is balanced at intervals.

The creditor keeps a record of all transactions involving the account holder. There will be a note of invoices sent, and debts incurred. There will also be a note of any payments made by the customer. The account is settled at agreed intervals, typically of one month. The supplier will issue a regular *statement* (see below), so that the customer can pay what is owed. The customer will first check that the statement accurately records the invoices received and payments made; this process is known as *reconciling* the statement.

3.2 Recording the issue of invoices

When an invoice is sent out, its issue is first recorded in the **sales journal** (see *Ledgers and jounals*, page 179). Where a customer account exists, it will be indicated on the invoice by an account number, a coding, or the customer's name. The information will be transferred from the journal to the relevant account. This is usually done daily. Only the basic information will be transferred, as the details will be found in the sales journal, and on the copy of the invoice itself, which will be kept on file.

3.3 The customer as a debtor

Though the customer can rightly be said to be the most important person in a business, he or she is nevertheless a debtor (see *Accounts: credit and debit*, page 73). If the supplier is to remain solvent it is important to keep track of what is owed, and to get payments in. Many firms therefore group the customer accounts into a debtors ledger (also called a sales ledger). The *debtors' ledger* will be used as summary of the state of affairs when preparing a profit and loss account (see *Final accounts*, page 147).

3.4 Aged debt analysis

Unfortunately, any business is likely from time to time to extend credit to customers who then find themselves unable to meet their debts at the agreed time. If this situation is allowed to continue, it can be a serious problem for a business. Their own debts to suppliers continue to fall due, but the flow into the firm of money owed by customers is less than is necessary to meet the payments outward which must be made. This is known as a *cashflow problem*.

It is important to realise that this type of difficulty does not only arise when customers have to default on their debts, that is that the debt is never paid. A long delay in payment can be sufficient to reduce cashflow to the point at which the firm which has offered credit can no longer fund its own trading. In recent years this has been a problem which has been as serious in its effect as falling sales.

Because of the above problem, businesses engage in *credit control*. One phase of credit control, the check on creditworthiness, is discussed earlier in this entry. But credit control has also to be applied after invoicing. In everyday terms, 'credit control' means that the accounts department keeps a close watch on the debts owing to them, so that they can take action quickly. To do this they create an aged debtors list. This is not a directory of customers who are pensioners; it is a listing, extracted from the customer accounts of:

- the *names of debtors* who have failed to pay according to the terms of business
- the *length of time by which the debt is overdue*
- the *amount* of the debt.

The findings will usually be grouped, especially according to the amount of time to which the debt is overdue. A common listing is: 1 month, 2 months, 3 months, 6 months, 1 year.

The process, which is known as *aged debt analysis*, may be carried out manually, but is made easier by the use of computerisation. Note that this record is a listing, and not an account. It is not part of the ledger, but a *control device* used by a business to monitor the extent of the credit which it has extended to customers.

Once the overdue debts has been listed, the supplier will then start to follow out the firm's procedure for the collection of debts. This will normally consist of reminders, followed by warnings and finally legal action to recover the debt. Sometimes the debt will be *written off* as a *bad debt,* that is the supplier will assume that the debt will never be paid. This too will be recorded in the accounts, as it is relevant to drawing up the final accounts (see *Final accounts*, page 147).

3.5 Suppliers' accounts

The same type of process applies to the situations in which a firm is the purchaser rather than the vendor. Incoming invoices are first recorded in the purchases journal (see *Ledgers and journals*, page 179). This information is then transferred from the journal to the Purchases Account, and an entry is made in the supplier's account. The firm will thus also have an accurate record of its own debts, and when they are due.

4. Statements of account

4.1 Format

Given below is a typical statement of account, sent in January by Kutkash to Boozers, a local off-license. It records transactions made in December.

KUTKASH

HIGHWORTH WAY CODLINGTON C02 1ZZ
TEL: 0201 82641 FAX: 0201 01210

Boozers
Pond Street,
High Wansted.

Credit limit: £1000

Account no: A12/456
Date: 31-12-91
Terms: 30 days

STATEMENT OF ACCOUNT

Date	Reference	Description	Debit	Credit	Balance
Dec 1		previous balance			142-00
Dec 7	722141	Invoice	158-60		300-60
Dec 10	722329	Invoice	210-00		510-60
Dec 14	2146	Credit Note		52-00	458-60
Dec 16	267389	Cheque		142-00	316-60
Dec 28	722414	Invoice	318-50		635-10
		Amount now due			635-10

VAT Reg. No. 130 774106

A statement will list the transactions, with dates. These will normally consist of:

1) The names and addresses of the parties involved

2) The customer account number

3) The date at which the statement was drawn up

4) A credit limit, if one exists

5) Sales to the account holder, listed according to their invoice number (recorded in the debit column)

6) Payments received from the customer (recorded in the credit column)

7) Credit notes issued (these are a form of refund, see page 170) - also recorded in the credit column

8) The balance at the start of the accounting period

9) Often, the balance after each transaction, known as a running balance

10) Most important, the balance at the close of the accounting period, which is the sum due.

Note: The choice of columns for recording the various transactions arises from the nature of double entry bookkeeping, and is explained in *Ledgers and Journals*, page 184.

4.2 Reconciliation

When the statement is received the customer will first reconcile it with the relevant records. In March the Kutkash accounts department employed a new clerk, a redundant college lecturer, who made a few errors. Boozers' comments, noted down during the reconciliation are given below.

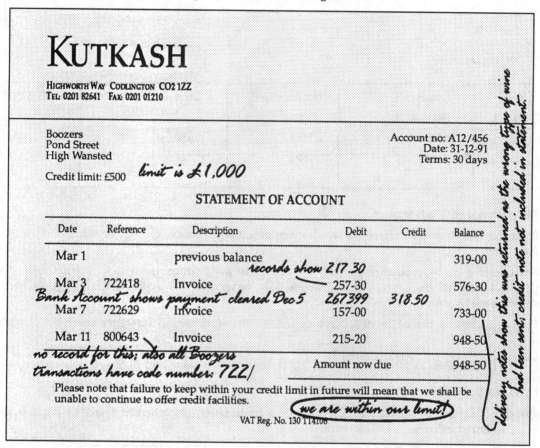

The reconciliation involves checking

- ❏ *purchases accounts* (ledger, possibly journal, occasionally original documents (invoice, delivery notes)
- ❏ *credit notes* with statement
- ❏ *bank account* for payments made.

4.3 Ledger cards

The customer account may be kept in books, on or computer, like any other account. However, many firms have found it convenient to use a system of ledger cards. An example is given below (Debora Allen opens an account with Eden Plants and Gardens):

Invoices

| | EDEN PLANTS & GARDENS
67 Pearmain Drive Codlington CO4 9BR
Telephone: 0201 946571 | CUSTOMER ACCOUNT CARD |

NAME: D. Allen

CREDIT LIMIT: £100

Date	Details	Ref number	Debit	Credit	Balance
May 1	Balance				0.00
May 15	Goods	R7456	11.50		11.50 DR
May 22	Goods	R7623	12.00		23.50 DR

This system has several advantages:

1) It permits quick and easy reference, which is important when ordering takes place face-to-face, or over the phone.

2) The use of a running balance permits the reader to see at once the state of the account, and in particular whether there is a large or growing debt, or whether the credit limit has been reached. It is an aid to credit control.

3) The basic format is that of the customer account. It is therefore easy to draw up a statement of account.

5. Credit notes

5.1 How they work

In *Statements of account*, page 167, mention is made of credit notes. In particular, there is a detail from the March statement as follows:

Mar 7	722629	Invoice	157-00	733-00

The comments of Boozers is:

"Delivery notes show this was returned as the wrong type of wine had been sent; credit note not included in statement."

If the Kutkash accounts had been accurate, the following would have happened:

1) Boozers check the delivery against the delivery note, and possibly their order form. They find that the wrong goods have been sent.

2) They notify Kutkash of this fact, by phone and possibly on paper. They certainly make a note on the delivery note. They then arrange for the return of the unwanted wine.

3) Kutkash then issue a credit note. Details will be entered in the sales returns journal, and later in the relevant sales ledger and customer account.

4) Boozers will enter the receipt of the credit note in the Purchases Returns journal, and file the credit note. Later the information will be transferred to the relevant purchases and supplier accounts.

5.2 Format of credit note

The credit note is often printed in red, and looks somewhat as follows:

KUTKASH

HIGHWORTH WAY CODLINGTON C14 CO2
TEL: 0201 82641   FAX: 0201 01210

CREDIT NOTE

Boozers
Pond Street,
High Wansted.

Account no: A12/456
Date: 08-03-91
Terms: 30 days

Re invoice:722629

Quantity	Item	Unit price	Total
2 case	6 x 75cl Liebfraumilch	13.75	27.50
		VAT ($17\frac{1}{2}$%)	4.81
		Total	32.31

Reason for credit:

Goods not as requested on Order Form BZ 76248.

VAT Reg. No. 130 774106

The credit note thus contains the following information.

☐ *Names and addresses* of parties

☐ *Reference numbers:* especially *customer account number* and *number of invoice* against which the credit note is being issued.

☐ *Details of goods* (as on invoice) against which the credit note is being issued

☐ VAT details and amount credited (if applicable)

☐ Reason for issue of credit note.

The commonest reasons for issuing a credit note are:

☐ the goods are not what was ordered

☐ the goods arrive damaged

☐ the goods were not included in the consignment which was delivered

☐ the customer has been overcharged.

6. Payment

6.1 Time and method of payment

Payment is due when requested either

a) by means of an invoice, for a single transaction, or

b) by means of a statement, as described earlier in this section.

When there is trading between businesses, the account is settled either by sending a cheque, or through a bank giro payment (see *Bank documents: bank giro*, page 79).

6.2 Remittance advice

At the time of payment the purchaser makes out a *remittance advice*. This is sent with a cheque, as an explanation of the nature of the payment, or it is sent separately, as notification that a bank giro payment is in hand.

The remittance advice which Boozers would send in settlement of their first statement (page 168) would then look as follows:

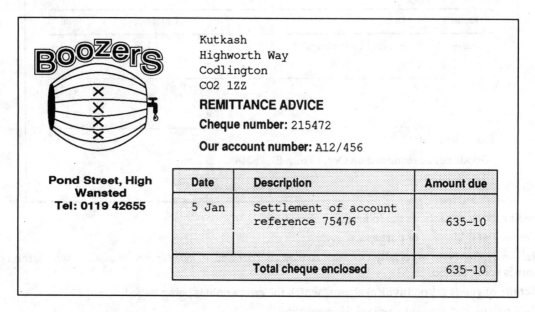

Date	Description	Amount due
5 Jan	Settlement of account reference 75476	635–10
	Total cheque enclosed	635–10

The remittance advice may serve the further purpose of itemising the transactions in relation to which payment is being made. In fact, Boozers decided to adopt this system, so their remittance advice looked as follows:

Kutkash
Highworth Way
Codlington
CO2 1ZZ

Our account number: A 12/456

REMITTANCE ADVICE

Cheque number: 215472

**Pond Street, High
Wansted
Tel: 0119 42655**

Date	Description	Ref number	Amount due	Balance
Dec 1	previous balance		142-00	142-00
Dec 7	Invoice	722141	158-60	300-60
Dec 10	Invoice	722329	210-00	510-60
Dec 14	Credit Note	2146	52-00	458-60
Dec 16	payment (cheque)	267389	142-00	316-60
Dec 28	Invoice	722414	318-50	635-10
Jan 5	**Total cheque enclosed**			635-10

You will see that this information follows that given in the statement of account. This makes the process of copying easier. Also the detail given makes it easier to transfer the information to the relevant ledger accounts.

6.3 Final action

The forwarding of a payment (also referred to as a *remittance*) is recorded in journals and ledger accounts by both parties. In businesses it is not generally thought necessary to acknowledge the receipt of the payment. This is because the payment will be recorded in bank statements (see *Bank documents: bank statements*, page 81), in the next statement of account, and the various accounts where a record of the transaction has been entered. As in the case of the March statement given earlier, errors and omissions will thus be picked up. The situation is different in the retail trade or in dealing with single cash transactions. Then a *receipt* is provided. This topic is dealt with under *Methods of payment: receipts*, page 206).

7. Invoicing – summary

7.1 Similarities and differences between stages of a purchase

If you have read through all the entries in this section, you will have noticed many similarities and repetitions between the various stages of the process. It has already been noted that such factors make much of the work mechanical, easily prone to error, and very suited to computerisation.

The similarities between the various documents in the stages from enquiry to delivery of goods have already been listed (see page 164). It is now necessary to do the same for the stages between the first recording of a debt owed, through invoicing, to the payment and forwarding of a remittance advice.

Though there are many similarities between these documents and those used in the quotation, ordering and delivery phases of a transaction, there are also important differences. These arise from two factors:

a) Payment is being requested and made. The handling of money is a matter in which it is notoriously easy to make errors, and for misunderstandings to arise. It a matter of great sensitivity when dealing with customers. It is therefore highly important that all documents are clear in the information they give, and of course, free of error.

b) The earlier stages in the purchasing of goods are supported by documents. The latter are part of the financial records of the business, and they also relate to the handling of stock (covered under *Stock control and valuation*, page 238). But they are not part of the accounts of the firm (see *Accounts*, page 71).

   By contrast, the issue and receipt of invoices is the first stage at which a transaction is recorded in the accounts of a firm. The keeping of the accounts and in particular of ledger accounts and journals has its own requirements. In particular it is essential to have a good system of retrieval (for instance, of a queried invoice) and cross reference (for instance between journals and ledgers, or between main accounts and personal (customer) accounts. The handling of these matters is dealt with in *Ledgers and journals*, page 177 forward.

7.2 Similarities between documents of payment phase

The documents used in the payment phase are:

invoice   statement   credit note   remittance advice

They contain:

1) **Parties involved in the transaction**
   - ☐ name and address of supplier
   - ☐ phone/telex/fax numbers (these will tend not to be on documents for internal use, ie customer account, ledger card)
   - ☐ name and address of purchaser.

2) **Reference number and code**
   - ☐ document number
   - ☐ account reference number (if any).

These are essential:

a) for quick retrieval of files and

b) in keeping accounts – they make cross reference possible, and keep down the amount of detail which needs to be copied from one account to another.

3) **Dates**
   - ❑ of transactions (all documents)
   - ❑ of drawing up (statements)
   - ❑ of sending of invoice or remittance.

These are crucial because accounts are drawn up to cover a given period, or at a certain point. Also, when credit is given, the customer is not liable for payment before a certain date. Various dates (including the tax point) are a legal requirement when VAT is payable (see *Value added tax*, page 259).

4) **Details of goods** and **cost** (invoice and credit note)
   - ❑ quantity
   - ❑ type of item
   - ❑ (sometimes) catalogue reference number
   - ❑ price per unit
   - ❑ subtotals for individual items
   - ❑ final total
   - ❑ reason for credit (credit note only).

5) **Other elements in the final total**
   - ❑ discount
   - ❑ VAT

Both are stated when applicable on the invoice, VAT only on the credit note. (Discount obviously does not apply to goods not purchased).

Discount and VAT are given special treatment in the drawing up of accounts (see *Value added tax*, page 251 and *Ledgers and journals* page 177).

6) **Making payments**
   - ❑ sum paid or credited (on remittance advice, credit note, customer account, statement, ledger card)
   - ❑ sum owing or debited (on invoice, customer account, statement, ledger card)

Except in the case of the invoice, credit note, and simple remittance advice, these sums are recorded by two column entry (see *Accounts: basic approach to record keeping*, page 74), and with the opening and final balance. Often a running balance is also included in a third column.

7) **Crucial elements**

You should make a habit of checking that the following are entered and correct.
   - ❑ **Purchaser's name**
   - ❑ **Reference numbers and codes** (document number; account reference number)
   - ❑ **Dates**
   - ❑ **Debits and credits in correct columns.**

7.3 Function of documents

As in the case of quotation and ordering, though the detail is often repeated, the functions of the different documents are different:

❒ the *invoice* itemises goods supplied and their cost, requests payment (if proforma) or notifies the customer of a debit to their account

❒ the *credit note* credits the customer's account when the customer would be entitled to a refund

❒ the *customer account* records the credits and debits in dealings with a particular customer

❒ the *ledger card* is a convenient practical way of recording the transactions of a customer account

❒ the *statement of account* summarises the state of a customer account and requests payment to settle the account

❒ the *remittance advice* notifies the supplier of a payment, and what that payment relates to.

Ledgers and journals

Information about journals, various ledger accounts (Sales, Purchases, Expenses and VAT) together with the record keeping procedures relating to those accounts

Preliminary reading

You should not try to use this section unless you have read *Accounts*, page 70.

Contents

1. Journals

1.1 Records of sales and purchases

A good way of considering the way in which the accounts of a business are kept is to start at the interface between the business and the outer world – the point at which goods are despatched to customers, or are received from suppliers.

There are two parts to this process:

1)   the recording of the *rise and fall in amount of the actual goods* (stock) which occurs each day

     This topic is dealt with under *Stock control and valuation*, page 238.

2)   the recording of the *changes in the financial position of the business* as a result of such sales or purchases.

     This is the topic dealt with in this section.

1.2 Sales and purchases journals

The *sales journal* and *purchases journal* are *books of original* (or *prime*) *entry*. They are also frequently referred to as *day books*.

These journals are mostly used to make a first record of credit transactions. They therefore include

❐   a *record of each transaction* together with an *invoice number*.

     The number is entered so as to make it easy to refer to the original invoice if necessary. At the same time it eliminates the need for including all the detail which is on the invoice.

❐   the *sums of money involved*.

     These journals do not include details of the sale or purchase of fixed assets – these are recorded in the relevant ledger accounts (see page 182).

     (If you need further explanation of the term 'assets' in order to carry out your task, turn to *Final accounts*, page 159).

The information which is given immediately below deals only with the making of entries in the journals. For information on the transfer of this information to the ledger see *Posting of journals to the ledger*, page 187.

1.3 Sales journal

The purpose of this journal (or day book) is to *record sales of goods that are traded in by the business*

A typical sales journal page looks as follows:

Date	Customer	Folio number	Invoice number	Total before VAT	VAT	Total including VAT
1991						
1 Jul	E Woodhouse	CW27	1816	57.00	9.97	66.97
2 Jul	J Knightley	CK14	1817	72.00	12.60	84.60
3 Jul	Boxhill Shrubs	CB56	1818	24.00	4.20	28.20
5 Jul	Totals			153.00	26.77	179.77

Information to be entered in the Sales Journal

1) *Date* — important for reference; required for VAT

2) *Name of customer* — crossrefers to name on customer account

3) *Folio number* — used for double entry bookkeeping (explained on page 187)

4) *Invoice number* — for filing and reference if details have to be checked

5) *Total before VAT*

6) *VAT* — These last three items are required by VAT legislation. For details see *Value added tax: The VAT invoice*, page 259.

7) *Total including VAT*

8) *Totals* — The columns are totalled at suitable intervals – in this case at the end of a week.

Notes:

1) These are sales which are on credit and will be entered into the customer accounts in the ledger. Payment will be made when a statement is presented (if unclear about this point see *Invoices: statements of account*, page 167).

2) The journals are most commonly used as a record of credit sales. However, in retail sales, where payments are often in cash, two changes might be made.

   a) For small numbers of sales per day (say in a car showroom), cash payments (that is, immediate payments in banknotes or by cheque) could be entered by hand. The 'invoice number' column might then be headed 'reference number' so as to include cheque serial numbers.

   b) When there are many sales in a day, say in a grocery store, the book would just contain a summary of the day's takings (see *Methods of payment: end of day procedure*, page 205). This would be supported by the till roll.

1.4 Purchases journal

This journal records *purchases of items directly used in the firm's trading*. These may be goods for resale (for instance, butter by a wholesaler in groceries) or they may be goods which will first be turned into a product which will then be sold (for instance, sugar for a chocolate manufacturer). As with sales, purchases of assets (for example a new building) are *not* included in the journal.

A typical purchases journal page might look as follows:

Date	Supplier	Folio number	Invoice number	Total before VAT	VAT	Total including VAT
1991						
21 Jun	F Churchill	SC71	A317	54.00	9.45	63.45
22 Jun	J Fairfax Ltd	SF13	1775	113.00	19.77	132.77
23 Jun	Highbury Landscaping	SH11	2/564	44.00	7.70	51.70
25 Jul	Totals			211.00	36.92	247.92

Entries to be made in the Purchases Journal (the points are much the same as for the Sales Journal).

1) *Date*

2) *Name of supplier*   crossrefers to name on supplier account

3) *Folio number*   used for double entry bookkeeping (explained on page 187)

4) *Invoice number*   different in format because different suppliers use different systems

5) *Total before VAT*

6) *VAT*

7) *Total including VAT*

8) *Totals*

Notes:

1) These are purchases which are on credit and will be entered into the supplier accounts in the ledger. Payment will be made when a statement is presented (if unclear about this point see *Invoices: customer accounts*, page 166).

2) In a small business there might also be a need to enter cash payments. Purchases of everyday needs, for small amounts, would be handled through petty cash (see *Petty cash*, page 219).

Some businesses enter the details of invoices in the purchases journal, while (as above) transferring only the totals to the ledger accounts.

An entry in such a journal would look as follows:

Date	Supplier	Folio no.	Invoice no.	Details	Total before VAT	VAT	Total incl. VAT	Invoice totals
1991								
21 Jun	F Churchill	SC71	A317	10 peat @ £1.10	11.00	1.87	12.87	
				5 compost @ £2.89	14.45	2.53	16.98	
								29.85

2. Returns journals

It happens from time to time that goods have to be returned to suppliers or are returned by customers. These situations are normally entered in separate journals: the *sales returns journal*, and the *purchases returns journal*. The reason for separating these transactions from the sales and purchases journals is that the calculation of debts is made more complicated by the issue of *credit notes*. The primary purpose of the returns books is thus to *record the arrival and issue of credit notes*.

The pattern of the journals is otherwise similar to that of the sales and purchases journals as the following two examples show

2.1 Purchases returns journal

A typical page in a purchases returns journal:

Date	Supplier	Folio number	Credit note number	Total before VAT	VAT	Total including VAT
1991						
13 May	Highbury Landscaping	SH11	4/774	32.00	5.60	37.60
14 May	J Fairfax Ltd	SF13	1805D	151.00	26.42	177.42
15 May	Totals			183.00	32.02	215.02

Entries to be made in the purchases returns journal (the points are much the same as for the purchases journal):

1) *Date*
2) *Name of supplier*
3) *Folio number*   used for double entry bookkeeping (explained on page 187)
4) *Credit note number*   different in format because different suppliers use different systems
5) *Total before VAT*
6) *VAT*
7) *Total including VAT*
8) *Totals*

Note that the receipt of credit notes will be entered into the supplier accounts in the ledger (see page 187). They will be set against any debts when a statement is presented (if unclear about this point see *Invoices: statement of account*, page 167).

2.2 Sales returns journal

The pattern is like that of the purchases returns journal:

Date	Customer	Folio number	Credit note number	Total before VAT	VAT	Total including VAT
1991						
8 Jul	Boxhill Shrubs	CB56	CX55	24.00	4.20	28.20
9 Jul	J Knightley	CK14	CX56	12.00	2.11	14.11
12 Jul	Totals			36.00	6.31	42.31

Again, the issue of credit notes will be recorded in the appropriate customer account in the ledger.

Entries to be made in sales returns journal

1) *Date*
2) *Name of customer*
3) *Folio number*   used for double entry bookkeeping (explained on page 187)
4) *Credit note number*
5) *Total before VAT*
6) *VAT*
7) *Total including VAT*
8) *Totals*

3. Making journal entries – summary

You need to enter:

1) Date
2) Name of customer or supplier
3) Folio number
4) Invoice or credit note number
5) Total before VAT
6) VAT
7) Total including VAT
8) Total for each column

Note that these documents are ones in which you can increase your accuracy by using an internal check (see *Work methods: accuracy* page 291). The total of the right hand column should be the same as the figure obtained by adding together the totals of the other columns.

4. Structure of the ledger

4.1 The ledger

The ledger consists of a set of accounts. As such it follows the basic principles set out in *Accounts: Basic approaches to record keeping*, page 74, that is:

☐ a *two column entry* (debit and credit)

☐ *calculation of balances* at regular intervals

☐ often, *three column entry*, to show a *running balance*.

If you are in doubt about any of the above points, you should reread *Accounts*, page 70, before going further.

Structure of ledger

The ledger can be imagined as a set of pigeon holes. These can be seen as being divided in various ways, according to the nature of the business. For the situations which are under discussion here, the ledger could be seen as having three main sections as follows:

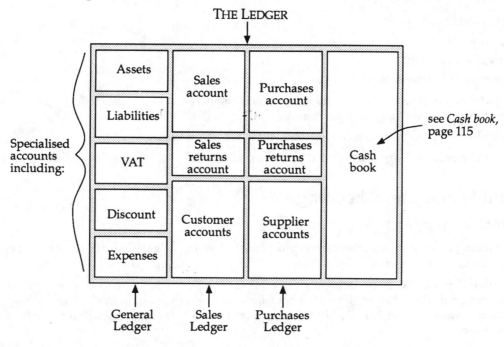

4.2 Relation of journals to the ledger

The day books serve the purpose of ensuring that transactions are entered quickly and conveniently in the financial records of the business. To become part of the accounts, they must be transferred into (posted to) the ledger. As shown above, this contains a *sales ledger*, and a *purchases ledger*, reflecting the concern of all accounts to record the two directions of the flow of money – into and out of the business.

4.3 The sales ledger

This ledge is concerned with the flow of money into the business, through sales. In particular its function is to record and monitor what credit has been extended to customers.

The sales ledger contains:

❑ *customers' individual accounts* (explained in *Invoices: customer accounts*, page 166)
❑ *the sales account*
❑ *the sales returns account.*

4.4 The sales and sales returns accounts

The latter two accounts contain simplified entries, as the purpose is to give an overview of the overall sales position. The use of crossreferences by use of the folio system (see page 187 below) makes it possible to go back to more detailed records (in the sales journal or in the original invoices) if this becomes necessary.

Note that in many businesses it is also necessary to record information in the VAT account (see page 188).

4.5 The purchases ledger

The purchases ledger deals with incoming goods and outgoing money, and the accumulation and paying off of debts to creditors. As might be expected, the structure of the purchases ledger entries is much the same as that of those in the sales ledger.

It therefore contains:

☐   *supplier accounts*

☐   *the purchases account*

☐   *the purchases returns account.*

The purchases and purchases returns account, like their counterparts in the sales ledger, give a simplified picture of the situation with regard to purchases.

Again, it is also often necessary to record information in the VAT account.

Both sales and purchases ledgers are created by using double entry bookkeeping (see following section).

5.   Double entry bookkeeping

5.1 Complementary entries

Double entry bookkeeping is the most central procedure in keeping ledger accounts. It is best to begin with an illustration of what is required.

Suppose Eden Plants and Gardens buy a lawn sweeper costing £125, from Hoxted Garden Equipment. It is a cash transaction paid by cheque. (If you are not sure how a cash transaction can be paid by cheque, read *Accounts: credit and debit*, page 73). The bookkeeper has to answer two questions in order to make a double entry. These are:

1)   *which accounts* do I enter the transactions in?

2)   *which columns* of those accounts are the ones in which I make the entries?

5.2 Which accounts?

The bookkeeper has first to identify the two accounts in which entries are to be made. In the case given above, the following accounts are involved:

1)   *Equipment account* (in the general ledger)
(Eden Plants and Gardens need to record that they have acquired the equipment. Because the lawn sweeper is not for resale, it is defined as an asset (see below) and its value is recorded (along with other equipment which are part of the assets of the business) in the Equipment account.

2)   *Bank account* (in the cash book)
The firm also needs to record the fact that money has been paid out. As the payment was made by cheque it will be recorded in the Bank Account columns of the cash book. There is therefore a *double entry. The link between these two entries is also recorded by means of the folio number system* (see page 187 below).

5.3 Assets and liabilities

It will help your understanding of the above actions, and of the choice of columns which is to follow, to be clear what is meant by 'assets' and 'liabilities'.

Assets are *the possessions or advantages of a business on which a money value can be placed*. Examples are: cash in the bank, motor vehicles, debts owed by customers (it is assumed that these will be paid).

Liabilities are basically *money which the business owes*; they can be seen as being to the disadvantage of the business. Examples are: a debt to a supplier, a bank loan. Note that capital is also classified as a liability, because it is money put into the business which the provider of the capital can require to be repaid.

This topic is explained more fully in *Final accounts*, page 147.

The choice of accounts in the lawn sweeper example above reflects the fact that the firm has had an increase in assets in the form of a lawn sweeper, but a reduction in assets in the form of money in the bank. The increase in assets in one account is a decrease in assets in another. This leads to the double entry rule:

❒ *Each entry of one type must be accompanied by a complementary entry of the opposite type.*

❒ *For each credit entry there must be a corresponding debit, and vice versa.*

5.4 Which column?

In each account there are two columns. The problem for many students when they first come to study bookkeeping is 'Which column do you enter the transaction in?'

It is therefore useful to give the answer in more than one way, as students seem able to grasp the problem from different angles. It should be noted that everyday, common sense interpretations can be misleading, as will be illustrated below.

The two sides have complementary purposes, which can be summed up as follows:

Debit side	Credit side
means	*means*
money coming in	money going out
debts owed by customers	debts owed to suppliers
credit notes received	credit notes issued
an increase in assets	a decrease in assets
a decrease in liabilities	an increase in liabilities

So the purchase of the lawn sweeper is recorded as follows:

Which accounts?

❒ *Equipment account*
because there is an increase in assets – a *debit entry*

❒ *Bank account*
must therefore have a *credit entry*

This also makes sense in everyday terms, as money is going out, and there is a decrease in cash assets.

5.5 Apparent exceptions

It is worth giving a couple of examples to show how our day-to-day experience can be misleading with regard to the recording of transactions.

Example 1

Eden Plants and Gardens buy 5 spades at £12 apiece on credit from Hoxted Garden Equipment. Where do the entries go?

Which accounts?   The purchases account and the supplier's account.

Which columns?

Debit	Credit
Purchases account	Supplier account

But since a purchase is money going out of the business, should not the entry be the other way round? The reason that the entry is correct is shown by considering the rules given above.

The sum owing to the supplier is certainly a debt owed by Eden Plants and Gardens and is entered, as expected, in the credit column of the supplier account. The corresponding entry must therefore be a debit.

If this still seems against common sense, consider the rule that

debit = increase in assets	**credit = decrease in assets**
or	or
decrease in liabilities	**increase in liabilities**

Eden Plants and Gardens have increased their assets in the form of stock, and increased their liabilities in the form of a debt owed.

Example 2

Bella Vista Apartments rent flats. Mr Mortimer pays rent of £90 by cheque at the end of April.

The accounts involved are: Bella Vista's Bank account and Mr Mortimer's rent account.

The entries are	Debit	Credit
	Bank	Customer account

Clearly the Bank account has money coming in (debit) so the customer account entry must be a credit. But isn't this money coming in? Again, by consulting the chart given on page 185 the answer can be seen. Bella Vista has not acquired a debt, but Mr Mortimer has reduced or cleared a debt owing to Bella Vista (that debt would be a debit entry). Bella Vista have lost the asset of a debt to them, but have acquired the asset of money in the bank.

It is worth drawing attention to another case in which the everyday use of words can mislead us. A debt tends to suggest something we do not want, or that might well not get paid. Though the handling of bad debts is a part of bookkeeping, it is assumed that normally debts will be paid. They are thus an asset which will at some point be realised, that is, they will be paid, and the money assets of the business will increase in amount.

5.6 Layout of ledger entries

There is nothing startling about the layout of a typical ledger entry. It fits the patterns already seen:

Debit					Account: Furniture and fittings			E7	Credit	
Date	Particulars	Folio number	£	p	Date	Particulars	Folio number	£	p	
1 May	Komfy Sofas	SA23	450.00							

5.7 Folio number

The important point to be noted here is the appearance of another column in the accounts. This is the *folio number* column. The entries in this column may be simple numbers, or they may be codes (as they are here).

'Folio' is an old word for the page of a book. Simple numbers therefore refer to the pages of the ledger on which the relevant accounts are to be found. In the present case, there are different books, which are coded. This entry is on folio (page) E7, that is page 7 of the Expenses account. The transaction which is recorded is the supply of office furniture (a sofa) by Komfy Sofas. Their account (in which the other part of the double entry will be made) is referenced by folio number SA23 (Suppliers Accounts page 23). It is very important to fill in the folio number, as they are the 'signposts' to where the other entries relating to the transaction are filed.

5.8 Summary of double entry procedure

1) Decide which accounts are affected.

2) Make the entry in the first account as follows:

Debit side	**Credit side**
means	*means*
money coming in	money going out
debts owed by customers	debts owed to suppliers
credit notes received	credit notes issued
an increase in assets	a decrease in assets
a decrease in liabilities	an increase in liabilities

3) *Make the entry in the second account in the complementary column* (that is, 1st entry credit, 2nd debit and vice versa)

4) Check that you have filled in the folio number

Rules of double entry:

1) Every transaction must have two entries.

2) For every debit entry there must be a corresponding credit entry.

6. Posting of journals to the ledger

The information which is first recorded in the journals must be transferred to the ledger. Clearly, one of the entries must be to ensure that the accounts of those with whom the firm does business on credit are properly credited or debited. But the double entry system will also require a complementary entry in another account. This will show the effect of the transaction on the firm's business (eg increase in sales).

The process of posting to the ledger may be illustrated by the diagram below showing what has to be done with regard to the Sales Journal entries for one week.

It should be noted that all transactions involving customers or suppliers are posted at once to the relevant personal (customer or supplier) accounts. At the end of a longer period (normally a week) the entries in the Sales Journal are totalled and that figure is transferred to the appropriate ledger account of the same name, that is:

Sales Journal	– Sales Account
Sales Returns Journal	– Sales Returns Account
Purchases Journal	– Purchases Account
Purchases Returns Journal	– Purchases Returns Account

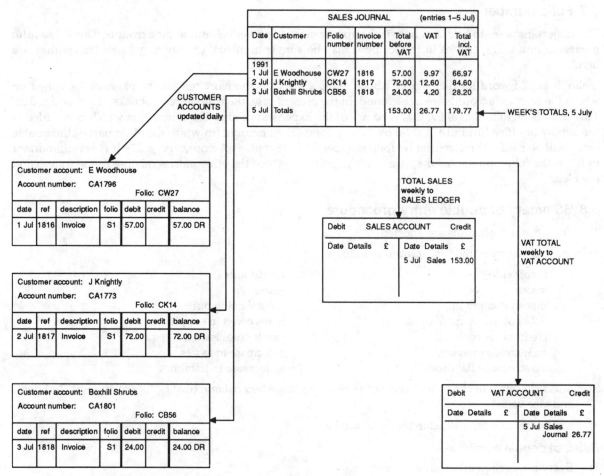

Sales journal

The ledger accounts thus contain only a summary of trading; details are recorded in the journals. The filed invoices and credit notes are kept on file as a last point of reference in the event of queries.

In most businesses there will also have to be an entry at the same time in the VAT account.

The same pattern applies to Purchases, Sales Returns and Purchases Returns, though the accounts involved are different. To decide which postings are needed, simply use the same diagram but label the boxes according to the table given below. This indicates both which account, and which column of that account will be involved:

Journal	Personal account	Sales or Purchases account	General Ledger account
Sales	Customer (Dr)	Sales (Cr)	VAT (Cr)
Purchases	Supplier (Cr)	Purchases (Dr)	VAT (Dr)
Sales Returns	Customer (Cr)	Sales Returns (Dr)	VAT (Dr)
Purchases Returns	Supplier (Dr)	Purchases Returns (Cr)	VAT (Cr)

7. The journal proper

This day book has not so far been discussed. It is a book of original entry, but is different in purpose and layout from the four sales and purchase journals.

The *journal proper* (sometimes referred to as 'the main journal' or just 'the journal') is used for transactions which are not part of the sales and purchases activity of the business, and which need further explanation. The commonest transactions which are entered in this journal are the acquisition or sale of assets (eg equipment), and the taking on of liabilities (eg a bank loan).

The pattern of entry is easy enough to understand.

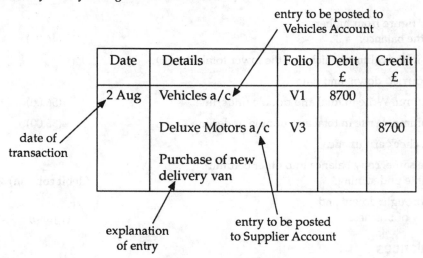

Date	Details	Folio	Debit £	Credit £
2 Aug	Vehicles a/c	V1	8700	
	Deluxe Motors a/c	V3		8700
	Purchase of new delivery van			

entry to be posted to Vehicles Account

date of transaction

explanation of entry

entry to be posted to Supplier Account

The journal proper

8. Balances

8.1 balancing the accounts

The process of balancing is described in *Accounts: basic approaches to record keeping*, page 74, and need not be repeated here. For convenience, here is a summary of the steps involved. The notes in brackets refer to the following example:

Debit				Account: Boxhill Shrubs		Credit	
Date	Details	£	p	Date	Details	£	p
17 May	Invoice	56.00		23 May	Sales returns	12.00	
				31 May	Balance c/d	44.00	
		56.00				56.00	
1 Jun	Balance brought down	44.00					

8.2 Method

1)	Total debit column.	(£56.00)
2)	Note this total on a separate piece of paper.	
3)	Total credit column.	(£12.00)
4)	Note this total on the same piece of paper. Write it above the debit total if it is higher; below the debit total if it is lower.	56.00 – 12.00
5)	Subtract lower figure from higher. This figure is the balance.	(44.00)
6)	Write balance in the column which had the lower total. (credit)	
7)	Add 'balance carried down' and date	
8)	Total debit column. Write in total and double underline.	(56.00)
9)	Total credit column. Write in total and double underline.	(56.00)
10)	If totals differ, check arithmetic.	
11)	If totals are the same, copy balance into other column under the double underlining.	(debit column)
12)	Add 'balance brought down' and date of next day of business.	(1 June)

8.3 Running balances

The three column method of entry, with a running balance, is described in *Accounts: basic approach to record keeping*, page 74. It is normal practice to indicate whether the running balance is a debit or a credit balance. These are abbreviated to Dr (Debit) and Cr (Credit). A summary of the method of calculation is given here for convenience.

8.4 Method

1) At the point when you make a new entry in the account the **previous balance** will be one of three types:

   a) Balance = £0.00 (a nil balance).

   b) Balance and entry are of same type (debit or credit).

   c) Balance and entry are different.

These are listed in column 1 of the table below.

2) Your *entry* must be in either the **Debit or Credit** columns. These are listed in column 2 of the table.

3) You then have to work out the *amount of the new balance*. How to do this is shown in column 3.

4) Finally, you have to indicate what *type of balance* (Dr and CR) you now have. What choice to make is shown in column 4.

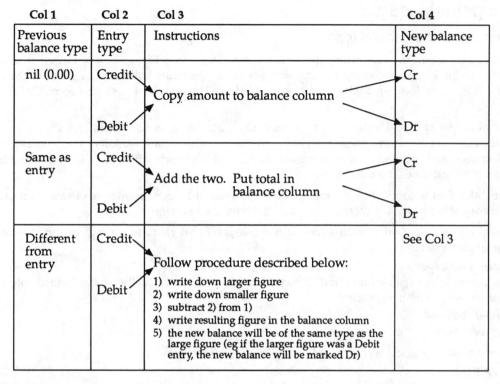

Col 1	Col 2	Col 3	Col 4
Previous balance type	Entry type	Instructions	New balance type
nil (0.00)	Credit	Copy amount to balance column	Cr
	Debit		Dr
Same as entry	Credit	Add the two. Put total in balance column	Cr
	Debit		Dr
Different from entry	Credit	Follow procedure described below:	See Col 3
	Debit	1) write down larger figure 2) write down smaller figure 3) subtract 2) from 1) 4) write resulting figure in the balance column 5) the new balance will be of the same type as the large figure (eg if the larger figure was a Debit entry, the new balance will be marked Dr)	

Example

Date	Debit	Credit	Balance	Notes	
1 Aug			0.00	Situation	1 – nil balance
2 Aug		150.00	150.00 Cr		
3 Aug		225.00	375.00 Cr		2 – same type
4 Aug	100.00		275.00 Cr		3 – different types
					375.00 –
					100.00
					275.00 Cr
					(larger figure was Cr)

8.5 Single entry

In certain cases there is only one entry in the account. The same pattern as described above is nevertheless followed:

Example

Debit			Account: J. Knightly			Credit
Date	Details	£ p	Date	Details	£ p	
7 Jul	Invoice	32.00	31 Jul	Balance c/d	32.00	
		32.00			56.00	
1 Aug	Balance brought down	32.00				

9. The general ledger

9.1 Structure of the general ledger

Many years ago, when the modern business world first came into being, it was sufficient to keep all accounts in one book – the ledger. At an early stage, bookkeepers and accountants decided for convenience to split the ledger into the cash book and the general ledger. The cash book is described in *Cash book*, page 115.

The general ledger can be divided up in various ways, according to the needs and purposes of those keeping the accounts. Whatever division is used, however, one important section of the general ledger will be that described earlier in this section: the group of accounts to which information is transferred from the journals dealing with sales and purchases.

Most firms also find it convenient to create within the general ledger summaries of sales and purchases activity: these are entered in the sales account and the purchases account.

The general ledger (often referred to as the nominal ledger) also contains a range of other accounts. Of particular importance are:

❏ *the expenses ledger*
   (This records the expenses involved in day-to-day trading, and usually be subdivided into separate accounts for each main expense).

❏ *an assets ledger*
   (This records the acquisition and sale of assets).

   (The discussion of assets will be found under *Final accounts*, page 159).

❏ *the VAT ledger*
   (This summarises the VAT situation. Total VAT paid and charged will be transferred from the ledgers dealing with sales and purchases. At the end of the VAT year this ledger is used to to compile the total of input and output tax paid, to be entered on the VAT return).

Some people find it useful to group accounts into three types:

1) *personal* accounts which record the debtors and creditors of the business

2) *real* accounts which set out the assets (for example, machinery owned) and capital (money or its equivalent) of the business

3) *nominal* accounts which deal with expenditure (money spent) and revenue (money coming in).

9.2 The expenses ledger

● What is an expense?

An expense is a payment made by a business which is *not part of the direct cost of the goods in which it trades,* but which is nevertheless essential to the running of the business. For example, a business premises needs heating and lighting, decoration, and repair at various times. These are all counted as expenses in the accounts. Most businesses find it convenient to keep separate accounts for different expenses. Examples are: heating and lighting, motor vehicles, advertising. There is further discussion of expenses in *Final Accounts*, page 150.

9.3 Example of an expense account entry in the general ledger

This follows the pattern already illustrated.

Eden Plants and Gardens receives a bill for £610.80 from Mercia Electricity which is paid by cheque on February 5. On February 8 work on altering the lighting is completed and invoiced by Volta Brothers Ltd for £350.

The entries in the general ledger account would be

Debit			Account: Electricity		Credit	
Date	Details	£ p	Date	Details	£ p	
5 Feb	Bank (ME)	610.80				
6 Feb	Bank (Volta)	350.00				

As in earlier cases, cheque payments are entered as 'Bank'. This is a crossreference to the Bank Account in the Cash Book, where the receipt of a payment would first be recorded.

You may again be puzzled that the entries are in the debit column. Surely, as the firm is paying out money, it should be entered in the credit column.

As with the examples given for the sales and purchase ledger, there are various ways of explaining the matter:

1) Eden Gardens certainly pays out money. But this payment would be entered in the credit column of the Bank account. The double entry therefore requires that a credit entry in the Bank account is balanced by a debit entry in the expense account.

2) Because both these payments are cash (rather than being debts owed in a credit arrangement) they reduce the assets of the company in the form of cash, but also reduce the liabilities of the firm (in the form of debts to the Electricity Company).

9.4 The VAT account

A firm which is registered for VAT is required to keep a VAT account. Input tax (on purchases) and output tax (on sales) must be totalled for the VAT return, and are calculated on the full price (before discount). It is therefore essential that the information from all relevant transactions should be extracted from those records and brought together in one account.

The account entries follow the standard pattern.

Debit			Account: Value Added Tax		Credit	
Date	Details	£ p	Date	Details	£ p	
31 Jul	Purchases Journal	142.00	31 Jul	Sales Journal	257.00	
31 Jul	Sales Returns	23.00	31 Jul	Purchases Returns	14.00	

Note that if this were all the information relating for the VAT tax year, input tax would be £165 and output tax £271. The balance of £106 would be owed to the Customs and Excise.

If you do not understand the above information, you are advised first to consider whether you need to deal with the VAT account for your present task. If not, you should ignore this information until a later date. If however, your task does require you to deal with the VAT account, you should first read *Value added tax*, page 261.

10.The trial balance

An important part of accountancy is the use of checks to see that the system is working properly. The first step in reviewing the accounts of a business for this purpose is to draw up a trial balance.

10.1 Method

The balance of each account in the ledger is either a debit balance or a credit balance. These are listed – a very simplified version might look like this:

	Debit balances	Credit balances
Premises		£20 000
Furniture and fittings £3 000		
Bank	£5 000	
Capital	£8 000	
Purchases	£10 000	
Sales	£30 000	
Totals	£38 000	£38 000

If the accounts balance, then the system is apparently in order. This method of testing the system arises from the nature of the double entry system, in which debits and credits must always balance exactly. (This is explained more fully below).

If the sides do not balance and there is a difference not accounted for, then further steps will have to be taken. These will usually involve tracking back in the accounts from which the problem is thought to arise.

10.2 Reason for using a trial balance

The reasoning behind the trial balance procedure is perfectly straightforward and runs as follows:

1) Each transaction entered in the accounts is given a double entry.

2) A double entry always credits one account and enters a corresponding debit in another.

3) For one entry, then, the accounts must balance.

4) Some accounts (for example supplies bought in) will be largely credit entries (money owed); others (sales, for example) will be largely debit entries (money coming into the firm).

5) But if each single entry balances, then the total number of entries should balance.

6) By totalling the balances for all the accounts, all entries will be taken into consideration.

7) The result of totalling the balances of all accounts (the trial balance) should be that

> **debit side = credit side**

proving that the accounts are in order (or unless someone has conducted a very clever fraud!).

A balance can thus have three functions

1) In single accounts, it show the *financial state of that account* (eg a customer is seriously in debt).

2) In final accounts (see *Final accounts*, page 147) it can show the *profitability of the business*.

3) In a trial balance, it can act as a check on the *accuracy of the accounting system*.

Letters

How to write letters dealing with financial business topics

Preliminary reading

The first time you use this entry, you should read the *Introduction*, below. Before using the entry *Useful phrases*, page 198, you should read *Basic principles*, page 197.

Note: letters dealing with the following topics are dealt with in other entries:
- asking for and giving a quotation – see *Quotations*, page 226.
- making or dealing with a complaint – see *Complaints*, page 126.

1. Introduction

1.1 Why you need to be able to write financial business letters

Unlike the secretary, the financial record keeper has to write relatively rarely, and usually very briefly. But there are a range of situations in which a simple accompanying statement is needed.

This may not always take the form of a letter – often only a standard slip is enclosed. When letter form is used, it will normally use a very standard pattern – often nowadays a stock letter produced on a word processor.

Nevertheless, you need to be able to compose your own letters for two main reasons:

a)   You will be able then to produce a letter when no standard document exists – for example in a very small firm

b)   You will also be able to rewrite a letter when necessary.

Increasingly, firms are becoming aware that letters put together from stock phrases, without thought as to the customer's reaction, can be very bad business. Such letters can seem to be offhand, to ignore totally what the customer is saying, or even to be threatening. Since we are dealing with money – a subject about which people are notoriously touchy – and are often trying to persuade people to part with money, it makes sense to try to be a little more appealing to them.

1.2 Your basic approach to writing

There are four stages in the creation of a piece of writing of any sort:

- ☐ **Creative**
- ☐ **Structuring**
- ☐ **Writing**
- ☐ **Polishing**

Professionals in fact tend to move constantly between one and the other, but inexperienced writers should separate them. Worrying about spelling, for example, often makes it difficult for many people to think about the meaning of what they are writing.

Creative: This is the stage in which the ideas come. It is the time when the writer gets the first insight or inspiration into how the piece is to be tackled.

The first thing to do is assemble all the relevant information: addresses, dates, figures, instructions from your boss and so on.

Next use 'brainstorming' – just let your mind run, and put down any ideas as they come – you can always change things later.

An important thing to remember is that this stage is interesting but very 'untidy'. Ideas don't always come in the best order, and many people find that their handwriting is poor, and they make spelling mistakes.

Structuring: Once the ideas have been gathered, you will have to put them into a *structure* and *order* which will make them clear to the reader. For many people, this is the most difficult phase of writing, requiring the most mental effort.

Writing: The next stage is to create a *draft* of the text. **Very few people can write out a text which is perfect first time.** Unless you are writing a completely standard letter you will need to think in terms of at least one draft and a fair copy.

However, there is no need to worry about fine detail at this stage. You are trying to decide on the order of what you will say, and the words you will use to say it, not to decide how many times you use 's' in 'disappointment'.

Polishing: When you have your draft, it becomes necessary to polish the work. Every day, reports in the media tell us that correct spelling and punctuation, clear handwriting (or good typing), and good layout are required by employers, and by the public.

Summary of method

- ☐ *Assemble* the data.
- ☐ Creative phase: use 'brainstorming' to *collect your ideas*.
- ☐ Structuring: put the ideas into an *order*.
- ☐ Writing: create a *draft* of the text.
- ☐ Polishing: attend to *layout*... correct *spelling* and *punctuation*.
- ☐ *Fair copy*: good handwriting/typing.

2. Basic principles

2.1 Common topics of financial business letters

Many situations come up again and again in this type of work. The commonest are:

- ❏ Sending for details about something
- ❏ Thanking someone for letter
- ❏ Enclosing a payment
- ❏ Telling the writer that the matter is being dealt with
- ❏ Asking for payment of a debt (dealt with under *Complaints*, page 126).

2.2 Style and language

What employers and customers do *not* want is pompous or old-fashioned 'business English'. What they do want is simple, direct, and above all clear and precise statements. You do not need to be a literary genius; in financial business letters you are required to invent very little. It is normal practice to use standard phrases, wherever these will truly meet the purpose. Examples are:

Thank you for your letter...

We regret that we cannot... However, ...

Some useful phrases are given in the next section.

For clarity, business letters often list what is to be said as separate points for clarity. The paragraphs are often only one sentence long, even though this would not be acceptable in most other forms of writing.

Remember finally, that, especially as you are dealing with money, the customer is likely to have more confidence in your skill, care and reliability, if your letters are accurately spelt and punctuated. It is reasonable to expect correctness in these matters, since the amount of writing to be checked is usually small.

3. Layout of a business letter

There is a standard layout for a business letter. It looks as follows:

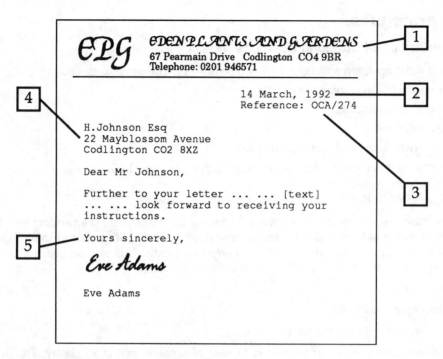

The elements, and the reasons why they are there, are as follows:

1	*Address:*	to show where to send any reply.
2	*Date:*	to show how recently letter was sent (this may be legally necessary, eg date of an agreement).
3	*Reference number:*	to help writer to identify any reply.
4	*Addressee's name and address:*	helps typist to address envelope, helps filing of copy, and reminds reader at later date of who it was sent to.
5	*Yours sincerely,*	(with a named addressee). Use 'Yours faithfully' with 'Dear Sir', 'Dear Sirs' or 'Dear Madam'.

4. Useful phrases

1) **Sending for details about something.**

   Please send me the leaflet "Holidays on the South Coast", which was advertised in last week's "Codlington Mercury".

   Note that it is worth repeating details (such as where the leaflet was advertised), as what is obvious to you may not be so to a business which receives many items of correspondence.

2) **Thanking someone for a letter.**

   Thank you for your letter dated June 30th, reference AD/123.

   Note that quoting the reference number which you have been given is helpful and often vital, when a business has many customers.

198

3) **Enclosing a payment.**

    Thank you for your payment (cheque/postal order) for £23.11 in response to (settlement of) our invoice (recent request).

    Note that it helps to state what the payment is in connection with; this may also be useful identifying a payment if there is a query some time afterwards. It is also sensible to give a confirmation of the sum paid – cheques can go astray, or be wrongly made out.

4) **Telling the writer that the matter is being dealt with.**

    Thank your for your letter of June 30th, which is receiving attention.

    Anyone who has written likes to know that the letter has been received, and if the matter cannot be dealt with at once, that it is at least in hand. For the amount of effort it takes it would be well worth while to add 'We shall be in contact with you as soon as we are able to answer your query/supply you with the goods', if you felt that it was especially important to stress that the matter was in hand.

5) **Asking for payment of a debt.**

    We are sorry to find that our invoice of...remains unpaid.

    We regret that, unless we receive your payment within seven days, we shall be obliged to...

    There are various alternative phrases: 'your debt of £25'; 'remittance' as formal term for payment.

    On such occasions invoice numbers and any other reference numbers, will be needed, and previous letters should be referred to, so that there can be no doubt that the payment is overdue.

    For further coverage of the last topic see *Complaints: importance of language used* and *useful phrases*, page 128–129.

Methods of payment

Information about various methods of payment which are available, and how to fill in the relevant documents

Preliminary reading

None. If you are looking for information about bank giro, cheques, cheque guarantee cards, standing orders or direct debits, you should look under those headings in the section *Bank documents*, page 79.

Contents

1. Ways of paying

There are a range of methods of payment which are available to individuals and businesses. They are listed below. Many are discussed in detail in other sections of this Information Bank, and will therefore only be mentioned here.

1.1 The options

1) *Payment in cash* (banknotes and coins)
This is an important method for *individuals*. It is much less important for businesses, who use other methods (a) for greater security and (b) because they make record keeping more effective. Note however that many businesses keep a small fund of cash on hand for everyday purchases; this is handled through petty cash (see *Petty cash*, page 219).

Note, though, that when *businesses* say they will pay cash, they mean they will pay immediately (probably by cheque) rather than take 'credit' and pay at a later date (see *Accounts: credit and debit*, page 73).

2) *Payment by cheque*
This is the commonest method of payment. See *Bank documents: cheques*, page 83.

3) *Payment by bank giro* (credit transfer)
A system of crediting accounts which minimises the need for sending cheques (see *Bank documents: bank giro*, page 79).

4) *Payment by standing order*
A convenient way to pay bills which are fixed and occur regularly (see *Bank documents: standing orders*, page 94).

5) *Payment by direct debit*
This method makes it easier to pay bills which occur regularly but which may vary in amount (see *Bank documents: direct debit*, page 92).

6) *Payment by postal order* (see below)

7) *Payment by a credit arrangement* (see below)

1.2 Postal orders

Most of us are familiar with the use of postal orders as a means of sending cash gifts. Many people, too, have used postal orders as a means of paying bills to firms located some distance away, as for example in buying from a mail order firm. However, for the most part, the facility is much more used by individuals than by business.

Postal Orders are sold at Post Offices; there are a range of values between 25p and £20. It is worth bearing in mind that a charge (poundage) is made, so that on small sums, one can end up paying substantially more than the amount to be sent. The example given below, worth only 25p to the receiver, cost 50p to buy!

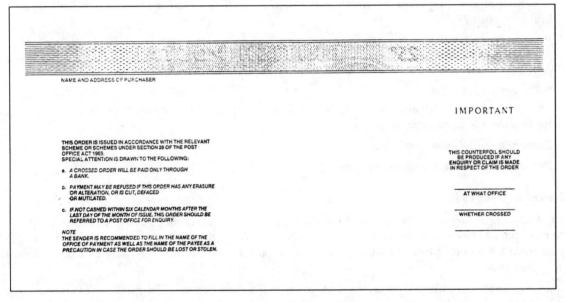

Postal order, front and back

The following features require action:

Front

1) Check order and counterfoil have been *stamped by the issuing office*

2) Purchaser to insert *name of payee*

3) Purchaser to insert *name of office to be paid at*

4) *Payee to sign* when presenting the order for payment

5) Purchaser may add *postage stamps* in order to make the order worth another value (in this case 26p to 49p)

6) The purchaser may *cross* the order if desired.

Back

1) Purchaser to write in *own name and address*

2) Purchaser to tear off and *keep counterfoil.*

Postal orders have various advantages.

1) The payee is guaranteed payment, because the postal order has already been paid for.

2) It is a safer way of sending small sums through the post, than by sending cash. In fact, the postal service does not accept responsibility for cash sent by ordinary mail.

3) There are various safeguards. The payee can be named, as can the post office at which payment is to be made. Also, the postal order can be crossed, like a cheque (see *Bank documents: crossing of cheques*, page 86). It can then only be paid into a bank account.

4) Like a cheque, too, a postal order has a limited life: a postal order becomes out of date six months after the date shown on the stamp of the issuing office.

1.3 Credit arrangements

In cash transactions, payment is immediate. With payment by credit, the date of settlement is delayed, or re-payment is by instalments (regular small amounts, until the debt is paid off). Payment may be made by any of the methods mentioned earlier. A credit arrangement is therefore not strictly a method of payment, that is, a way of transferring money. Instead it is a type of agreement about when such transfers should take place.

The commonest form of credit arrangement for *individuals* is hire purchase. Normally a deposit is paid, though in difficult times some businesses do not require one, so as to encourage buyers. The debt is then paid off by instalments, typically over a period of one or two years. Legally, the goods do not become the property of the buyer until all payments are made; instead they have the hire of the goods. Though nowadays many firms compete by offering 'interest-free' credit, normally the payments to be made will also include interest. This should always be looked into before buying, since it can amount to a massive increase in the price (see *Credit cards*, page 207). Businesses offering hire purchase in fact are now legally required to make quite clear what their conditions and charges are, and to allow the buyer a 'cooling-off' period before the agreement is made during which the buyer can consider the financial commitment he or she is making.

For *businesses*, credit takes two main forms:

☐ loans, which the business pays back according to agreed conditions

☐ customer accounts, which tend to be settled monthly on receipt of a statement.

Loans are explained in *Banking facilities: borrowing money*, page 98; customer accounts are explained in *Invoices: customer accounts*, page 166.

2. Retail trading

2.1 Methods of payment

The retailer is involved in two sorts of dealings, with somewhat different patterns of payment. On the one hand, the retailer must deal with suppliers (see *Quotations*, page 226). Payment in these cases follows the usual business pattern involving customer accounts and payment by cheque.

On the other hand, the retailer deals directly with the general public, often involving very small amounts of money. The methods of payment used are therefore rather different from those used by other areas of the business world. The main methods of payment are:

☐ payment in cash (see page 204)

☐ payment by cheque.
The retailer will normally expect a cheque to be supported by a *cheque guarantee card*. (For details see *Bank documents: cheques*, page 83 and *Bank documents: cheque guarantee cards*, page 89).

☐ payment by credit card (see page 207).

☐ payment by electronic credit transfer (see below).

2.2 Electronic credit transfer

This option is used by some shops and stores, by arrangement with banks, building societies, and credit card companies. The topic is not covered in any detail in this book, as firms which offer the facility have their own training courses on the use of such methods. The system works as follows:

1) The customer has a special card which he or she offers to the cashier

2) The cashier passes the card through an electronic card reader

3) The reader transmits the data to the computer of the relevant organisation (bank or credit card company)

4) The computer checks the card holder's details, including his or her credit limit

5) The computer transmits back whether the sale is authorised

6) If it is, the customer usually signs a sales slip to show that he or she has agreed to the sale

7) The cashier then uses the terminal to confirm the sale to the computer

8) The customer's account is debited, and the retailer's credited accordingly (ie the transaction is another form of credit transfer between two accounts).

The latter point is important to business people, as it means that payment is immediate and guaranteed.

The card which is read is either a credit card (see page 207), or, if the account to be drawn on is with a bank or building society, the customer will use a *debit card*, designed for this purpose. The debit card facility is sometimes combined with a cheque guarantee card.

3. Retail cash payments

3.1 Giving change

We are all familiar with the process of going into a shop, paying and being given change. Though it is important to be able to work out the change required for oneself, the life of the salesperson or cashier is made much easier these days by the existence of tills which show the amount to be given automatically. The cashier merely keys in the cost of each item, and the amount of cash offered. The machine does all the adding and subtraction.

What it does not do (except in vending machines) is to work out what coins and notes are to be given, and to count them out.

The practical approach used by many cashiers is:

1) start from the amount being charged

2) build up the change from the currency of the lowest denomination (value)

3)   as soon as it is possible to use a higher value coin or note, do so

4)   when you reach the amount offered by the customer, stop!

Example

Thomas Arne has just come from being paid at work. He goes into a minimarket and buys various small items for his supper. The bill is £3.12, but Thomas has only a £50 note to pay with. The change was counted out as follows:

Sale		£3.12 paid
Change (start with lowest coin)	1p	£3.13
can move into	2p	£3.15
	5p	£3.20
	10p	£3.30
	20p	£3.50
	50p	£4.00
	£1	£5.00
can move into notes	£5	£10.00
The cashier could go to	£10	£20.00
	£10	£30.00
	and £20	£50.00

or it would be possible to jump from £5 to £20 and give two £20 notes.

3.2 End of day procedure

Machines also help at the end of the day. Instead of the cashier having to total up manually a day's receipts, it is done automatically, and printed on the *till roll*, on which all the day's sales have been recorded. But the cashier will still need to count up what is in the till and see that it matches. If not, there has been an error somewhere. This is most likely to have occurred:

1)   when counting the cash in the till

2)   when checking money offered by customers

3)   when giving change.

When you are the customer, you should remember that though the till roll will show that there has been an error during the day, it will not prove that the error arose in connection with your purchase.

The amount of cash in the till will not necessarily be the day's takings, because the cashier may well have started the day with a float (loose change for early customers). This will have to be subtracted, before it is known if the cash in the till on the total on the roll agree. The calculation is:

total on roll − float = cash in till.

The takings are paid in to a bank, using a deposit slip (see *Bank documents: deposit slips*, page 91). Because banks are often closed by the time that trading ends, many shops use the night safes which you can see on the outside of many banks. To use the night safe the procedure is:

1)   'bag up' the cash, putting it into packs according to denomination (for example all pound coins together)

2)   fill in a deposit slip

3)   put cash and slip into a bag or wallet, which is taken to the night safe.

Because cash can be used immediately and anywhere and is very hard to identify, it is always tempting to thieves. Attention to security is therefore very important wherever there are cash dealings. The cashier should always lock the till when it is not in use, and keep the key safely. For further discussion of security see *Work methods: security*, page 293.

4. Receipts

4.1 Use of receipts

An important advantage of payment by cheque or credit transfer is that the transaction is recorded in various places. By contrast, there is no clear evidence of a cash payment, except the word of the parties concerned. Yet there are many occasions when such evidence is needed. One example is when the buyer wishes to return faulty goods. Another is to prove that cash has been laid out, when you wish to claim it back (see *Petty cash*, page 219 and *Expenses*, page 140). It is for this reason that *receipts* came into use. They are a record made by the person receiving cash, that payment has been made.

It should not need stressing that it is important to check your receipt at the time of issue: errors are very hard to prove later. Also, you should keep receipts carefully and label them for your own reference if necessary.

4.2 Format and content of a receipt

Receipts may be hand written or produced by machine. Here are examples of both types:

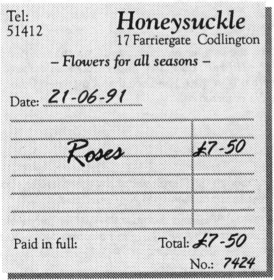

Hand-written receipt   Printed receipt

Though receipts are far from standard in format, they tend to contain the following information:

- ☐ the date
- ☐ a reference number (in large stores there may be more than one)
- ☐ a listing of purchases
- ☐ (often) a subtotal
- ☐ VAT (as appropriate)

- a total (or 'balance due')
- the amount tendered by the customer (on machines, this is needed as part of the information for calculating change and takings – see above)
- an indication of whether payment was in cash or by cheque
- the amount of change given (in the case of a cash payment)

4.3 Filing and recording of receipts

There are various ways in which receipts may be filed. The most obvious are:

- type of expense (eg equipment, plants)
- date of payment
- a reference number which is allotted when the receipt is entered into the firm's financial records.

The system will be linked closely to the structure of the ledger, since the receipts are part of the back-up for the less detailed entries in the various ledger accounts (see *Ledgers and journals*, page 177).

5. Credit cards

5.1 What they are

The person who does not wish to pay a bill at once by means of cash or a cheque, may choose to do so by using a *credit card*. This should not be confused with cheque guarantee and cash dispenser cards (see *Bank documents: cheques* page 83).

The credit card does two things:

1) It allows the cardholder to defer payment, that is to buy things on credit.
2) It allows the user to obtain cash up to an agreed limit (see below).

There are four sets of people involved in the use of credit cards:

1) the customer (or cardholder)
2) the person or firm providing services or goods (known as the vendor)
3) the vendor's bank
4) the credit card company.

In the UK the cards most commonly used are those issued by companies which were set up by the clearing banks. The first of these was Barclaycard; this was followed by Access, a facility set up in 1972 by the other main banks (Lloyds, Midland, Natwest). There are other companies which are now trying to break into the UK market – perhaps the best known is American Express. Some big stores (eg Marks and Spencer) also issue store cards, which allow credit for goods purchased from them.

In order to obtain a credit card, you fill in a form. The questions ask for a range of information which allows the card company to decide upon your *credit rating*. This sets a limit on the amount of money that the cardholder can owe at any one time, as well as the length of time which he or she can be allowed for repayment.

5.2 How credit cards are used at the time of the sale

In order to carry out a payment by credit card instead of cash, the following procedure is needed:

1) The cardholder must first check that the vendor accepts the type of card he or she has (there will usually be a sign on display).

2)   The customer hands over the card.

3)   It is processed as described below and a voucher is made out.

4)   The customer is then given back the card and a copy of the voucher.

From the point of view of financial record keeping this is important, because it acts as a record of the transaction for accounting and tax purposes.

To carry out the processing the vendor has several things to do. If there is any doubt about the customer's right or ability to pay, the vendor will telephone the card company's authorisation centre in order to check. The vendor will also have a list of stolen cards, against which the card will be checked.

If all is well, the next stage is to use either an *imprinter* (a manual system) or a *card reader* (an automatic system) to read and record the card.

5.3 Using an imprinter

This simple, manual machine makes it possible to avoid clerical errors in copying crucial details, and especially numbers. It is used as follows:

1)   The card is placed in the machine, and then the voucher slips are laid on top.

2)   The assistant writes in:
- the details of the sale (articles, cost, total due)
- the date
- any details required for internal record keeping (for example, assistant's code number).

3)   The assistant works a roller, which imprints the details which on the customer's card onto the voucher and copies.

4)   The customer is asked to check and sign the voucher.

5)   The vendor then checks the signature against that on the card.

6)   If all is well, the assistant hands back the card together with the customer's copy of the sales voucher.

7)   The remaining three copies are processed according to the vendor's normal procedures. Two will be filed, as a record of the sale. The white copy is handled as though it were a cheque and is taken to the bank along with cheques and cash.

Any employee who has to handle credit cards should be especially careful about security, as there is a great deal of credit card fraud. In particular:
- check the stolen cards list
- do not hesitate to seek authorisation if in doubt.

5.4 Using a card reader

This is also known as a 'swipe machine', because of the way that the card is passed through it!

The basic account of how it works is given in *Electronic credit transfer*, page 204.

The steps taken by the cashier are:

1)   pass the card through the reader

2)   check that the card is accepted as valid

3)   key in the amount due

4)   check that the computer authorises the purchase as being within the purchaser's credit limit

5)   wait for the till to print out the receipt

6)   obtain the customer's signature

7)   compare the signature with that on the credit card

8)   give the customer the top copy

9)   file the second copy according to your firm's normal procedures.

5.5 How the accounts are adjusted

The 'swipe machine' is a terminal for a computer (see *Computerisation*, page 131): the accounts are therefore altered immediately authorisation is given from the terminal.

When an imprinter is used, the transaction proceeds as follows.

1)   The vendor separates the voucher and sends on the white copy to the firm's bank, who credit the firm's account with the relevant amount. The other part is kept for the firm's financial records.

2)   The bank first credits the vendor's account, and then forwards the slip to the credit card company in order to retrieve this amount.

3)   The credit card company pays the bank, because the card holder has an account with them (see *Accounts: basic approaches to record keeping*, page 74 and *Invoices: customer accounts*, page 166).

4)   The credit card company records the payment which is owed in the cardholder's account (debits the account).

5)   The cardholder is sent a statement of what he or she owes every month, and is required to make a repayment.

5.6 Other facilities

A credit card can also be very useful in two other ways. First, some organisations will allow customers to phone through their credit card details in order to pay; this saves having to travel in order to pay in person. Second, holders of credit cards, such as Access, can obtain cash from the bank up to the limit of their credit rating. This is, in effect, another way of obtaining a loan.

6. Repayment of credit

6.1 Longer term repayments

The entry which follows describes repayment on a credit card account. It does however illustrate points which apply to various other forms of credit.

Once a credit cardholder has made purchases or drawn cash by means of a credit card, he or she is in debt to the credit card company.

Typically, the customer is given the option to pay back what is owed in full within 25 days. Anyone who can do this has in fact had a short-term interest-free loan.

Most people wish, however, to spread payment over a longer period, particularly if the sum is large. In these circumstances the credit card company charges for the service and for the loan (and so makes its profits) by means of adding interest to the amount owed. This is calculated and charged monthly, and is included in the monthly statement.

6.2 Interpreting the interest charges

It is important to be clear about the main ways in which interest can be calculated. Research by consumers' organisations shows that most people are unaware of just how much they are being charged in order to borrow money. Because they are do not understand the information which they are given, purchasers frequently pay much more than they need.

For example, if you borrow £2,000 for five years on a fixed interest loan, you pay the same rate of interest and do so over the whole period, no matter how much you pay back. If your repayments are £50 per month, over the period you pay back

£50 (monthly payment) x 12 (months) x 5 (years) = £3,000.

You pay £1,000 to borrow £2,000, and so over the whole period you pay 50% interest on the sum loaned. (If you are not clear about these calculations refer to the entry *Calculations: Interest,* page 000).

Credit cards work differently; instead you pay interest on what you owe. You would think this must be cheaper, but for this to be so, it is essential to keep up payments, or the addition of interest can soon mean that you are worse off than when you first started. For example, Mr Jones spends £2,000:

Month 1:	spend	£2,000
	end of month: interest at 2%	£40
	owed	£2,040
	repay	£50
Month 2:	owed	£1,990
	end of month: interest at 2%	£39.80
	no repayment	
Month 3:	owed	£2,029.80
	end of month: interest at 2%	£40.60
	no repayment	
Month 4:	owed	£2,070.40

Mr Jones now owes more than he originally spent and has paid £50 to be £70.40 more in debt!

6.3 APR

In credit sales, interest is quoted and calculated on a monthly basis. For instance, if the monthly rate is 2%, over one year that means an interest rate of 26.8%*. This means that to borrow £2,000 as above for one year (not a lot for someone investing in furniture or a kitchen unit for a new home), you would have to find an additional £536 (which is £10.30 a week more on top of the amount borrowed).

[* It will not be 24% (which is 12 months x 2%) because it is *compound* interest.]

Interest calculated over the year is known as the ***Annual Percentage Rate (APR)***. Fortunately, customers do not have to have the complication of calculating the APR for themselves; the law requires that all who provide credit card services and hire purchase transactions must display the APR prominently.

Even so, it is still wise to look at several options for borrowing money before making a decision, or you can have a virtually endless burden of debt.

If you are unsure about the calculations of interest payments and especially compound interest, refer to *Calculations: Interest,* page 107.

Orders

Explanation of the process of ordering goods or services

Preliminary reading

It is assumed that you have read the entry *Quotations*, page 226.

Contents

1. Ordering goods

When customers wish to purchase goods, they place an order. To aid the decision about what to buy, the customer may request a quotation, as described earlier, or may consult a price list or catalogue.

Normally, the customer then completes an *order form* (see page 212). They will enter details of:

- the quantity
- the type of item
- (often) a catalogue reference number.

There are also spaces for

- the price per unit
- the subtotals for individual items
- the final total.

At this stage the customer makes a commitment to buy.

The supplier will pack the goods, and send them off according to the *terms of business*. This process will be accompanied by appropriate documents – which may include an *acknowledgement of order*, an *advice note*, and a *delivery note* (see entries below under those headings).

Finally the supplier will request payment by means of an *invoice* (see page 161).

2. The Order Form

Though there are differences of detail between companies, an order form looks basically like this:

STAR ☆ Minimarket

Middle Lane
Hoxted

VAT Reg. No.: 129 44053   ✆ **0191 23456**

Order form

To: Kutkash, Highworth Way, Codlington   Order No. C742
    Highworth Way   22 Mar, 1991
    C14

Quantity	Item	Unit	Price	Total
28	streaky bacon	(4)	2.06	14.42
24	(80) tea bags	(6)	3.42	13.68
80	cornflakes	(10)	5.99	47.92
24	tomato sauce	(12)	4.05	8.10
36	1 ltr washing up liquid	(12)	3.15	9.45
36	(250ml) cola	(12)	1.45	4.35
36	(250ml) lemonade	(12)	1.45	4.35
20	steak and kidney pies	(5)	3.60	14.40
20	tomato and cheese pizza	(4)	0.75	3.75
108	(4) beefburgers	(12)	6.30	56.70
72	(10) cod fish fingers	(12)	6.48	38.88

TOTAL   216.00

Delivery: Wed 26 March 1991
              Carriage paid

J Smith

John Smith
Manager

Information to be included:

❏ name and address of supplier
❏ order form reference number

- ❏ account reference number (if any)
- ❏ date
- ❏ quantity of goods
- ❏ type of item
- ❏ (sometimes) catalogue reference number
- ❏ price per unit
- ❏ place of delivery (if relevant)
- ❏ date of delivery
- ❏ terms of delivery
- ❏ signature of person authorising the purchase.

All the above will be entered by the employee responsible for making out purchase orders.

3. Delivery of goods

3.1 Check on creditworthiness

Once an order form has been received, the supplier's accounts department checks the financial arrangements:

1) Most important, they check the *creditworthiness* (see *Accounts: credit and debit*, page 73) of the customer

2) In the case of cash payments, the accounts department will check the suppliers stop list to see if there is any history of bad debts. In the case of a large cheque they may contact the bank to obtain *special clearance* (that is, the bank hurries up the normal process of clearance in order to state whether or not the drawer is in a position to issue the cheque). For businesses, there is also a special service which gives an immediate statement of creditworthiness up to a certain limit. This is helpful to companies who have to accept cheques for some hundreds of pounds.

3) When dealings are on a credit basis, the supplier will check to see if *aged debt analysis* (see *Invoices: aged debt analysis*, page 167) has revealed that the customer's account is in arrears. In the case of a new account, money will be owed for a period; the supplier will usually seek some indication, such as a banker's reference, that the customer can be trusted to have such credit. The above types of activity are part of what is termed *credit control*.

3.2 Process of delivery

Assuming that the question of payment raises no problems, the department may send out an *acknowledgement of order* (see below). The stores and packaging personnel with then make up the order, and pass it on for delivery. This will involve the *despatch documents* (see *Advice note*, page 215 and *Delivery note*, page 216).

4. The Acknowledgement of Order

4.1 Format of acknowledgement

An acknowledgement of the order is often made, though in the case of small orders, or delivery by mail, this stage may be dispensed with in the interests of economy. Acknowledgement may be made on a form very similar to the order form. However, with simple orders, acknowledgement may be made by means of a letter. As in other business correspondence, the letter will use the standard layout and phrases, and will be clear and courteous. For guidance see *Letters*, page 197 forward.

4.2 Letter of acknowledgement

A typical letter might read:

KUTKASH

HIGHWORTH WAY CODLINGTON Co2 1ZZ
TEL: 0201 82641   FAX: 0201 01210

```
Mr J. Smith                              Your ref: ABC 123
Star Minimarket                          Our ref: DEF 678
Middle Lane
Hoxted                                   23 March 1991
```

Dear Mr Smith,

Thank you for your order of 22 March, reference C742, requesting the supply of the following:

Quantity	Item	Unit	Unit	price
28	streaky bacon	(4)	2.06	14.42
24	(80) tea bags	(6)	3.42	13.68
80	cornflakes	(10)	5.99	47.92
24	tomato sauce	(12)	4.05	8.10
36	1 ltr washing up liquid	(12)	3.15	9.45
36	(250ml) cola	(12)	1.45	4.35
36	(250ml) lemonade	(12)	1.45	4.35
20	steak and kidney pies	(5)	3.60	14.40
20	tomato and cheese pizza	(4)	0.75	3.75
108	(4) beefburgers	(12)	6.30	56.70
72	(10) cod fish fingers	(12)	6.48	38.88

We can arrange delivery either am or pm on 26 March. Perhaps you would be kind enough to phone us before 25 March, if you have a preference.

Yours faithfully,

A Johnson

A Johnson,
Manager

VAT Reg. No. 130 774106

4.3 Information to be included

- [ ] name and address of customer
- [ ] order form reference number
- [ ] account reference number (if any)
- [ ] date
- [ ] quantity of goods
- [ ] type of item

- ☐ (sometimes) catalogue reference number
- ☐ price per unit
- ☐ place of delivery (if relevant)
- ☐ date of delivery
- ☐ terms of delivery
- ☐ signature of person acknowledging the order

5. Advice note

5.1 Despatch documents

Before goods are sent ('despatched'), the firm will draw up the *despatch documents*. These may include an *advice note*, which informs the customer that the order has been received and dealt with, and how the goods have been sent. Increasingly nowadays suppliers economise by sending only a *delivery note* (see page 216). For example, as delivery is local, and is to take place so soon, there would be no point in Kutkash sending an advice note.

5.2 Advice note

The advice note looks like this:

215

It contains the following information:

- ☐ name and address of customer
- ☐ order form reference number
- ☐ account reference number (if any)
- ☐ date
- ☐ quantity of goods
- ☐ type of item
- ☐ (sometimes) catalogue reference number
- ☐ price per unit
- ☐ place of delivery (if relevant)
- ☐ date of delivery
- ☐ terms of delivery
- ☐ despatch details (type of transport, number of packages)
- ☐ signature of person acknowledging the order.

You will notice that this list is very similar to that given for the order form and the acknowledgement of order. In fact there is just one difference, which you should look for.

6. Delivery note

6.1 What it is

The delivery note lists the goods which have been sent. It is therefore an essential part of the checking, first by the supplier's despatch department and then by the customer. Sometimes it is sent with the goods, and sometimes separately. When the goods are not delivered by the supplier's own transport, but by an independent carrier, the delivery note is usually referred to as a *consignment note*.

The delivery note is a very useful document, because it allows the recipient of the goods to check what they have received against what the supplier claims to have sent. They can then, if necessary, raise queries or make complaints, for example about errors, omissions or damage.

The person responsible for receiving the goods will be asked to sign a copy of the delivery note to acknowledge the delivery. Both as an employee and as a private individual you are likely to have to deal with delivery notes. Consequently, it is worth remembering that, when you sign, you are acknowledging the safe delivery of what you have requested. You should therefore always check the delivery for visible damage or omission. In the case of very expensive or fragile deliveries you should also check the contents before signing.

This action will not always make you popular! Delivery staff often have many calls to make, and tend to want to be off quickly. But you should bear in mind that you are committed to paying for the goods, and that once they have come into your possession, it becomes increasingly hard to prove that any damage occurred before you received the goods. Fortunately, many firms will in practice accept your word that goods were found to be damaged when the package was opened. What is certain is that visible damage should be reported at once to both the delivery staff and the supplier, and that damaged goods should normally be returned at once. What action you take should be recorded on the delivery note. Similarly, damage discovered on opening packages should be reported to the supplier at once by phone and confirmed in writing.

There is a further stage of checking which is widely undertaken. Imagine that the delivery note has been compared with the actual goods delivered, and is found to be a correct record of what has been sent. As human beings can make mistakes, what has been sent may nevertheless not be the same as what has been ordered, or what is charged for. Firms will therefore tend to check a correct delivery note against a copy of the order form, and against the invoice, when it is received. The latter process is called the *reconciliation of delivery form with invoice*.

6.2 Format

A delivery note looks as follows:

KUTKASH

HIGHWORTH WAY CODLINGTON CO2 1ZZ
TEL: 0201 82641   FAX: 0201 01210

DELIVERY NOTE

26 March 1991   ORDER No.: C742
Star Minimarket
Middle Lane
Huxted

QUANTITY	ITEM	UNIT
28	streaky bacon	(4)
24	(80) tea bags	(6)
80	cornflakes	(10)
24	tomato sauce	(12)
36	1 ltr washing up liquid	(12)
36	(250ml) cola	(12)
36	(250ml) lemonade	(12)
20	steak and kidney pies	(5)
20	tomato and cheese pizza	(4)
108	(4) beefburgers	(12)
72	(10) cod fish fingers	(12)

DESPATCH DETAILS: Road, 5 packages

DELIVERY   above address
Wed, 26 March, a.m.

A Johnson

A Johnson,
Manager

RECEIVED: _____

SIGNED: _____

FIRM: _____

VAT Reg. No. 130 774106

It contains the following information:

- ❏ name and address of customer
- ❏ order form reference number
- ❏ account reference number (if any)
- ❏ date
- ❏ quantity of goods
- ❏ type of item
- ❏ (sometimes) catalogue reference number
- ❏ price per unit (often omitted)
- ❏ place of delivery (if relevant)
- ❏ date of delivery
- ❏ terms of delivery
- ❏ signature of person taking the delivery

The signature will acknowledge the receipt of the goods. In the event of payment having to be made to the carrier (ie terms of delivery: COD), there will be either a place on the delivery note or a separate receipt (see *Methods of payment: Receipts,* page 206) to show that payment has been made.

6.3 The next stages

1) You will notice similarities between this and the other documents in this entry. For a summary of the information required on these documents see *Invoices: Similarities between documents,* page 164).

2) The transaction now moves into the payment stage. How this is handled is described in *Invoices* (page 161).

Petty cash

Information about the nature and operation of a standard petty cash system

Preliminary reading

Before reading the section on the Petty Cash Book, you should have read *Accounts: basic approach to record keeping*, page 74.

Contents

1. The petty cash system

The ledger accounts deal with the main transactions of a business. However, there is a steady need for dealing with small amounts of cash for the day-to-day running of a business. Examples are postage, stationery, and travel expenses. Such sums are money are known as *petty cash* (from the French petit, meaning small). They are handled by the petty cashier – usually a senior member of the office staff.

1.1 The imprest system

In order to run a petty cash system there must be cash available in coins and notes, to meet the various expenses which will be paid for in cash. This is rather like the position in retail trading, in which the cashier starts the day with a float (see *Methods of payment: retail cash payments*, page 204).

In the petty cash system used in many businesses, this start-up fund of money is called the *imprest*, and the method for controlling petty cash is called (naturally enough) the imprest system. The reason for not calling this sum a float is that the system has the following features, which do not necessarily apply to a float:

1)   A fixed sum is given to the petty cashier;

2)   This sum is expected to cover payments for a set period, usually a week or a month;

3)   The petty cashier must keep records, including *vouchers*; these are proof that the expenses claimed have actually been made

4)   At the end of the period (or before if the imprest is exhausted) the petty cashier receives a sum of money equal to the amount spent. This restores the imprest to the original sum;

5)   This topping up *(reimbursement of the imprest)* depends on the production of satisfactory records, and vouchers accounting for what has been spent.

1.2 The petty cashier

The petty cashier has the following responsibilities:

1)   to ensure the security of the cash on the premises;

2)   to handle the petty cash vouchers (see below);

3)   to keep receipts and records for all amounts spent;

4)   to make the necessary entries in the petty cash book (see below).

1.3 Security

As with any system of cash handling, security is very important. The following procedures should be followed to ensure that the cash is secure.

1)   The petty cash is usually kept in a cash box and is locked in a safe place when not in use.

2)   The petty cashier keeps and is responsible for the key.

3)   The petty cashier keeps accurate records.

4)   Employees who wish to be reimbursed for money spent must fill in a voucher, which must be properly authorised before payment is made.

5)   At intervals the petty cash book will usually be checked by a member of the accounts department. There will also be checks from time to time, made without warning, (known as *spot checks*) to ensure that all is well.

2. Vouchers

Any employee who wishes to obtain money or be paid back for the sort of expense covered by petty cash can only do so when a petty cash voucher has been properly completed. Such a voucher looks like this:

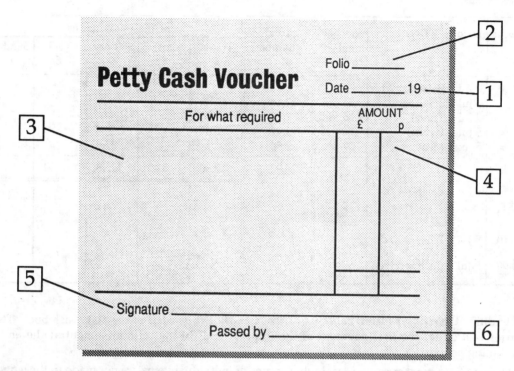

A properly completed voucher will contain:

1. *date* of payment
2. a *serial number* for easy identification
3. a *description* of the item of expenditure
4. the *amount* (inclusive of VAT, if relevant) of money spent
5. *signature* by the member of staff who is making (or has made) the expenditure
6. *signature of the person who authorises the payment* (usually the petty cashier)

When a receipt has been given to the person who is requesting a repayment, this should be attached to the petty cash voucher.

3. The petty cash book

3.1 Layout

A page from a typical petty cash book looks as follows:

Receipts £	Date	Details	Voucher number	Total payment £	Travel £	Post £	Stat'nry £	VAT £	Sundry £
					Analysis columns				
50.00	2 Jul	Balance b/d							
	3 Jul	Stationery	34	12.48			12.48		
	4 Jul	Travel	35	2.50	2.50				
	5 Jul	Postage	36	5.42		5.42			
	5 Jul	Meal	37	3.50				3.50	
				23.90	2.50	5.42	12.48	3.50	
	6 Jul	Balance c/d	26.10						
50.00			50.00						
26.10	9 Jul	Balance b/d							
23.90	9 Jul	Cash received							

Notes:

- By tradition the *receipts (debit) column is always on the extreme left* of the petty cash book. The only entries will be (a) the first payment of the imprest and (b) the reimbursement at the end of an accounting period.

- There is *no folio number column,* as double entries of individual items are not made in the ledger. It is to save such labour that the petty cash system was devised.

- *Voucher number.* This is explained above.

- *Analysis columns,* as in the analysed cash book (see *Cash book,* page 118).

- *VAT column.* This is explained separately (page 223).

- *'Sundry' column.* This column is for entering all expenses not entered in the other analysis columns.

- *Totals line.* This gives the total expenses paid out. To the right are the totals for the individual columns.

- *'Balance carried down'.* This figure is the amount of cash which should be left in the cash box.

- *Balance line.* The two totals, receipts and expenditure (expenses plus cash left in cashbox) are equal. The account balances.

- *'Balance b/d'* is the amount which is actually left in the cash box.

The lower entries are explained in the section *Making entries,* page 224.

- *'Cash received'* is the reimbursement from the chief cashier. This equals the expenses paid out, and restores the imprest to its original total for the start of the new accounting period.

3.2 Analysis columns

The petty cash book is really a form of analysed cash book (see *Cash book: analysed cash book,* page 118). As such it contains debit and credit columns, which are part of the ledger. These are totalled and balanced like any other accounts (see *Ledgers and journals: balances,* page 177). A summary of these columns will be included in the final accounts.

As with the analysed cash book, the analysis columns are for the convenience of those keeping the records. There are no set headings. They are *not balanced,* but they are totalled from time to time, and these totals are then posted to the relevant expense accounts.

The nature of the petty cash book means that it is possible to carry out an internal check. The result of adding the column totals should be the same as that of adding the debit (payments column).

3.3 VAT columns

It is required by law that all businesses registered for VAT must keep records of all transactions involving VAT. This also applies to petty cash.

When VAT has been applied to a purchase, there will be two situations which the petty cashier will encounter:

1) **VAT has been separately calculated, and is stated on the receipt.** In these cases, the petty cashier will enter:

   ❑ **total actually paid** – Total payment column

   ❑ **cost before VAT** is added – entered in the appropriate analysis column

   ❑ **VAT paid** – in the VAT column

2) When purchases which are subject to VAT are ones which are for small amounts, and frequently made, **the vendor does not always give a separate statement of what VAT has been added.** The price will merely be described as 'inclusive of VAT'. (When the vendor needs to know the total VAT paid, ie for his accounts, this can be calculated easily using the total sales figure.)

3.4 Calculating VAT paid

The petty cashier has, however, the chore of working out what the actual sum was, so that it can be entered in the VAT column of the petty cash book. This will be the first stage towards including it in the VAT return.

To work out the sums involved (an example is given in brackets to the right of the page) assuming the VAT rate is 17.5%.

1) Write down (or enter on your calculator) the total payment (£3.75)
2) Divide this figure by 117.5 (£0.031914)
3) Multiply by 100 (£3.1914)
4) Subtract total (3) from total (1) (£0.5586)
5) If the VAT amount includes fractions of a penny, round* to a whole number (£0.55)
6) Calculate the remainder – this is the price paid. (£3.20)

* In this book we have decided to simplify matters by rounding *down* in all VAT calculations. However, you should be aware that in reality the Customs and Excise regulations are more complex, and can involve rounding up *or* down. You should therefore follow the guidelines that laid down by your employer or lecturer.

If working manually and you wish to check, calculate and add $17\frac{1}{2}\%$ to the sale price. It may help to remember that

❑ 10% moves the decimal point one place to the left

❑ 5% is half of 10%

❑ $2\frac{1}{2}\%$ is half of 5%

❑ $10 + 5 + 2\frac{1}{2} = 17\frac{1}{2}$

> **Example: VAT on £10.50**
>
> | | |
> |---|---|
> | 10% | 1.0500 |
> | 5% | 0.5250 |
> | $2\frac{1}{2}$ % | 0.2625 |
> | VAT: | £ 1.8375   (£1.83) |

The VAT columns will be totalled at the same time as the other columns, and the amount of VAT paid, being input tax, will be entered in the debit column of the VAT account.

If you are unsure about any aspect of the above information, you will need to refer to *Value added tax*, page 251.

4. Making entries in the petty cash book

Before making the entry, make the payment and complete the voucher (see page 221).

❑ In the petty cash book enter:

1) *date*

2) *details*

3) *voucher number*

4) *total amount paid out*

5) Note whether VAT has been paid, then carry out one of the following:

   a) if there was *no VAT payment*

   enter *total amount paid under one of the analysis columns*

   b) if there was a *VAT payment*, and this is *known*

   enter *VAT paid in the VAT column*

   amount paid (net of VAT) in an analysis column

   c) if there was a *VAT payment*, but it is *not known* how much

   work out VAT (see page 113 above)

   then *carry out b)*

6) You should then *file* the voucher.

❑ At the end of the accounting period:

1) *total all columns*

2) *balance the petty cash book*.

5. Balancing the petty cash book

5.1 Method

The method of balancing the petty cash book is the same as that used in other accounts. As the petty cash book is often kept by those who do not otherwise keep accounts, the method is also given here for convenience.

1) Rule a line right across the page, starting at the *Total Payment* column.

2) Total each of the analysis columns. Enter the totals in the appropriate columns, under the ruled line.

3) Total the *Total Payment* column. Enter it under the ruled line.

4) Carry out an internal check on your addition as follows:

   a) add together the totals of the analysis columns

   b) check that this is the same as the total for the *Total Payment* column.

   c) If the figure is not the same,
- check your arithmetic
- if the totals are correct, check your voucher entries – are both entries the same?

5) On the line below the totals enter the date.

6) In the *Details* column write '*Balance b/d*'.

7) In the *Total Payment* column enter the sum of money which is still in the petty cash box.

8) Rule a line across the *Receipts* column and the *Total Payment* column.

9) Total the *Receipts* column.

10) Write this under the ruled line.

11) Add the total of the *Total Payment* column to the *Balance b/d*.

12) Write it under the ruled line.

13) The figures in 10 and 12 should be the same.
- If they are, draw a double line across these two columns.
- If they are not, there has been an error. The amount left in the cash box is not that which should be there according to the entries. Try

   a) checking the cash in the box and

   b) checking your arithmetic.

If there is still a problem, it will probably be necessary to examine the vouchers and check them against the entries.

5.2 Restoring the Imprest

1) Take the petty cash vouchers to the cashier as proof of money spent.

2) Obtain cash to the value of the *Total Payments* made.

3) In the petty cash book enter
- date of next day of business
- under Details 'balance b/d'
  in Receipts column the amount which was in the petty cash box
- under Details 'To cash'
  in Receipts column sum reimbursed by the cashier.

The petty cash book is now ready for the next week's entries.

Quotations

Explanation of the process of requesting and preparing a quotation

Preliminary reading

The first time you use this entry on Quotations, you should begin by reading *Quotations – the process.*

Contents

1. Requesting a quotation

1.1 Quotations – the process

Finding what things will cost

When a customer – either an individual, or a firm – is considering making a purchase, they will frequently begin by making enquiries about how much it will cost to supply the goods. The customer will first want to get a rough idea of the outlay which will be required, and will then look for the best bargain. The latter may be the lowest price, or it may be the best 'package'. For example, a company which charges more may nevertheless be a better buy because they offer some other advantage, such as after sales service.

The first step is to ask for an estimate or a quotation. This may be done over the phone in the first instance, but this is frequently followed by a *letter of enquiry*. This is both more convenient with enquiries that are at all complicated, and ensures that there is a record of what the enquiry was and when it was made. How to write a letter of enquiry is explained in *Letter of enquiry*, page 228.

Estimates and quotations

An *estimate* may be given in writing or by word of mouth ('verbally'). It is a *rough guide as to how much the work will cost*, so that the customer can see whether the price is reasonable, competitive, and affordable. For example, an experienced small builder might estimate the cost of a proposed extension to a house at £5 000. This does not commit the builder to providing the extension for exactly that sum, but gives the enquirer an idea as to whether the amount is within his or her means.

If the enquirer is still interested, he or she will then ask for a *quotation*. At that point the builder would calculate in detail, the cost of materials, labour etc. so as to arrive at a *precise figure for which the work could be done*. In the case of the house extension it might be, say, £5 275 (ie the estimate was too low). The customer then decides whether to enter into a contract with the builder. A range of conditions may then apply. One to be considered would be whether the quotation would be the guaranteed cost, or whether the builder could change it, in the light of new circumstances, eg a rise in the price of materials.

A quotation may be given in writing or verbally, but in jobs of any complexity, a written statement of how the quotation is arrived at is usually required. A quotation *lists in detail* what factors are taken into account. It is also *usually a fixed price*; a customer will normally request this, since he or she will wish to know exactly how much they are going to have to pay out. However, this can be a cause of difficulty to the person or firm giving the quotation, since to underestimate will mean that the business will lose money. On the other hand, to quote too high may well mean that the customer goes elsewhere.

Quoting for goods and services

GOODS   When the supplier is selling goods, various factors will be taken into account:

    a)   the cost per unit (eg per box of light bulbs, per pound of sugar)

    b)   the total cost of all that has been ordered

    c)   any additional charges (notably terms of business (see page 232) and Value Added Tax (see *Value added tax*, page 251)).

    d)   any reductions in cost (usually discount, see page 233).

SERVICES   In the scenario used in this book, Eve Adams is often not selling goods, but is doing work for someone, such as mowing a lawn, or planting a rose bed. She is therefore not selling an article at a fixed price, as she would if she were selling cakes in a cake shop. She is selling a service, which involves costing, but for which there is no set price. If your task or assignment involves quoting for a service to be supplied, you should therefore read the entry on *Costing*, page 230.

Preparing the quotation

The detailed steps on how to prepare a quotation are given separately, in *Preparing a quotation*, page 234, but basically what happens is that a company of any reasonable size will have a catalogue or at least a price list. The task of the employee making out the quotations will thus be to extract information from a catalogue, so as to give a quotation for goods.

A quotation which is quite simple (say, just a couple of items) may well be incorporated into a letter, replying to the enquiry. When there is a lot of detail, the supplier may well put the quotation onto a special form, and send with it a covering letter (for how to write this see *Covering letter*, page 237).

Quotation or order?

It is important to be clear that when a customer asks for and a supplier gives a quotation, this means

1) that the figure gives in detail the cost of the required goods, but

2) the customer has *not yet placed an order*.

Quotations are not binding commitments on either side – indeed many quotations have 'let-out clauses' to protect the supplier against various types of risk. The firm commitment to buy will come when the customer sends in a completed order form (see *Orders: order form*, page 212).

In some cases the quotation may contain a warning that the price quoted may be altered after the order has been placed, in the light of a change of circumstances. (This is regularly done in the travel industry, where air fuel may be subject to sharp and unexpected increases in cost).

From the employee's point of view, the good thing is that much of a quotation merely contains the same information which has been received, with prices added. This makes the work easy – but it also means that the writer of the quotation can become inattentive and make mistakes in copying. For a summary of the similarities between quotations and orders see *Invoices: similarities between documents*, page 164).

1.2 Letter of enquiry, requesting a quotation

Suggested method for writing the letter

1) **Map out on rough paper the layout of the letter**
   This will be a standard business letter, and can use standard phrases. If you are uncertain about these topics turn to the entries headed *Letters*, page 195.

2) **Make notes of what points are to be made**
   You may wish to know or state:
   - ❏ *details of the goods* (what type, quality are available)
   - ❏ *number or amount required*
   - ❏ the *price* (per unit, and in total)
   - ❏ when the goods can be *delivered*

   Also you often need to know:
   - ❏ if any *taxation* (notably VAT) is to be added
   - ❏ whether the supplier can offer a *discount* (a reduction in price)

3) **Decide what order these points go in**

4) **Arrange the data systematically.** One possibility is:

Number of items	type of item	details of item	comments
20	switch fuses	20 amp, metal clad	British Standard

5) **Work out how you will say what you want**
Are there any standard phrases?

6) **Check your spelling and punctuation**

7) **Make your fair copy**

8) **Check spelling and punctuation again**

Example

STAR ☆ Minimarket

Middle Lane
Hoxted

VAT Reg. No.: 129 44053   © 0191 23456

```
Kutkash
Highworth Way
Codlington

20 March 1991

Our ref: ABC 123

Dear Sirs,

Please send me a quotation for the supply of the following:

24 packets tea bags (80 bags per packet)
80 packets cornflakes
36 1 litre washing up liquid
24 jars tomato sauce
36 cans lemonade
20 tomato and cheese pizza
108 packets beefburgers (packets of 4)
72 packets cod fish fingers (packts of 10)
28 packets streaky bacon
36 cans cola
20 steak and kidney pies

Could you at the same time please inform me of any discount
offered, as well as the terms of delivery, including your normal
day of delivery in this area.

Yours faithfully,

J Smith

J Smith,
Manager.
```

1.3 Costing

What is costing?

The person in business has to decide how much to charge the customer. This charge will be the cost of an article ('goods') or the price of work done. We refer to the latter as the service performed. To decide what the charge should be, it is necessary to *cost* the goods or service. At all levels of business, costing is one of the most important and complicated tasks.

Costing is normally done by management in large firms, and not by the financial record keeper. But it makes the work more meaningful and interesting if you understand why certain charges are being added. Also, this work is the detail which provides the data which is summarised in the profit and loss account (see *Final accounts: the profit and loss account*, page 150).

Costing of goods

Consider first the costing of goods – for example, the groceries mentioned in *Letter of enquiry*, page 228.

There are some obvious things to be taken into account: the *purchase price* of, say, cornflakes, to the supplier, and the *profit* which the supplier adds on. But a little thought will show that the supplier has in fact spent more than just the price paid for the cornflakes.

1) There is *handling*. Someone has to receive the cornflakes when they arrive, put them where they are to be stored, move them when they are to be sent out, and possibly package them. These workers will receive wages.

2) There is *record keeping and administration*. Someone has to keep a record that the goods have been ordered and paid for by the supplier, and then that they have been ordered, sent, an invoice sent out, and payment received from the customer (for details of these operations see *Orders*, page 211 and *Invoices*, page 161). These employees, too, will have to be paid, and their materials and equipment (paper, possibly a computer) will have to be bought.

3) Someone needs to note how much of each article the supplier has in stock, and whether new supplies are needed to meet customer demand. This is called *stock control* and is dealt with in the entry *Stock control and valuation*, page 238. Here is another source of wages and of payments for materials.

4) There are *premises* involved. The goods must be kept somewhere, such as a warehouse, and those keeping the records will need an office to work in. The premises may be bought or rented. They will certainly need heating and lighting. There may well be a need for security.

5) Finally the goods have to be moved to the customer. Many firms (for example mail order companies) could not run without some system of *delivery*, either by their own vehicles, by a carrier, or through the postal system.

6) On certain goods, in certain situations, *Value Added Tax* (see page 251) will have to be added. Though this may well be refunded, a record has to be kept.

All the above things cost money, which has to be accounted for in working out the profit and loss of a business (see page 150). Items 1 to 6 are all part of the *expenses* which will be included in drawing up such an account. There are various ways of dealing with these costs, but one of them is to include a suitable proportion of the costs to each article sold. Only then can a decision be made about how much to add as profit.

Costing of services – the Eve Adams scenario

Eve Adams begins by offering gardening services; only later does she begin to sell goods as well. However, she has to consider similar factors to those listed above in deciding what her charges should be.

When Eve starts out, it is not obvious that this is so. She does not have to handle goods, though she does have to spend time administering her accounts. This is time she has to spend on her business, which she can't spend earning, but which she still has to find. In reality she will probably just add it to her working day.

She will keep small amounts of stock (fertiliser etc) at first, so she doesn't need a system of stock control. And in the early days she can probably keep her equipment in her own garden shed. She certainly won't be earning enough to be liable for VAT.

These matters will change, though, if she starts to do a large volume of business, and certainly when she takes on an employee (whose wages must also be found).

But even in the earliest days there are matters which Eve must think about. If she lays out money in order to do the job, but doesn't add it to the bill, she is really paying to do the work, and earning less than she thinks. These are her *expenses*, which she must take account of.

Some things which Eve will always or sometimes have to pay for to do a day's work are as follows.

Always

1) Travel to and from the work

2) Have lunch (will she need to go out for lunch?)

3) Charge for her time. She will therefore need to decide how long the work is likely to take.

Sometimes

1) Buy or replace tools

2) Buy necessary items which are disposable or used up, such as rubbish bags or fertiliser

3) Buy plants or other garden equipment, to be left with the customer

    The latter will involve:

    a) spending time and money choosing and buying those things

    b) the cost of delivering them

Costing and giving a quotation

Note that when someone is selling a service, which is costed as described above, there is no set price. Some of the expenses described involve financial questions which will be dealt with elsewhere in this course, for example under *Wages*, page 266. Some are questions of accountancy, and are beyond the scope of this book.

As an example, a customer will not be prepared to buy Eve the equipment assumed to do the job – she will be expected to have the tools she needs. Yet Eve will in fact have to lay out the money. And again, the customer can hardly be expected to add the cost of a slap-up lunch with wine to the bill – he or she is paying for the work done in the garden. Yet Eve will need to eat.

In real life, Eve Adams will need to consider other factors, too, in arriving at her final quotation. If she names too low a price, she may fail to make a profit; but too high a figure may mean that the prospective customer will go elsewhere. She will certainly be advised to to go and look over a garden (or other place of work) before she names her price – perhaps first in the form of an estimate (see earlier). Though to do this will cost her time and money, it will make her costing more accurate, and she is likely to be better off in the long run.

2. Terms of business

2.1 Introduction

Parties involved in sales

The phrase 'terms of business' refers to various aspects of a sale, which both sides need to agree upon and be clear about. It is therefore important to be clear who is involved in such dealings.

There are typically four sets of people involved in the manufacture and sale of goods. These are:

- the *manufacturer*, who actually makes the goods (for example, lawnmowers, or refined sugar)
- the *wholesaler*, who buys the goods from the manufacturer and sells and distributes them to the retailer (for instance, dealers in garden equipment, or groceries)
- the *retailer*, who buys goods from the wholesaler and sells them to the general public (for example a local garden centre, or grocery shop)
- the *customer*, the ordinary person, or the business which is actually going to use the goods (in the case of Eve Adams' business, buying a lawnmower, or Eve herself, buying a pound of sugar).

Note that businesses often deal directly with the wholesaler, as the prices are frequently very attractive. Eve might well do this in buying supplies for her business.

At each stage, one side is the *supplier* and the other, the *purchaser*.

Matters covered by 'terms of business'

The aspects of sales which the phrase 'terms of business' refers to are:

a) who is responsible for paying for the delivery of the goods (the 'terms of delivery')

b) when and how payment is due (the 'terms of payment')

c) discounts

d) taxation.

At the present time, the latter refers to VAT (see *Value added tax*, page 251). It will not therefore be dealt with in this entry.

2.2 Terms of delivery

The 'terms of business' include the 'terms of delivery'.

Both sides need to agree how the delivery is to be paid for. The options are:

supplier pays in full	known as	**carriage paid**
customer pays in full		**ex works or**
		ex warehouse
		(according to the type of goods involved)
customer pays part		**free on rail**
		(the commonest option)

The latter term means that the supplier transports the goods free to the nearest railway station, after which the cost is borne by the customer.

2.3 Terms of payment

The two parties in a sale also need to agree when and how goods are to be paid for. The options are:

☐   at the time of placing the order   known as   **cash with order**
                                                  (usually shortened to CWO)

☐   at the time of delivery   known as   **cash on delivery**
                                                  (usually shortened to COD)

☐   later, at the end of a set period, by   (see *Invoices: customer accounts*, page 166).
      using a customer account

2.4 Discount

The terms of business commonly include a statement of discount offered. *A discount is a reduction in price, usually stated in the form of a percentage of that price.*

Types of discount

Discounts are used as an incentive to the purchaser in various circumstances:

1)   to encourage purchasers when trade is poor or the goods are moving slowly

2)   for bulk purchases (known as *quantity discount*)

     Suppliers are keen to encourage purchasers to buy large quantities, as this means that they recover quickly the money which they have laid out on goods.

3)   for regular customers (known as *customer discount*)

     Regular customers are very important to a business, as they help to keep the volume of business done and the cashflow (movement of money in and out of the business) more stable. Regular customers ensure that there are less likely to be periods when no money is coming in, while overheads (such as rent) still have to be paid. To encourage customers to keep coming back, a discount may be given.

4)   to members of the trade (known as *trade discount*). One example is the 'educational discount' given to schools and similar institutions on educational books and supplies.

     Another common situation is when a wholesaler offers goods to the retail trade at a substantially lower price than the retail price, so as to allow the retailer to make a profit. For example, a video costing £10 in a shop, may well be bought in at half that price (that is, the trade discount is 50%).

5)   to encourage prompt payment (known as *cash discount*)

     This is perhaps the commonest form of discount. There is a major problem for many companies, especially during an economic recession, in ensuring that they receive quickly any money owed to them. To encourage prompt payment many firms will offer a discount for payment within a set time (typically within a fortnight or a month). A cash discount is used to encourage customers not to request credit over a long period on their customer account.

Retailers, too, frequently offer a cash discount for similar reasons. Many small businesses will make a substantial reduction for a cash payment. For instance, a person who is buying a refrigerator will often seek to do so by means of a credit agreement, under which repayment will take months, or even years. To offer to pay in cash in return for a discount (and so complete the payment at once) will very often bring about a reduction in price of 10%.

Note that a cash discount does not mean that the buyer must produce banknotes. Payment by cheque is perfectly acceptable, since the process of clearance (see *Banking facilities: clearance of cheques*, page 100) will mean that the money is received by the supplier within a few days.

If you are still uncertain about the meaning of the terms 'cash' and 'credit', read the entry *Accounts: Credit and debit*, page 73.

How discount is indicated in documents

A discount which is being offered may be described in a full sentence, for example in a letter accompanying a quotation. Very often (for instance, on an invoice) it is expressed through an abbreviation such as

`Terms: 5%, 14 days, otherwise net.`

This means that a discount of 5% will be allowed, if payment is made within 14 days. Otherwise the figure owed is net, that is, there will be no reduction.

Calculation of discount

Example
Hinstone Garden Centre gives a discount to members of the trade of 5% for purchases totalling over £20. Eve Adams buys compost and a spade costing £24.00. What will she pay?

	£
Cost of goods	24.00
Discount (5%)	1.20
Balance to pay	22.80

If you are unsure how this discount was arrived at, you should read the entry on percentages (*Calculations: percentages*, page113).

3. Preparing a quotation

3.1 Preparation

Preparing the information

1) List the *items* requested and look them up in the *catalogue*.

2) Note any items which are *out of stock*.

3) Calculate the *cost of an order*:

   a) write down *cost per item*

   b) calculate *cost of each batch*

   c) calculate *total cost* of proposed order.

4) Decide whether *VAT* is payable or whether the quotation will be VAT exclusive. (Your employer will normally have provided you with the answer to this question.)

5) *Calculate VAT.*

   Important note: VAT is calculated on the total **before** discount is given.

6) Calculate

   a) what the *discount* (if any) will be

   b) the *sum due* would be with such a discount.

7) Make a note of any *terms of delivery*.

Note: If you are in doubt about:

5)   refer to the entry *Value added tax*, page 251.

6)   refer to *Discount*, page 233.

7)   refer to the entry *Terms of delivery*, page 232.

Planning the letter

1)   Decide whether the quotation can be included in a *short letter*, or whether you will need a *separate quotation*, with an accompanying letter. (In many companies there may be a set procedure for this matter).

2)   *Plan the letter*. Put the information into a suitable order. Use standard business layout, and suitable standard phrases.

3)   *Writing out the quotation*

   a)   List items according to format of catalogue entry

   b)   Give

   ❑   number of units

   ❑   item

   ❑   cost per item

   ❑   cost of each batch

   ❑   subtotal cost of proposed order

   ❑   include VAT information (if any) (for details see *Value added tax*, page 251)

   ❑   discount

   ❑   sometimes the quotation will make clear the total cost after discount.

A possible layout is as follows:

Quantity	Item	Unit Price	Total
......			
Total			
Discount (2%, 30 days)			

Sometimes there is also:

Total (after discount)			£206.43

Write to the customer

Bear in mind that it makes for good relations not just to give the information, but to present it in a simple but courteous framework.

If you are in doubt about planning the letter refer to the entries *Letters: layout*, page 197, and *Useful phrases*, page 198.

3.2 Quotation – an example

This is the sort of quotation which might be sent in response to the letter of enquiry given earlier (see page 229).

KUTKASH

HIGHWORTH WAY CODLINGTON C02 1ZZ
TEL: 0201 82641   FAX: 0201 01210

QUOTATION for supply of goods to: Star Minimarket
                                                     Middle Lane
                                                        Hoxted

Quantity	Item	Unit	Price	Total
28	streaky bacon	(4)	2.06	14.42
24	(80) tea bags	(6)	3.42	13.68
80	cornflakes	(10)	5.99	47.92
24	tomato sauce	(12)	4.05	8.10
36	1 ltr washing up liquid	(12)	3.15	9.45
36	(250ml) cola	(12)	1.45	4.35
36	(250ml) lemonade	(12)	1.45	4.35
20	steak and kidney pies	(5)	3.60	14.40
20	tomato and cheese pizza	(4)	0.75	3.75
108	(4) beefburgers	(12)	6.30	56.70
72	(10) cod fish fingers	(12)	6.48	38.88

TOTAL   216.00

DISCOUNT for cash, 30 days: $7\frac{1}{2}$%

Carriage paid

VAT Reg. No. 130 774106

Notes:

1) You should be clear what the pattern of the entries means. For example

      108   (4) beefburgers   (12)   6.30   56.70

means that the customer will receive 108 packets of beefburgers. As requested, these are sold in packets containing 4 beefburgers each. However, wholesalers do not tend to deal in single items, but in bulk purchases, and minimum quantities. The smallest amount you can buy is known as the *unit*. For example, Sainsbury's do not sell single cans of lager: the pack of 4 is their unit of sale. In this case the unit in which beefburgers are sold is boxes of twelve packs, each containing 4 beefburgers. This means that 1 unit = 12 packs = 48 beefburgers. Since the customer wants 108 single packs, he or she will have to buy 9 units.

This supplier listed the quantity as specified by the *customer*. Many suppliers would, however, have listed the quotation as seen by *them*, that is, the quantity column would show 9 (9 units in which the unit is a pack of 12 is 108 single packets).

Note that the prices will seem low to you, compared with your local shop. This is because the quotation is for the retailer's buying-in price, not the price to the public, which includes profit.

2) The quotation includes the statement of discount offered (how this is arrived at is explained in the firm's covering letter (see page 237). Note that it does not state the sum, or subtract it from the total. Quotations are frequently made in this way for the following reasons:

a) Discount is normally entered into accounts as a separate entry.

b) Customers who have an account with a supplier (see *Invoices: customer accounts*, page 166) will not need to settle a particular bill immediately, and so do not need a figure to write onto a cheque.

3.3 Covering letter sent with quotation

Contents

1) Should follow the standard layout of a business letter.

2) Must state that 'a quotation is enclosed'.

3) Other topics which might be included are:

    a) discount for cash and for new customer

    b) enclose a copy of the firm's catalogue

Example

KUTKASH

HIGHWORTH WAY CODLINGTON C02 1ZZ
TEL: 0201 82641   FAX: 0201 01210

Your ref: ABC 123
Our ref: DEF 678
Mr J. Smith
Star Minimarket
Middle Lane
Hoxted
21 March 1991
Dear Mr Smith,

Thank you for your letter of 20th March. We have pleasure in enclosing a quotation as requested.

Please note that we offer a 5 percent discount to all customers who settle their accounts in cash within one month. In addition we are also able on this occasion to offer you a $2\frac{1}{2}$ per cent discount as a new customer.

Please note also that the order will be delivered carriage paid for routine deliveries. Our normal day of delivery in the Hoxted area is Wednesday.

We look forward to receiving your order, together with an indication of your preference as to date of payment. We hope that you will find our prices attractive, and look forward to enjoying your future custom. We enclose a copy of our catalogue for your inspection.

Yours sincerely,

A Johnson

A Johnson,
Manager

VAT Reg. No. 130 774106

Stock control and valuation

Methods of recording the movement of stock, and of valuing stock

Contents

1. The physical factors

Stock is the term we use to refer to physical goods actually possessed by a business, which are intended to be sold or re-sold. A moment's thought will show that there are a vast variety of things which count as stock: cylinder heads and chocolate bars, sides of beef and staplers – these only begin the list. Clearly, too, the problems of moving and storing stock would fill many books.

Stock is needed at all stages of the production and marketing process. This fact leads accountants to classify stock under various headings.

1) First there are *raw materials* from which goods will be manufactured. Examples are wood for furniture and cocoa for chocolate.

2) Next the raw materials are turned into *finished products* – the furniture and the chocolate.

3) Finished products are made by manufacturers. There will then need to be a stage at which retailers become involved. Their stocks are *goods for resale*.

4) Finally, some businesses (for example, certain motor vehicle dealers) will keep goods which are sold as *spare parts*.

5) It is important at times in accounting also to have a classification of stocks as being a part of *work in progress*. An example would be whisky, which can take ten or more years to mature. After distillation it is no longer 'raw materials', yet nor is it a finished product.

238

Some businesses will be involved with (and so hold stocks for) all these phases; others may only be involved in one of them.

The term 'stock' is also used to refer to items which are used up over a fairly short period, but which are not part of the goods which the firm sells. A good example is the stationery used by the office. The fact that such goods are not intended for resale becomes important when a valuation is being made.

From the point of view of keeping accounts, it is important that the movement of all stock is accurately recorded, since it is all part of the *assets* of a business. It is also important that an accurate calculation of the value of the stock is made at appropriate times.

However, the recording of the purchase, sale or replacement of stock is handled by different parts of the accounts system. Stock bought or sold as a direct contribution to the firm's trading (eg stationery bought for resale) is part of the sales and purchases documentation. By contrast, stationery bought for administrative purposes is recorded in the expense accounts. These matters are explained in *Ledgers and journals*, page 177.

2. Recording the movement of stock

In reality, the recording of stock movements is increasingly done by computer. This is described in *Computerisation*, page 131. However, as with other forms of record keeping, the principles remain much the same as when things were done manually. The process and documents needed are therefore described as though they were kept on paper, and by hand.

2.1 Stock record cards

The existence and movement of stock is recorded on *stock record cards*. A typical card is shown overleaf.

The entries which must be made are:

1) **Stock description** – this is the *type of item*, eg bed, bunk bed, double bed

2) **Unit –** *stock is issued or sold in units*
   These vary greatly: beds come in single units, photocopying paper is regularly sold in packs of 500 sheets.

3) **Ref –** *the reference code or number*
   This can be vital when dealing, say, with a wide range spares for cars, the nature of which may not be obvious to the warehouse staff. This code or number is most usually the catalogue number of the item.

   Catalogues frequently adopt a coding system, to make things easier. For examples, suppose your firm sells stationery. Among your stock will be envelopes. Now a person making an order could be careful to ensure that they wanted white rather than buff, to hold A4 unfolded rather than folded, and without windows rather than with. But miss out any of these characteristics and the order might not be clear. Miss out the colour and you might receive buff envelopes rather than white. It is more efficient to have a unique code for each type of item.

STOCK RECORD CARD					

Description envelopes, brown manilla, plain 90mm x 150mm

Unit box 1000   Min level 3 boxes

Ref SE1424   Max level 15 boxes

Location E4/24   Re-order level 5 boxes

Date	Received		Issued		Balance
	Ref	quantity	Ref	quantity	
1 Jun					12
7 Jun			AB189	3	9
15 Jun			AB197	5	4
17 Jun			AB204	1	3
23 June	SP1124	5			8

4) **Location –** *where the stock is kept*
There will some system of coding, for instance to identify shelves, cupboards or drawers. In a warehouse of any size this is crucial if the stock is to be found quickly (or at all!)

5) **Min level –** *the minimum number of units to be kept in stock*
If stocks run out, the result can mean anything from slight inconvenience to the loss of major orders. Management will therefore take a decision on how low the stock can get before there is a problem. This point is the minimum level. It will be one of the duties of the store or warehouse keeper to check regularly whether this point has been reached.

6) **Re-order level –** *the number of units in stock at which a new order to the supplier should be placed*
This will tend to be higher than the minimum level, because the replacement of stock is not necessarily something which can be done immediately. For this reason the re-order level is calculated by *adding to the minimum level the amount of stock which will be needed over the period between ordering new stock and its arrival.*

7) **Max level –** *the maximum number of units to be kept in stock*
Just as the business cannot afford to let stocks get too low, it is equally important not to have too much stock on hand. A management decision has to be made about the rate at which stocks will be used or sold. Holding stocks uses up space, and ties up money, which is not brought back into the business until the goods are sold. With some goods there are also very serious problems of the deterioration of the stock, or of it becoming much less saleable, because of changes in fashion.

8) **(Re-order) quantity –** *the number of units to be be requested when re-ordering*
This will be decided by management or buyers in the light of the maximum level and the predicted rate at which stocks will be issued or sold. It will be necessary to strike a balance between letting stocks run too low, and keeping too much stock in hand.

9) **Date –** *the date of the receipt or issue of goods*

10) **Received –** *the columns for recording the receipt of goods*

11) **(Received) Ref –** *reference number of the purchase order* (see *Orders*, page 211).
This links the physical arrival of the goods into the whole recording process, including the order form, delivery note, and invoice.

12) (Received) **quantity** – *the number of units of goods received*

13) (Issued) **Ref** – *reference of requisition order* (see next section)

14) (Issued) **quantity** – *number of units issued*

15) **Balance** – *the number of goods which are currently in stock*, according to the records

Since the stock record card refers only to a single type of item in the stocks, it is possible to keep a note of how many units are in stock. to achieve this, the person filling in the card will need to update this number by

❏ adding the number of goods received to the previous balance

❏ subtracting the number of goods issued from the previous balance.

This type of procedure is known as *keeping a running balance*.

Notes on the record card entries:

When this card was started, on 1 June, there were 12 units in stock. Requisitions (see below) on 7 and 15 June took the stocks below the re-order level, and an order was placed.

A requisition on 17 June could be met, because it did not go below the minimum level. On 23 June new stocks arrived, in response to purchase order SP1124. Note that at this rate of usage, stocks are likely to hover constantly around the re-order level. It would probably make sense for the number to be increased, say, to 10 units.

2.2 Stores requisitions

On 7 June the storekeeper entered the following on the record card reproduced on page 240.

7 Jun	AB189	3	9

This was in response to the arrival of the following *stores requisition*:

STORES REQUISITION		No. AB 189
From: Sales Dept		
To: General Admin		

Quantity	Details	Ref
3 boxes (1000)	plain brown manila envelopes	SE1424

Signed: *H Green* Date: 6 June 1991

The whole process was as follows.

Hazel Green in the Sales Department was organising the mailing of prospective customers. She decided that at least 2200 envelopes would be needed. She therefore filled in a stores requisition form giving:

1) the *reference number*

2) her *department*

3) the *quantity* (number of boxes of 1000 envelopes) required

4) the *item required*

5) the *reference number or code of the item,* as given in the supplier's catalogue or the firm's own stock catalogue

6) her *signature*

7) the *date*

8) the *department* responsible for approving and organising such supplies (in this company, General Administration

From them the stores requisition was sent to the storekeeper, who arranged for the issue and entered it as seen earlier on the appropriate stock record card. At this stage the requisition is 'cancelled', often by drawing a line through it. A rubber stamp could also be used.

3. Stock valuation

3.1 What it is

It will be noticed that the first part of the entry does not mention prices. Stock control is concerned only with the physical movement of stock in, out of or within the business. It is not concerned with the buying and selling process, nor with the keeping of accounts.

The actual buying in of goods will be a matter for the purchases department, and the sale of goods that of the sales department.

The accounts department, by contrast, are not concerned with the physical storage and movement of goods, but only with their value. In particular, the firm's accountant needs to know the total value of the stock at the beginning and end of the accounting period, which is usually one year (see *Final accounts*, page 147).

This is achieved by *stock taking.* The stock records are consulted, but staff will also physically count and check what stock there is. This process also acts as a check against error in the records, and against theft or damage.

3.2 Basic calculation

The process of valuation is quite straightforward in principle. Each *type of item* is noted, together with the *number of units* and the *purchase price.* An example in a wine merchant's might be Riesling, 18 cases (12 bottles per case) plus 4 uncased bottles, cost 1.78 per bottle. The value of the Riesling would then be

> **number of units x purchase price**

> **[(18 x 12) + 4] x 1.78 = £391.60**

3.3 Complicating factors

As with so many things, however, the real process is not quite so simple. For despite the fact that the business has laid out a definite cost price, which normally they would wish to get back, with a profit added, this is not always possible. Common reasons are:

❐ deterioration of stock (food nearing sell-by date, rusting of machinery)

❐ changes in the market due to fashion (eg clothes, records) or to recession ('do-it-yourself' products tends to be much more popular when the housing market is buoyant).

On occasion the changes in situation are so acute that it is no longer possible to sell the stock even at cost price, let alone at a profit. The normal principle in such circumstances is:

> **valuation = purchase price** or **selling price**, whichever is lower

This method of valuation is arrived at by applying a fundamental principle of accountancy, that of *prudence*. In this case the principle to be followed is that losses should be accounted for as they are foreseen.

Another factor which has to be taken into account during stock valuation is inflation. If the Riesling did cost £1.78, but now costs £1.98, management has to decide which should be taken as the purchase price. The firm actually paid £1.78 per unit, but to *replace* the wine would now lost 20p more.

4. Valuation – the three common approaches

There are three methods by which businesses commonly value their stock. The choice of which to use will depend on the management's assessment of what is most efficient and in the best interests of the business. The methods are:

1) Average cost system (AVCO)

2) 'First in first out' (FIFO)

3) 'Last in first out' (LIFO)

4.1 Average cost system

The basic principle is that you find an average price per unit. The procedure can be shown by an example:

Date	transaction	unit cost	value of batch	total stock	valuation
2 Jul	buy in 50 bottles red table wine	1.50	75.00	50	75.00
9 Jul	sell 10 bottles	1.50	15.00	40	(40 x 1.50) 60.00
	The price changes				
16 Jul	new delivery 20 bottles	2.00	40.00	60	??

To calculate the new stock valuation:

1) Find *average cost per unit*

2) Multiply by number of *units*.

The formula for calculating the average cost per unit is calculated as

> **value of old stock + value of new stock**
> ───
> **number of items of old stock + number of items of new stock**

In the above case

$$\frac{60.00 + 40.00}{40 + 20} = \frac{100}{60} = £1.66$$

valuation   = items x average cost per unit

                   = 60 x 1.66 = £99.60

4.2 FIFO and LIFO – general points

You may be familiar with these terms if you have studied computing or information technology. In those fields data which is waiting to be handled is treated as though it were in a *stack* or a *queue*.

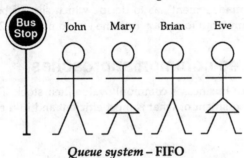

Queue system – FIFO

FIFO stands for 'first in, first out'. This is what happens (or should happen) in a bus queue. John arrives at the stop first, so he gets on the bus first. Eve arrives last, and must therefore wait until last.

Stack – (bricks delivered on June 3rd removed first) – LIFO

LIFO stands for 'last in, first out'. This is made clearer by imagining a stack. Bricks are being delivered to a building site. Delivery 1 goes on the ground. Delivery 2 goes on top of 1, and 3 on top of 2. When bricks are needed, the most convenient bricks are those which came in Delivery 3.

These two systems are frequently applied in stock valuation. Note that the valuation may or may not reflect what actually happens in stock control. For example, in the physical handling of stock, perishable goods are probably best moved according to the FIFO principle. The movement of coal will probably tend to use LIFO.

In stock valuation, however, FIFO, LIFO and AVCO are *methods of accounting*. They are adopted for accountancy purposes, and may not at all reflect the reality of stock movement.

4.3 Calculation by FIFO and LIFO

The same example will be used because accountants will often value stock by all three methods before deciding what system will be adopted in the accounts.

Date	transaction	unit cost	value of batch	total stock	valuation
2 Jul	buy in 50 bottles red table wine	1.50	75.00	50	75.00
9 Jul	sell 10 bottles	1.50	15.00	40	(40 x 1.50) 60.00
The price changes					
16 Jul	new delivery 20 bottles	2.00	40.00	60	??

So far there are no differences from AVCO. However, *to calculate the new stock valuation by FIFO:*

Find the cost of each batch and add them

old stock   40 @ 1.50 =   60.00
new stock   20 @ 2.00 =   40.00
valuation £100.

This is straightforward enough. Where it becomes important to decide whether you are adopting FIFO or LIFO as your method can be shown, by taking the following example.

On 23 July you sell 50 bottles. What purchase price do you assume?

❐   With *FIFO, you use up all old stocks first*, so the order is made up of:

        40 bottles @ 1.50 =   60.00
        10 bottles @ 2.00 =   20.00

Your purchase costs are taken to be £80.

❐   With *LIFO*, you assume that you use up your *new* stocks first, so the order is made up of:

        20 bottles @ 2.00 =   £40.00
        30 bottles @ 1.50 =   £45.00

So your purchase costs are taken as £85.00.

❐   What if you had used *AVCO*?
        Before this sale, the position was

Date	transaction	unit cost	value of batch	total stock	valuation
16 Jul	new delivery 20 bottles	2.00	40.00	60	99.60

Unit cost was £1.66.

So 50 bottles @ £1.66 = £83.00.

245

4.4 Why have different systems?

Two of the final accounts (see *Final accounts*, page 147) are the trading and profit and loss accounts. Basically, these show how well trading is going. An important part of the process of drawing up these accounts is to calculate

$$\text{sales} - \text{cost of sales}$$

so as to arrive at the *gross profit*.

In the example given above, according to which system you adopted, your profit would be

- ❑ FIFO £20
- ❑ LIFO £15
- ❑ AVCO £17

When you start to apply these differences to large numbers, this could make quite a difference to (a) how much the owners of the business could take for themselves and (b) how much tax had to be paid. Then again, which system would you choose if you were trying to sell the business?

Note: The results do not always work out in the same relation as above. For example, LIFO does not necessarily produce the lowest valuation. Other factors, such as the direction in which prices change are relevant. These are outside the scope of this book.

You might think that the obvious thing to do would be to select the system which gives the largest profit. This option looks even more appealing if you think of what it might mean in the stores and at the counter. You buy in bottles at £1.50 and sell them for £1.75. Inflation then means that after a few months your selling price can be raised to £2.00, but you have old stock which was bought in at £1.50. An extra 25p a bottle just like that – instant wealth!

In everyday terms this might make sense. But a business runs from year to year. Meanwhile, inflation has hit the suppliers, too, so they are now charging £1.85, while you are acting as though the old price still held. In such circumstances, your instant profit can easily turn out not even to be sufficient to meet your costs of replacing stock.

As an accountant in the UK you can adopt any system you like for your internal workings, but LIFO is not accepted by the Inland Revenue in the public statement of accounts. Also it is required that your system of valuation should be consistent. You have to choose one and stick to it.

5. Calculating turnover

Another factor which is crucial in making decisions about what to buy is, naturally enough, what is selling. The optimum position would be to buy in supplies at a rate which matched exactly the flow of sales. In this situation there will be a steady *turnover*. Ideally, turnover would be rapid, as the business would then be recouping its outlay on purchases very quickly, as well as adding to its profits. But the rate of stock turnover will vary partly according to the nature of the business. Eggs, being highly perishable, will move quickly; the rate of turnover of pianos will be much slower. But the rate of turnover may be slow too because of trading conditions or because of poor judgement about stock levels by management.

For the above reasons, the management of a business need to have a measure of rate of turnover. This is calculated as follows:

$$\text{Rate of turnover} = \frac{\text{cost of sales}}{\text{average stock}}$$

The *cost of sales* is defined as *opening stock + purchases – closing stock*

The calculation of average stock is made by using the formula:

$$\frac{\text{opening stock} + \text{closing stock}}{2} = \text{average stock}$$

Example

At a garden centre the trading in potted plants began with opening stock which was valued at £962. Closing stock was valued at £648. Purchases during the accounting period were £5620. Then

cost of sales = 962 + 7620 – 648 = £7934

average stock for that period is $\dfrac{962 + 648}{2} = \dfrac{1610}{2} = 805$

rate of turnover = $\dfrac{7934}{805}$ = 9.86 times per year.

This rate can be expressed as the average number of days which it took to sell the stock, by using the formula

$$\frac{365}{\text{rate of turnover}} = \frac{365}{9.86} = 37 \text{ days approx.}$$

This means that the stock turned over in just over a month on average, or, or put another way, it took just over a month to sell stock after it had been purchased.

Texts

How to read and summarise texts dealing with financial business matters

Preliminary reading

The first time you use this entry, you should read *Reading and understanding - basic approach*, below, before consulting other entries.

Contents

---

1. Reading and understanding

1.1 Basic approach

1) *The problem*

   Anyone who has to deal with financial matters has sooner or later to read information about the subject. This may be come in the form of a reference book, or it may be a leaflet, for example dealing with taxation.

   Many people find difficulties in reading such material at first. There are often two reasons for this:

   ☐ lack of a suitable method or approach

   ☐ Lack of understanding of what causes the difficulty

2) *Basic approach to financial texts*

   Until they come to study this or any other technical subject, many people have only had to read simple documents, newspapers, or novels. They are therefore used to material which is carefully written so that it can be understood quickly, allowing the reader to read on without stopping or going back over the text.

   Technical books are different. They contain a lot of information, much of which is there for reference. They also contain complicated ideas, and need to be studied. The reader must therefore expect to have to do three things:

   ☐ go back over what has been read

   ☐ sift out what is important for the immediate purpose

   ☐ study and think about what is left.

   To help you do this, the next two sections suggest methods for approaching financial texts. If you find a text which does not respond to these approaches, it may be that the difficulty is *not in your method, but in the text itself*. In that case you should read section 1.4.

1.2 Technique I – skimming and sifting

One method of approaching a text is 'sifting and skimming'. You read the text quickly to identify what matters to you, and eliminate the rest, before you try to read the text more carefully.

Method

❏ Read through the text quickly

❏ As you read: tick any points to which you can definitely answer 'yes';

  cross out any points which don't apply;

  put a cross against points to which the answer is 'no';

  put a question mark against points to which you don't know the answer.

❏ Put aside the text, and to try to think of four or five things which the text deals with

❏ Expand those points, so that you have four or five main points with a few details about each.

1.3 Technique II – close reading

At a certain point it will be necessary to study the text more carefully: this is known as close reading. You have cut out the irrelevant material, but you still have to understand what is left.

1) *Structure of texts*

In order to get at what a text means it helps to understand how a piece of writing is constructed. Technical texts are carefully put together, as are machines or pieces of furniture: they have a structure.

Usually, a writer makes a series of short points, usually of a sentence or so apiece. These short points will concern one topic. Each topic lasts for a paragraph, which is normally about four or five sentences long. All the topics will be about one main subject, which is usually summed up in the title.

What you are looking for, then, are:

❏ the *topic* of the text

❏ the *main points* of the text (usually four or five)

❏ the *topics of each paragraph*

❏ the *'questions'* which the sentences are answering.

What you end up with is a set of structured notes, which is often what the writer works from when creating the text.

2) *'Signposts'*

Good writers of technical material help their readers. They do this by being logical and systematic about paragraphing. Often they indicate in an introductory paragraph what is to be said next. This is often brought together at the end of the chapter in a summary. Get into the habit of looking for these first – it can save a lot of work!

A good technical writer will also indicate how many points are to be made, and then head them with words such as 'first', 'second', or even number (tabulate) them. The writer will also indicate when different sides of an argument are being put, but using words such as 'however', 'a contrasting view is...' and so on. Watch for these: they can help you to see clearly what you are supposed to get from the text.

1.4 Sources of difficulty

Even if you have studied a text carefully, you will still sometimes find that it is very hard to read. It is important to remember that sometimes the problem is not in you, the reader, but in the text itself. There are various common sources of difficulty in a piece of writing. The main ones are:

1) The reader does not understand the words used (the *vocabulary*)

2) The reader is confused by the way the words are put together (the *sentence structure*)

3) The reader finds it hard to distinguish

❐ *background information* from

❐ *main points.*

Note that when point 3) is a problem, it is often the fault of the writer, who has not given a clear indication of what is important – that is, has not used 'signposts' (see entry 1.3 above).

In order to deal with the two main sources of difficulty – the words (vocabulary) and the way they are put together (sentence structure), try the following approach.

❐ Underline all words *which you do not understand*

❐ Of the words which are underlined, *start with those which are familiar*

❐ Try to *work out* what the *familiar words* might mean

❐ *Break down difficult groups* of words in the same way

❐ Identify words which seem to *involve knowledge that you don't have*

❐ Decide *where you will get this knowledge*

Value added tax (VAT)

Information about the basic structure and workings of VAT, together with guidance on how to deal with VAT invoices, VAT accounts, and the VAT return

Contents

1. Outline of the system

1.1 Who is involved?

'VAT' stands for 'value added tax'. It is a tax which is applied by the Government to most business transactions in the UK.

VAT is a form of indirect taxation. This means that people do not pay the tax directly to the Government. Instead, they pay it as part of the purchase price on goods or services which are subject to VAT (not all are). The VAT is then collected for the government from businesses by the Customs and Excise Department. This situation stands in contrast to direct taxation, which the individual pays directly to the Government. The most well known example is Income Tax, which is collected for the Government from individuals by the Department of Inland Revenue.

When dealing with VAT the term 'business' refers to a very wide range of activities. The sale of new or used goods, the hire of goods, services provided for payment (for example accountancy) and the charging of admission (for example to theatres) all count as business.

1.2. Taxable supplies

However, not all activities within a firm are liable for VAT. The types of transaction which interest the VAT authorities are known as *supplies*. The use of this word may at first be a little confusing, because in everyday language we think of supplies as being something concrete – something we can see and carry away. This clearly isn't true, for example, of an accountant who is interpreting a point of tax legislation. Yet the provision of such a service counts as 'supplies' for VAT purposes.

Not all 'supplies' (transactions) are liable for VAT. Those which are not are known as *exempt supplies*. In contrast, those which are liable for VAT are called *taxable supplies*.

Exempt supplies

The range of exempt supplies is interesting but does not always fit an obvious pattern. It is easy to see why, for example, medical services and various educational services do not have tax added. But why insurance, the provision of credit, or membership benefits of unions should be exempt is less clear. Even more baffling is the fact that betting, gaming and lotteries are exempt, but charges for admission to Bingo and takings from gaming machines are not. No employee can be expected to know all the answers. The only advice which can be given is

1)   consult the works of reference provided by the Customs and Excise; and

2)   call in an accountant.

1.3 Rate of VAT

At any given time, the VAT which the government requires is calculated at a given *rate*. The rate is stated and worked out as a percentage of the cost of the supplies. The main rate set by the government is called the *standard rate*. This can vary according to Government policy. At the rate of $17\frac{1}{2}\%$ set in 1991, the buyer must pay a further $17\frac{1}{2}$ pence on every pound of the purchase price.

The other rate is the *zero rate*; this means that no extra charge is laid upon the customer. It may seem strange to talk about a tax which involves no payments. The reasons for this situation is made clear below.

Zero-rating

The public sometimes have strong feelings about what should be subject to tax, and wise governments try to take note of this – at least at election times. This situation explains the existence of a zero rate.

Examples of zero-rated supplies include: books and newspapers; dispensing of medical prescriptions, and young children's clothing and footwear. One can see why the latter two, especially, are in this class. The burden of prescriptions usually comes at a time which is difficult. The cost of children's clothing, too, is already very high in comparison to the incomes of many parents, so that a further increase in cost would be very unacceptable.

1.4 Taxable turnover

Not everyone who is in business is liable for VAT. Whether you are liable or not depends on the level of your *taxable turnover*. Taxable turnover is the total value of all your taxable supplies. Note that it is the *full value* of those supplies which is taken into account, and not just the *profit* on them, unlike, say the Inland Revenue taxes on the earnings of individuals and businesses.

Once your taxable turnover reaches a certain level, you become a *taxable person*, and must register with the authorities. This matter is explained more fully in *VAT registration*, page 255.

1.5 Taxable person

As with the word 'supplies', the word 'person' is used somewhat differently from the way it is in everyday life. In the case of a 'one-man business' (for example a small shop), the *taxable person* is the individual who owns and runs that business.

However, many businesses are more complex. They have a *legally constituted structure*, that is, they are governed by rules which are laid down by Parliament. The most well-known example is the limited company. In this case the business does not belong to one individual, but involves at least two people. Again, in a company, money is not provided just by one individual, but by two or more shareholders. As far as VAT is concerned, it is the *company* which is considered to be the 'taxable person' and must be registered and must pay the tax. Other examples of 'taxable persons' include a partnership, a club or a registered charity.

A taxable person has to account for all occasions on which a taxable supply is made. This therefore means that you have to account for and pay tax on what you sell – (because this is what goes out, this is referred to as your *output tax*). But the taxable person has also to account for and pay tax on what is purchased – what comes in, and hence called your *input tax*.

2. Input and output tax

2.1 What input tax applies to

Those who are registered for VAT can usually claim back the VAT which they have paid on their business purchases and expenses. The money which is being claimed is referred to as their *input tax*.

Input tax applies not only to goods bought for resale, or to raw materials, but also to other transactions, so long as they are made as part of the conduct of that business. For a business ('taxable person') a telephone bill includes a charge for VAT, as does an accountant's bill. Both of these charges can be reclaimed. But if a person uses the phone privately as well, he or she can't reclaim VAT on that part of their bill.

2.2 Claiming back input tax

To claim back the input tax you have paid, you have to keep accounts, total up your input tax and declar it on your VAT return.

In order to make such a claim you must keep records. Furthermore you must keep evidence (such voices) in support of those records. This applies to nearly all transactions on which you paid inp

There are a few exceptions. Certain small expenses such as business calls from payphones may be included without documentary evidence.

2.3 Charging output tax

Once you are registered for VAT, you have to charge all customers VAT on all taxable supplies which you make. The tax you charge is your output tax.

Output tax is not only charged on goods (because the term 'supplies' does not only refer to goods). So VAT is also charged on meals sold to employees, gifts of more than £10 value, and the commission received by agents and salesmen.

2.4 Declaration of output tax

Your output tax has to be declared on your VAT return at the same time as you claim your input tax. As with input tax, you must keep detailed records of all charges made.

On your VAT return you give two totals – input tax and output tax. One of these will nearly always be greater than the other. If your output tax is greater, you owe that sum to the Customs and Excise. However, if your input tax is greater, you claim the difference from the Customs and Excise.

3. Summary

Who is involved?
- ☐ applies to most business transactions in the UK
- ☐ collected for the government from businesses by the Customs and Excise Department

Taxable supplies
- ☐ name for the types of transaction which interest the VAT authorities
- ☐ supplies which are not taxable are exempt supplies

Rate of VAT
- ☐ rate stated and worked out as a percentage of the cost of the supplies.
- ☐ standard rate: $17\frac{1}{2}$ % (from April 1991)
- ☐ zero rate: no charge laid upon the customer

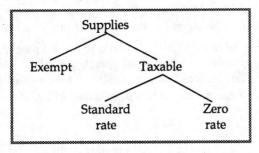

Taxable turnover

❏ business must register for VAT when it reaches a certain level of taxable turnover

❏ taxable turnover is the total value of (*not* profit on) all your taxable supplies

Taxable person

❏ person liable to register for VAT is known as a taxable person

❏ 'person' may refer to an individual or to a legally constituted structure (such as a company)

Input and output tax

❏ Input tax: the VAT paid on purchases and expenses made entirely as part of the conduct of a business.

❏ To claim back input tax, must keep accounts, and declare total on VAT return

❏ Output tax: charge made to all customers by a VAT registered business on taxable supplies

  must keep detailed records and declare total on VAT return

❏ On VAT return calculate difference between the two totals:

if output tax is greater, difference is owed to Customs and Excise

if input tax is greater, claim difference from Customs and Excise.

4. VAT registration

The law requires that all 'taxable persons' must

❏ register for VAT

❏ keep records

❏ make VAT returns

❏ when output tax for a given period exceeds input tax, pay the difference to the Customs and Excise.

You must register either

1) when your taxable turnover has already reached the appropriate level, or

2) when there are 'reasonable grounds' for believing that your taxable turnover is about to reach that level.

4.1 Past turnover

The first situation which a business may find itself in is that taxable turnover has already reached the relevant level. The Customs and Excise makes the position quite clear. You have to register if 'at the end of any month, the value of the taxable supplies you made in the past 12 months has exceeded £35 000'. (This was the level set in 1991.)

4.2 Future turnover

The VAT regulations also require you to consider not only the business you have done, but what you think you are likely to do. The law requires you to register

> *if at any time you find that you have 'reasonable grounds' for believing that 'the value of the taxable supplies you will make in the next 30 days will exceed £35 000'.*

The VAT year is considered to start from 'the first day from which grounds existed'.

4.3 Reasonable grounds

What are 'reasonable grounds' and why should this apparently complicated or vague way of doing things have been adopted?

Basically, 'reasonable grounds' are the evidence you will get from sales, information about the market and so on, which allow you to estimate what business will be like in the near future.

This phrase is chosen because the aim of the Customs and Excise is to collect all VAT which is due to them; if necessary they use the courts to do this. By setting the condition of 'reasonable grounds' they can deal with one type of tax evasion. It will not be sufficient for 'taxable persons' to claim that they did not think VAT would become payable. Other people (such as a jury) will need to be convinced by the evidence, that it was not reasonable to suppose that the business would grow to that extent.

4.4 Form VAT 1

Form VAT1 is the registration form. Basically, you are obliged to obtain and complete it as soon as you realise that you should now register for VAT.

This will be either

a)   when at the end of a month you you find that you have made over £35 000 worth of taxable supplies over the past 12 months; or

b)   when you realise that there are 'reasonable grounds' that your taxable turnover will exceed £35 000 over the next 30 days.

At this point you must within 30 days send for, fill in and return Form VAT 1 to the Customs and Excise.

In case a) your registration starts at the beginning of the second month after you realised that you should register. For example, 31 January, turnover reaches the right level, get and send off VAT 1 during February, and registration starts from 1 March.

In case b), the date of your sudden insight that 'grounds existed' (not after returning the form) is deemed by the Customs and Excise to be your first day of registration. For example, you realise on 1 February that you are going to have the relevant turnover during February, so you must get the form in by March, and you will be registered from 1 February.

Once Form VAT 1 has been checked, the Customs and Excise send you an advice of registration. This shows your date of registration and your VAT number.

The Customs and Excise also stress the importance of not delaying registration once 'reasonable grounds exist'. If afterwards it is found that you should have registered earlier, you have to account for VAT which was payable from the earlier date, pay any tax due and may well be liable to a 'financial penalty'.

VALUE ADDED TAX
Application for Registration

HM Customs and Excise

You should open up this form and read the notes before you answer these questions. Please write clearly in ink.

For official use

Local office code and issuing number	
Date of receipt	1
Local office code and registration number	
Name	
Trade name	
Taxable turnover	E D R D M Y Stagger Status

Rept.	Vol.	Oversize name address	Computer user	Group Div.	Intg.	Overseas

Bn   D M Y

Applicant and business

1 Full name

2 Trading name

3 Address of principal place of business

Phone no.

Postcode

Business details

4 Status of business

Limited company ☐ Company incorporation certificate no. _____ and date [day] [month] [year] 19

Sole proprietor ☐ Partnership ☐ Other—specify _____

Business activity _____ Trade classification _____

5 Other VAT registrations ☐

6 Do you use a computer for accounting? ☐

7 Repayments of VAT ☐

Bank account details

8 Bank sorting code and account no. _____ National Girobank account no. _____

VAT 1

please continue overleaf ⟶

Form VAT 1 – side 1

Compulsory registrations

9 Are you required to be registered because the value of the taxable supplies:

YES   NO

(a) you **have made** in the past 12 months or less has exceeded the registration limit? ☐ ☐
OR
(b) you **expect to make** in the next 30 days will exceed the registration limit? ☐ ☐

10 • Date from which you:

day	month	year
		19

(a) are required to be registered

(b) wish to be registered if earlier than (a)

day	month	year
		19

• Value of expected taxable supplies in the 12 months from date of registration – (a) or (b) above   £ _____

11 Exemption from compulsory registration ☐

expected value of zero-rated supplies in the next 12 months   £ _____

Voluntary and intending registration

12 Taxable supplies below registration limits ☐

value of taxable supplies in the last 12 months   £ _____

13 No taxable supplies made yet ☐

(a) expected annual value of taxable supplies   £ _____

(b) expected date of first taxable supply

day	month	year
		19

Business changes and transfers

14 Business transferred as a going concern ☐

(a) date of transfer or change of legal status

day	month	year
		19

(b) name of previous owner _____

(c) previous VAT registration number (if known) _____

15 Transfer of VAT registration number
(You must also complete a form VAT 68) ☐

Declaration – You must complete this declaration

16 I _____
(Full name in BLOCK LETTERS)

declare that all the entered details and information in any accompanying documents are correct and complete

Signature _____ Date _____

Proprietor ☐   Partner ☐   Director ☐   Company Secretary ☐   Authorised Official ☐   Trustee ☐

For Official Use

Registration	Obligatory	Exemption	Voluntary	Intending	Transfer of Regn. no.
Approved – Initial/Date					
Refused – Initial/Date					
Form Issued – Initial/Date	VAT 9/ Other	VAT 8	VAT 7	Letter	Approval Letter

VAT1 F3733

Form VAT 1 – side 2

5. The VAT tax invoice

5.1 What it is

Once you have registered for VAT, you must keep records.

The first stage and central document in VAT record keeping is the tax invoice. An example of the invoice and how to fill it in is given in the last section of this entry. The tax invoice shows that you were charged VAT by a VAT registered supplier, and gives details of that transaction.

5.2 Issue of invoice

If you are registered for VAT you must issue a tax invoice to all VAT registered customers for all standard-rated sales. You also need to be given one for all standard-rated purchases.

It is absolutely essential to obtain a tax invoice for all transactions which are liable for input tax, since without the evidence provided by a tax invoice, the Customs and Excise will not accept your claim for the repayment of input tax.

5.3 Original copy

It is important to remember that the tax invoice *must be an original, not a photocopy*. If you lose an original, you have to get the supplier to make a you a copy, headed 'duplicate'. Also to the Customs and Excise, a pro forma invoice (see *Invoices*, page 163) does not count as a tax invoice. In order to claim back VAT you must also be supplied with a properly drawn up tax invoice.

5.4 Tax point

The tax invoice has to state the 'time of supply'. This is the time at which the Customs and Excise consider the transaction to have taken place. For this reason it is also called the *tax point*. The tax point determines in which tax period the transaction belongs. Even if the rate of VAT later changes, it is the rate in force at the tax point which is payable. The tax point is usually the time at which goods become available for the customer to use, or the time at which you perform a service.

5.5 Exceptional situations

The Customs and Excise recognise that in certain types of business, it may be difficult or impossible to issue an invoice for each sale. They have therefore arranged for retail schemes which will satisfy their requirements. Businesses which use a retail scheme do not normally provide invoices, but they are obliged to do so if someone asks for one.

A registered business must issue a tax invoice to every VAT registered customer. However, there is no need to do so to members of the general public unless asked. In the latter case the invoice is less detailed than the one used between registered persons. Also, whereas a business must keep all tax invoices used between registered persons, the Customs and Excise do not require this to be done with the less detailed invoices which are issued to members of the public on request.

It is worth remembering that *a tax invoice can only be issued by a registered person*. An individual or unregistered business cannot give you such an invoice. But as a consequence they should not be charging you VAT, since they are not liable to pass it on to the Customs and Excise. Such a charge would amount to taking an extra profit.

5.6 Filling in the invoice

A VAT tax invoice looks like this:

Value added tax (VAT)

```
┌─────────────────────────────────────────────────────────────┐
│  Sales Invoice No. 172                                        │
│                                                               │
│  From: HOT BOPPIN,          VAT Regd. No. 947 4649 22         │
│        133 ASHMONGER ST, CODLINGTON                           │
│  To: MUSIC TODAY,                                             │
│      14 QUEENS PARADE, CODLINGTON                             │
│                                                               │
│  Sale                       Tax point: 22/10/91               │
└─────────────────────────────────────────────────────────────┘
```

Quantity	Description and Price	Amount exclusive of VAT	VAT Rate	VAT Net
		£	%	£
1	SPANISH GUITAR	118.00	17.5	20.65
1	NEUMANN MICROPHONE	570.00	17.5	99.75
1	ROLAND D20 SYNTHESISER	1250.00	17.5	218.75
		1938.00		339.15

Terms: *for immediate settlement only*

VAT 339.15

TOTAL £2277.15

It must show:

1) an identifying number

2) name and address of supplier

3) VAT registration number of supplier

4) time of supply (the tax point)

5) customer's name and address

6) type of supply (sale, rental etc)

7) description of goods or services supplied

   (Note: the Customs and Excise specify that this should identify the supplies – vague entries are not acceptable)

8) Quantity of each item supplied

9) Charge for each item exclusive of VAT

10) rate of VAT

11) total charge excluding VAT

12) total VAT payable

13) rate of cash discount (if any)

14) for cash payments, statement that payment has been received and date when received.

15) total including VAT.

6. VAT record keeping

6.1 Basic requirements

The Customs and Excise require all registered persons to keep records of all taxable supplies. Failure to do so can result in financial penalties.

Your records must include a record of all taxable goods or services received or supplied, whether standard or zero rated. There must also be a separate record of any exempt supplies.

6.2 Safe keeping of invoices

All registered persons are obliged to give all VAT registered customers a tax invoice giving details of the transaction. Without this evidence the Customs and Excise will not accept a claim for repayment of input tax. Consequently those engaged in financial record keeping must make arrangements to give, receive and keep safely the VAT invoices arising from the business. Keeping the documents safely is important, as the Customs and Excise will not accept a photocopy as evidence.

6.3 VAT account

The Customs and Excise also expect you to keep a *VAT account*. This is built up from your records. It is a summary of your output and input tax for the tax period. The account will include not only tax paid and tax charged, but also errors, credits and bad debts.

At appropriate points the record keeper will add up the VAT shown in the sales records and transfer the information to the VAT account (see *Ledgers and journals*, page 177). This will be output tax. In the same way the accounts department will keep invoices for purchases, record them in the purchases record, and later enter the input tax in the VAT account.

The Customs and Excise require that all records be kept for six years. The records to be kept include not only VAT records but other types of record, such as cash books, delivery notes, credit notes, and import/export documents. The documents must be available for inspection by a VAT officer if required.

6.4 VAT return

At the end of the tax period the trader is obliged to fill in a VAT return. This is a form which is sent by the Customs and Excise. On it they require you to summarise your position. The VAT account is used to fill in the form. The return will accompany either a claim for input tax due to the trader, or a cheque for output tax due to them.

6.5 Visits by VAT officers

Once you are registered for VAT you are likely to be visited by a VAT officer from the Customs and Excise. These visits are made partly to check that you are applying VAT correctly and are keeping proper records. Partly of course, the intention is to check the accuracy of your returns.

Value added tax (VAT)

There is a visit fairly early after registration; after that it depends on circumstances. The Customs and Excise stress that 'Traders who send in late, incorrect or seemingly inconsistent VAT returns or who don't send in returns at all are visited more frequently.'

Visits are made during normal business hours, and may last for anything between a few hours and a few days, according to the size of the business. The visiting officer will carry an identification card, which the trader is entitled to see.

The VAT officer discusses with those responsible for the VAT accounts any matters which arise. The officer also examines the records to see that they are accurate and being properly kept. The officer points out problems and discusses them. The officer can ask to see all business records, not just those to do with VAT. So bank statements, balance sheets and even correspondence can be examined. The officer can ask to see how day-to-day maintenance of accounts is handled. The officer can even ask a trader to open up a gaming machine. Businesses are required to produce information of the above types: failure to do so can incur penalties.

In the event of a disagreement, the trader can appeal to the local VAT collector.

7. Filling in the VAT return

Even though the VAT Return has recently been greatly simplified, when you first meet it, it can still be somewhat mind-boggling! It is a good example of the problems of reading documents giving financial information (see *Texts*, page 248).

The basic problem is that there is a lot of detail, and no clear, simple instructions about what to do. Also much of the information given relates to procedures which must certainly be acted upon by those who keep the VAT account. But such matters should have been taken care of before the Return is filled in. For example, if you have calculated your tax totals having wrongly claimed repayment of VAT on motor cars, you are going to have to go over your accounts and amend them before you can arrive at an accurate total.

Method
1) **Entering information on the form**
    a) Don't alter any details already on the form.
    b) Entering amounts
        1) Each box should contain an amount or the word 'none'.
        2) If you are entering an exact number of pounds enter '00' in the pence column.
        3) If you make a mistake, cross out the figure, write in the new one, and initial it.

2) **Amounts misdeclared on previous returns**

    Check whether in a previous return you have declared too much (overdeclaration) or too little (underdelaration). If not, go on to section (C) below.

    Do not include: past payments, VAT declared previously but unpaid, repayments not yet received, or misdeclarations about which the Customs and Excise have written to you.

    If there has been a misdeclaration, you must act as follows:

    ☐ amount under £500:   a) show the amount in your VAT account;
                            b) include it in the totals which you enter in either

                               Box 1 – money payable to the Customs and Excise, or

                               Box 2 – money repayable to you.

❏   amount over £500:   a)   do not adjust VAT account;

                                          b)   notify your local VAT office in writing at once, as you will be charged default interest until the sum owed by you is paid.

Note that normally you would be informed if any misdeclaration is to be included by the person responsible for a firm's accounts. It is not something you would decide for yourself, unless you were preparing accounts for your own business.

3)   **Boxes 1 to 5:**

Box 1: enter Output Tax from VAT account

Box 2: enter Input Tax from VAT account

Box 4: enter total outputs (excluding VAT).

Box 5: enter total inputs (excluding VAT).

(The information for both Boxes 4 and 5 comes from the accounts of the business. There are reminders of what is included on the back of the form. These should have been included (or excluded) during the preparation of the accounts, before a total was arrived at).

If you are in doubt what these terms mean, you will need to re-read the relevant parts of this section (for list of contents see page 251).

4)   **Retail schemes**

A trader who has used one of the schemes for retailers enters the appropriate letters in this box.

5)   **Payment**

If Box 1 is the larger amount, decide by what means you will be making a payment.

   a) If you are enclosing a payment:

       ❏   tick the box on the left

       ❏   make out the remittance as follows:

           cheque or postal order; cross 'A/C Payee only'; pay to 'HM Customs and Excise'; write VAT number on back

       ❏   return the form and remittance by the due date (see top of form).

   b) If you are paying by credit transfer:

       ❏   apply to local VAT office for pre-printed credit transfer slips

       ❏   fill in and write VAT number on back.

6)   **Making the declaration**

The registered person, or person authorised by them, fills in, signs and dates the declaration.

7)   **Check entries**

   a)   Is there a figure or the word 'none' in Boxes 1 to 5?

   b)   If enclosing a payment:

       ❏   has the left hand box been ticked?

       ❏   is the cheque properly made out?

       ❏   is your VAT number on the back?

   c)   If you have used a retail scheme, have you filled in the relevant box?

   4)   Has the appropriate person signed and dated the declaration?

Value Added Tax Return

For the period
to

HM Customs and Excise

Registration number

Period

You could be liable to a financial penalty if your completed return and all the VAT payable are not received by the due date.

Due date:

For official use

Before you fill in this form please read the notes on the back. Complete all boxes clearly in ink, writing 'none' where necessary. Don't put a dash or leave any box blank. If there are no pence write "00" in the pence column. Do not enter more than one amount in any box.

		£	p
VAT due in this period on **sales** and other outputs	1		
VAT reclaimed in this period on **purchases** and other inputs	2		
Net VAT to be paid to Customs or reclaimed by you **(Difference between boxes 1 and 2)**	3		
Value of **outputs** (pounds only) excluding any VAT	4		00
Value of **inputs** (pounds only) excluding any VAT	5		00

Retail schemes. If you have used any of the schemes in the period covered by this return please enter the appropriate letter(s) in this box.

If you are enclosing a payment please tick (✓) this box.	DECLARATION by the signatory to be completed by or on behalf of the person named above.
	I, ...declare that the
	(Full name of signatory in BLOCK LETTERS)
	information given above is true and complete.
	Signature ....Date ....19..........

VAT 100   CD 1942/N1 (8.89)   F 3790 (JANUARY 1990)

VAT return form

264

8. What to do

The following instructions are based on information supplied by the London Enterprise Agency to people who are thinking of starting their own business. Much of this section gives information for reference, to be drawn on as you need it. There is no point, for example, in spending time on working out the difference between exempt and zero-rated supplies, unless you need to do so. Studying VAT documents can damage your mental health!

But these instructions tell you what to do, especially in small and new businesses. When you need to follow up a point, consult the *Contents* list of this section.

---

1) Decide whether you need to register

a)   If your taxable turnover has reached a specified limit (at the time of going to press this is £35 000) within the last twelve months, or if it is likely to do so within the next 30 days, you must register for VAT.

b)   If your turnover is less than those figures, decide whether you wish to register voluntarily.

---

2) When you are registered

Keep records of all VAT transactions.

(This means: file VAT invoices safely

• note all transactions in the relevant journal

• keep a VAT account

For the latter two points see *Ledgers and journals,* page 177.)

Show your registration number on all sales invoices.

(For instructions on how to fill in a VAT tax invoice see page 262).

Charge VAT (currently at the rate of $17\frac{1}{2}$ %) on all goods and services unless

☐   they are zero-rated

☐   they are exempt.

(For explanations see *Taxable supplies,* page 254).

In the case of goods for export

☐   do not charge VAT

☐   keep evidence of export papers.

☐   At the end of each quarter complete your VAT return.

☐   a)   Show what you have charged on your sales.

　　b)   Show the VAT charged to you by suppliers.

☐   If a) is greater than b), enclose a cheque for the difference.

☐   Send the return to the Customs and Excise department.

(Full details of how to fill in the return are given in the entry *Filling in the VAT return,* page 262).

Wages and salaries

The calculation of payments to employees (including bonuses, deductions, and repayment of expenses) and the recording of those payments both for the employer and for Income Tax and National Insurance authorities

Contents

1. Main methods of calculating pay

1.1 Wages and salaries

Payment for work done can be classified and calculated in various ways. The commonest differences which people think of are:

Wages	**Salary**
manual workers	non-manual workers
production or service industries	administration, management, professions (eg teachers)
paid weekly	paid monthly
paid in cash	paid by cheque or credit transfer

Calculation of payment

❏ *Salary*

Income set as annual sum. This is divided into twelve equal payments which are paid monthly.

Example

A teacher is paid £14 100 *pa* (*pa* stands for the Latin words 'per annum' meaning 'for a year'). What is her monthly salary cheque?

$$\frac{14\ 100}{12} = \text{£1175 per month}$$

❏ *Fixed wage*

Income set as weekly sum, usually paid towards the end of the week.

Example

Jane Turner works in a bakery shop. Each Friday she is paid £162.50.

❏ *Variable wage*

There is no guaranteed sum. Instead the worker is paid according to work actually done. The normal ways of calculating this are given below.

❏ *Hourly rate* (also known as *time rate*)

The worker is paid for the hours actually worked.

Example

George Herbert is paid £3.16 per hour. In the week ending May 23 he worked 35 hours. What was his wage?

$35 \times 3.16 = \text{£110.60}$

In many jobs there is a set rate up to a certain number of hours (usually between 35 and 40 per week). After that the hours worked are known as *overtime,* and are paid at a higher rate. The commonest rates are 'time and a half' ($1\frac{1}{2}$ times the basic or normal rate) and 'double time' (twice the basic rate).

Example

George Herbert is saving up to buy a house. So in the next week he again works 35 hours at the basic rate of £3.16. He then puts in an extra two hours a day (10 hours in all) at the overtime rate, which is time and a half. What does he earn?

1) *find the rates per hour*
   basic rate £3.16
   overtime = £3.16 x 1.5 = £4.74

2) *find the amounts earned at the different rates*
   basic wage 35 x 3.16   =   £110.60
   overtime 10 x 4.74   =   £47.40

3) . add them together to get the total pay   £158.00

Piece rate

Another form of variable wage is piece work. This is work paid at a piece rate, which means that the worker is paid for the number of items produced, irrespective of time taken.

Example

Maria Georgiou is an outworker, that is, she works at home for a manufacturer. She sews together children's clothes, and is paid £1.25 per item. In her first week she sews 20. How much did she earn?

   20 x 1.25 = £25

She can sew a dress together in half an hour. She is offered work as a cleaner at £28.50 per week, for two hours cleaning a day, and a five day week. Will she be better off?

To decide, compare hours worked, rate per hour, and total earned.

	hours	rate	total wage
sewing	20 dresses at $\frac{1}{2}$ hour = 10 hours	2 x 1.25 = 2.50 hourly	£25.00
cleaner	5 x 2 = 10 hours	28.50 ÷ 10 = 2.85 hourly	£28.50

So she will work the same number of hours but get more money.

The important thing when comparing payment made hourly or on piece work is not to look at just one factor. For instance, if the cleaning job had required her to work three hours a day, Maria would have earned more money, but her rate per hour would have been less and the hours she worked would have been more. (Hours 15, rate 28.50 ÷ 15 = £1.90). Sewing for the same time she would earn another 5 hours at £2.50, that is £12.50 or a total wage of £37.50. The above calculations only take account of course of Maria's earnings. Whether she would have to spend money on travelling to her work, or whether she prefers one type of work would also affect her choice.

Bonuses

Wages may also vary as a result of a bonus. This is an extra payment, offered as an incentive, if workers exceed a set target.

Example

Azure computers have an important contract to complete and offer their workers a bonus of 15 per cent if the work is completed on time. This happens. Fenella Greenfield normally earns £255 weekly. What will be her payment on this occasion?

   basic wage   255.00
   bonus   255.00 x 15 =   38.25
                 total wage   £293.25

Commission

This is an incentive to sales staff. It is calculated as a percentage of the sales made. Some sales staff are paid only the commission they earn; some earn a basic salary to which commission is added.

Example

Robert Bruce works for Cable Codlington selling telephone installations. He is paid a basic rate of £60.00 weekly and commission at 20% of his sales. These are calculated according to the installation charges. Subscribers can opt for 1 line only to be installed, or they can have several lines (3, 7, or 12). One week he signs up new subscribers as follows:

Number of subscribers	Number of lines required
3	1 line @ £100
1	3 line @ £150
2	7 line @ £300
4	12 line @ £550

What does he earn?

1) **Note basic rate**   60.00

2) **Calculate total sales**   3 @ £100 =   300
                                 1 @ £150 =   150
                                 2 @ £300 =   600
                                 4 @ £550 =   2200
                                 total   3250.00

3) **Work out commission**

$$\frac{\text{total sales}}{\text{percentage}} = \frac{3250 \times 20}{100} = \quad\quad 650.00$$

4) **Add basic wage and commission**   £710.00 total wage

2. Records of attendance

2.1 Types of record

When the pay of employees is calculated according to the hours worked, there is a need for a record of the times at which they actually started and finished work. There are various ways in which this can be done:

❑   *time book*: the employees sign on and off

❑   *time sheets*: completed by the employee and authorised by the signature of a suitable member of staff. Some firms will allow claims for time spent travelling or waiting (eg in the event of a breakdown of works machinery).

❑   *clock cards*: in which a card is stamped automatically (described below)

❑   *computer cards*: a computer system records automatically the times at which the employee inserted his or her card to record arrival or departure.

2.2 Clock cards

Basic principles

This system is a traditional one for industrial workers. It illustrates the basic principles which apply to all records of attendance for workers on an hourly rate, namely:

1) times of arrival and departure are noted

2) total hours worked are calculated

3) wages are calculated by multiplying hours by rate per hour.

Clocking in and out

When the workers arrive, they take a personal record card (the clock card from an 'out' rack. They place the card into a special time recorder clock, which is designed so that the card can be stamped. The workers then place their cards into an 'in' rack, which shows that there are at the place of work. The process is reversed when they leave.

The clock card

Hourly rates are usually calculated on the basis of a *basic rate* for a certain number of hours eg 40 hours per week. Any hours worked above the basic 40 are counted as *overtime*. Overtime is usually paid at time and half, or on special occasions, double time.

No:	122				
Name:	A. Crashaw				
Week ending:	29.02.91				
Day	In	Out	In	Out	Total hours
Mon	8.00	12.30	13.30	16.30	7.30
Tue	8.00	12.30	13.30	18.30	9.30
Wed	9.30	12.30	13.30	16.30	6.00
Thur	8.00	12.00	14.00	17.30	7.30
Fri	8.00	12.30	13.30	19.30	10.30
Total					41.00
Basic rate: 4.52	Hours:	35			158.20
Overtime: 6.78	Hours:	6			40.68
		GROSS PAY	198.88		

The clock card

Notes:

1) Andrew Crashaw's basic week is a $37\frac{1}{2}$ hour week, at a rate of £4.52 an hour. The normal day is from 8.00 until 12.30, an hour for lunch, and then 1.30 pm to 4.30 pm.

2) In the week ending 29 February, Andrew's clock card shows some differences from the normal pattern as follows:

Day	am	pm
Monday	normal day	
Tuesday	normal hours	2 hours overtime (4.30 to 6.30)
Wednesday	started work $1\frac{1}{2}$ hours later (9.30) owing to visit to doctor	normal hours
Thursday	Finished work $\frac{1}{2}$ hour early	started $\frac{1}{2}$ hour late (long lunch break); worked 1 hour overtime
Friday	normal hours	worked 2 hours overtime

3) Note that in the total hours column, four entries of .30 give a total of .00 rather than (1).20, because you are adding minutes.

4) Hours at basic rate. These are the hours spent at work during normal working hours. Andrew took $2\frac{1}{2}$ hours off.

5) Hours on overtime. For Andrew's firm, these are hours outside normal working hours. Some firms will simply allow overtime as hours worked above the basic working week (here $37\frac{1}{2}$).

6) **Gross pay** is the **amount earned before any deductions are made**. **Net pay** is the **amount due after deductions**.

Completing the clock card

The wages of each employee will be totalled up by the wages clerk.

The procedure is as follows:

1) For each day, **calculate the hours worked**. Enter this figure in the 'Total hours' column.

2) **Add up the 'Total hours' column**. Enter the total at the bottom.

3) Calculate the number of **hours worked as overtime** and enter this at the appropriate point on the card.

4) **Calculate and enter the wages payable at the basic rate** (hours x rate).

5) Calculate and enter the wages payable at the **overtime rate**.

6) Add the figures for ordinary time and overtime together to calculate the **Gross pay**.

7) Enter this figure and **forward the card** (or a gross wages sheet, according to the procedures of the company) for the next stage of wage calculations – the making of deductions.

3. Statutory deductions

3.1 Statutory and voluntary deductions

Before an employee is paid a salary or a wage, it is the employer's responsibility to make any **deductions**. These are of two types: **statutory** (or compulsory) and **voluntary**.

Statutory deductions

These are so called because they are required by statutes (laws) made by Parliament. They are:

1) **Income tax**
This is tax which is paid to the Inland Revenue. How much is paid depends on how much the employee earns, and also what allowances he or she is entitled to.

2) **National Insurance**
These are the payments which are collected to pay for various social and welfare services. The most important of these are medical care under the National Health Service, and the Retirement Pension. This is the 'old age pension' which everyone collects when they reach the end of their working life.

How much is deducted depends on whether the employee is required to pay full National Insurance contributions, or has instead contracted out of full payment in order to contribute to a private pension scheme.

Voluntary deductions

Voluntary deductions are not required by law: the employee agrees to have them made. The commonest are:

1) *pension scheme contributions*
    Unlike the retirement pension, these are occupational pensions. They are only paid to people who have been employed and have contributed to a specially set up scheme. For example, teachers may have a percentage of their money deducted in order to provide a pension when they retire. (This will mean that they receive two pensions: the occupational pension and the Retirement Pension). Some firms run their own pension schemes, feeling that it makes their company more attractive to workers.

2) *trade union contributions*

3) *savings schemes*

4) *social club subscriptions* (if the firm offers sports and leisure facilities)

5) Sometimes *payments to charities* can be paid at this point.

These deductions are known as *deductions at source*, that is, they are made at the point when wages are being calculated and paid, rather than being collected separately later.

3.2 The PAYE (Pay As You Earn) scheme

Income tax is a tax on what you earn. It goes to the Government, but it is collected by the Department of Inland Revenue. For them, there are many sources of money which count as income – it is not just a matter of the money for which you work. For instance pensions are subject to taxation. Income may not even take the form of money: certain types of benefits, for example a car made available by an employer to encourage employees with skills in short supply, may well count as income. There are also surprising exceptions. For example, football pools wins do not count as income: the Inland Revenue classify them as 'gambling windfall gains'. Not surprisingly, perhaps, taxation is a specialist field in accountancy.

For most employees, though, income tax is much simpler to understand, though no more welcome. Their gross pay is calculated, certain allowances are made (see below) and then tax is deducted at source by their employer, and forwarded in due course to the Inland Revenue. The scheme by which this happens is called *PAYE (Pay As You Earn)*.

3.3 Taxation of the self-employed

A person such as Eve Adams is classified differently by the Inland Revenue: she is self-employed. As such she is still liable for taxation and for National Insurance contributions. However, these are collected differently. National Insurance is paid directly to the Department of Social Security; the rates and conditions are calculated somewhat differently from the situation explained elsewhere in this entry.

Schedule D

Eve Adams will pay tax under this form of taxation has some important differences from the PAYE system.

❏   Tax is not deducted weekly or monthly. Instead an assessment is made annually, and the sum due paid in one or two lump sums.

❏   The self-employed person declares all untaxed income from his or her business. They also declare a wide range of *allowable expenses* which were incurred in pursuit of that business. These are deducted from the total income to arrive at the taxable income. By contrast, the PAYE scheme does permit a limited range of expenses, such as specialised clothing. A good example of the difference in the status of expenses is that of travel. A full-time teacher employed at a school cannot claim travel to and from work, whereas a self-employed private tutor can make such a claim. In the scenario used in this book, it is therefore important to Eve to log carefully travel costs. She would otherwise have to pay tax on that amount of her income.

272

3.4 Basic requirements of the Inland Revenue under PAYE

The Inland Revenue sees the process of calculating PAYE taxation as follows.

1) Take the gross income.

2) Subtract allowances.

The commonest of these is the *personal allowance*. This is an amount which everyone is allowed to earn before they have to pay tax.

There are various other allowances which some people can claim. Among them are allowances for dependent relatives, and for necessary clothing (in certain types of work).

3) The remainder is the *taxable income*. Tax is calculated as a percentage of this.

4) Deduct the tax due. The rest (net income) is what is actually paid to the employee.

The calculation of gross income is explained earlier (page 267). The details of how allowances and tax payable are calculated in practice are explained in *Filling in Form P11*, page 275 below.

3.5 Tax codes

Life could rapidly become unworkably difficult if the employer had to work out all the allowances weekly. It is also likely that there would be disputes. The Inland Revenue avoids these complications as follows.

❏ All allowances have to be agreed with them. The taxpayer has to claim allowances

a) by filling in a tax return form each year and

b) by writing to the local Inspector of Taxes, if circumstances change.

Note that it is up to the taxpayer to claim allowances: if you don't claim, they will not automatically be included in the calculation.

❏ Once allowances have been agreed, they are summed up in a *tax code*. This consists of a number and a letter. The number is obtained by calculating your allowances, and omitting the last figure. The letter indicates your status (eg married or unmarried), according to a system devised by the Inland Revenue. For example an unmarried person whose allowances were £2375, would have the code 2375L. L is the code letter for an unmarried person.

❏ The amount of tax which is payable for any given income is calculated by the Inland Revenue and set out in *Tax Tables*.

The tax tables are issued to Employers by the Inland Revenue. They consist of two books:

Table A: This shows the Free Pay Tables for each week or month of the financial year (6 April – 5 April)

Tables B to D show the amount of tax to be paid on taxable pay.

(The use of these is explained below).

Note that the amount of tax to be paid is *determined* by the government; it is only collected by the Inland Revenue.

3.6 How tax is calculated: the principle

Note: *This section does not tell you how to work out your tax as you would if you were a wages clerk*. To do that, you follow the instructions given in *Filling in Form P11* below. But if you wish to understand what is happening, and what calculations the Tax Tables are based upon, the following explanation will be of interest.

The examples given below reflect the situation when there are two rates of income tax: 25% and 40%, with the higher rate applying to taxable income of £20 700 and above. To say that a person 'pays income tax at the lower rate' means that of their pay which is subject to tax, they pay 25% in income tax. The pay which is subject to tax at the lower rate is the pay between the allowances, and £20 700. It should be noted, though, that the number of rates of income tax can and does vary according to Government policy, as do the points (thresholds) at which they become applicable. Thus the figures used in the examples were later amended to £3 295 and £23 700.

Students are sometimes confused about the principle of how tax is deducted, especially when several levels of income are involved. What happens is illustrated in the following table. In it you have three people with different incomes. For the sake of simplicity, it is assumed that they all have the same allowances of £3000.

name	gross income	allow-ance	25% tax	40% tax	total tax	net income
Thompson	2 500	3000	none	none	none	2 500

(Thompson pays no tax because he has not even used up all his allowances)

Richardson	12 500	3000	2375	none	2375	10 125

25% of £9 500   12 500
= 12 500 − 3000   − 2 375

(Richardson has allowances and pays tax at the lower rate, but does not earn enough to pay at the higher rate)

Harrison	22 500	3000	4425	320	4745	15 955

25% of £17 700   40% of £800   12 500
= 20 700 − 3000   = 320   − 2 375

(Harrison has an allowance. He then pays tax at 25% on the balance of his income up to £20 700. To that is added tax at 40% on his earnings above £20 700)

The steps in the calculation are:
1) calculate gross pay
2) subtract allowances
3) take result of 3 from income or £20 700, whichever is the lower
4) calculate 25% of this figure
5) if there is any income above £20 700, subtract £20 700
6) calculate 40% of this figure
7) add the answers to 4 and 6: this is the tax payable
8) to find net pay, subtract tax payable from gross income.

In brief: *Net income = gross income − tax payable*

but the latter may have to be calculated in several stages.

Fortunately, the tax tables have already worked all this out for you!

3.7 National Insurance contributions

The employee's position is in important ways similar to that which obtains with regard to income tax in that:
☐ there is a lower limit below which no deduction is made (in the examples used here £43 per week);
☐ there are bands of payments, which are calculated as a percentage of earnings;
☐ but unlike with income tax:

274

a) if you are liable for contributions, you pay a percentage (in these examples 2%) of your earnings up to £43, as well as a different percentage (here 9%) on the remainder of your earnings up to £325 per week

b) there is an upper limit (here £325 per week) above which no contribution is required.

As with income tax, various tables are provided to enable wages staff to read off what deduction should be made. The most commonly used is Table A, which gives Standard Rate contributions for employees who are not contracted out (that is, who have not made other arrangements to pay contributions).

The employer is also required to pay a contribution on behalf of the employee. It is also calculated as a percentage of the employee's earnings basis, though the percentages are not the same ones as are used for employees. Though this concerns the accounts or wages department, it is not part of the wage calculation, since it is not deducted from the employee's earnings.

4. Filling in Form P11

4.1 Method

The method of calculating and recording the deductions and net pay for an employee is explained below. The explanation is illustrated by an example, the recording of a week for Alexander Pope, an assistant at the EPG Garden Centre. Following tradition in such explanations, the example makes the unlikely assumption that Mr Pope starts work with EPG on Monday, April 6, which is the first day of the tax year.

Employee's surname *in CAPITALS* POPE				First two forenames ALEXANDER ALOYSIUS				
National Insurance no. CC 11 22 33 C		Date of birth *in figures* Day 28 Month 09 Year 62		Works no. etc 17			Date of leaving *in figures* Day Month Year	
Tax code † 254L	Amended code † Wk/Mth in which applied							

Week no	Pay in the week or month including Statutory Sick Pay/Statutory Maternity Pay 2	Total pay to date 3	Total free pay to date as shown by Table A 4	Total taxable pay to date Ø 5	Total tax due to date as shown by Taxable Pay Tables 6	Tax deducted or refunded in the week or month *Mark refunds 'R'* 7	For employer's use
1	172 60	172 60	49 02	123 58	30 75	30 75	
2							
3							
4							
5							
6							
7							
8							
9							
10							
11							
12							

Alexander Pope's Form P11 (extract)

1) **Obtain Form P11**
   This is a record of the tax and NI contributions deducted from the employee's gross wage. It is provided for employers by the Inland Revenue.

2) **When you first create a new P11 record, enter**
   a) *employee's details*
      (Name: Alexander Augustine Aloysius Pope (do you write it in full? – look closely at the form); National Insurance Number is CC 11 22 33C; date of birth: 28 September 1962; works number: 17); tax code number: 254L).
   b) *employer's details*
      (Name: Eden Plants and Gardens; Tax reference: 888/E123M.

3) **Enter the gross pay for the week in column 2 of the P11**
   (£172.60)

4) **Enter total pay to date in column 3**
   Being the first week of the tax year, Mr Pope's total pay to date will be the same as his week's pay. For any other week:
   ❏ add week's pay (column 2) to last figure in column 3 (total to last week)
   ❏ enter the result in column 3 as the new total pay to date

5) **Find the Total Free Pay to date and enter this figure in column 4**
   To find Total Free Pay (that is untaxed pay):
   ❏ note tax code number (254)
   ❏ turn to Tax Table A – this is used for the calculation of free pay
   ❏ turn to the relevant week of the tax year (in this case week 1)
   ❏ read off the Free Pay figure opposite the code (£49.02)

   Note that, unlike in the case of gross pay, you do not have to calculate this yourself.

WEEK 1
Apr 6 to Apr 12

TABLE A—FREE PAY

Code	Total free pay to date	Code	Total free pay to date	Code	Total free pay to date	Code	Total free pay to date	Code	Total free pay to date	Code	Total free pay to date	Code	Total free pay to date	Code	Total free pay to date
	£		£		£		£		£		£		£		£
0	NIL														
1	0·37	61	11·91	121	23·45	181	34·99	241	46·52	301	58·06	361	69·60	421	81·14
2	0·56	62	12·10	122	23·64	182	35·18	242	46·72	302	58·25	362	69·79	422	81·33
3	0·75	63	12·29	123	23·83	183	35·37	243	46·91	303	58·45	363	69·99	423	81·52
4	0·95	64	12·49	124	24·02	184	35·56	244	47·10	304	58·64	364	70·18	424	81·72
5	1·14	65	12·68	125	24·22	185	35·75	245	47·29	305	58·83	365	70·37	425	81·91
6	1·33	66	12·87	126	24·41	186	35·95	246	47·49	306	59·02	366	70·56	426	82·10
7	1·52	67	13·06	127	24·60	187	36·14	247	47·68	307	59·22	367	70·75	427	82·29
8	1·72	68	13·25	128	24·79	188	36·33	248	47·87	308	59·41	368	70·95	428	82·49
9	1·91	69	13·45	129	24·99	189	36·52	249	48·06	309	59·60	369	71·14	429	82·68
10	2·10	70	13·64	130	25·18	190	36·72	250	48·25	310	59·79	370	71·33	430	82·87
11	2·29	71	13·83	131	25·37	191	36·91	251	48·45	311	59·99	371	71·52	431	83·06
12	2·49	72	14·02	132	25·56	192	37·10	252	48·64	312	60·18	372	71·72	432	83·25
13	2·68	73	14·22	133	25·75	193	37·29	253	48·83	313	60·37	373	71·91	433	83·45
14	2·87	74	14·41	134	25·95	194	37·49	254	49·02	314	60·56	374	72·10	434	83·64
15	3·06	75	14·60	135	26·14	195	37·68	255	49·22	315	60·75	375	72·29	435	83·83

Tax tables: extract 1

6) **Find the Total Taxable Pay to date. Enter this in column 5**
To find Total Taxable Pay to date:
☐   subtract the figure in column 4 (Total Free Pay to date – 49.02) from the figure in column 3 (Total Pay to date – 172.60) (So Total Taxable Pay to date = £123.58)

7) **Find the Total Tax due, and enter this in column 6**
To find Total Tax due (so far, for this tax year):
☐   turn to Table B
☐   take figure from column 5 (£123.58)
☐   ignore pence (£123)
☐   read off figure £30.75 (this is the tax due)

TABLE B

TAX DUE ON TAXABLE PAY FROM £1 TO £360

Total TAXABLE PAY to date	Total TAX DUE to date	Total TAXABLE PAY to date	Total TAX DUE to date	Total TAXABLE PAY to date	Total TAX DUE to date	Total TAXABLE PAY to date	Total TAX DUE to date	Total TAXABLE PAY to date	Total TAX DUE to date	Total TAXABLE PAY to date	Total TAX DUE to date
£	£	£	£	£	£	£	£	£	£	£	£
1	0.25	61	15.25	121	30.25	181	45.25	241	60.25	301	75.25
2	0.50	62	15.50	122	30.50	182	45.50	242	60.50	302	75.50
3	0.75	63	15.75	123	30.75	183	45.75	243	60.75	303	75.75
4	1.00	64	16.00	124	31.00	184	46.00	244	61.00	304	76.00
5	1.25	65	16.25	125	31.25	185	46.25	245	61.25	305	76.25
6	1.50	66	16.50	126	31.50	186	46.50	246	61.50	306	76.50
7	1.75	67	16.75	127	31.75	187	46.75	247	61.75	307	76.75
8	2.00	68	17.00	128	32.00	188	47.00	248	62.00	308	77.00
9	2.25	69	17.25	129	32.25	189	47.25	249	62.25	309	77.25
10	2.50	70	17.50	130	32.50	190	47.50	250	62.50	310	77.50

Tax tables: extract 2

8) **Calculate tax deducted this week. Enter this in column 7**
Because this is Week 1 this figure will be the same as the Total Tax due.

Normally:
☐   subtract lowest figure in column 6 (the most recent figure for Total Tax due) from the figure above it (last week's Total tax due). This gives this week's tax due.

9) **Move across form P11 and in column 1a enter the Gross Pay figure (omitting pence)** (£172.60).

10) **Find the total of employee's and employer's contributions and enter it in column 1b**
To find total NI contributions
☐   turn to the National Insurance Tables (in this case Weekly A)
☐   find the Gross Pay figure and read off the amount of the total contribution (£26.71)

Earnings on which employee's contributions payable 1a	Total of employee's and employer's contributions payable 1b	Employee's contributions payable 1c	Employer's contributions*
£	£	£	£
152	23·19	10·08	13·11
153	23·37	10·17	13·20
154	23·55	10·26	13·29
155	23·72	10·35	13·37
156	23·90	10·44	13·46
157	24·07	10·53	13·54
158	24·25	10·62	13·63
159	24·43	10·71	13·72
160	24·60	10·80	13·80
161	24·78	10·89	13·89
162	24·95	10·98	13·97
163	25·13	11·07	14·06
164	25·31	11·16	14·15
165	25·48	11·25	14·23
166	25·66	11·34	14·32
167	25·83	11·43	14·40
168	26·01	11·52	14·49
169	26·19	11·61	14·58
170	26·36	11·70	14·66
171	26·54	11·79	14·75
172	26·71	11·88	14·83
173	26·89	11·97	14·92
174	27·07	12·06	15·01
175	27·24	12·15	15·09
176	27·42	12·24	15·18
177	27·59	12·33	15·26

Tax tables: extract 3

11) **Find the employee's NI contribution payable and enter this figure in column 1c**

   ❑ turn to the same NI table
   ❑ from the Gross Pay figure read off the employee's contribution (£11.18).

Though it is not entered in the P11, you could now calculate net pay as follows:

gross pay			172.60
less	income tax	30.75	
	NI contribution	11.88	
	total deductions	42.63	
net pay			£129.97

4.2 Summary

New record

enter:

a) employee's details
   (name; National Insurance Number; date of birth; works number; tax code number)

b) employer's details
   (name; tax reference number)

278

Weekly record of deductions

enter:

1) gross pay in column 2

2) total pay to date in column 3
(add week's pay (column 2) to last figure in column 3 (total to last week)

3) total free pay to date in column 4
(use tax code number in Tax Table A for relevant week of the tax year to read off the free pay)

4) total taxable pay to date in column 5
(Subtract figure in column 4 (Total Free Pay to date) from figure in column 3 (Total Pay to date)

5) total tax due in column 6
(In Table B use Total Taxable Pay (ignore pence) to read off Total Tax Due)

6) tax deducted this week in column 7
(subtract lowest figure in column 6 from the figure above it to give this week's tax due)

7) gross pay in column 1a

8) total of employee's and employer's contributions in column 1b
(In National Insurance Tables use Gross Pay figure to read off the total contribution)

9) employee's NI contribution payable in column 1c
(In NI table, use gross pay figure to read off employee's contribution).

5. Other deductions and payments

Apart from the statutory deductions there are various other aspects of pay which the wages clerk will frequently encounter. The main ones are:

❑ Entered on Form P11:   *Statutory Sick Pay*

                                   Statutory Maternity Pay

❑ Voluntary Deductions: *Holiday Pay*

                                   Pension Schemes

5.1 Statutory sick pay

The conditions relating to statutory sick pay (abbreviated to SSP) cannot be discussed here. The important point is that all sick pay (including Statutory Sick Pay) counts as pay for tax and National Insurance purposes, and is entered on the P11.

It affects two entries:

❑ *column 2*, where the gross amount must be entered; it is either added to or instead of the wage

❑ *column 1f*, where only the SSP received is entered.

5.2 Statutory Maternity Pay (column 1g)

Again the conditions for the award of maternity pay (money paid while a woman is absent from work in the period around childbirth) cannot be discussed here. But again, maternity pay is entered on the P11 as follows:

❑ column 2, gross amount added to or instead of wages

❑ column 1g gross amount of maternity pay only

5.3 Holiday pay

Some firms operate schemes in which voluntary deductions are made from pay and repaid to the employee at holiday time. In certain schemes tax is deducted before repayments are made to employees; the income is not then taxed again.

5.4 Pension schemes (also known as superannuation schemes)

These are a benefit which the employer arranges, so that the employee will have extra income on retirement. The employer first obtains authorisation from the Superannuation Funds Office; the employee's contributions to a pension fund are then not taxed. This means that the wages clerk will have to deduct such contributions from the gross pay *before* working out the tax.

6. Paying the employee

6.1 Methods of payment

The ways which are most commonly used by businesses to pay wages and salaries are:

- cash
- cheque
- credit transfer direct to an account held at a bank, building society or the National Girobank.

(These are described under the relevant headings in *Bank documents*, page 79).

Larger businesses handle pay in bulk by sending the data, prepared for computerisation and recorded on tape, direct to BACS (the Clearing House) (see *Banking facilities: clearance of cheques*, page 100).

Companies who do not have the appropriate computer facilities can still arrange to make use of the system by filling in a form giving details of account numbers and amounts due for all employees who are to be paid. The entry into the computer is then handled by a bank or a computer bureau.

6.2 The pay slip

At the time of payment, the wages clerk prepares the *pay slips*. A pay slip is a statement of what payment is being made and how it is calculated. The slip also serves as a record of what has been paid. The employee should of course check at once that the pay slip is accurate, and agrees with the amount in the pay packet. The longer the delay in the event of a complaint, the more difficult it will be to put right.

The pay slips of Eden Plants and Gardens are a model of clarity, and look as follows:

EDEN PLANTS AND GARDENS			
Pay advice			
Date	Employee	Tax code	Week
17-04-92	A.A POPE	272L	2
Payments		**Deductions**	
Basic Pay:	172.60	Income tax:	26.50
Overtime:	32.18	Nat Ins.	14.76
Gross pay:	204-78	Total:	41.26
Net pay:	163.52		
Gross pay to date:	376-68	Tax paid this year:	57.25
Taxable pay:	271-30	NI paid:	26.64

Sadly, the reality of some pay slips is far from the above, especially when they come from a computerised system. The information is often printed in a type so faint that it is virtually illegible, and the format of the pay slip, instead of making clear the gross and net pay and deductions, is such that it would flummux even the Brain of Britain to decipher.

7. Payroll

The employer will keep a record of wages and salaries paid to employees. This is known as the payroll. The payroll sheet will be designed to meet the employer's needs but will basically take the form: overleaf.

The columns permit an internal check (a crosscheck, see *Work methods: accuracy*, page 291).

8. Cash analysis

8.1 Preparation of wage packets

If employees are to be paid in cash, it is important that the right notes and coins are available to put into their wage packets. They don't want to be fishing in their pockets for change on pay day!

The task of the wages clerk is therefore to ensure that this problem does not arise, by taking the following steps.

1) Find which employees are to be paid, and the net pay for each.
   This is achieved by looking at the payroll sheet.

2) Calculate for each employee what denominations (values) of cash will be needed.
   This process is known as making a *cash analysis*, and is explained below.

3) Total up how much of each denomination will be needed in order to pay all the employees.

4) Arrange with the bank for the preparation and collection of the cash, with each denomination being packaged separately.

5) Use this cash to make up each wage packet.

Week ending:　　　　　　　Week number:

Worker number	Name	Earnings				Deductions				Net pay	Employer NI
		Basic	Overtime	Bonus	Gross pay	PAYE	NI	Pension scheme	Total de-ductions		
TOTAL											

Payroll

8.2 The cash analysis sheet

The process is aided by using a cash analysis sheet:

CASH ANALYSIS SHEET

Employee	Wage £	p	£50	£20	£10	£5	£1	50p	20p	10p	5p	2p	1p
Total													

8.3 Cash analysis of one wage

The method can usefully be presented in the form of a flowchart:

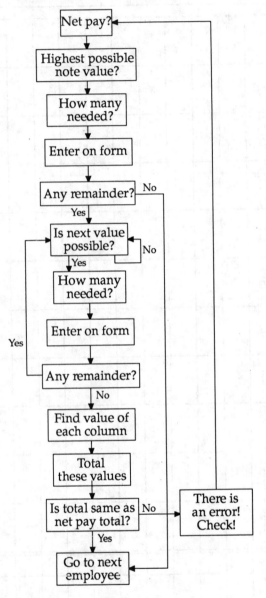

Applying this to the case of Alexander Pope it works as follows:

Pay £116.88

denomination	number	value	remainder
£20	5	£100	£16.88
£10	1	£10	£6.88
£5	1	£5	£1.88
£1	1	£1	88p
50p	1	50p	38p
20p	1	20p	18p
10p	1	10p	8p
5p	1	5p	3p
2p	1	2p	1p
1p	1	1p	£0.00

The pay packet is complete.

So Mr Pope's wage packet will include five £20 notes and one each of all the other denominations. An amazingly helpful coincidence!

Note: The analysis could be carried out in other ways. For example, 18p could be broken up into 3 x 5p, a 2p piece and a 1p piece. If you can see a possibility such as this, or if it makes the rest of the work more convenient, there is no reason why you should not use a different analysis. But the above method will ensure that you end up with a satisfactory result if you are unsure what to do.

8.4 Completing the cash analysis sheet

A very simple cash analysis sheet might look as follows:

Employee	Wage £	P	£50	£20	£10	£5	£1	50p	20p	10p	5p	2p	1p
Johnson S	111	55		5	1		1	1			1		
Pope AA	86	32		4		1			1	1		1	
Swift J	85	33		4		1			1	1		1	1
Total				260.00	10.00	10.00	2.00	0.50	0.40	0.20	0.05	0.04	0.01

CASH ANALYSIS SHEET

Method

After each wage packet has been analysed:

1) total up the figures in the far left column
2) multiply this total by the value (£20 in this case)
3) enter the total value at the bottom of the column
4) repeat for the other columns

5) cross check. The total of the right hand column should be the same as the result of adding together the totals of the denomination columns. If is not, there is an error.

6) draw up a request for the bank on the following lines:

13 x £20	260.00
1 x £10	10.00
2 x £5	10.00
2 x £1	2.00
1 x 50p	0.50
2 x 20p	0.40
2 x 10p	0.20
1 x 5p	0.05
2 x 2p	0.04
1 x1p	0.01
Total cash	283.20

A cheque for this amount may be taken to the counter, or the sum may be debited from the firm's accounts.

9. Summary forms

There are various times at which the information on the P11 has to be summarised. These are explained below.

9.1 Form P60

Example

After the end of the tax year on April 5, the employer is required to give a certificate of pay and tax deductions to each employee. This does not apply to those who have paid no tax. This document is Form P60 which is provided by the Inland Revenue for the purpose.

The form shows:

☐ the total amount paid to the employee during the tax year which has just ended

☐ total tax and National Insurance contributions deducted.

The form can be used by the employee when he or she has to complete a tax return for the Inland Revenue.

Filling in the form:

This follows naturally enough from keeping the Form P11 record of pay and deductions.

1) The various personal details and tax references are all (with the exception of the employer's address) to be found on Form P11.

2) The relevant columns of Form P11 which deal with National Insurance are indicated on the P60 (1a, 1b, 1c).

3) The total pay and total tax deducted are shown in special boxes at the bottom of columns 3 and 6, on side 2 of the P11.

4) The box headed 'Week 53 payment indicator' has to be filled in as described in the 'Employer's Guide to PAYE' and is not within the scope of this book.

Form P60

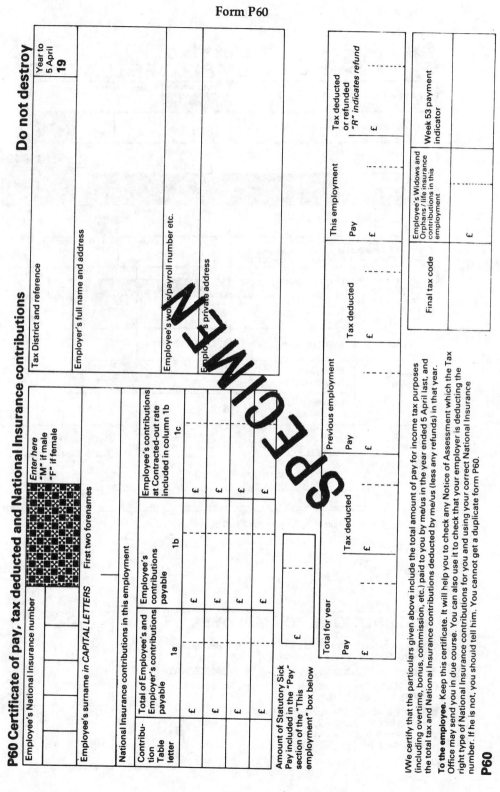

Form P45

P45 — Details of EMPLOYEE LEAVING — PART 1

		District number	Reference number
1.	PAYE reference		
2.	National Insurance number		
3.	Surname *(Use BLOCK letters)*		Mr. Mrs. Miss
	First two forenames *(Use BLOCK letters)*		

		Day	Month	Year
4.	Date of leaving *(in figures)*			

5.	Code at date of leaving	Code	Week 1 or Month 1
	If Week 1 or Month 1 basis applies, please also write "X" in the box marked "Week 1 or Month 1"		

			Week	Month
6.	Last entries on Deductions Working Sheet *If Week 1 or Month 1 basis applies, complete item 7 instead*	Week or Month number		
		Total pay to date	£	p
		Total tax to date	£	p
7.	Week 1 or Month 1 basis applies	Total pay in this employment	£	p
		Total tax in this employment	£	p

8.	Works Number	9. Branch, Contract Department, etc.

10. Employee's private address ....
....
.... Postcode ....

11. I certify that the details entered at items 1 to 9 above are correct.

Employer

Address

Date   Postcode

INSTRUCTIONS TO EMPLOYER

- Complete this form according to the "Employee leaving" instructions on the P8 (BLUE CARD).
- Detach Part 1 and send it to your Tax Office IMMEDIATELY.
- Hand Parts 2 and 3 (unseparated) to your employee WHEN HE LEAVES.
- IF THE EMPLOYEE HAS DIED, please write "D" in this box and send ALL THREE PARTS of this form (unseparated) to your Tax Office IMMEDIATELY.

For Tax Office use

For Central use		
Amended	M.E	P

P45   HPB 1439 9/84

Form P46

Inland Revenue PAYE

Instructions to Employer

- **Employee without a P45**

  If a **new** employee does not give you Parts 2 and 3 of form P45
  - ask him to read the Note to Employee below and complete Certificate A or B if appropriate
  - fill in the back of this form yourself and follow the instructions on form P8. If this tells you to send form P46 to your Tax Office please do this straight away.

- **Employee previously paid below the limit**

  If an **existing** employee's pay rises above the taxable limits
  - fill in the back of this form and follow the instructions on form P8.

Note to Employee

As you have not been able to give your employer Parts 2 and 3 of form P45, you should consider Certificates A and B below.

If this is your first regular job since leaving full-time education and you have **not** claimed unemployment benefit* since then, you should sign Certificate **A** below. This may enable your employer to operate a correct PAYE code for you straight away.

If this is your only job or your main job, you should sign Certificate B below. Your employer will use the emergency code.

If you are unable, or do not want to sign either Certificate, your employer will deduct tax at the basic rate.

- **Certificate A**

  I declare that this is my first regular job since leaving full-time education and that I have not claimed unemployment benefit* since then.

  Signature _____ Date _____ 19 ___

- **Certificate B**

  I declare that this is my only or my main job.

  Signature _____ Date _____ 19 ___

P46(1990)   *including income support paid because of unemployment

---

Please use CAPITALS

Employer's PAYE reference

Employee's National Insurance number

Employee's surname   Mr/Mrs/Miss/Ms

Employee's first names

Employee's private address

Postcode

Works or payroll number, if any

Branch or department, if any

Nature of employment

Date employment started   Day Month Year 19
Please use figures

Class of employee - *please tick the box which applies. If you tick Class 1, 2 or 3 please show the code you have used in the 'Code in use' box.*

Class 1 - **New employee** coming from school or college who has signed Certificate A

Class 2 - **New employee** who has signed Certificate B

Class 3 - **New employee** who has not signed either certificate

Class 4 - **Existing employee** previously paid below the taxable limit and now paid above it

Code in use
If week 1 or Month 1 basis applies please write 'X' in this box

Code | Wk 1 or Mth 1

Employer's name

Address

Postcode

Date _____ 19 ___

Please do not write in this space

HMSO. Dd. 8134656. 2/90. C190000. 40371. (74113).

289

9.2 Form P45 and P46

The example given to illustrate how to deal with Form P11 was carefully chosen so as to have a new employee, beginning work on the first day of the Tax Year. In fact, of course, many employees begin work in the middle of the tax year. How does the wages clerk proceed then?

There are two possibilities.

1) *The employee arrives without a P45.*
   The employer is required to ask the employee to attempt to obtain Form P45. Meanwhile the employer is required to use Form P46. The employee fills in side 1 unless neither Certificate A nor Certificate B is inapplicable (for instance, if the employee has another job which is his or her main employment). The employer fills in Side 2 and sends it to the Inland Revenue.

   Employees do not always understand the importance of obtaining and producing Form P45. They are often then surprised and irritated at the level of stoppages which are made until their tax coding is decided by the Inland Revenue. This is because an emergency coding is applied which is in excess of what is really due from the employee. Any overpayment of tax is refunded at a later stage.

2) *The employee arrives with Form P45.*
   To enable employers to begin at once to use Form P11 charging the correct deductions, the Inland Revenue has devised Form P45. This issued by an employer to an employee who is leaving, provided that the employer has been filling in Form P11. The form gives details of pay and deductions made so far during the current tax year.

Form P45 is in three parts. The top copy (Part 1) must be filled in by the employer – not the employee. Parts 2 and 3 are carbon copies of the top copy.

The parts are used as follows:

Part 1   This is sent by the employer to the local Tax Office.

Parts 2 and 3   These are given to the employee, who passes them on to the new employer. It is then possible for the new employer to begin using Form P11 in the normal way.

As with the P60 the various information required is taken from Form P11. The use of the 'Week 1 or Month 1' boxes are described in the 'Employer's guide to PAYE'.

9.3 Importance of following Inland Revenue requirements

One final point should be made, which holds whether you are acting as a wages clerk or dealing with your own pay and tax.

The amount of paper work involved in making deductions sometimes seems unnecessary or tedious. But it is not possible to avoid doing it. The employee whose affairs have not been properly documented will be taxed at the Emergency Rate until it is proved that he or she is entitled to another coding. Refunds are likely to be delayed until matters have been cleared up to the satisfaction of the authorities. Not least important, the statutory deductions are required by law, and to fail to make them intentionally is a crime (known as tax evasion). In order to discourage such situations the Government have given the Inland Revenue considerable powers to enforce the legislation. These powers can lead to heavy fines and even imprisonment.

Work methods

Information and suggestions on how to carry out work with efficiency, accuracy and security

Contents

1. Accuracy

1.1 Attention to accuracy

Attitudes to accuracy

Every examiner and every employer emphasises the need for work which is accurate. You can easily see why. Would you like to be charged too much for a purchase, or to be paid less than you had earned?

Everyone makes mistakes, but you can reduce them greatly by acquiring good habits. In particular remember that, though employees have to become quick and efficient in their work, it is better, if you are uncertain, to go slowly and carefully. A quite staggering amount of work can be caused by a wrong calculation at an early stage, which is not picked up until later. There is also the problem of restoring the goodwill of customers who have been inconvenienced.

Good work methods

There are two points at which you can take care to eliminate error. One is when preparing for or carrying out the task (by good work methods); the other is by careful checking.

Some of the things you can do to help ensure accuracy are:

1) *Use a systematic approach.* In this book there are many checklists and other aids to carrying out tasks systematically. Using such methods has both two advantages. First, you are less likely to miss out important steps. Second, you are more likely to be accurate under pressure, because you are not constantly having to think how to carry out the task.

2) *Get into the habit of laying out your work neatly.* If your figures are hard to read, or if your calculations are cramped, you are more likely to make mistakes.

3) *If in doubt, make a rough copy.* Until you are used to a job, it often helps to rough it out first. Very often something arises in the task which means that the work you have done before has to be changed.

4) *Consult reference sources.* Most people find that it is easy to get numbers wrong (for instance, remembering 1067 as 1076). If in doubt, look up figures – the job isn't a memory test. This is also true of multiplication tables. The authors believe that these should be known by heart – it makes life much easier. But if you don't know them well it is better to look them up, than to make an error.

1.2 Rough estimates – procedure

1) *Make a rough estimate*
   Once you have completed a task, you can often avoid errors by careful checking of what you have done. There are various techniques which can be helpful. One of these is to make a *rough estimate* of the answer.

   Making such an estimate may be made easier by using **round figures**, that it, an easier number handle which is close to the number you are dealing with.

   For example, you calculate that VAT on £20.00 is £15.30. The rate of VAT is $17\frac{1}{2}$% – roughly 20%, or one fifth. A fifth of 20 is 4, so the VAT can't be more than £4.00. You need to check your calculations.

2) *Repeat your calculations*
   Once you have completed your calculations, you should check what you have done. You may do this by using a calculator to check manual results and vice versa. Or you may go over the working again.

3) *Use standard checking procedures where these exist*
   One such procedure is the *internal check*, in this case a *crosscheck*. It is a standard technique used by auditors.

   An example can be given by listing a simple set of everyday office expenses as follows:

Day	Postage	Stationery	Travel	Total
Monday	2.50	3.50	3.50	9.50
Tuesday	3.50	1.50	2.50	7.50
totals	6.00	5.00	6.50	17.00

You first total across the columns. You then total down the columns.

Next total the right hand column. Finally total the bottom line. They should be the same. (They aren't – can you find out why?) This is a very valuable technique when dealing with payroll and cash analysis.

Note: The table above is given to illustrate a principle. It is not a standard way of recording petty cash expenditure (see *Petty Cash*, page 219 forward).

4) *'Proof reading'*
   Even the most experienced person can make mistakes when writing words or numbers. The problem is made worse by the fact that we often fail to see our own errors, even when we would spot them straight away in the work of others. If possible, get another person to check your work. It's worth remembering that publishers always do this. It is also a technique often used by secretaries when working on long or complicated pieces of typing. The person who typed it reads it aloud, while a colleague follows it on the page. This technique is know as 'proof reading'.

   Another useful tip is to cover all lines except the one you are reading, so as to concentrate your eye.

5)   *Error analysis*

It is a good idea to make a note of your errors: you will often find a pattern there. Very often, one or two difficulties will account for most of your problems. You may think this is a rather tedious and use-less exercise. If so, bear in mind that American banks did just this, to find out the causes of error in the work of clerks who enter data into computers. It has already saved them millions of dollars.

Naturally, it will not always be possible to follow out any, let alone all of the above advice. But if you are in doubt, you should remember the following:

a)   Examiners think it is of the highest importance

b)   So do employers

c)   If you do find a problem that keeps on coming up, trying the above methods is quite likely to pin-point the source of the difficulty.

2. Organising your work

2.1 The need to organise

Employers look for people who can work independently and efficiently. The key to meeting this require-ment is the ability to organise your work. For this reason examining bodies, and especially BTEC, stress the importance of acquiring this skill. If you have ever had to deal with an inefficient organisation, you will know how costly it can be in terms of time and temper.

Some useful techniques are:

1)   *Make a list*

Take the burden off your memory!

2)   *Prioritise*

a)   Note which tasks are **urgent** and which must be done at a **set time**.

b)   Put tasks in order of the **seniority** of the person requiring the action.

3)   *Group tasks which need to be done*

a)   in the same **place**

b)   at the same **time** or as **part of one job.**

4)   *Estimate time required*

5)   *Make a plan*

This may take the form of:

a)   a list in order of priority

b)   a flowchart

c)   a timetable.

3. Security

3.1 Outline of problem

There is perhaps no aspect of financial record keeping which both examining bodies and employers stress more than the need to be attentive to security. It seems to be a permanent problem that where there is money, there will also be those who seek to get hold of it by illegal means.

With regard to security there are two basic situations in which it becomes possible to obtain money illegally:

(a) fraud

(b) theft (including burglary and robbery with violence).

It is important to remember that many crimes involving money are not planned in advance; they are 'opportunist crimes'. This means that the criminal happens to see an opening, and exploits it. Attention to the procedures which are used can ensure that the risk of loss of money may be greatly reduced.

3.2 Fraud

Nowadays we hear a great deal about crime, and especially armed robbery, in connection with money. These are rightly regarded as serious matters, and they are undoubtedly very disturbing to those who suffer such incidents. Yet in terms of loss fraud is probably a far greater problem.

There are limits to what the ordinary employee can do; serious fraud is a matter for the police. Nevertheless, everyone can help in reducing fraud. The danger of fraud may be reduced by various means:

Some important ways of doing this are:

1) *Reduce the ease of access to cash,* for instance by using crossed cheques (see *Bank documents: cheques,* page 83).

2) There should be *careful checking of all documents* by both senders and recipients. For this purpose, the sorts of checklist given in this book can be very valuable.

3) The financial record keeper should normally *refuse to accept inaccurately completed documents.*

4) Check **credit limits**. This means that it is more difficult for customers to spend money which they cannot repay.

5) Require a *cheque to be supported by a cheque guarantee card* (see *Bank documents: cheque guarantee cards,* page 89), containing various data, and notably a signature. It is very important for anyone who is going to be accepting cheques (for instance a shop assistant or a receptionist) to follow the correct procedures to ensure that a cheque is valid (see *Bank documents: cheques,* page 83).

3.3 Theft

There are of course very great limits to what the ordinary employee can do or is expected to do about theft, and especially about armed robbery. These are matters for the police and security organisations. The employee should always follow the guidelines and instructions laid down concerning such incidents.

Nevertheless, we can all help to reduce theft as follows:

1) Both firms and individuals can *avoid holding cash* by the use of cheques, standing orders, direct debit and credit facilities (for details see the relevant entries under *Bank documents,* page 79).

2) Individuals should keep *cheque guarantee cards and cheque books separately* (see *Bank documents: cheque guarantee cards,* page 89).

3) It is important to *exercise care in keeping credit cards.* A remarkable amount of fraud is made possible because opportunist thieves find credit cards lying about, rather than obtaining them by breaking and entering.

4) As far as possible, firms should *not hold or transport large amounts of cash.*

5) Where the holding of cash is unavoidable, there is a need for the *use of safes, alarms and security personnel.* Even when dealing with the relatively small amounts of money involved in petty cash (see *petty cash,* page 219), it is normal practice to keep the cash locked in a box. To this there should a restricted number of keys, which are kept in a safe and secure place.

6) Firms are also advised by the police to keep a *low profile on the movement of cash.* More than one person should go to collect it. The times of withdrawals should be varied to avoid a routine becoming known to criminals.

Section 3

PRACTICE AND DEVELOPMENT OF SKILLS AND KNOWLEDGE

How to use this section

This section of the book gives you the chance to apply and develop what you have learned in Section 1. It does so by presenting a series of simulations of financial record keeping in the workplace. You are given an indication of the circumstances in which you are working, and your brief. There is then a set of tasks to be worked at.

The best way to work is as follows:

1) **Read the list of topics** covered by the simulation. **Decide if you need to refresh your knowledge** before setting to work.

2) **Look over the whole simulation to see what you have to do and how the tasks link up.**

3) **Start on the first task.** Take your time, and **work carefully**: at this point in your career accuracy is far more important than speed.

4) It will usually be wise to **make drafts or rough copies** before you create your final version of a task.

5) **Use any checks** you can on your calculations.

There are two other points worth making:

6) **Use The Information Bank** (Section 2)
   When you learn something new, it usually makes sense to take things in easy stages and to keep things simple. That is how Section 1 is built up. Unfortunately, the real world is not quite so neatly packaged. The types of skill and knowledge are likely to come from any point in the course you have been through.

   For this reason, the simulation is headed by a list of the topics which will arise. As suggested above, you may wish to refresh some of these. You should also remember that the Information Bank is intended to be your own personal source of reference. Unless your lecturer indicates otherwise, you should not hesitate to use it to look up information or procedures.

7) **Read the tasks you are given very carefully**
   In order to make the simulation more realistic, and to develop your confidence in handling the various procedures, **errors have been built into some of the tasks**. You are quite likely to find, for example, that the addition on an incoming invoice is wrong. As a person handling financial records, whether as a student or an employee, you will always need to be on the lookout for such errors, and to take the appropriate action.

Section contents

Petty cash

(corresponding to NVQ Element 20.1)

Topics covered: *petty cash (imprest, vouchers, cash book); balancing an account; calculating VAT.*
Forms needed: *petty cash voucher*, page 221; *petty cash sheet*, The Forms Bank, page 359.

Practice in the calculation of balances

Task 1: enter the missing details:

Number	Imprest	Total payments	Balance c/d	Balance b/d	Sum needed to restore imprest
1	40.00	32.73			
2	60.00	14.45			
3	100.00	64.91			
4	20.00	19.79			

Practice in the calculation of VAT

Task 2: adding VAT

Sum	VAT Rate (%)	VAT payable	Total
1.94	10		
2.15	$12\frac{1}{2}$		
3.45	15		
0.65	$17\frac{1}{2}$		
1.37	$17\frac{1}{2}$		
5.76	$17\frac{1}{2}$		
10.50	$17\frac{1}{2}$		

Task 3: calculating VAT included (at rate $17\frac{1}{2}$%)

Total Sum	VAT payable	Price before VAT
2.52		
1.66		
6.52		
7.17		
2.92		

Simulation

Task 4

You are asked to handle petty cash by an employer. Your task is to deal with petty cash requests during the month of September, as listed below.

Your brief is:

1) Record the receipt of the imprest (£75.00) on 1 September.

2) If a request is for less than £5.00 and is supported by a receipt, you are authorised to make out a petty cash voucher. Otherwise the payment is referred to the Cashier.

3) Vouchers should be dated and numbered in sequence, contain the relevant details, including VAT paid when relevant, and should indicate who authorised the payment.

4) Indicate clearly when authorisation has to be sought.

5) Assume that all payments are authorised and make the relevant entries on the petty cash sheet.

6) Ensure that VAT output tax paid is entered on the sheet, calculating this yourself when appropriate.

7) Total and balance the sheet, and also record the restoration of the imprest for the following month.

Claims made (a receipt was produced unless otherwise indicated):

1st	postage £2.52
2nd	travel by car (25 miles): firm allows 35p per mile
3rd	pencils £1.80 plus 0.31p VAT
4th	window cleaner £4.50
5th	travel by bus £0.85 (no receipt offered)
8th	envelopes £3.64 (including VAT)
9th	pens £2.15 plus 0.37p VAT
11th	postage £1.85
12th	labels £2.58 (including VAT)
15th	travel: £7.70 (bus £1.20 (no receipt), taxi £6.50 (with receipt))
17th	meal: £6.38 (including VAT; no receipt produced)
18th	postage £1.10
19th	travel by bus £0.80 (no receipt produced)
22nd	pot plant for office £7.95 + VAT £1.39
23rd	envelopes £1.99 (£1.70 + VAT 0.29p)
24th	postage £3.72
25th	coffee for office £2.42
26th	travel: car £4.65 (13 miles)
29th	stationery £2.70 (£2.30 plus 0.40p VAT)
30th	postage £0.90

To carry out this task use the voucher form, page 221 and petty cash sheet from The Forms Bank, *page 359.*

Help ?

See Section 2: The Information Bank

Accounts: balancing an account, page 77.

Calculations: percentages, page 113.

Petty cash, page 219.

Receiving payments

(corresponding to NVQ Element 20.2)

Topics covered: *giving change; VAT calculations; issuing receipts; validity of cheques; end of day routine; giving discounts; cheque guarentee cards; credit card payments.*

Forms needed: *receipt, credit card sales voucher,* The Forms Bank, page 359; *deposit slip,* page 5.

Situation 1

The date is 1 June 1991. You are working in Codlington's major department store, Renshaws. A customer may offer payment in three ways: in cash, by cheque supported with a cheque guarantee card, or by credit card.

Task 1: giving change

Calculate the change to be given, and the minimum number of notes and coins which will make up that change in the following transactions:

Cost of goods	Customer tenders	Change due	Analysis
3.25	5.00		
3.19	5.00		
2.09	2.50		
1.16	5.00		
4.17	10.00		

Task 2: adding VAT and making out a receipt

For the following transactions make the calculations indicated and then make out receipts. You may invent items or simply write 'goods'.

Cost of goods	Total less VAT	VAT	Total includ- ing VAT
18.50			
18.50; 23.50			
4.25; 6.30; 5.00			
9.50; 6.40			
3.50; 2.65; 4.25			

Task 3: validity of cheques

During the day you are offered the following cheques and guarantee cards. What action should you take? You should also decide how you will present the situation to the customer.

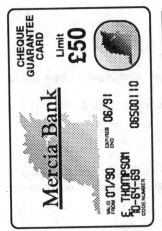

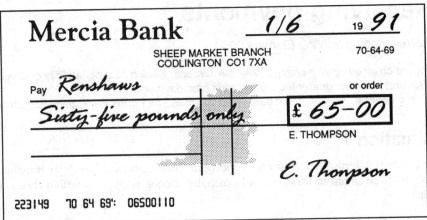

Mercia Bank

1/6   19 **91**

SHEEP MARKET BRANCH
CODLINGTON CO1 7XA

70-64-69

Pay *Renshaws*   or order

Sixty-five pounds only   £ **65—00**

E. THOMPSON

E. Thompson

223149   70 64 69':   06500110

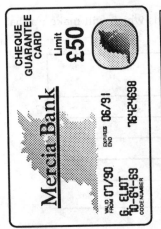

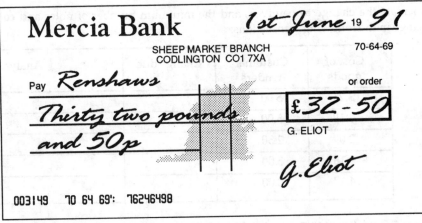

Mercia Bank

1st June 19 **91**

SHEEP MARKET BRANCH
CODLINGTON CO1 7XA

70-64-69

Pay *Renshaws*   or order

Thirty two pounds and 50p   £**32—50**

G. ELIOT

G. Eliot

003149   70 64 69':   76246498

Mercia Bank

1 June 19 **91**

SHEEP MARKET BRANCH
CODLINGTON CO1 7XA

70-64-69

Pay *Renshaws*   or order

Forty-one pounds only   £**41—00**

W. COLLINS

W. COLLINS

004121   70 64 69':   76123400

 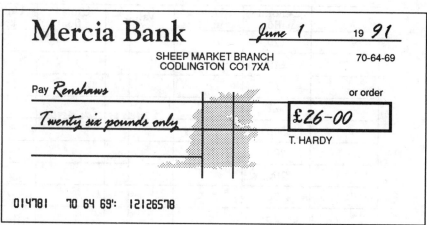

Task 4

Make out sales vouchers for the following credit card sales. Details are Department Code: CS; sales number: E2; description: table linen.

1) Goods worth £15.40

2) Goods worth £23.95; customer's signature does not match that on the card

Once again, decide exactly what you will say to the customer.

Task 5: end of day routine.

You start the day with a float as listed below.

At the end of the day, you have coins, notes and cheques in the till, also listed below.

1) Work out the total amount in the till.

2) Leave the original float in the till.

3) Work out:

   a) the number of units of each denomination which is left over to be banked;

   b) the value of each denomination to be banked;

   c) the total value of the cheques;

   d) the total amount (cash and cheques) to be banked.

4) Make out a deposit slip accordingly.

5) Make out a summary of the day's takings as indicated below.

Float: Total: £30, consisting of 1 x £10; 2 x £5; 5 x £1; 4 x 50p; 5 x 20p; 10 x 10p; 10 x 5p; 20 x 2p; 20 x 1p.

In till at end of day: 1 x £20; 3 x £10; 6 x £5; 22 x £1; 11 x 50p; 8 x 20p; 14 x 10p; 10 x 5p; 22 x 2p; 23 x 1p.

Cheques: £15.31; £16.10; £14.95; £14.95

Use the following table so as to make a crosscheck of your calculations.

	Denomi-nation	Units in till	Value		Units in float	Units to bank	Value to bank	
	£20							
	£10							
	£5							
	£1							
	50p							
	20p							
	10p							
	5p							
	2p							
	1p							
subtotals								
cheques								
Totals (values only)								

Summary of takings		
In till at end of day	£	p
cash:		
cheques:		
total takings:		
less float		
Total at bank:		

Situation 2

Task 6: giving change

Calculate the change to be given, and the minimum number of notes and coins which will make up that change in the following transactions:

Cost of goods	Customer tenders	Change due	Analysis
26.50	50.00		
31.20	40.00 (2 x £20)		
19.91	20.00		
37.40	50.00		
9.75	20.00		

Task 7: deducting discount and making out a receipt

For certain sales the firm offers a discount. In the following transactions make the calculations indicated and then make out receipts. You may invent items or simply write 'goods'.

Cost of goods	total value	Discount (%)	value of discount	Total after discount
28.50		2		
28.50; 13.25		$2\frac{1}{2}$		
5.90; 46.30; 7.00		5		
6.50; 8.40		$7\frac{1}{2}$		
5.50; 3.15; 4.95		10		

Task 8: validity of cheques

The date is 1 June 1991. You are selling an item costing £32.25. During the day you are offered the following cheques and guarantee cards. What action should you take? You should also decide how you will present the situation to the customer.

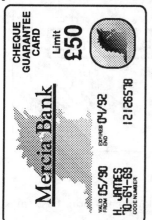

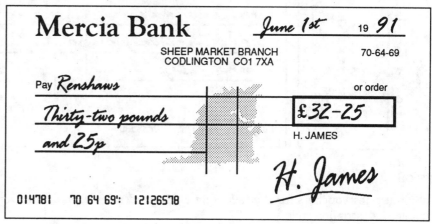

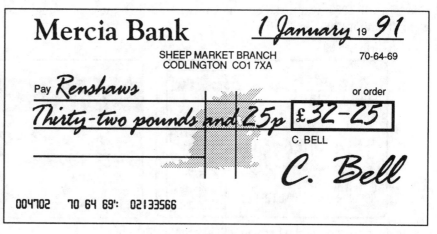

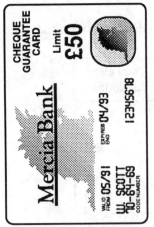

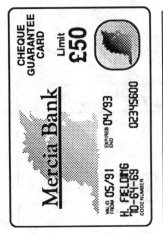
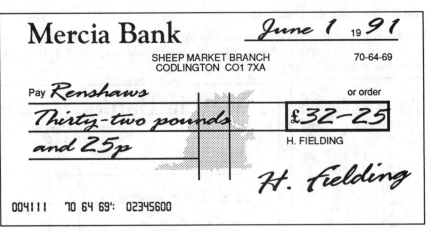

Task 9

Make out sales vouchers for the following credit card sales. Details are Department Code: DH; sales number 44; description cutlery.

3 Goods worth £250; you make out the voucher and then the confirming phone call, which indicates that the credit limit is £200

4 Goods worth £65.00

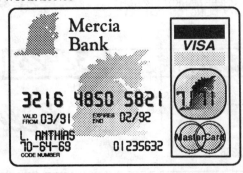
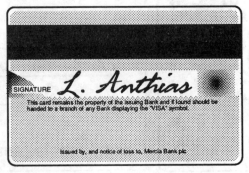

Once again, decide exactly what you will say to the customer.

Task 10: end of day routine.

You start the day with a float as listed below.

At the end of the day, you have coins, notes and cheques in the till, also listed below.

1)   Work out the total amount in the till.
2)   Leave the original float in the till.
3)   Work out
     a)   the number of units of each denomination which is left over to be banked;
     b)   the value of each denomination to be banked;
     c)   the total value of the cheques;
     d)   the total amount (cash and cheques) to be banked.
4)   Make out a deposit slip accordingly.
5)   Make out a summary of the day's takings as indicated below.

Float: Total: £75, consisting of 1 x £20 2 x £10; 5 x £5; 5 x £1; 4 x 50p; 5 x 20p; 10 x 10p; 10 x 5p; 20 x 2p; 10 x 1p.

In till at end of day: 6 x £20; 5 x £10; 9 x £5; 12 x £1; 5 x 50p; 10 x 20p; 10 x 10p; 15 x 5p; 30 x 2p; 21 x 1p.

Cheques: £25.34; £17.99; £23.95; £14.15

Use the following table so as to make a crosscheck of your calculations.

	Denomi-nation	Units in till	Value		Units in float	Units to bank	Value to bank	
	£20							
	£10							
	£5							
	£1							
	50p							
	20p							
	10p							
	5p							
	2p							
	1p							
subtotals								
cheques								
Totals (values only)								

Summary of takings		
In till at end of day	£	p
cash:		
cheques:		
total takings:		
less float		
Total at bank:		

305

Help ?

See Section 2: The Information Bank

Bank documents: cheques, page 83; *cheque guarantee cards,* page 89.

Calculations: percentages, page 113.

Quotations: calculation of discount, page 234.

Methods of payment: retail trading, page 203; *receipts,* page 206; *credit cards,* page 207.

Paying in and withdrawing money at the bank

Corresponding to NVQ Element 20.3

Topics covered: *filling in cheques; validity of cheques; deposit slips, postal orders, credit cards; cash analysis; foreign currency.*
Forms needed: *deposit slip,* page 5; *cash analysis sheet,* page 283; *cheque,* The Forms Bank, page 359.

Situation 1

Task 1: paying in cash

You receive the following cash from the till, together with the total indicated:

3 x £50; 4 x £20; 10 x £10; 14 x £5; 21 x £1; 10 x 50p; 16 x 20p; 45 x 10p; 9 x 5p; 24 x 2p; 16 x 1p; total 449.91

a)   Check and if necessary amend the total.

b)   You receive 8 cheques, total £142.00

   One of the cheques is as shown below; what should you do?

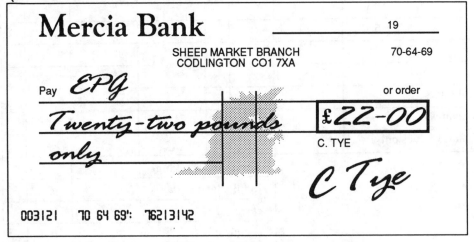

c)   Make out a deposit slip to bank the money.

Task 2: you are required to obtain some foreign currency as listed below:

- ❏ £25 worth of French francs
- ❏ £15 Dutch guilders
- ❏ 50 000 Italian lire

a) Make out the cheque with which you will pay for the currency so that it is ready for signature by your cashier.

b) At the bank the clerk gives you the following currency. Is this correct? (Ignore charges).

- ❏ 250 francs; 50 guilders, 50 000 lire.

The exchange rates are as shown below:

Exchange rates

French franc	10.03
Deutschmark	2.9553
Lira	2 197
Peseta	184.18
Guilder	3.3287
Ruritanian doubloon	87.87

Situation 2

Task 3: paying in to the bank

a) You receive two postal orders as follows:

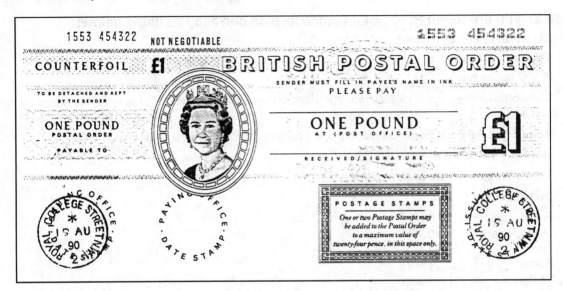

What will be your action?

b) You receive cheques, with totals, as follows:

- ❐ Till 1: 6 cheques 85.60
- ❐ Till 2: 5 cheques 210.00
- ❐ Till 3: 5 cheques 171.25

One of the cheques is as shown below; what should you do?

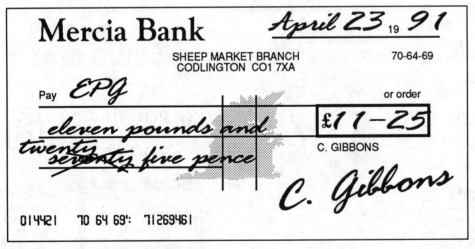

c) Make out a deposit slip to bank the money.

Task 4: You are required to obtain cash for the wages of various casual workers. They are to receive the following net pay:

Name	Net pay
C Hawkins	52.50
L Young	104.15
C Parker	99.90

a)   Make a cash analysis of your requirements (highest note value £20)

b)   Make out the necessary cheque

Situation 3

Task 5: paying in money

You receive the following cash from the tills, together with the totals indicated:

❏   Till 1:   2 x £50; 5 x £20; 13 x £10; 25 x £5; 47 x £1; 30 x 50p; 54 x 20p; 31 x 10p; 23 x 5p; 24 x 2p; 32 x 1p; total: £512.85

❏   Till 2:   4 x £50; 7 x £20; 11 x £10; 64 x £5; 33 x £1; 22 x 50p; 4 x 20p; 32 x 10p; 18 x 5p; 11 x 2p; 17 x 1p; total £879.80

a)   Check for errors, and if necessary amend the totals

b)   You receive cheques, with totals, as follows:

   ❏   Till 1: 8 cheques 190.50

   ❏   Till 2: 3 cheques 99.00

One of the cheques is as shown below; what should you do?

Task 6: you are required to obtain some foreign currency as listed below:

❏   £150 worth of Deutschmarks

❏   10 000 Spanish pesetas

You are also to pay in 120 guilders.

Practice and development of skills and knowledge

a)   How much foreign currency will you receive?

b)   Calculate how much you will need to pay for currency, and what you will receive in sterling.

c)   Make out a cheque for the difference ready for signature by your cashier.

The exchange rates are as shown earlier.

Situation 4

Task 7: paying in to the bank

You receive credit card voucher slips and a total as follows:

☐   Till 1:   89.50

☐   Till 2:   105.00

☐   Till 3:   167.50

a)   You notice that the signature of Mrs Knight has hardly come through the carbon and is unlikely to be accepted. The sale was for £45.00 What will you do? Make any amendments to the total.

b)   You also receive cheques, with totals, as follows:

☐   Till 1:   £99.00

☐   Till 2:   £165.50

☐   Till 3:   £192.25

One of the cheques is as shown below. What should you do?

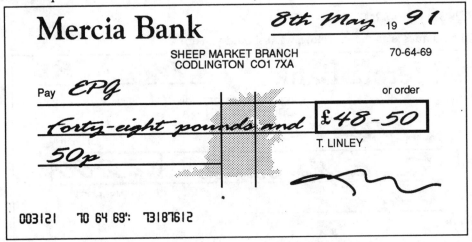

c)   Make out a deposit slip to bank the money.

Task 8: you are again required to obtain cash for the wages of various casual workers. They are to receive the following net pay:

Name	Net pay
C Hawkins	68.73
L Young	131.17
C Parker	89.10

a)   Make a cash analysis of your requirements.

b)   Make a summary for the bank.

c)   At the bank, you are given the following by the assistant:

       ❐   13 x £20; 1 x £10 ; 2 x £5; 9 x £1.

    What would you do?

Situation 5

Task 9: bagging up and paying in money

You receive the following cash from the tills, together with the totals indicated:

❐   Till 1:   1 x £50; 6 x £20; 11 x £10; 22 x £5; 43 x £1; 40 x 50p; 24 x 20p; 37 x 10p; 13 x 5p; 54 x 2p; 18 x 1p; total: £463.41

❐   Till 2:   2 x £50; 4 x £20; 13 x £10; 12 x £5; 33 x £1; 30 x 50p; 26 x 20p; 39 x 10p; 18 x 5p; 44 x 2p; 27 x 1p; total 449.15

❐   Till 3:   8 x £50; 6 x £20; 21 x £10; 14 x £5; 13 x £1; 18 x 50p; 14 x 20p; 12 x 10p; 8 x 5p; 31 x 2p; 15 x 1p; total £827.15

a)   Check for errors, and if necessary amend the totals.

b)   You are required to 'bag up' the cash according to the following specifications:

       ❐   £50: batches of 10; £20 batches of 25; £10 batches of 10; £5 batches of 20; £1 bags of 20; 50p bags of 20; 20p bags of 50; 10p bags of 50; 5p bags of 20; 2p bags of 50; 1p bags of 100.

    Indicate what you will have at the end of the process.

c)   You receive cheques, with totals, as follows:

       ❐   Till 1:   8 cheques 190.50

       ❐   Till 2:   4 cheques 142.00

       ❐   Till 3:   3 cheques 99.00

    One of the cheques is as shown below; what should you do?

d)   Make out a deposit slip to bank the money.

Task 10: you are required to obtain some foreign currency as listed below:

a) Calculate how much the currency will cost.

French francs	1800
Lira	2 000 000
Guilder	300
Ruritanian doubloon	10 000

b) Make out a cheque for that sum ready for signature by your cashier.

c) At the bank the clerk informs you that owing to a political crisis, the exchange rate for the Ruritanian doubloon has changed sharply overnight. The exchange rate is now 47.50.

    1) How many will you now receive for your money?

    2) You phone the cashier who says that she will amend the cheque.

        a) What sum will now be needed to acquire the required amount?

        b) What sum must the cheque now be for?

Help ?

See Section 2: The Information Bank

Bank documents: cheques, page 83; *deposit slips*, page 91.

Methods of payment: postal orders, page 201; *credit cards*, page 207.

Wages: cash analysis page 281.

Calculations: foreign currency, page 106.

Making payments

(corresponding to NVQ Element 20.4)

Topics covered: *reconciliation of invoices; delivery notes; reconciliation of customer statements; VAT registration; VAT calculations; terms of business (delivery, discount);` foreign currencies.*
Forms needed: *cheque, remittance advice*, The Forms Bank, page 359.

You are working in the accounts section of Eden Plants and Gardens. At the end of October the invoices and statements given below arrive for payment. Your task is to make any necessary checks on accuracy, and then to prepare cheques or giro slips for signature. When cheques are made out, you should also fill in the counterfoil.

To avoid unnecessary or irrelevant labour, addresses and reference numbers can be omitted except when stated. Also much unimportant detail is omitted from the invoices. However, in certain cases, the invoice is reproduced in full. On such occasions it is important to check the whole document carefully.

The VAT rate is taken to be $17\frac{1}{2}$% throughout.

Your brief:

1) Where instructed, reconcile the documents given.

2) Check the calculations (including VAT and discount where relevant).

3) In the event of error by the firm forwarding the invoice or statement, draft the appropriate letter.

4) Where there is no error, make payment of the type indicated.

5) Where there is error, make the necessary amendments, assume that the changes have been approved by both sides, and make payment of the type indicated.

6) In the case of payment by cheque, make out a remittance advice.

Stage 1

Task 1

Reconcile the following invoice with the relevant delivery note and then follow your brief.

			INVOICE			

A EDENS
Shepherd's Way, Appleton
Date: 31 October

VAT reg no: 197 8345 23

Quantity	Item	Unit	Unit cost	total before VAT	VAT ($17\frac{1}{2}$%)	total including VAT
200	snowdrop	10	2.00	40.00	7.00	47.00
4	rhododendron	1	5.00	20.00	3.50	23.50
400	daffodil	10	1.80	72.00	12.60	84.60
100	narcissus	10	1.95	19.50	3.41	22.91
6	winter jasmine	1	8.50	51.00	8.92	59.92
2	flowering pear	1	17.50	35.00	6.12	41.12
9	flowering cherry	9	12.00	108.00	18.90	126.90
	totals			345.50	60.45	405.95

DELIVERY NOTE

A. EDENS
Shepherd's Way, Appleton
Date: 12 October

Quantity	Item	Unit
200	snowdrop	10
4	rhododendron	1
400	daffodil	10
100	narcissus	10
6	winter jasmine	1
2	flowering pear	1
9	flowering cherry	9

Goods received as stated

Signature: *Dean Cuffey*

Task 2

You receive the following statement:

Harmonious Blacksmith
- all kinds of ironwork -
Handley's Edge

Customer: EPG
Credit limit: £500

Account no: GC42
Date: 16 November 1991
Terms: 30 days

STATEMENT OF ACCOUNT

Date	Description	Debit	Credit	Balance
Oct 1	Balance b/d			427.50 DR
Oct 2	Invoice HB182	36.19		463.69 DR
Oct 4	Remittance		427.50	36.19 DR
Oct 5	Invoice HB184	42.00		78.19 DR
Oct 8	Invoice HB187	76.00		154.19 DR
Oct 10	Invoice HB191	102.75		256.94 DR
Oct 17	Invoice HB194	80.00		336.94 DR
Oct 20	Invoice HB195	36.19		373.13 DR
Oct 23	Invoice HB197	19.50		392.63 DR
Oct 30	Balance due			392.63 DR

A check on invoices received and other records yields the following information.

Invoices received:

❏   2 Oct HB182   36.19;   8 Oct HB187   76.00;   17 Oct HB194   80.00;   23 Oct HB197   19.50.
    5 Oct HB184   42.00;   10 Oct HB191   102.75;   20 Oct HB195   36.19.

❏   3 Oct Remittance sent 427.50.

❏   Credit notes received: 21 Oct HBCN83 14.40.

The invoices of 2 October and 20 October are as follows:

Harmonious Blacksmith
- all kinds of ironwork -
Handley's Edge

Date: 2 October 1991

VAT reg. no. 201 8697 23

INVOICE

Quantity	Item	Unit	Unit cost	Cost net of VAT	VAT	Balance
2	lamp brackets	1	15.40	30.80	5.39	36.19
totals				30.80	5.39	36.19

Delivery: 2 October, a.m., to Honeysuckle, Farriergate, Codlington, carriage paid

314

Harmonious Blacksmith

- all kinds of ironwork -
Handley's Edge

Date: 20 October 1991

VAT reg. no. 201 8697 23

INVOICE

Quantity	Item	Unit	Unit cost	Cost net of VAT	VAT	Balance
2	lamp brackets	1	15.40	30.80	5.39	36.19
totals				30.80	5.39	36.19

Delivery: 2 October, a.m., to Honeysuckle, Farriergate, Codlington, carriage paid

Task 3

Check the following invoice carefully. Note that the firm is not registered for VAT.

Sabrina Fair
Garden Pools

INVOICE

Date: 31 October

Riverside walk, Ashton St John

Quantity	Item	Unit	Unit cost	Balance
1	Kent pool	1	25.00	25.00
1	Norfolk pool	1	60.00	60.00
2	Hampshire pool	1	58.00	126.00
2	Wiltshire pool	1	55.00	110.00
total				321.00
less discount $2\frac{1}{2}$%				6.42
Amount due				314.58

Terms: carriage paid, discount $2\frac{1}{2}$%, 30 days

Take any necessary action according to your brief.

Task 4

You receive the following invoice. Carry out your brief. What should you do about the costs of delivery?

Cowslip Wild Flowers

Mare's Dell, Wanstead St Mark

Date: 28 October

INVOICE

Quantity	Item	Unit	Unit cost	Balance
10	Shepherd's purse	packet	0.50	5.00
10	Mixed wild flowers	packet	0.40	4.00
10	Conflower	packet	0.50	5.00
5	Wild rose	bush	2.00	10.00
		subtotal		24.00
		delivery		3.50
		total amount due		27.50

Task 5

You receive the following invoice. Follow your brief.

BYE BYE FLY
INSECTICIDES

Date: 31 October

INVOICE

Quantity	Item	Unit	Unit cost	Total before VAT	VAT	Total incl. VAT
10	Flygo powder	750g	2.99	14.95	2.61	17.56
10	Zappawasp spray	750ml	4.99	49.90	8.73	58.63
10	Anti-caterpillar smoke	2 cone pack	3.99	19.95	3.49	23.44
5						
			Totals	84.80	14.83	99.63

VAT registered number: 313 2412 31

Stage 2 – Credit transfer

You have been instructed that the following invoices and statements are to be settled by credit transfer. Your brief is as follows.

a) Check the documents.

b) If they are not filled in correctly, indicate what needs to be done.

Task 6

You receive the following statement:

HOXTED HORTICULTURE

LITTLE ACRE, HOXTED

Customer: EPG
Credit limit: £2000

Account no: CT 112
Date: 31 October 1991
Terms: 30 days

STATEMENT OF ACCOUNT

Date	Reference	Description	Debit	Credit	Balance
Oct 1		Balance b/d			872.00 DR
Oct 1	CT112/50	Invoice HH1096	85.00		957.00 DR
Oct 6	CT112/51	Invoice HH1111	72.50		1029.50 DR
Oct 7	CT112/52	Remittance		872.00	157.50 DR
Oct 9	CT112/53	Invoice HH1113	16.75		173.25 DR
Oct 15	CT112/54	Invoice HH1129	101.50		274.75 DR
Oct 16	CT112/55	Credit note HHCN1474	48.50		226.25 DR
Oct 17	CT112/56	Invoice HH1134	94.60		320.85 DR
Oct 21	CT112/57	Invoice HH1135	32.50		353.35 DR
Oct 25	CT112/58	Invoice HH1136	46.75		400.10 DR
			Amount now due		400.10

A check on invoices received and other records yields the following information.

Invoices received:

☐ 1 Oct HH1096 85.00; 9 Oct HH1113 16.75; 17 Oct HH1134 94.60; 25 Oct HH1136 46.75.
6 Oct HH1111 72.50; 15 Oct HH1129 101.50; 21 Oct HH1135 32.50;

☐ 6 Oct Remittance sent 872.00.

☐ Credit notes received: 16 Oct HHCN1474 48.50.

Task 7

You receive the following statement:

WILLIAM MORRIS
GARDEN ORNAMENTS

Customer: EPG
Account no.: E12
Credit limit: £1000

STATEMENT

Date	Details	Debit	Credit	Balance
1 Oct	Balance b/d			110.50 DR
2 Oct	Invoice WM1075	25.00		135.50 DR
4 Oct	Remittance		110.50	25.00 DR
6 Oct	Invoice WM1028	18.50		43.50 DR
11 Oct	Invoice WM1032	30.00		73.50 DR
13 Oct	Credit note 84		24.50	49.00 DR
17 Oct	Invoice WM1041	21.00		70.00 DR
24 Oct	Invoice WM1046	17.50		87.50 DR
26 Oct	Credit note 86		12.50	75.00 DR
30 Oct	Invoice WM1047	21.50		96.50 DR
31 Oct	Balance due			96.50

A check on invoices received and other records yields the following information:

Invoices received:

☐ 2 Oct WM1075   25.00;   11 Oct WM1032   30.00;   24 Oct WM1046   17.50;
    6 Oct WM1028   18.50;   17 Oct WM1041   21.00;   30 Oct WM1047   21.50.

☐ 4 Oct Remittance sent 110.50.
☐ Credit notes received: 13 Oct 84 24.50; 26 Oct 86 12.50.

Task 8

You receive the following statement:

Pick & Fawkes Ltd

Superior garden tools
Levellers Common, Digby
VAT reg no 12 3412 56

Customer: EPG
A/c no.: ED21
Credit limit: £400

Date	Details	Debit	Credit	Balance
1 Oct	Balance b/d			221.00 DR
3 Oct	Invoice SEC07	120.00		341.00 DR
7 Oct	Invoice SEC09	26.50		367.50 DR
8 Oct	Remittance		221.00	146.50 DR
14 Oct	Invoice SEC15	65.00		211.50 DR
18 Oct	Invoice SEC16	48.50		260.00 DR
20 Oct	Credit note CN53		48.50	211.50 DR
21 Oct	Invoice SEC30	62.25		273.75 DR
30 Oct	Balance due			273.75

A check on invoices received and other records yields the following information:

Invoices received:

☐ 3 Oct SEC07   120.00;   14 Oct SEC15   65.00;   21 Oct SEC30   62.25.
    7 Oct SEC09   26.50;   18 Oct SEC16   48.50;

☐ 8 Oct Remittance sent 221.00.
☐ Credit notes received: 20 Oct CN53 48.50.

Task 9

Invoices are also received from the suppliers listed below. The calculations are found to be correct, with amounts due as indicated. All the invoices offer a discount of $2\frac{1}{2}\%$ for payment within 30 days, which EPG is entitled to claim.

Name	Invoice total	discount $2\frac{1}{2}\%$	remittance needed
G Campbell	85.60		
R Finlay	101.20		
G Hyde	19.67		
A Payne	55.90		
G Weston	42.00		

Work out the amounts due.

Task 10

You receive the following invoice for goods and materials used during EPG's work on the French holiday home of Mr Claude Shannon.

FACTURE   No: 1254

JARDINS BOVARY-FLAUBERT
Rue Voltaire 177, Plume de Matante, CALVADOS 24250

Référence	Quantité	Désignation produits	Unité	Prix unitaire	Montant hors taxes	Montant TTC
77	1	pompe	1	652.00		652.00
79	1	filtre	1	180.00		180.00
81	2	gicleur fontaine	1	255.00		510.00
83	1	cascade	1	510.00		510.00
		montant total				1852.00

Conditions de paiement: par virement bancaire sur notre compte No 303 056 171 22 du BANQUE BEAUJOLAIS NOUVEAU, Place Descartes 17, Plume de Matante, CALVADOS 24250 au 30 NOVEMBRE. Avec nos remerciments.

---

a) You are more than a little anxious at being confronted with a document in French, but you consult the dictionary which Eve has brought back and find the following:

facture	*invoice*	unité	*unit*
référence	*reference number*	prix unitaire	*price per unit*
quantité	*quantity*	montant	*total*
désignation produits	*description of goods*	hors taxes	*net of taxes*

You know that Mr Shannon is having a pool put into the garden, and so are not surprised to find the following too:

pompe	*pump*
filtre	*filter*
fontaine	*fountain*
gicleur	*jet*
cascade	*waterfall*

Your task is then to check the calculations.

b) Work out the sterling which will be needed to buy the relevant number of French francs. The exchange rate is 10.07 to the pound.

c) More work at the dictionary reveals:

conditions de paiement	*method of payment*
virement bancaire	*credit transfer*
compte	*account*

It should be clear which is the account number and which the address. How will you arrange the international credit transfer?

Help ?

See Section 2: The Information Bank

Invoices, page 161.

VAT, page 251.

Quotations: terms of business, page 232.

Calculations: foreign currency, page 106.

Petty cash: calculating VAT, page 223.

Banking facilities: foreign dealings, page 102.

Reconciliation

(corresponding to NVQ Element 21.1)

Topics covered: *reconciliation of invoices; delivery notes; reconciliation of customer statements; VAT registration; VAT calculations; terms of Business: delivery, discount; foreign currencies.*
Forms needed: *none.*

You are working in the accounts section of Eden Plants and Gardens. At the end of October the invoices and statements given below arrive for payment. Your task is to make any necessary checks on accuracy, and to reconcile the various documents involved.

To avoid unnecessary or irrelevant labour, addresses and reference numbers can be omitted except when stated. Also much unimportant detail is omitted from the invoices. However, in certain cases, the invoice is reproduced in full. On such occasions it is important to check the whole document carefully.

The VAT rate is taken to be $17\frac{1}{2}$% throughout.

Task 1

a) Reconcile the following invoice with the relevant delivery note.

INVOICE

ORGANIC FERTILISERS LTD

Meadowcote

Date: 30 October

VAT reg no 197 4553 52

Quantity	Item	Unit	Unit cost	total before VAT	VAT	total including VAT
20	All purpose liquid feed	250ml	1.49	29.80	5.21	35.01
5	Geranium liquid fertiliser	1 ltr	5.50	27.50	4.81	32.31
5	Rose liquid fertiliser	1 ltr	5.50	27.50	4.81	32.31
3	Tomato liquid fertiliser	1 ltr	6.99	20.97	3.66	24.63
15	House plant liquid fertiliser	500ml	5.75	86.25	15.09	101.34
50	Cut flower preservative	250ml	2.49	124.50	21.78	146.28
totals				316.52	55.36	371.88

b) You decide to check the invoice against the catalogue. The relevant extract reads:

FERTILISERS		*Organic Fertilisers Ltd*
All purpose liquid feed	250ml	1.49
	1 ltr	6.25
	5 ltr	25.55
Geranium liquid fertiliser	1 ltr	5.50
Rose liquid fertiliser	1 ltr	5.50
Tomato liquid fertiliser	1 ltr	6.99
House plant liquid fertiliser	500ml	5.25
Lawn feed	2.5kg (60sq m)	7.25
Cut flower preservative	250ml	2.49

DELIVERY NOTE

ORGANIC FERTILISERS LTD

Meadowcote
Date: 18 October

Quantity	Item	Unit
20	All purpose liquid feed	250ml
5	Geranium liquid fertiliser	1 ltr
5	Rose liquid fertiliser	1 ltr
15	House plant liquid fertiliser	500ml
30	Cut flower preservative	250ml

Goods received as stated

Signature: *Dean Cuffey*

What steps should be taken? Write the appropriate letter.

Task 2

You receive the following statement:

BOXHILL SHRUBS

Customer: EPG
Account number: E14
Credit limit: £500

Date	Details	Debit	Credit	Balance
1 Oct	Balance b/d			292.50 DR
1 Oct	Invoice BSE4/71	19.50		312.00 DR
3 Oct	Invoice BSE4/72	11.25		323.25 DR
4 Oct	Remittance		272.50	50.75 DR
7 Oct	Invoice BSE4/73	36.10		86.85 DR
15 Oct	Invoice BSE4/74	98.40		185.25 DR
17 Oct	Credit Note C18		16.40	168.85 DR
24 Oct	Invoice BSE4/75	14.95		183.80 DR
26 Oct	Invoice BSE4/76	20.10		203.90 DR
31 Oct	Balance due			203.90

A check on invoices received and other records yields the following information

Invoices received:

❏   1 Oct BSE4/71   19.50;   7 Oct BSE4/73   36.10;   24 Oct BSE4/75   14.95;
   3 Oct BSE4/72   11.25;   15 Oct BSE4/74   98.40;   26 Oct BSE4/76   20.10.

❏   3 Oct Remittance despatched 292.50.
❏   Credit notes received: 5 Oct C17 11.25; 17 Oct C18 16.40.

a)   Reconcile your records with the statement.

b)   Draft a suitable accompanying letter.

Task 3

a)   Examine the following invoice closely. (You may find it necessary to refresh your knowledge of invoices and VAT invoices). Check the calculations.

G OAK

Market Gardener, Hillcot, Appleton

Invoice no: 387
To: Eden Plants and Gardens Garden Centre, Codlington

Quantity	Item	Unit	Unit cost	total before VAT	VAT $(17\frac{1}{2}\%)$	total including VAT
20	Parsley	pot	0.40	8.00	1.40	9.40
20	Sage	pot	0.70	14.00	2.45	16.45
20	Rosemary	large pot	4.50	90.00	15.75	105.75
20	Thyme	pot	1.20	24.00	4.20	28.20
totals				136.00	23.80	159.80

b) Draft a suitable letter.

Task 4

a) Check the calculations on the following invoice.

F Churchill

GARDEN WOODWORK

VAT reg no 334 4212 66

Quantity	Item	Unit	Unit cost	total before VAT	VAT (17½%)	total including VAT
10	Diamond trellis 6ft x 1 ft	1	2.40	24.00	3.00	27.00
5	Fan trellis 6 ft x 1 ft	1	5.50	27.50	3.53	30.93
10	Diamond trellis 6ft x 6 ft	1	15.00	150.00	18.75	168.75
		totals		201.50	25.28	226.68

b) Draft a suitable letter.

Task 5

a) Check the following invoice. (Use a cross check on the columns). You should also refer to the extract from Brunel's catalogue which is given.

BRUNEL GARDEN EQUIPMENT
Eldercote

VAT no 232 5546 71

Catalogue number	Quantity	Item	Unit	Unit cost	total before VAT	VAT (17½%)	total including VAT
BH02	10	tap connector	1	1.70	17.00	1.70	18.70
BH03	5	screw tap connector	1	5.50	55.00	9.62	64.62
BH01	5	square tap connector	1	3.99	19.95	3.19	23.44
BH04	10	twin tap connector	1	6.80	68.00	11.90	79.90
BH05	10	standard hose connector	1	11.79	117.90	20.63	138.53
BH06	5	push/pull hose connector	1	3.99	17.95	50.18	21.09
totals					294.60	50.18	346.28

Extract from supplier's catalogue

	Brunel Garden Equipment
Hose adaptors	
BH01 tap connector	3.99
BH02 screw tap connector	1.70
BH03 square tap connector	5.50
BH04 twin tap connector	6.50
BH05 standard hose connector	1.79
BH06 push/pull hose connector	3.99

b)   Draft a suitable letter.

Task 6

a)   Check the calculations on the following invoice.

LONGMEADOW MANURE AND COMPOST LTD
Great Byre, Longmeadow
VAT reg no 211 2362 31

Date: 31 October

Qty	Item	Unit	Unit cost	total before VAT	VAT ($17\frac{1}{2}$%)	total including VAT
1	Low peat multipurpose	80ltr	10.33	10.33	1.90	12.13
1	Fish blood and bone	25kg	13.91	13.91	2.43	16.34
2	Sulphate of potash	25kg	15.65	31.30	6.36	37.66
4	Irish moss	200 ltr	11.25	48.00	8.40	56.40
6	Cow manure	15 ltr	3.69	21.42	3.74	25.16
		totals		124.96	22.83	147.69

b)   Draw up what the invoice should have been.

c)   Draft a suitable letter.

Task 7

a)   You receive the following invoice. You find from the file that the order was to be delivered carriage paid, with a cash discount of 2%. There is also a special offer of a further 5% reduction on the Terracotta 'Bird in Hand' bird feeding novelty. Check the invoice for errors.

WILD BIRD PRODUCTS

Lark Rise, Hedgesparrow Magna

VAT reg no 124 5456 23

Ref no.	Q'ty	Item	Unit	Unit cost	total before VAT	VAT (17½%)	total incl. VAT
UL07	2	Bird Haven	1	17.95	35.90	6.28	48.18
UL09	6	Hanging feeds	1	2.75	16.50	2.88	19.38
UL10	2	Bird Kitchen	1	3.15	6.30	1.10	7.40
UL13	2	Feedabird peanut dispenser	1	2.25	4.70	0.82	5.52
UL14	2	Terracotta bell feeder	1	7.45	14.90	2.60	17.50
UL15	2	Bird Lodge feeding station	1	28.95	57.90	10.13	68.03
UL21	2	Terracotta 'Bird in Hand' Bird feeder	1	9.95	18.90	3.30	22.20
		totals			155.10	27.11	182.21
		cash discount 2%, 30 days					3.64
		amount due					178.57

Terms: carriage paid; 2%, 30 days else net

b) Draft a suitable letter.

Task 8

You receive the following invoice. Check the calculations. What should you do about payment?

PRO FORMA INVOICE

Trevi Fountains

VAT reg no 124 5456 23

Uptown Lane, Meadowcote

Date/tax point: 31 October 1991

Ref no.	Quantity	Item	Unit	Unit cost	total before VAT	VAT (17½%)	total incl. VAT
TF17	1	amphibious pump (105 watts)	1	113.20	113.20	19.81	133.01
TF19	1	Biological filter (1000/1500 gall)	1	131.40	131.40	22.99	154.39
TF23	1	Brass fountain jet	1	23.65	23.65	4.13	27.78
totals					268.25	46.93	315.18

Task 9

You receive the following invoice. Check the calculations. What should you do about the costs of delivery?

Cowslip Wild Flowers

Mare's Dell, Wanstead St Mark
Date: 31 October

INVOICE

Quantity	Item	Unit	Unit cost	Balance
5	Wild rose	bush	2.00	10.00
20	Blue bell	pack (5)	1.00	20.00
10	Mixed wild flowers	packet	0.40	4.00
		subtotal		34.00
		delivery		3.50
		total amount due		37.50

Terms: 2.5%, 30 days, carriage paid

Task 10

You receive the following invoice. Check the calculations. What should you do about payment?

Cat and Cauldron

VAT reg. no. 13 6669 99

brooms and brushes

Date: 31 October

Quantity	Item	Unit	Unit cost	total before VAT	VAT ($17\frac{1}{2}\%$)	total including VAT
2	Heavy duty broom	1	7.45	14.90	2.60	17.50
5	All purpose broom	1	4.45	22.25	3.89	26.14
2	Patio/pool surround broom	1	3.75	7.50	1.31	8.81
5	Lawn/leaf broom	1	3.75	18.75	3.28	22.03
10	Small garden broom	1	4.45	44.50	7.78	52.28
5	Stiff brush	1	2.65	13.25	2.31	15.56
10	Yard broom	1	4.85	48.50	8.48	56.98
	totals			169.65	29.65	199.30

Terms: COD

326

Help ?

See Section 2: The Information Bank

Invoices, page 161.

VAT, page 251.

Quotations: terms of business, page 232.

Calculations: foreign currency, page 106.

Petty cash: calculating VAT, page 223.

Banking facilities: foreign dealings, page 102.

Supply of goods

Corresponding to NVQ Element 21.2

Topics covered: *quotations(preparing a quotation, terms of business, covering letter); orders (check on credit worthiness); invoices (types of invoice); customer accounts; statements of accounts; complaints; calculating percentages; aged debtors list; stock record cards.*
Forms needed: *quotation, invoice, customer statement, The Forms Bank, page 359.*

Eden Plants and Gardens supplies many businesses and organisations. Your task is to process those detailed below. Note that for convenience all activities of one type are given together (eg quotations to be prepared). You may well find it preferable to follow through one transaction, by taking the relevant task from each section.

To carry out these tasks, select the necessary documents from The Forms Bank, page 359.

Task 1: preparing a quotation

The following requests are received on 1 May, 1992.

☐   From: P Grimes, The Old Vicarage, Long Compton.

> 10 litres all purpose liquid feed
>
> 5 litre tomato liquid fertiliser

☐   From: A Herring, 49 St Johns Road, Eastcote.

> diamond trellis
>
> 2 6ft x 1ft
>
> 4 6 ft x 3 ft

❐   From: L Anthias, The Old Manor House, Upper Carsholt.

> Customer account number: EPGCA14
>
> 1 Hampshire pool
>
> pool liner (rubber)

❐   From Codlington Council Gardens Department, Council House, Codlington.

> Customer account number: EPGCA109
>
> 2 Heavy duty max-min thermometers
>
> Three way light/plant/ph meter

❐   From Azure Computers, Azure Estate, Appleton.

> Customer account number: EPGCA274
>
> the largest pool available
>
> pool liner
>
> a large waterfall
>
> a stream

a)   Refer to the extract from the catalogue given on page 331, to find whether the request can be met, and if so, under what conditions (cost, terms of delivery etc).

b)   Make out the quotations. Include catalogue numbers.

c)   Where appropriate, draft a covering letter. Explain reasons for what is offered, where this differs from what was requested.

Task 2: orders from customers

You receive orders from customers which follow without changes the details of the quotation.

a)   Carry out credit control. First consult this extract from the aged debtors list to ascertain the customer's creditworthiness. Because of increasing cashflow problems, a discount of 5 per cent is offered if (but only if) payment is made within 30 days. Customers with debts outstanding for more than 60 days must be referred to a superior. Those with debts of over 90 days must be refused further credit until they have settled their account.

You should decide:

1)   Which customers without an account can be offered a discount.

2)   Which orders if any should be referred to your superior.

3)   Which customers if any cannot be extended further credit.

```
EDEN PLANTS AND GARDENS
AGED DEBTORS LIST      as at 07-06-91
```

Account no	Name	Balance	up to 30 days	over 30 days	over 60 days	over 90 days
53	Eastcote Leisure	402.50	397.00	0.00	5.50	0.00
14	L Anthias	307.00	85.00	65.00	101.00	56.00
91	St Martin's	115.00	115.00	0.00	0.00	0.00
109	Codlington Council	398.00	187.00	211.00	0.00	0.00
274	Azure Computers	320.50	302.50	0.00	118.00	0.00

b) Draft letters where appropriate. Assume that your superior approves the supply of the order, in cases where you have made a query.

c) Update and amend the following stock record card (which has not been kept up to date) in the light of the despatch to Mr Grimes of 10 litres of all purpose liquid feed. State what action you would take if any. Is any future action likely?

STOCK RECORD CARD

Item all purpose liquid feed	Min level 10 units
Unit 5 ltr	Max level 60 units
Ref EPGF003	Re-order level 15 units
Location HR12	Re-order quantity 45 units

Date	Received		Issued		Balance
	Ref	quantity	Ref	quantity	
15 May		45			60
20 May				10	
23 May				10	
24 May				5	
28 May				2	
6 June				2	

d) Draft invoices for the supply of the above orders.

You are instructed that all orders have now been approved, as all customers have now settled their accounts. However Mr Herring is an old friend of Eve Adams, who has said that he can be allowed goods on approval.

Task 3: Invoices requesting payment by customers

The following invoices outstanding from the previous day's business should also be made out (addresses can be ignored for this purpose). Articles are sold in single units, except for liquid products, which are sold in the quantity indicated. Prices per unit are in the catalogue (page 331). VAT is charged on all items.

☐ G Oak 1 EPGT001 spade; 4 EPGF001 All purpose liquid feed; 3 EPGT001 diamond trellis 6ft x 1 ft; cash discount offered (5%, 30 days)

☐ A Edens 1 EPGT002 fork; cash discount offered (2%, 30 days)

☐ C Woodcroft 6 EPGT008 fan trellis 6ft x 1 ft; 10 EPGF002 All purpose liquid feed; terms of delivery: free on rail

☐ T Mortimer 1 EPGT003 rake; 1 EPGM002 Outdoor wall thermometer; on approval (pro-forma)

☐ J Dillon 20 EPGF004 All purpose liquid feed; terms: ex warehouse

☐ G Adie 1 EPGT004 hoe; 1 EPGW008 pool liner PVC 8ft x 6ft; terms: COD

☐ C Jones 2 EPGF003 All purpose liquid feed; terms of delivery: carriage paid

☐ M Bampton 10 EPGT005 trowel; 8 EPGF006 Tomato liquid fertiliser; 4 EPGW008 pool liner PVC 8ft x 6ft; terms: carriage paid, discount 5%, 30 days

☐ R Jones 2 EPGF007 House plant liquid fertiliser; terms: COD

☐ L Hampton 1 EPGT006 secateurs; 1 EPGM002 Outdoor wall thermometer; 4 EPGT008 fan trellis 6ft x 1 ft; carriage paid

☐ J Jones 2 EPGF007 House plant liquid fertiliser; 2 EPGT001 Diamond trellis 6ft x 1 ft; COD

☐ R Brown 1 EPGT002 fork; on approval

☐ W Cobham 1 EPGF009 Cut flower preservative; 6 EPGT008 fan trellis 6ft x 1 ft; COD

☐ A Maxwell 1 EPGT005 trowel; 2 EPGF002 All purpose liquid feed; 5 EPGT001 Diamond trellis 6ft x 1 ft; terms: carriage paid

☐ C Bird 1 EPGT001 spade; 1 EPGF007 House plant liquid fertiliser; 3 EPGT001 Diamond trellis 6ft x 1 ft; terms: discount 2%, 30 days

Task 4

On 31 May the customer statements have to be drawn up. Among them are the ones to cover the transactions detailed below.

☐ Codlington Council: Customer account number: EPGCA109; credit limit: £1500.00
opening balance £956.00 DR
invoices issued: 5 May 912/368, £40.58; 10 May 912/371, 184.50; 19 May 912/378, £92.00; 23 May 912/379 £ 560.00
remittance received 7 May £956.00

☐ Azure Computers (Customer account number: EPGCA274, £1000)
opening balance: £454.00 DR
invoices issued: 4 May 912/367 £379.49; 11 May 912/375, £ 105.25;
17 May 912/378, £215.60
remittance received 9 May £454.00
credit note issued CN214 20 May £215.60

☐ A Edens (CA17, £300)
opening balance: £0.00
invoices issued: 7 May 912/369, £28.72; 10 May 912/373, £ 15.00; 15 May 912/377, £18.00; 25 May 912/382, £ 31.00
remittance received 13 May £43.72

❏ M Bampton (CA242, £800)
opening balance £137.50 DR
invoices issued: 4 May 912/367, £207.66; 7 May 912/370, £102.00; 10 May 912/74, £51.50; 15 May 912/376 £ 137.50
credit note issued CN215 25 May £42.75

❏ C Bird (CA321, £400)
opening balance £85.00 CR
invoices issued: 8 May 912/372, £ 51.86; 22 May 912/380, £102.00; 25 May 912/381, £21.80
credit note issued CN213 15 May £10.20
remittance received: 23 May £85.00

❏ Extract from the catalogue of:

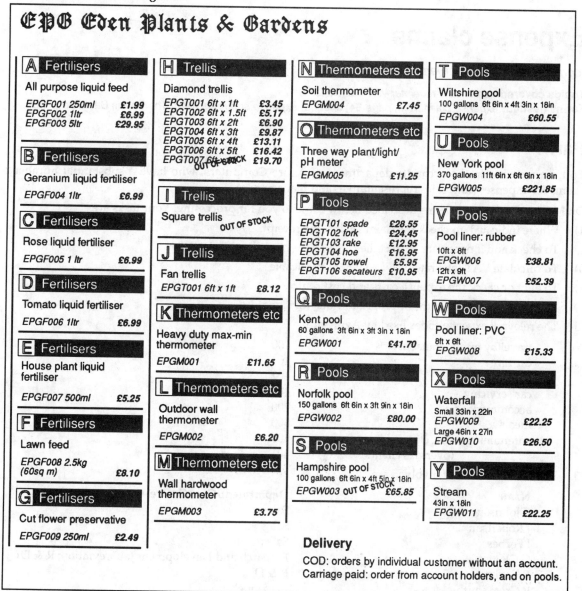

EPG Eden Plants & Gardens

A Fertilisers
All purpose liquid feed
EPGF001 250ml	£1.99
EPGF002 1ltr	£6.99
EPGF003 5ltr	£29.95

B Fertilisers
Geranium liquid fertiliser
| EPGF004 1ltr | £6.99 |

C Fertilisers
Rose liquid fertiliser
| EPGF005 1 ltr | £6.99 |

D Fertilisers
Tomato liquid fertiliser
| EPGF006 1ltr | £6.99 |

E Fertilisers
House plant liquid fertiliser
| EPGF007 500ml | £5.25 |

F Fertilisers
Lawn feed
| EPGF008 2.5kg (60sq m) | £8.10 |

G Fertilisers
Cut flower preservative
| EPGF009 250ml | £2.49 |

H Trellis
Diamond trellis
EPGT001 6ft x 1ft	£3.45
EPGT002 6ft x 1.5ft	£5.17
EPGT003 6ft x 2ft	£6.90
EPGT004 6ft x 3ft	£9.87
EPGT005 6ft x 4ft	£13.11
EPGT006 6ft x 5ft	£16.42
EPGT007 6ft x 6ft OUT OF STOCK	£19.70

I Trellis
Square trellis OUT OF STOCK

J Trellis
Fan trellis
| EPGT001 6ft x 1ft | £8.12 |

K Thermometers etc
Heavy duty max-min thermometer
| EPGM001 | £11.65 |

L Thermometers etc
Outdoor wall thermometer
| EPGM002 | £6.20 |

M Thermometers etc
Wall hardwood thermometer
| EPGM003 | £3.75 |

N Thermometers etc
Soil thermometer
| EPGM004 | £7.45 |

O Thermometers etc
Three way plant/light/pH meter
| EPGM005 | £11.25 |

P Tools
EPGT101 spade	£28.55
EPGT102 fork	£24.45
EPGT103 rake	£12.95
EPGT104 hoe	£16.95
EPGT105 trowel	£5.95
EPGT106 secateurs	£10.95

Q Pools
Kent pool
60 gallons 3ft 6in x 3ft 3in x 18in
| EPGW001 | £41.70 |

R Pools
Norfolk pool
150 gallons 6ft 6in x 3ft 9in x 18in
| EPGW002 | £80.00 |

S Pools
Hampshire pool
100 gallons 6ft 6in x 4ft 5in x 18in
| EPGW003 OUT OF STOCK | £65.85 |

T Pools
Wiltshire pool
100 gallons 6ft 6in x 4ft 3in x 18in
| EPGW004 | £60.55 |

U Pools
New York pool
370 gallons 11ft 6in x 6ft 6in x 18in
| EPGW005 | £221.85 |

V Pools
Pool liner: rubber
10ft x 8ft
| EPGW006 | £38.81 |
12ft x 9ft
| EPGW007 | £52.39 |

W Pools
Pool liner: PVC
8ft x 6ft
| EPGW008 | £15.33 |

X Pools
Waterfall
Small 33in x 22in
| EPGW009 | £22.25 |
Large 46in x 27in
| EPGW010 | £26.50 |

Y Pools
Stream
43in x 18in
| EPGW011 | £22.25 |

Delivery
COD: orders by individual customer without an account.
Carriage paid: order from account holders, and on pools.

Help ?

See Section 2: The Information Bank

Quotations, page 226.

Invoices, page 161.

Complaints, page 126.

Stock control and valuation, page 238.

Calculations: percentages, page 113.

Expense claims

(corresponding to NVQ Element 21.3)

Topics covered: *expenses; receipts; VAT calculations.*
Forms needed: *expense claim from*, page 64; *cheque, expense summary form*, The Forms Bank, page 359.

Part 1

You are working in the accounts department of Azure Computers, who have a substantial number of claims for expenses from sales representatives and management.

On 31 May the expense claims described below come to you for processing. Your tasks are:

1) Where indicated, to check the claim against the receipt.

2) To check and if necessary correct the calculations made by the claimant.

3) To calculate VAT (at a rate of $17\frac{1}{2}\%$) where applicable

4) To allot or check the expense costs and cost centre.

5) To prepare a cheque of the appropriate value for signature.

☐ The relevant expense codes used by Azure are:

travel by public transport	100
car hire	101
petrol	102
car servicing	103
accommodation	200
meals	300
entertaining (UK clients)	400
(overseas clients)	401

☐ The members of staff involved are

Name	Department/Cost Centre
E Johnson	Sales
J Robertson	Sales
I Forbes	Sales
G Clayton	Research and Development (abbreviation: R & D)
R Taylor	R & D
B Greensmith	Personnel

332

Name	Department/Cost Centre
R Franks	General Administration
J Richards	Purchases
G Simpson	Purchases
N Davies	R & D

Note: As far as this simulation is concerned, the relevant Customs and Excise rulings are:

Public transport – no VAT payable

Entertaining UK clients – VAT cannot be reclaimed

Entertaining Overseas clients – VAT can be reclaimed

VAT payable is rounded down to the nearest penny.

Task 1

EXPENSES CLAIM FORM

Claimant's name (BLOCK CAPITALS): E.Johnson

Month: May   Cost centre: Sales

Date	Details	Code	Total paid		Total net of VAT		VAT paid	
2–4 May	Southampton	102	16	50				
		200	18	40				
		300	36	20				
		400	28	50				
	Totals		99	60				

Task 2

Check the claim form against the receipt and carry out all other instructions as above.

EXPENSES CLAIM FORM

Claimant's name (BLOCK CAPITALS): J.Robertson

Month: May   Cost centre: Sales

Date	Details	Code	Total paid		Total net of VAT		VAT paid	
5 May	Entertaining overseas client	401	123	67				
	Totals							

```
┌─────────────────────────────────────────────────┐
│                                                   │
│     𝓗𝓸𝓽𝓮𝓵  𝓜𝓮𝓽𝓻𝓸𝓹𝓸𝓵𝓮                          │
│                                                   │
│    Codlington            VAT Reg.No. 12 3176 22   │
│                                                   │
│                  5/5/91                           │
│    Date:................................          │
│                                                   │
│    ┌─────────────────────────┬──────────────┐     │
│    │ Drinks                  │      4.80    │     │
│    │ First courses           │     10.50    │     │
│    │ Main courses            │     32.85    │     │
│    │ Desserts                │      8.60    │     │
│    │ Wines                   │     28.90    │     │
│    │ Coffee                  │      3.10    │     │
│    │ Drinks                  │     16.50    │     │
│    │ Subtotal                │    105.25    │     │
│    │ VAT 17½%                │     18.42    │     │
│    │ Total                   │    123.67    │     │
│    └─────────────────────────┴──────────────┘     │
│                                                   │
└─────────────────────────────────────────────────┘
```

Tasks 3-6

The following group of claims may be entered onto the relevant form or the calculations may be completed in tabular form as below.

Task	Name	Cost centre	Details	code	total	total net of VAT	VAT paid
3	I Forbes	Sales	Travel (train) (5 May)	100		14.30	
			Accommodation (5 May)	200		22.00	
			Meal (5 May)	300		8.50	
			Meal (6 May)	300		4.50	
totals						49.30	
4	G Clayton	R & D	Meal (7 May)			3.50	
			Meal (10 May)			4.20	
			Meal (17 May)			3.70	
			Entertaining (UK client)			22.75	
totals						34.15	
5	R Taylor	R & D	Car hire (17 May)	101		25.00	
			Petrol (17 May)	102		12.00	
			Car hire (25 May)	101		25.00	
			Petrol (25 May)	102		10.50	
totals						72.50	
6	B Greensmith	Personnel	Car hire (14 May)			35.00	
			petrol (14 May)			6.50	
			Accommodation (14 May)			17.50	
			Meal (14 May)			8.20	
			Entertaining (overseas client 15 May)			45.60	
totals						122.60	

Task 7

You have received an expense claim with the following details. One of the accompanying receipts is as shown. Check all the details and complete the calculations (either enter the details on the relevant form or complete the calculations in tabular form, as below.)

Name	Cost centre	Details	code	total paid	total net of VAT	VAT paid
R Franks	Gen Admin	Travel (1/5)	100	12.60		
		Accomodation (1/5)		26.00		
		Meal (1/5)		9.55		
		Travel (7/5)	100	10.40		
		Meal (7/5)		8.75		
		Entertaining UK client		28.75		
totals				96.05		

```
   HEARTBREAK HOTEL
VAT reg no 55 2323 16




    02-05-91

Room B&B       15.50
Lunch           5.75
Newspapers      1.35
Phone calls     3.40

Total          26.00

(VAT included)
```

Task 8

Mr Richards of Purchases has fallen ill and has not collected a claim form. He sends in his receipts, which are in order. The Cashier decides that you can fill in a form on Mr Richards' behalf, and that the claim can be forwarded without Mr Richards needing to sign it until his return to work, so that he can receive his money. Make out the claim form. The expenses are:

☐ 13 May train fare 15.50; taxi fare 2.50; Meal 3.25; hotel 27.30; 14 entertaining overseas clients 44.10; taxi 2.50

Task 9

Mr G Simpson of Purchases is a man who is always in a hurry.

The important parts of his May claim are:

☐ 13 May   train   12.50
☐ 17 May   train   2.50
☐ 18 May   train   14.00
☐   taxi   3.50

| ☐ | 25 May | taxi | 14.80 |
| ☐ | total | | 62.10 |

Unfortunately he has not learned the virtue of checking his calculations. Amend the claim and suggest how his error may have arisen. What are the figures for VAT?

Task 10

Check and complete the following claim.

EXPENSES CLAIM FORM

Claimant's name (BLOCK CAPITALS): N.Davies

Month: May   Cost centre: R&D

Date	Details	Code	Total paid	Total net of VAT	VAT paid
1 May	train	100	12.00		
	taxi	100	3.20		
	meal	300	6.50		
5 May	car hire	101	25.00		
	petrol	102	10.30		
	meal	300	8.50		
12 May	car hire	101	25.00		
	petrol	102	16.50		
	accommo-dation	200	46.50		
15 May	train	100	10.00		
	taxi	100	2.15		
	entertaining UK client	400	47.50		
17 May	entertaining overseas client	401	110.30		
Totals			323.45		

Task 11

Fill in summary forms for May as follows:

a)   for the Sales Cost Centre

b)   for expense code 100 (public transport).

Part 2

On 30 June the expense claims described below come to you for processing. Your tasks are as for Part 1:

Task 12

You have received an expense claim with the following details. One of the accompanying receipts is as shown. Check all the details and complete the calculations (either enter the details on the relevant form or complete the calculations in tabular form, as below.)

Name	Cost centre	Details	code	total paid	total net of VAT	VAT paid
B. Greensmith	Personnel	Car hire (22/6)	101	25.00		
		petrol (22/6)	102	8.25		
		accomodation (22/6)	200	30.00		
		entertaining o/seas (24/6)	401	65.00		
totals				128.25		

```
--------------------------------
|                              |
|         SANDY BAY            |
|          HOTEL               |
|        VAT REG. NO.          |
|         61 2552 13           |
|                              |
|                              |
|         22-06-91             |
|                              |
|                              |
|  Room B&B        14.50       |
|  Lunch            5.50       |
|  Ticket -                    |
|  festival                    |
|  dance           10.00       |
|                  30.00       |
|                              |
|  (VAT included)              |
--------------------------------
```

Tasks 13-16

The following group of claims may be entered onto the revelant form or the calculations may be completed in tabular form as below.

Task	Name	Cost centre	Details	code	total	total net of VAT	VAT paid
13	G Simpson	Purchases	Entertaining (overseas client 8 Jun)	401		54.60	
			Car hire (17 Jun)	101		25.00	
			Meal (18 Jun)	300		8.50	
			Car hire (23 Jun)	101		25.00	
totals						113.10	
14	G Clayton	R & D	Travel (train) (6 Jun)	100		14.30	
			Meal (7 Jun)	300		3.50	
			Travel (train) (15 Jun)	100		14.30	
			Accommodation (15 Jun)	200		22.00	
			Meal (16 Jun)	300		6.50	
totals						60.60	

Task	Name	Cost centre	Details	code total	total net of VAT	VAT paid
15	N Davies	R & D	Travel (train) (9 Jun)	100	14.30	
			Car hire (14 Jun)	101	25.00	
			Petrol (14 Jun)	102	10.00	
			Meal (14 Jun)	300	8.50	
			Accommodation (24 Jun)	200	17.50	
totals					75.10	
16	E Johnson	Sales	Car hire (2 Jun)	101	35.00	
			Meal (10 Jun)	300	6.00	
			Entertaining (UK client 12 Jun)	400	45.00	
			Meal (14 Jun)	300	8.40	
			Travel (train) (5 Jun)	100	14.30	
totals					108.70	

Task 17

Check an expense claim with the following details, and complete the calculations (either enter the details on the relevant form or complete the calculations in tabular form, as below.)

Name	Cost centre	Details	code	total paid	total net of VAT	VAT paid
J.Robertson	Sales	Travel (3/6)		12.60		
		Accomodation (3/6)		21.25		
		Entertaining UK client (10/6)		48.75		
		Travel (15/6)		12.60		
		Accomodation (15/6)		21.25		
totals				116.45		

Task 18

You have received an expense claim with the following details. One of the accompanying receipts is as shown. Check all the details and complete the calculations (either enter the details on the relevant form or complete the calculations in tabular form, as below.)

Name	Cost centre	Details	code	total paid	total net of VAT	VAT paid
R Franks	Gen admin	Entertaining o/seas client (12/6)	401	63.65		
		Exeter	100	26.50		
			200	16.40		
			400	58.50		
totals				165.05		

338

```
          HOTEL METROPOLE
    Codlington          VAT Reg.No. 12 3176 22

    Date: ......6/91...........

    ----------------------------------------
    | Drinks          |        2.80 |
    | First courses   |        6.50 |
    | Main courses    |       22.75 |
    | Desserts        |        4.60 |
    | Wines           |       18.90 |
    | Coffee          |        2.10 |
    | Drinks          |        6.00 |
    | Subtotal        |       63.65 |
    | VAT 17½%        |       11.13 |
    | Total           |       74.78 |
    ----------------------------------------
```

Task 19

Check and complete the following claim form.

EXPENSES CLAIM FORM

Claimant's name (BLOCK CAPITALS): .....I.Forbes.....

Month: June   Cost centre: Sales

Date	Details	Code	Total paid		Total net of VAT		VAT paid	
4-6 Jun	Birmingham	100	18	50	18	50		
		200	18	40	15	66	2	74
		300	16	00	13	62	2	38
		401	38	00	38	00		
totals			90	90	85	78	5	12

Task 20

Check an expense claim with the following details, and complete the calculations (either enter the details on the relevant form or complete the calculations in tabular form, as below.)

Name	Cost centre	Details	code	total paid	total net of VAT	VAT paid
R Taylor	R & D	Travel (9/6)	100	12.60		
		Accomodation (9/6)	200	21.25		
		Meal (9/6)	300	5.55		
		Entertaining UK client (9/6)	401	38.75		
totals				78.15		

Task 21

Check an expense claim with the following details, and complete the calculations (either enter the details on the relevant form or complete the calculations in tabular form, as below.)

Name	Cost centre	Details	code	total paid	total net of VAT	VAT paid
G Richards	Purchases	car hire (6/6)	101	25.00		
		petrol (6/6)		10.30		
		meal (6/6)	300	6.50	5.54	0.96
		train (8/6)	100	12.00		
		taxi (8/6)	100	2.20		
		meal (8/6)	300	8.50		
		entertaining o/sea client (11/6)		35.60		
		car hire (22/6)	101	25.00	21.28	3.72
		petrol (22/6)		12.50		
		accomodation (22/6)	200	46.50		
		train (25/6)	100	10.00		
		taxi(25/6)	100	3.25		
		entertaining UK client (25/6)	400	35.50	35.50	
totals						

Task 22

Fill in summary forms for May as follows:

a)   for the R & D Cost Centre

b)   for expense code 400 (entertaining UK).

Help ?

See Section 2: The Information Bank

Expenses, page 140.

Methods of payment: receipts, page 206.

Petty cash: calculating VAT, page 223.

Ordering goods

(corresponding to NVQ Element 21.4)

Topics covered: *stock control; requesting a quotation; order forms; covering letters; discount.*
Forms needed: *order form*, The Forms Bank, page 359.

Situation 1: ordering stationery

Task 1: stock levels

In the office of Eden Plants and Gardens Mary Douglas is responsible for stock control. During one of her regular checks she notes the following information:

Item	Unit	Balance	Re-order level	Re-order quantity
paper white bond A4, 85gm	box (500)	12	10	10
paper white bank A4, 45gm	box (500)	21	15	20
paper white copier A4, 80gm	box (500)	20	20	30
paper white duplicator A4, 70gm	box (500)	25	20	20
paper coloured bond A4, 85gm	box (500)	5	5	5
paper coloured bank A4, 45gm	box (500)	4	3	2
envelopes brown manila plain 110mm x 220mm	box (1000)	2	2	3
envelopes brown manila window 110mm x 220mm	box (1000)	3	2	2
envelopes brown manila plain 110mm x 220mm	box (1000)	4	2	2
envelopes white plain 110mm x 220mm	box (1000)	3	2	3
envelopes white window 110mm x 220mm	box (1000)	3	2	2
envelopes white plain 110mm x 220mm	box (1000)	3	2	2

What action should Mary take?

Task 2: requesting a quotation

Write the letter requesting a quotation which Mary will send to each of the following suppliers:

❑ Central Stationers, 132 High Street Hoxted HO4 7TG

❑ Super Supplies, Unit 18A, Codlington Industrial Estate, Appleton

❑ Mightier than the Sword, Recycled paper suppliers, 11 The Grove, Eastcote.

Task 3: choice of supplier

Two suppliers reply by sending a price list; the relevant extracts are on page 345. Central Stationers are also currently offering a discount of 5% to all new customers. Mightier than the Sword write a letter, naming the following prices:

❑ white copier paper £3.60 (box of 500); coloured bond paper (box of 500) £6.90; envelopes (per 1000) £20.45.

Which supplier will offer the goods at the cheapest cost?

Task 4

Make out the order form for the goods to the supplier making the lowest quotation

Task 5

Amend the stock record cards in the light of this delivery (on 11 June, invoice ref CS1234):

STOCK RECORD CARD

Item: paper white copier A4, 80gsm
Re-order level: 20

Unit: box 500
Re-order quantity: 30

Date	Received		Issued		Balance
	ref	quantity	ref	quantity	
1 Jun					25
3 Jun			SR45	5	20

STOCK RECORD CARD

Item: paper coloured bond A4, 80gsm
Re-order level: 5

Unit: box 500
Re-order quantity: 5

Date	Received		Issued		Balance
	ref	quantity	ref	quantity	
1 Jun					6
2 Jun			SRA12	1	5

STOCK RECORD CARD

Item: envelopes brown manilla plain box 110mm x 220mm
Re-order level: 2

Unit: box 1000
Re-order quantity: 3

Date	Received		Issued		Balance
	ref	quantity	ref	quantity	
1 Jun					3
2 Jun			HS132	1	2

Situation 2 ordering stationery

Task 6: stock levels

On another occasion Mary Douglas notes the following information:

Item	Unit	Balance	Re-order level	Re-order quantity
paper white bond A4, 85gm	box (500)	13	10	10
paper white bank A4, 45gm	box (500)	15	15	20
paper white copier A4, 80gm	box (500)	25	20	30
paper white duplicator A4, 70gm	box (500)	25	20	20
paper coloured bond A4, 85gm	box (500)	5	5	5
paper coloured bank A4, 45gm	box (500)	4	3	2
envelopes brown manila plain 110mm x 220mm	box (1000)	4	2	3
envelopes brown manila window 110mm x 220mm	box (1000) 3	2	2	
envelopes brown manila plain 110mm x 220mm	box (1000)	3	2	2
envelopes white plain 110mm x 220mm	box (1000)	3	2	3
envelopes white window 110mm x 220mm	box (1000)	2	2	2
envelopes white plain 110mm x 220mm	box (1000)	3	2	2

What action should Mary take?

Task 7: requesting a quotation

EPG were satisfied with their last dealings with Central Stationers and so decide to go back to them. Draft the letter, making the following points:

a) EPG are satisfied with the service.

b) Have prices changed?

c) If so, request the new price list.

d) In particular, EPG wish to purchase white bank paper and white window envelopes.

Task 8

Prices are unchanged, so EPG continue to trade with Central Stationers. Make out the order form for the above requirements.

Situation 3

Task 9

Write a letter to Super Supplies asking for quotations for an electronic typewriter for the EPG office.

Task 10

EPG decide to buy a Gonzales Superspeed 123. This is currently offered at £210.50 (exclusive of VAT). Place the necessary order.

Situation 4

Task 11

Write a letter to Bumph, Photocopy House, Railway Approach, Hoxted, asking for a quotation for photocopying facilities. You wish to know whether machines can be bought or hired. EPG are considering various options, including a machine which can collate documents, and which can produce good quality colour copies.

Task 12

Bumph are able to make a special trial offer of a Paperguzzla Plus 709. This machine gives high quality black and white and colour photocopies, will collate, and will give a print out of number of copies provided and cost. The 709X will also make coffee. In order to introduce the machine it is offered at a hire fee of only £95.00 per week (£97.50 for the 709X). The 709X can be delivered within 3 weeks. EPG decide definitely to hire one of the machines; Eve Adams says they will take a 709X, but only if it is delivered within 7 days.

Write a letter placing the order, and enclose an order form.

Situation 5

Task 13

Write a letter to Lazybones, the Codlington temp agency, which is at 132 Farriergate. You wish to know about rates for holiday cover for

1)   an audiotypist
2)   general office duties (the temp must be widely experienced) and
3)   a bookkeeper (2 weeks in August only).

Task 14

Lazybones are able to offer an audiotypist for a fee of £195 per week (the fee includes the agency's fee, and they will pay the employee). A suitably experienced office worker is available for a fee of £215. In the case of the bookkeeper they are only able to offer someone for the week beginning August 1st (fee £245).

Since goods are not being ordered, the order will be placed by letter. It must therefore detail clearly what is being requested and agreed to. EPG want the audiotypist for 5 weeks beginning July 14th. The office worker is to start on July 21st and to finish at the same time. EPG will accept the bookkeeper, but wish to says that, if someone becomes available for the second week, they will accept that arrangement. EPG also wish to be sure that the Lazybones fee includes not only paying the workers, but making the relevant stoppages, and the Lazybones will pay the employer's NI contribution.

Situation 6

Task 15

Write a letter of enquiry to Spick and Span, 56 St Agnes Lane, Appleton. EPG are looking for a firm to handle the cleaning of the offices and possibly various outdoor duties, including the collection of litter left by visitors. EPG really want work to be done on Sundays, as well as at other times, since this is a very busy day at the garden centre.

Task 16

Spick and Span reply that they can provide cleaning services for any normal office requirements. They can also provide workers to deal with outside cleaning, but wish to know whether, since EPG is a garden centre, there would be any especially heavy or dirty work. Service can be provided on Sundays, but double time has to be charged. A charge of £15 would be made for sending a vehicle for removing rubbish bags etc. Spick and Span offer cleaners at a standard rate of £4.50 per hour (this includes provision of equipment, materials, and the agency's overheads).

Write the letter on behalf of EPG requesting Spick and Span to provide a cleaning service (two cleaners for 2 hours, Monday to Friday); cleaning outside Saturday and Sunday (two workers, two hours daily). There will be no heavy or dirty work, as this is handled by garden centre staff, and a vehicle will not be needed, as rubbish bags can form part of the normal collection by the Council on Mondays.

Extracts from price lists

CENTRAL STATIONERS
132 High Street
Hoxted HO4 7TG

P109	coloured bond 85g	7.20
P110	coloured bank 45g	3.95
P111	coloured copier 80g	4.80
P112	coloured duplicator, 70g	6.20

☐ Paper: A4 size office paper, price per box of 500 sheets

P105	white bond 85g	7.70
P106	white bank 45g	4.30
P107	white copier 80g	3.70
P108	white duplicator, 70g	6.50

☐ Envelopes: gummed, business 110mm x 220mm, box of 1000

E43	Brown manila plain	22.00
E44	Brown manila window	26.50
E45	White plain	27.10
E46	White window	31.05

SUPER SUPPLIES Unit 18A,
Codlington Industrial Estate, Appleton

● Business envelopes (110mm x 220mm, box of 500)

EB1	Brown manila plain	10.25
EB2	Brown manila window	13.00
EW1	White plain	13.10
EW2	White window	14.95

● Paper (box of 500)

○ bond 85g

PW1	white	7.60
PC1	coloured	7.10

○ bank 45g

PW2	white	4.25
PC2	coloured	3.95

○ copier 80g

PW3	white	3.55
PC3	coloured	4.70

○ duplicator 70g

PW4	white	6.40
PC4	coloured	6.15

Practice and development of skills and knowledge

Help ?

See Section 2: The Information Bank

Quotations: requesting a quotation, page 227.

Orders, page 211.

Quotations: discounts, page 233.

Documentation of wages

(corresponding to NVQ Element 22.1)

Topics covered: *calculation of pay; clock cards; time sheets; Form P11; payroll sheet; payslips; forms P45, P46, and P60.*

Forms needed: *Form P11*, page 275; *payroll sheet*, page 282; *payslip*, The Forms Bank, page 359; *Form P60*, page 287; *Form P45, Form P46*, page 288–289.

You have taken up a post in the accounts department of Azure Computers and have been given the job of handling part of their wages bill. You will be dealing with the affairs of the following employees:

F Atkins, C Barnes, T Charlton, A Donaldson, R Edwards, H Finlay, G Gresham, M Handley, P Ingham, J Jackson, E King, W Long, B Morley, T Nason, A Ogilvy, T Patrick, S Quentin, T Ross, N Smith, K Thomson.

Simulation: Stage 1 – calculation of basic pay

Task 1

Many of the employees record their hours of work by means of clock cards.

Here are two of the ones you have to complete.

Mr Atkins and Miss Ingham work in the Warehouse. Their basic day is from 9am until 12.30pm and from 1.30 pm until 5pm. The basic rate of pay is £4.96 an hour. Overtime is calculated as time and a half.

No: 47
Name: F Atkins
Week ending: 12 April 1991

Day	In	Out	In	Out	Total hours
Mon	9.00	12.30	1.30	5.00	
Tue	9.00	12.30	1.30	5.00	
Wed	9.00	12.30	1.30	5.00	
Thur	9.00	12.30	1.30	6.00	
Fri	9.00	12.30	1.30	7.00	
Total					

Basic rate:
Overtime:
GROSS PAY

Day	In	Out	In	Out	Total hours
Mon	9.00	12.30	1.30	5.30	
Tue	9.00	12.30	1.30	5.00	
Wed	9.00	12.30	1.30	6.00	
Thur	9.00	12.30	1.30	7.00	
Fri	9.00	12.30	1.30	5.00	
Total					

No: 112
Name: P Ingham
Week ending: 12 April 1991

Basic rate:
Overtime:
GROSS PAY

Task 2

Certain Azure staff, such as the service engineers, do not clock in, but instead complete a time sheet. On this they list the hours worked on each job. They also include travelling time. The sheet is checked and signed by the Service Manager, Mr Singh, before it is forwarded to the wages section.

Two of the timesheets you receive are as shown below. Calculate the gross wages of the employees. They are paid at a rate of 9.00 per hour for 35 hours a week to include up 10 hours travelling. Hours spent over that time (but not travelling) are paid at time and a quarter. Emergency work on Saturday is paid at time and a half and on Sundays at double the basic rate.

Complete the time sheets, calculate the gross pay and state what other action you need to take (if any)

Name: E King
Works no: 245
Week ending: 12 April 1991

Job	Mon	Tue	Wed	Thu	Fri	Sat	Sun
Codlington Council	6	7	6				
James and James				6	7	4	
Travel	1	1	1	1	1	1	
Total	7	8	7	7	8	5	

Signature of Service Manager: *K Singh*   Date: *12 April*

FOR OFFICE USE ONLY

Rate   Total hours worked   Wages due
basic rate
overtime
Saturday
Sunday
GROSS PAY

```
Name:          W.Long
Works no:      246
Week ending:   10 April 1991
```

Job	Mon	Tue	Wed	Thu	Fri	Sat	Sun
Codlington Council	6	7	6				
James and James				6	6		2
Travel	1	1	1	1	1		1
Total	7	8	7	7	7		3

Signature of Service Manager: Date:

FOR OFFICE USE ONLY

Rate	Total hours worked	Wages due
basic rate		
overtime		
Saturday		
Sunday		
GROSS PAY		

Task 3

Mrs Barnes and Mrs Charlton work in the Assembly Section. They are paid 4.20 an hour, for a 38 hour week, with overtime at time an a quarter. As an incentive for the current project Azure are paying a bonus. For the current week it is 8%. For the current week (ending 10 April) the relevant details from their clock cards are:

☐ Mrs C Barnes (works number 321)   basic: 38 hours
                                          overtime: 4 hours

☐ Mrs T Charlton (works number 337)   basic: 38 hours
                                          overtime: 7 hours

Calculate their gross pay.

Task 4

Graham Gresham and June Jackson work for Sales as representatives. They are paid a basic wage of £110 per week, and a commission of 18% on their gross sales. For the current week their sales achieved were

☐ Gresham: £1800
☐ Jackson: £3150

There is a further bonus on the week's wages of 5% for the representative who sells the most each week. This time June Jackson wins the bonus.

Calculate their gross wages.

Stage 2 – Form P11

The gross wages of the remaining employees for the week ending 12 April are as follows:

Name	works number	gross wages
A Donaldson	116	87.50
R Edwards	118	95.00
H Finlay	205	110.00
M Handley	207	105.40
B Morley	208	156.00
A Ogilvy	411	154.00
T Patrick	425	132.50
S Quentin	439	110.00
T Ross	456	98.75
K Thomson	565	99.90

The following member of staff was off ill and received Statutory Sick Pay:

N Smith	522	92.00

The following member of staff was away on Maternity Leave and received Statutory Maternity Pay.

T Nason	312	67.00

Task 5

Fill in Form P11 for the above employees and those mentioned in Stage 1.

a) Fill in the income tax entries, using the Tax Tables given on page 365–374.

b) Fill in the National Insurance contributions using Weekly Table A (given on page 276). Ignore columns 1d and 1e – none of these employees are contracted out. For the purpose of this task the figure for column 1a is taken from column 2. Ignore pence in deciding on the employee's earnings. If the employee earns £390.00 or more, write 390 in Column 1a.

The tax codes are:

- 278L for C Barnes, T Charlton, R Edwards, G Gresham, M Handley, P Ingham, J Jackson, W Long, T Nason, A Ogilvy, T Patrick, S Quentin, T Ross, N Smith, K Thomson.
- 437H for F Atkins, A Donaldson, H Finlay, E King, B Morley,

Stage 3 – The payroll sheet and payslips

Task 6

Make out the payroll sheet for the wages and deductions so far calculated.

Ignore entries for overtime, bonus or commission except in the examples already given.

Apart from the statutory contributions, the following other deductions should also be applied:

Pension scheme:

- rate £15 per week: Jackson, King
- rate £10 per week: Gresham

You will find the Employer's National Insurance contributions for each gross wage in the Weekly Tables

Crosscheck your calculations.

Stage 4 – Further income tax documentation

Task 7

Make out payslips for the employees on the payroll.

Task 8

As it is the end of the year, you have to issue Form P60. Make out the form for Mr Anthony John Hainsworth, born 5 May 1962, NI number AD 34 67 23V. The totals on his P11 are:

column	1a	4680
	1b	544.44
	1c	234.00
	3	4680.00
	6	1170.00

Task 9

Update Form P11 for the following employees, at the end of Week 2.

F Atkins, C Barnes, T Charlton, A Donaldson, R Edwards.

Task 10

The Form is filled in for week 3 as follows during your absence. Check the entries. (The gross wages are correct).

Name	code	week	column					
			2	3	4	5	6	7
F Atkins	437H	1	195.92	195.92	84.22	111.70	27.75	27.75
		2	190.50	386.42	168.44	217.98	54.25	26.50
		3	193.00	579.42	252.66	326.76	81.50	27.25
C Barnes	278L	1	195.05	195.05	53.64	141.41	35.25	35.25
		2	195.00	390.05	107.28	282.77	70.50	35.25
		3	195.00	565.05	140.92	424.13	106.00	35.50
T Charlton	278L	1	211.06	211.06	53.64	157.42	39.25	39.25
		2	201.50	412.56	107.28	305.28	76.25	37.00
		3	210.50	623.06	160.92	462.14	115.50	39.25
A Donaldson	437	1	87.50	87.50	84.22	3.28	0.75	0.75
		2	87.50	175.00	168.44	6.56	1.50	0.75
		3	87.50	262.50	252.66	9.84	2.25	0.75
R Edwards	278L	1	95.00	95.00	53.64	41.36	10.25	10.25
		2	95.00	190.00	107.28	82.72	20.50	10.25
		3	95.00	190.00	107.28	82.72	20.50	10.25

Name	week	1a	1b	1c
F Atkins	1	195	34.28	13.95
	2	190	33.31	13.50
	3	193	33.89	13.77
C Barnes	1	195	34.28	13.95
	2	195	34.28	13.95
	3	195	34.28	13.95
T Charlton	1	211	37.39	15.39
	2	201	35.45	14.49
	3	210	37.39	15.39
A Donaldson	1	87	10.00	4.23
	2	87	10.00	4.23
	3	87	10.00	4.23
R Edwards	1	95	11.25	4.95
	2	95	11.25	4.95
	3	95	11.25	4.95

Task 11

Fill in Form P11 for the same employees for week 4.

Wages earned:

Atkins £190.00; Barnes £195.00; Charlton £200.00; Donaldson £87.50; Edwards £95.00

Task 12

Mr Atkins leaves at the end of that week. Make out his P45.

Task 13

Mr Atkins is replaced by Miss Paula Sugden, who was eighteen on February 9th, has NI number EF 13 25 67 E, and has just left college. She has no tax documentation. Take the necessary action.

Help ?

See Section 2: The Information Bank

Wages and salaries, page 266.

Payment of wages

(corresponding to NVQ Element 22.2)

Topics covered: *payment of wages in cash and by cheque; cash analysis.*
Forms needed: *cash analysis sheet*, page 283; *cheque*, The Forms Bank, page 359.

You have taken up a post in the accounts department of Azure Computers and have been given the job of handling part of their wages bill. You will be dealing with the affairs of the following employees:

F Atkins, C Barnes, T Charlton, A Donaldson, R Edwards, H Finlay, G Gresham, M Handley, P Ingham, J Jackson, E King, W Long, B Morley, T Nason, A Ogilvy, T Patrick, S Quentin, T Ross, N Smith, K Thomson.

Task 1

Make out cheques for:

F Atkins, C Barnes, T Charlton, G Gresham, P Ingham, J Jackson, E King, W Long, B Morley, A Ogilvy, T Patrick.

Task 2

The following employees are to be paid in cash. Make out a cash analysis of what will be required.

A Donaldson, R Edwards, H Finlay, G Gresham, M Handley, T Nason, S Quentin, T Ross, N Smith, K Thomson.

The highest value note should be £20. Calculate both the number of each denomination needed and their value.

Help ?

See Section 2: The Information Bank

Wages and salaries, page 281–286.

Credit transfer

(corresponding to NVQ Element 22.3)

Topics covered: *bank giro, foreign dealings.*
Forms needed: *bank giro slip*, page 11; *cheque* , page 8.

Your brief:

You are working in the accounts section of Eden Plants and Gardens. At the end of October invoices and statements arrived for payment. The following are to be settled by credit transfer

Task 1

A customer statement arrives from Hoxted Horticulture for £400.10. Assume that it is authorised for payment, and prepare a giro slip. The Hoxted account (number 35621768) is with the Mercia Bank, King's Parade, Hoxted (sort code 56-23-77).

Task 2

A customer statement arrives from William Morris Garden Ornaments for £400.10. Assume that it is authorised for payment, and prepare a giro slip. The William Morris account (number 35621768) is with the Working Men's Bank, Tolpuddle Lane, East Lynn (sort code 88-21-16).

Task 3

A customer statement arrives from Pick and Fawkes Ltd, Levellers Common, Digby. The balance due is £273.75. Assume that you have reconciled your records with the statement and prepare a giro slip to make the payment. The Pick and Fawkes account (number 82425674) is with the Rochdale and Wigan Bank, Formby Street, Digby (sort code 44-15-98).

Task 4

Invoices are also received from the suppliers listed below. The calculations are found correct, with amounts due as indicated. All the invoices offer a discount of $2\frac{1}{2}$% for payment within 30 days, which EPG is entitled to claim.

Name	Invoice total	discount $2\frac{1}{2}$%	remittance needed
G Campbell	85.60		
R finlay	101.20		
G Hyde	19.67		
A Payne	55.90		
G Weston	42.00		

a) Work out the amounts due.

b) Prepare giro slips to settle the invoice.

c) Prepare a cheque to cover the amount being paid out by bank giro.

Name	bank	branch	account number	sort code number
G Campbell	Mercia	West Codlington	2314 9326	20-65-44
R finlay	Mercia	Eastcote	1739 2856	20-44-33
G Hyde	Wessex and Cornwall	Longmeadow	4732 8561	77-33-51
A Payne	Working Men's	Hoxted	8375 9120	50-43-80
G Weston	Mercia	Baker's Alley	0127 6345	20-45-11

Task 5

Prepare a cheque to cover the amount being paid out by bank giro in the above transactions.

Task 6

You receive an invoice from Jardins Bovary-Flaubert, Rue Voltaire 177, Plume de Matante, CALVADOS 24250, France. It is for 1850.00 francs. It contains the information:

❐ Conditions de paiement; par virement bancaire sur notre compte No 303 056 171 22 du BANQUE BEAUJOLAIS NOUVEAU, Place Descartes 17, Plume de Matante, CALVADOS 24250 au 30 Novembre. Avec nos remerciments.

Supply EPG's bank with the details which they will need to make an international transfer.

Help ?

See Section 2: The Information Bank

Bank documents: bank giro, page 79.

Banking facilities: foreign dealings, page 102.

Cash book, journals and ledger

(corresponding to NVQ Element 23.1)

Topics covered: *two-column cash book; contra entry; journals (sales, purchases, sales returns, purchases returns); customer and supplier accounts; double entry bookkeeping; ledger accounts (sales, purchases, sales returns, purchases returns, VAT); aged debtors list.*

Forms needed: *cash book sheet, customer statement, journals sheet, ledger account sheet,* The Form Bank, page 359.

Warning: Read the instructions carefully before you begin work, or you are likely to end up in a serious muddle!

Moira Faraday, the senior bookkeeper at Eden Plants and Gardens has decided to alter the procedures at Honeysuckle, Eve Adams' flower shop. She appoints you as her assistant to carry out the work.

The period concerned is January and February. For your convenience, here is a calendar of that period.

	Mon	Tue	Wed	Thu	Fri	Sat	Sun		Mon	Tue	Wed	Thu	Fri	Sat	Sun
January					1	2	3	February	1	2	3	4	5	6	7
	4	5	6	7	8	9	10		8	9	10	11	12	13	14
	11	12	13	14	15	16	17		15	16	17	18	19	20	21
	18	19	20	21	22	23	24		22	23	24	25	26	27	28
	25	26	27	28	29	30	31								

Listed below are all the transactions which are to be recorded at Honeysuckle.

Your brief is to record two sorts of activity: cash sales, and credit dealings.

1) *Cash sales*

Customers who come into the shop pay in cash or by cheque.

The cash taken is handled through the till, and the figure given for each working day is the total shown on the till roll.

Cheques are totalled up manually at the end of the day.

Cheques are banked daily. Cash is put in the safe, and banked weekly after the end of Saturday's trading, through the night safe of the Mercia Bank. The float of £50 is always left at the shop.

Following standard practice, these transactions are recorded in the Cash Book. This will open with a cash float of £50.00 and a Bank Account balance of £1865.00. The Cash Book is to be balanced at the end of the month.

2) *Credit dealings*

These are handled in the standard way, in the first instance being recorded in the books of original entry, that is the Sales Journal, Purchases Journal, Sales Returns Journal and Purchases Returns Journal.

EPG post the contents of the journals weekly to the ledger, that is to the personal (customer and supplier accounts).

Summaries of the transactions are posted at the end of the month to the four ledger accounts corresponding to the journals, and to the VAT account.

Payments received and made by EPG in settlement of credit dealings are first recorded in the Cash Book. A double entry is then made to the relevant customer or supplier account.

Moira suggests that you first deal with cash transactions, then credit dealings and finally occasions on which settlements of credit are made.

Stage 1 – January

Invoices issued and received are set out in the following format:

Anthias: H100; 24.00; 4.20; 28.20.

This means that on the invoice (ref: H100) relating to the account of Mrs Anthias the invoice totals were:

before VAT 24.00

VAT charged: 4.20

total invoice: 28.20

The receipt and issue of credit notes follows the same pattern.

Transactions:

4 Jan   Sales cash: 32.00 cheques: 57.00

5 Jan   Sales cash: 18.00 cheques: 61.00
          Invoice issued: Anthias: H100 24.00; 4.20; 28.20

6 Jan   Sales cash: 40.00 cheques: 70.00
          Invoice received: Hoxted: HH792; 36.00; 6.30; 42.30

7 Jan   Sales cash: 25.00 cheques: 15.00
          Invoice issued: Edens: H101; 34.00; 5.95; 39.95
          Credit note received: Hoxted: HCN32; 36.00; 6.30; 42.30

8 Jan   Sales cash: 35.00 cheques: 80.00
          Invoice received: Boxhill: BH345; 27.00; 4.72; 31.72
          Credit note issued: Edens: HC100; 10.00; 1.75; 11.75

9 Jan   Sales cash: 45.00 cheques: 75.00

11 Jan   Sales cash: 24.00 cheques: 30.00
          Invoice issued: Metropole: H102; 56.00; 9.80; 65.80

12 Jan   Sales cash: 31.00 cheques: 25.00
          Invoice received: Hoxted: HH800; 52.00; 9.10; 61.10

13 Jan   Sales cash: 23.00 cheques: 14.00
          Invoice issued: Metropole: H103; 65.00; 11.37; 76.37

14 Jan   Sales cash: 15.00 cheques: 27.00
          Invoice received: Churchill: FC233; 60.00; 10.50; 70.50
          Credit note issued: Metropole: HC101; 15.00; 2.62; 17.62

15 Jan   Sales cash: 40.00 cheques: 39.00

16 Jan   Sales cash: 50.00 cheques: 61.00
          Invoice received: Churchill: FC237; 48.00; 8.40; 56.40

18 Jan   Sales cash: 20.00 cheques: 17.00
          Invoice received: Boxhill: BH352; 22.00; 3.85; 25.85

19 Jan   Sales cash: 18.00 cheques: 29.00
          Invoice issued: Anthias: H104; 17.00; 2.97; 19.97
          Credit note received: Boxhill: BC72; 22.00; 3.85; 25.85

20 Jan   Sales cash: 30.00 cheques: 10.00
          Invoice issued: Edens: H105; 12.00; 2.10; 14.10

21 Jan   Sales cash: 32.00 cheques: 15.00
          Invoice received: Boxhill: BH357; 18.00; 3.15; 21.15
          Credit note issued: Edens: HC102; 12.00; 2.10; 14.10

22 Jan   Sales cash: 45.00 cheques: 37.00
          Credit note received: Boxhill: BC74; 18.00; 3.15; 21,15

23 Jan   Sales cash: 55.00 cheques: 60.00
          Invoice issued: Metropole: H106; 50.00; 8.75; 58.75

25 Jan   Sales cash: 24.00 cheques: 30.00
          Invoice received: Hoxted: HH815; 34.00; 5.95; 39.95

26 Jan   Sales cash: 31.00 cheques: 25.00
          Invoice issued: Edens: H107; 10.00; 1.75; 11.75

27 Jan   Sales cash: 23.00 cheques: 14.00
          Invoice received: Churchill: FC251: 61.00; 6.51; 67.51

28 Jan   Sales cash: 15.00 cheques: 27.00
          Credit note received: Churchill: FCN84; 21.00; 3.67; 24.67

29 Jan   Sales cash: 40.00 cheques: 39.00
          Invoice received: Boxhill: BH365; 46.00; 8.05; 54.05

30 Jan   Sales cash: 50.00 cheques: 61.00
          Invoice issued: Metropole: H108; 40.00; 7.00; 47.00

Task 1

Make the cash book entries for January.

Task 2

Make the journals entries for January.

Task 3

Make the ledger accounts entries for January.

Folio numbers:

Sales S1; Sales Returns S2; Purchases P1; Purchases Returns P2

Customer accounts: Anthias C12; Edens C32; Hotel Metropole C65

Supplier Accounts: Hoxted Horticulture SP11; Boxhill Shrubs SP17; Frank

Churchill Ltd SP35

VAT account: V1

Task 4

Draw up the statements of account which are to be sent out to customers. Assume all the accounts are new.

Task 5

Moira Faraday wishes to review the accounts held with suppliers. Make up statements of position for her to look at.

356

Stage 2 – February

Your brief is as before with one addition. During the month payments are made and received in settlement of credit accounts as indicated in the list of transactions. These payments are made by cheque.

Transactions

1 Feb   Sales cash: 15.00 cheques: 9.00
Invoice issued: Anthias: H109 14.00; 2.45; 16.45

2 Feb   Sales cash: 22.00 cheques: 30.00

3 Feb   Sales cash: 18.00 cheques: 21.00
Cheques issued: Hoxted: £101.05; Boxhill: £85.77; Churchill: £169.74

4 Feb   Sales cash: 26.00 cheques: 17.00
Invoice received: Boxhill: BH375: 22.00; 3.85; 25.85
Credit note issued: Anthias: HC103 6.00; 1.05; 7.05

5 Feb   Sales cash: 34.00 cheques: 23.00
Invoice issued: Anthias: H110 21.00; 3.67; 24.67
Credit note received: Boxhill: BC82; 11.00; 1.92; 12.92
Cheque received: Edens: £65.80

6 Feb   Sales cash: 45.00 cheques: 52.00
Invoice received: Churchill: FC264; 33.00; 5.77; 38.77

8 Feb   Sales cash: 10.00 cheques: 5.00
Invoice issued: Edens: H111; 10.00; 1.75; 11.75
Credit note received: Churchill: FCN91 33.00; 5.77; 38.77

9 Feb   Sales cash: 20.00 cheques: 22.00
Invoice received: Hoxted; HH827; 11.00; 1.92; 12.92
Cheque received: Metropole: £247.92

10 Feb   Sales cash: 15.00 cheques: 7.00
Invoice issued: Metropole: H112; 45.00; 7.87; 52.87
Credit note received: Hoxted; HCN40 11.00; 1.92; 12.92

11 Feb   Sales cash: 34.00 cheques: 17.00
Invoice received: Hoxted: HH832; 41.00; 7.17; 48.17

12 Feb   Sales cash: 42.00 cheques: 28.00
Credit note issued: Metropole: HC104; 20.00; 3.50; 23.50

13 Feb   Sales cash: 51.00 cheques: 44.00
Invoice issued: Metropole: H113; 35.00; 6.12; 41.12

15 Feb   Sales cash: 18.00 cheques: 15.00
Invoice received: Hoxted: HH837; 64.00; 11.20; 75.20

16 Feb   Sales cash: 40.00 cheques: 14.00
Invoice issued: Anthias: H114 7.00; 1.22; 8.22
Credit note received: Hoxted: HCN45; 24.00; 4.20; 28.20

17 Feb   Sales cash: 35.00 cheques: 27.00

18 Feb   Sales cash: 23.00 cheques: 37.00
Invoice received: Boxhill: BH386; 17.00; 2.97; 19.97

19 Feb   Sales cash: 40.00 cheques: 21.00
Credit note issued: Anthias: HC105; 7.00; 1.22; 8.22

20 Feb   Sales cash: 50.00 cheques: 24.00
         Invoice issued: Edens: H115; 14.00; 2.45; 16.45
         Invoice received: Churchill: FC282; 28.00; 4.90; 32.90

22 Feb   Sales cash: 24.00 cheques: 8.00
         Invoice issued: Metropole: H116; 15.00; 2.62; 17.62

23 Feb   Sales cash: 18.00 cheques: 24.00
         Invoice received: Churchill: FC285; 19.00; 3.32; 22.32

24 Feb   Sales cash: 16.00 cheques: 16.00

25 Feb   Sales cash: 31.00 cheques: 27.00
         Invoice issued: Metropole: H117; 25.00; 4.37; 29.37

26 Feb   Sales cash: 38.00 cheques: 17.00
         Invoice received: Boxhill: BH397; 34.00; 5.95; 39.95
         Credit note issued: Edens: HC106; 14.00; 2.45; 16.45

27 Feb   Sales cash: 47.00 cheques: 29.00
         Credit note received: Boxhill: BC85; 12.00; 2.10; 14.10
         Invoice issued: Metropole: H118; 32.00; 5.60; 37.60

Task 1

Make the cash book entries for February.

Task 2

Eve Adams asks for a breakdown of the sales made in the shop. Draw up the totals for the week and the month for payments in cash, by cheque, and the total of the two.

Task 3

Make the journals entries for February.

Task 4

Make the ledger account entries for February.

Task 5

Draw up customer account statements. Make an aged debt analysis of these accounts.

Task 6

Draw up statements of the supplier accounts, as before, for Moira Faraday.

Help ?

*See **Section 2: The Information Bank***

Cash book, page 115.

Ledgers and journals: journals, page 178; *returns journals,* page 181; *double entry bookkeeping,* page 184; *posting of journals to the ledger,* page 187.

Invoices: aged debtors list, page 167; *statements of account,* page 167.

Section 4

THE FORMS BANK

The forms in this Section can be photocopied as required.

Journals

Date			Total before VAT	VAT	Total including VAT
	Totals				

Blank receipt

Date: ....

....

....

....

....

....

....

....

....

....

Paid in full: Total:

                                    No.:

Cash book

Debit					Credit				
Date	Details	Folio	Cash	Bank	Date	Details	Folio	Cash	Bank

Customer statement

ЄDЄN PLANTS AND GARDENS

Credit limit: ....   Date: ....

Account no.: ....   Terms: ....

STATEMENT OF ACCOUNT

Date	Reference	Description	Debit	Credit	Balance
				Amount now due	

Credit card voucher

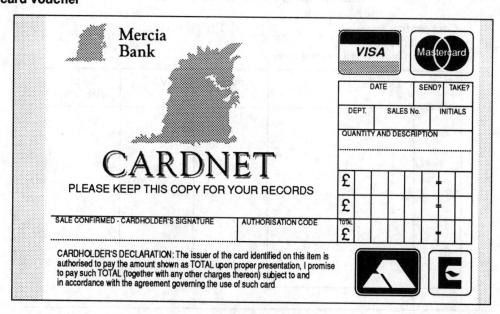

Petty cash

Debits £	Date	Details	Voucher number	Credit £	Analysis columns				
					£	£	£	£	£
		Totals							

Expenses summary form

EXPENSES SUMMARY FORM

Cost centre/ ------------------------- Period ending: ----------------
Expense code:
(Cross out whichever is not appropriate)

Date	Details	Amount less VAT	VAT	Total with VAT

Blank cheque

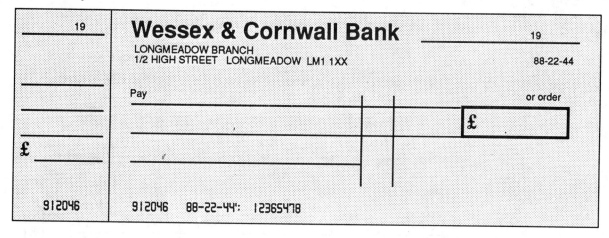

	19

£ _____

912046

Wessex & Cornwall Bank
LONGMEADOW BRANCH
1/2 HIGH STREET LONGMEADOW LM1 1XX

	19

88-22-44

Pay _____ or order

£

912046   88⁻22⁻44ꞌ: 12365478

Ledger

Debit			Credit		
Date	Details	£	Date	Details	£

Pay slip

Pay advice			
Date	Employee	Tax code	Week

Payments	Deductions
Basic Pay:	Income tax:
Overtime:	Nat Ins.
Gross pay:	Total:
Net pay:	
Gross pay to date:	Tax paid this year:
Taxable pay:	NI paid:

Standing order mandate

<table>
<tr><td colspan="3" align="center">**STANDING ORDER MANDATE**</td></tr>
</table>

To _

Address _

	Bank	Branch title (not address)	Code Number
Please pay			
	Beneficiary		Account Number
for the credit of			
	Amount in figures	Amount in words	
the sum of			

	Date and amount of 1st payment			Date and frequency
commencing	*now		and thereafter every	
	Date and amount of last payment			
*until				
quoting the reference			and debit my/our account accordingly	

* This instruction cancels any previous order in favour of the beneficiary named above, under this reference
† If the amount of the periodic payments vary they should be incorporated in a schedule overleaf

Special instructions

Signature(s) _____ Date _____

Title and number of
account to be debited _____

*Delete if not applicable

Note: The Bank will not undertake to
   (i)   make any reference to Value Added Tax or pay a stated sum "plus VAT"
   (ii) advise payer's address to beneficiary
   (iii) advise beneficiary of inability to pay
   (iv) request beneficiary's banker to advise beneficiary of receipt

Order form

<table>
<tr><td colspan="5" style="text-align:center">Order form</td></tr>
<tr><td colspan="3">VAT Reg. No.: 129 44053</td><td colspan="2">✆ 0191 23456</td></tr>
<tr><td colspan="3">To:......................................
...................................</td><td colspan="2">Order No. ....
Date: ....</td></tr>
<tr><td>Quantity</td><td>Item</td><td>Unit</td><td>Price</td><td>Total</td></tr>
<tr><td></td><td></td><td></td><td></td><td></td></tr>
<tr><td colspan="4">TOTAL</td><td></td></tr>
<tr><td colspan="5">Delivery : ....

Signed: ....</td></tr>
</table>

Invoice

<table>
<tr><td colspan="5" style="text-align:center">Invoice</td></tr>
<tr><td colspan="3">DATE :
CUSTOMER NAME :</td><td colspan="2">ORDER NO.:</td></tr>
<tr><td>Quantity</td><td>Item</td><td>Unit</td><td>Price</td><td>Total</td></tr>
<tr><td></td><td></td><td></td><td></td><td></td></tr>
<tr><td colspan="4">TOTAL excl. VAT</td><td></td></tr>
<tr><td colspan="4">VAT</td><td></td></tr>
<tr><td colspan="4">TOTAL</td><td></td></tr>
<tr><td colspan="5" style="text-align:center">VAT Reg. No. 130 774106</td></tr>
</table>

Credit note

Credit note

Customer name: Account no:
Date: Terms:

Re invoice:

Quantity	Item	Unit price	Total
		VAT ($17\frac{1}{2}\%$)	
		Total	

Reason for credit:

....

VAT Reg. No. 130 774106

Delivery note

Delivery note

DATE: ORDER No.:
CUSTOMER NAME:

QUANTITY	ITEM	UNIT

DESPATCH DETAILS: _____

DELIVERY: _____

RECEIVED: _____

SIGNED: _____

FIRM: _____

VAT Reg. No. 130 774106

Remittance note

Customer

REMITTANCE ADVICE
Cheque number:
Our account number:

Date	Description	Amount due
	Total cheque enclosed	

Quotation

Name:.. Ref:...

Address:.. Date:...

....

Quantity	Item	Unit Price	Total

Total

Discount

Total (after discount)

WEEK 1
Apr 6 to Apr 12

TABLE A—FREE PAY

Code	Total free pay to date	Code	Total free pay to date	Code	Total free pay to date	Code	Total free pay to date	Code	Total free pay to date	Code	Total free pay to date	Code	Total free pay to date	Code	Total free pay to date
	£		£		£		£		£		£		£		£
0	NIL														
1	0·37	61	11·91	121	23·45	181	34·99	241	46·52	301	58·06	361	69·60	421	81·14
2	0·56	62	12·10	122	23·64	182	35·18	242	46·72	302	58·25	362	69·79	422	81·33
3	0·75	63	12·29	123	23·83	183	35·37	243	46·91	303	58·45	363	69·99	423	81·52
4	0·95	64	12·49	124	24·02	184	35·56	244	47·10	304	58·64	364	70·18	424	81·72
5	1·14	65	12·68	125	24·22	185	35·75	245	47·29	305	58·83	365	70·37	425	81·91
6	1·33	66	12·87	126	24·41	186	35·95	246	47·49	306	59·02	366	70·56	426	82·10
7	1·52	67	13·06	127	24·60	187	36·14	247	47·68	307	59·22	367	70·75	427	82·29
8	1·72	68	13·25	128	24·79	188	36·33	248	47·87	308	59·41	368	70·95	428	82·49
9	1·91	69	13·45	129	24·99	189	36·52	249	48·06	309	59·60	369	71·14	429	82·68
10	2·10	70	13·64	130	25·18	190	36·72	250	48·25	310	59·79	370	71·33	430	82·87
11	2·29	71	13·83	131	25·37	191	36·91	251	48·45	311	59·99	371	71·52	431	83·06
12	2·49	72	14·02	132	25·56	192	37·10	252	48·64	312	60·18	372	71·72	432	83·25
13	2·68	73	14·22	133	25·75	193	37·29	253	48·83	313	60·37	373	71·91	433	83·45
14	2·87	74	14·41	134	25·95	194	37·49	254	49·02	314	60·56	374	72·10	434	83·64
15	3·06	75	14·60	135	26·14	195	37·68	255	49·22	315	60·75	375	72·29	435	83·83
16	3·25	76	14·79	136	26·33	196	37·87	256	49·41	316	60·95	376	72·49	436	84·02
17	3·45	77	14·99	137	26·52	197	38·06	257	49·60	317	61·14	377	72·68	437	84·22
18	3·64	78	15·18	138	26·72	198	38·25	258	49·79	318	61·33	378	72·87	438	84·41
19	3·83	79	15·37	139	26·91	199	38·45	259	49·99	319	61·52	379	73·06	439	84·60
20	4·02	80	15·56	140	27·10	200	38·64	260	50·18	320	61·72	380	73·25	440	84·79
21	4·22	81	15·75	141	27·29	201	38·83	261	50·37	321	61·91	381	73·45	441	84·99
22	4·41	82	15·95	142	27·49	202	39·02	262	50·56	322	62·10	382	73·64	442	85·18
23	4·60	83	16·14	143	27·68	203	39·22	263	50·75	323	62·29	383	73·83	443	85·37
24	4·79	84	16·33	144	27·87	204	39·41	264	50·95	324	62·49	384	74·02	444	85·56
25	4·99	85	16·52	145	28·06	205	39·60	265	51·14	325	62·68	385	74·22	445	85·75
26	5·18	86	16·72	146	28·25	206	39·79	266	51·33	326	62·87	386	74·41	446	85·95
27	5·37	87	16·91	147	28·45	207	39·99	267	51·52	327	63·06	387	74·60	447	86·14
28	5·56	88	17·10	148	28·64	208	40·18	268	51·72	328	63·25	388	74·79	448	86·33
29	5·75	89	17·29	149	28·83	209	40·37	269	51·91	329	63·45	389	74·99	449	86·52
30	5·95	90	17·49	150	29·02	210	40·56	270	52·10	330	63·64	390	75·18	450	86·72
31	6·14	91	17·68	151	29·22	211	40·75	271	52·29	331	63·83	391	75·37	451	86·91
32	6·33	92	17·87	152	29·41	212	40·95	272	52·49	332	64·02	392	75·56	452	87·10
33	6·52	93	18·06	153	29·60	213	41·14	273	52·68	333	64·22	393	75·75	453	87·29
34	6·72	94	18·25	154	29·79	214	41·33	274	52·87	334	64·41	394	75·95	454	87·49
35	6·91	95	18·45	155	29·99	215	41·52	275	53·06	335	64·60	395	76·14	455	87·68
36	7·10	96	18·64	156	30·18	216	41·72	276	53·25	336	64·79	396	76·33	456	87·87
37	7·29	97	18·83	157	30·37	217	41·91	277	53·45	337	64·99	397	76·52	457	88·06
38	7·49	98	19·02	158	30·56	218	42·10	278	53·64	338	65·18	398	76·72	458	88·25
39	7·68	99	19·22	159	30·75	219	42·29	279	53·83	339	65·37	399	76·91	459	88·45
40	7·87	100	19·41	160	30·95	220	42·49	280	54·02	340	65·56	400	77·10	460	88·64
41	8·06	101	19·60	161	31·14	221	42·68	281	54·22	341	65·75	401	77·29	461	88·83
42	8·25	102	19·79	162	31·33	222	42·87	282	54·41	342	65·95	402	77·49	462	89·02
43	8·45	103	19·99	163	31·52	223	43·06	283	54·60	343	66·14	403	77·68	463	89·22
44	8·64	104	20·18	164	31·72	224	43·25	284	54·79	344	66·33	404	77·87	464	89·41
45	8·83	105	20·37	165	31·91	225	43·45	285	54·99	345	66·52	405	78·06	465	89·60
46	9·02	106	20·56	166	32·10	226	43·64	286	55·18	346	66·72	406	78·25	466	89·79
47	9·22	107	20·75	167	32·29	227	43·83	287	55·37	347	66·91	407	78·45	467	89·99
48	9·41	108	20·95	168	32·49	228	44·02	288	55·56	348	67·10	408	78·64	468	90·18
49	9·60	109	21·14	169	32·68	229	44·22	289	55·75	349	67·29	409	78·83	469	90·37
50	9·79	110	21·33	170	32·87	230	44·41	290	55·95	350	67·49	410	79·02	470	90·56
51	9·99	111	21·52	171	33·06	231	44·60	291	56·14	351	67·68	411	79·22	471	90·75
52	10·18	112	21·72	172	33·25	232	44·79	292	56·33	352	67·87	412	79·41	472	90·95
53	10·37	113	21·91	173	33·45	233	44·99	293	56·52	353	68·06	413	79·60	473	91·14
54	10·56	114	22·10	174	33·64	234	45·18	294	56·72	354	68·25	414	79·79	474	91·33
55	10·75	115	22·29	175	33·83	235	45·37	295	56·91	355	68·45	415	79·99	475	91·52
56	10·95	116	22·49	176	34·02	236	45·56	296	57·10	356	68·64	416	80·18	476	91·72
57	11·14	117	22·68	177	34·22	237	45·75	297	57·29	357	68·83	417	80·37	477	91·91
58	11·33	118	22·87	178	34·41	238	45·95	298	57·49	358	69·02	418	80·56	478	92·10
59	11·52	119	23·06	179	34·60	239	46·14	299	57·68	359	69·22	419	80·75	479	92·29
60	11·72	120	23·25	180	34·79	240	46·33	300	57·87	360	69·41	420	80·95	480	92·49

TABLE A—FREE PAY

Code	Total free pay to date	Code	Total free pay to date	Code	Total free pay to date	Code	Total free pay to date	Code	Total free pay to date	Code	Total free pay to date	Code	Total free pay to date	Code	Total free pay to date
	£		£		£		£		£		£		£		£
0	NIL														
1	0·74	61	23·82	121	46·90	181	69·98	241	93·04	301	116·12	361	139·20	421	162·28
2	1·12	62	24·20	122	47·28	182	70·36	242	93·44	302	116·50	362	139·58	422	162·66
3	1·50	63	24·58	123	47·66	183	70·74	243	93·82	303	116·90	363	139·98	423	163·04
4	1·90	64	24·98	124	48·04	184	71·12	244	94·20	304	117·28	364	140·36	424	163·44
5	2·28	65	25·36	125	48·44	185	71·50	245	94·58	305	117·66	365	140·74	425	163·82
6	2·66	66	25·74	126	48·82	186	71·90	246	94·98	306	118·04	366	141·12	426	164·20
7	3·04	67	26·12	127	49·20	187	72·28	247	95·36	307	118·44	367	141·50	427	164·58
8	3·44	68	26·50	128	49·58	188	72·66	248	95·74	308	118·82	368	141·90	428	164·98
9	3·82	69	26·90	129	49·98	189	73·04	249	96·12	309	119·20	369	142·28	429	165·36
10	4·20	70	27·28	130	50·36	190	73·44	250	96·50	310	119·58	370	142·66	430	165·74
11	4·58	71	27·66	131	50·74	191	73·82	251	96·90	311	119·98	371	143·04	431	166·12
12	4·98	72	28·04	132	51·12	192	74·20	252	97·28	312	120·36	372	143·44	432	166·50
13	5·36	73	28·44	133	51·50	193	74·58	253	97·66	313	120·74	373	143·82	433	166·90
14	5·74	74	28·82	134	51·90	194	74·98	254	98·04	314	121·12	374	144·20	434	167·28
15	6·12	75	29·20	135	52·28	195	75·36	255	98·44	315	121·50	375	144·58	435	167·66
16	6·50	76	29·58	136	52·66	196	75·74	256	98·82	316	121·90	376	144·98	436	168·04
17	6·90	77	29·98	137	53·04	197	76·12	257	99·20	317	122·28	377	145·36	437	168·44
18	7·28	78	30·36	138	53·44	198	76·50	258	99·58	318	122·66	378	145·74	438	168·82
19	7·66	79	30·74	139	53·82	199	76·90	259	99·98	319	123·04	379	146·12	439	169·20
20	8·04	80	31·12	140	54·20	200	77·28	260	100·36	320	123·44	380	146·50	440	169·58
21	8·44	81	31·50	141	54·58	201	77·66	261	100·74	321	123·82	381	146·90	441	169·98
22	8·82	82	31·90	142	54·98	202	78·04	262	101·12	322	124·20	382	147·28	442	170·36
23	9·20	83	32·28	143	55·36	203	78·44	263	101·50	323	124·58	383	147·66	443	170·74
24	9·58	84	32·66	144	55·74	204	78·82	264	101·90	324	124·98	384	148·04	444	171·12
25	9·98	85	33·04	145	56·12	205	79·20	265	102·28	325	125·36	385	148·44	445	171·50
26	10·36	86	33·44	146	56·50	206	79·58	266	102·66	326	125·74	386	148·82	446	171·90
27	10·74	87	33·82	147	56·90	207	79·98	267	103·04	327	126·12	387	149·20	447	172·28
28	11·12	88	34·20	148	57·28	208	80·36	268	103·44	328	126·50	388	149·58	448	172·66
29	11·50	89	34·58	149	57·66	209	80·74	269	103·82	329	126·90	389	149·98	449	173·04
30	11·90	90	34·98	150	58·04	210	81·12	270	104·20	330	127·28	390	150·36	450	173·44
31	12·28	91	35·36	151	58·44	211	81·50	271	104·58	331	127·66	391	150·74	451	173·82
32	12·66	92	35·74	152	58·82	212	81·90	272	104·98	332	128·04	392	151·12	452	174·20
33	13·04	93	36·12	153	59·20	213	82·28	273	105·36	333	128·44	393	151·50	453	174·58
34	13·44	94	36·50	154	59·58	214	82·66	274	105·74	334	128·82	394	151·90	454	174·98
35	13·82	95	36·90	155	59·98	215	83·04	275	106·12	335	129·20	395	152·28	455	175·36
36	14·20	96	37·28	156	60·36	216	83·44	276	106·50	336	129·58	396	152·66	456	175·74
37	14·58	97	37·66	157	60·74	217	83·82	277	106·90	337	129·98	397	153·04	457	176·12
38	14·98	98	38·04	158	61·12	218	84·20	278	107·28	338	130·36	398	153·44	458	176·50
39	15·36	99	38·44	159	61·50	219	84·58	279	107·66	339	130·74	399	153·82	459	176·90
40	15·74	100	38·82	160	61·90	220	84·98	280	108·04	340	131·12	400	154·20	460	177·28
41	16·12	101	39·20	161	62·28	221	85·36	281	108·44	341	131·50	401	154·58	461	177·66
42	16·50	102	39·58	162	62·66	222	85·74	282	108·82	342	131·90	402	154·98	462	178·04
43	16·90	103	39·98	163	63·04	223	86·12	283	109·20	343	132·28	403	155·36	463	178·44
44	17·28	104	40·36	164	63·44	224	86·50	284	109·58	344	132·66	404	155·74	464	178·82
45	17·66	105	40·74	165	63·82	225	86·90	285	109·98	345	133·04	405	156·12	465	179·20
46	18·04	106	41·12	166	64·20	226	87·28	286	110·36	346	133·44	406	156·50	466	179·58
47	18·44	107	41·50	167	64·58	227	87·66	287	110·74	347	133·82	407	156·90	467	179·98
48	18·82	108	41·90	168	64·98	228	88·04	288	111·12	348	134·20	408	157·28	468	180·36
49	19·20	109	42·28	169	65·36	229	88·44	289	111·50	349	134·58	409	157·66	469	180·74
50	19·58	110	42·66	170	65·74	230	88·82	290	111·90	350	134·98	410	158·04	470	181·12
51	19·98	111	43·04	171	66·12	231	89·20	291	112·28	351	135·36	411	158·44	471	181·50
52	20·36	112	43·44	172	66·50	232	89·58	292	112·66	352	135·74	412	158·82	472	181·90
53	20·74	113	43·82	173	66·90	233	89·98	293	113·04	353	136·12	413	159·20	473	182·28
54	21·12	114	44·20	174	67·28	234	90·36	294	113·44	354	136·50	414	159·58	474	182·66
55	21·50	115	44·58	175	67·66	235	90·74	295	113·82	355	136·90	415	159·98	475	183·04
56	21·90	116	44·98	176	68·04	236	91·12	296	114·20	356	137·28	416	160·36	476	183·44
57	22·28	117	45·36	177	68·44	237	91·50	297	114·58	357	137·66	417	160·74	477	183·82
58	22·66	118	45·74	178	68·82	238	91·90	298	114·98	358	138·04	418	161·12	478	184·20
59	23·04	119	46·12	179	69·20	239	92·28	299	115·36	359	138·44	419	161·50	479	184·58
60	23·44	120	46·50	180	69·58	240	92·66	300	115·74	360	138·82	420	161·90	480	184·98

3

WEEK 3
Apr 20 to Apr 26

TABLE A—FREE PAY

Code	Total free pay to date	Code	Total free pay to date	Code	Total free pay to date	Code	Total free pay to date	Code	Total free pay to date	Code	Total free pay to date	Code	Total free pay to date	Code	Total free pay to date
	£		£		£		£		£		£		£		£
0	NIL														
1	1·11	61	35·73	121	70·35	181	104·97	241	139·56	301	174·18	361	208·80	421	243·42
2	1·68	62	36·30	122	70·92	182	105·54	242	140·16	302	174·75	362	209·37	422	243·99
3	2·25	63	36·87	123	71·49	183	106·11	243	140·73	303	175·35	363	209·97	423	244·56
4	2·85	64	37·47	124	72·06	184	106·68	244	141·30	304	175·92	364	210·54	424	245·16
5	3·42	65	38·04	125	72·66	185	107·25	245	141·87	305	176·49	365	211·11	425	245·73
6	3·99	66	38·61	126	73·23	186	107·85	246	142·47	306	177·06	366	211·68	426	246·30
7	4·56	67	39·18	127	73·80	187	108·42	247	143·04	307	177·66	367	212·25	427	246·87
8	5·16	68	39·75	128	74·37	188	108·99	248	143·61	308	178·23	368	212·85	428	247·47
9	5·73	69	40·35	129	74·97	189	109·56	249	144·18	309	178·80	369	213·42	429	248·04
10	6·30	70	40·92	130	75·54	190	110·16	250	144·75	310	179·37	370	213·99	430	248·61
11	6·87	71	41·49	131	76·11	191	110·73	251	145·35	311	179·97	371	214·56	431	249·18
12	7·47	72	42·06	132	76·68	192	111·30	252	145·92	312	180·54	372	215·16	432	249·75
13	8·04	73	42·66	133	77·25	193	111·87	253	146·49	313	181·11	373	215·73	433	250·35
14	8·61	74	43·23	134	77·85	194	112·47	254	147·06	314	181·68	374	216·30	434	250·92
15	9·18	75	43·80	135	78·42	195	113·04	255	147·66	315	182·25	375	216·87	435	251·49
16	9·75	76	44·37	136	78·99	196	113·61	256	148·23	316	182·85	376	217·47	436	252·06
17	10·35	77	44·97	137	79·56	197	114·18	257	148·80	317	183·42	377	218·04	437	252·66
18	10·92	78	45·54	138	80·16	198	114·75	258	149·37	318	183·99	378	218·61	438	253·23
19	11·49	79	46·11	139	80·73	199	115·35	259	149·97	319	184·56	379	219·18	439	253·80
20	12·06	80	46·68	140	81·30	200	115·92	260	150·54	320	185·16	380	219·75	440	254·37
21	12·66	81	47·25	141	81·87	201	116·49	261	151·11	321	185·73	381	220·35	441	254·97
22	13·23	82	47·85	142	82·47	202	117·06	262	151·68	322	186·30	382	220·92	442	255·54
23	13·80	83	48·42	143	83·04	203	117·66	263	152·25	323	186·87	383	221·49	443	256·11
24	14·37	84	48·99	144	83·61	204	118·23	264	152·85	324	187·47	384	222·06	444	256·68
25	14·97	85	49·56	145	84·18	205	118·80	265	153·42	325	188·04	385	222·66	445	257·25
26	15·54	86	50·16	146	84·75	206	119·37	266	153·99	326	188·61	386	223·23	446	257·85
27	16·11	87	50·73	147	85·35	207	119·97	267	154·56	327	189·18	387	223·80	447	258·42
28	16·68	88	51·30	148	85·92	208	120·54	268	155·16	328	189·75	388	224·37	448	258·99
29	17·25	89	51·87	149	86·49	209	121·11	269	155·73	329	190·35	389	224·97	449	259·56
30	17·85	90	52·47	150	87·06	210	121·68	270	156·30	330	190·92	390	225·54	450	260·16
31	18·42	91	53·04	151	87·66	211	122·25	271	156·87	331	191·49	391	226·11	451	260·73
32	18·99	92	53·61	152	88·23	212	122·85	272	157·47	332	192·06	392	226·68	452	261·30
33	19·56	93	54·18	153	88·80	213	123·42	273	158·04	333	192·66	393	227·25	453	261·87
34	20·16	94	54·75	154	89·37	214	123·99	274	158·61	334	193·23	394	227·85	454	262·47
35	20·73	95	55·35	155	89·97	215	124·56	275	159·18	335	193·80	395	228·42	455	263·04
36	21·30	96	55·92	156	90·54	216	125·16	276	159·75	336	194·37	396	228·99	456	263·61
37	21·87	97	56·49	157	91·11	217	125·73	277	160·35	337	194·97	397	229·56	457	264·18
38	22·47	98	57·06	158	91·68	218	126·30	278	160·92	338	195·54	398	230·16	458	264·75
39	23·04	99	57·66	159	92·25	219	126·87	279	161·49	339	196·11	399	230·73	459	265·35
40	23·61	100	58·23	160	92·85	220	127·47	280	162·06	340	196·68	400	231·30	460	265·92
41	24·18	101	58·80	161	93·42	221	128·04	281	162·66	341	197·25	401	231·87	461	266·49
42	24·75	102	59·37	162	93·99	222	128·61	282	163·23	342	197·85	402	232·47	462	267·06
43	25·35	103	59·97	163	94·56	223	129·18	283	163·80	343	198·42	403	233·04	463	267·66
44	25·92	104	60·54	164	95·16	224	129·75	284	164·37	344	198·99	404	233·61	464	268·23
45	26·49	105	61·11	165	95·73	225	130·35	285	164·97	345	199·56	405	234·18	465	268·80
46	27·06	106	61·68	166	96·30	226	130·92	286	165·54	346	200·16	406	234·75	466	269·37
47	27·66	107	62·25	167	96·87	227	131·49	287	166·11	347	200·73	407	235·35	467	269·97
48	28·23	108	62·85	168	97·47	228	132·06	288	166·68	348	201·30	408	235·92	468	270·54
49	28·80	109	63·42	169	98·04	229	132·66	289	167·25	349	201·87	409	236·49	469	271·11
50	29·37	110	63·99	170	98·61	230	133·23	290	167·85	350	202·47	410	237·06	470	271·68
51	29·97	111	64·56	171	99·18	231	133·80	291	168·42	351	203·04	411	237·66	471	272·25
52	30·54	112	65·16	172	99·75	232	134·37	292	168·99	352	203·61	412	238·23	472	272·85
53	31·11	113	65·73	173	100·35	233	134·97	293	169·56	353	204·18	413	238·80	473	273·42
54	31·68	114	66·30	174	100·92	234	135·54	294	170·16	354	204·75	414	239·37	474	273·99
55	32·25	115	66·87	175	101·49	235	136·11	295	170·73	355	205·35	415	239·97	475	274·56
56	32·85	116	67·47	176	102·06	236	136·68	296	171·30	356	205·92	416	240·54	476	275·16
57	33·42	117	68·04	177	102·66	237	137·25	297	171·87	357	206·49	417	241·11	477	275·73
58	33·99	118	68·61	178	103·23	238	137·85	298	172·47	358	207·06	418	241·68	478	276·30
59	34·56	119	69·18	179	103·80	239	138·42	299	173·04	359	207·66	419	242·25	479	276·87
60	35·16	120	69·75	180	104·37	240	138·99	300	173·61	360	208·23	420	242·85	480	277·47

4

TABLE A—FREE PAY

WEEK 4
Apr 27 to May 3

Code	Total free pay to date	Code	Total free pay to date	Code	Total free pay to date	Code	Total free pay to date	Code	Total free pay to date	Code	Total free pay to date	Code	Total free pay to date	Code	Total free pay to date
	£		£		£		£		£		£		£		£
0	NIL														
1	1·48	61	47·64	121	93·80	181	139·96	241	186·08	301	232·24	361	278·40	421	324·56
2	2·24	62	48·40	122	94·56	182	140·72	242	186·88	302	233·00	362	279·16	422	325·32
3	3·00	63	49·16	123	95·32	183	141·48	243	187·64	303	233·80	363	279·96	423	326·08
4	3·80	64	49·96	124	96·08	184	142·24	244	188·40	304	234·56	364	280·72	424	326·88
5	4·56	65	50·72	125	96·88	185	143·00	245	189·16	305	235·32	365	281·48	425	327·64
6	5·32	66	51·48	126	97·64	186	143·80	246	189·96	306	236·08	366	282·24	426	328·40
7	6·08	67	52·24	127	98·40	187	144·56	247	190·72	307	236·88	367	283·00	427	329·16
8	6·88	68	53·00	128	99·16	188	145·32	248	191·48	308	237·64	368	283·80	428	329·96
9	7·64	69	53·80	129	99·96	189	146·08	249	192·24	309	238·40	369	284·56	429	330·72
10	8·40	70	54·56	130	100·72	190	146·88	250	193·00	310	239·16	370	285·32	430	331·48
11	9·16	71	55·32	131	101·48	191	147·64	251	193·80	311	239·96	371	286·08	431	332·24
12	9·96	72	56·08	132	102·24	192	148·40	252	194·56	312	240·72	372	286·88	432	333·00
13	10·72	73	56·88	133	103·00	193	149·16	253	195·32	313	241·48	373	287·64	433	333·80
14	11·48	74	57·64	134	103·80	194	149·96	254	196·08	314	242·24	374	288·40	434	334·56
15	12·24	75	58·40	135	104·56	195	150·72	255	196·88	315	243·00	375	289·16	435	335·32
16	13·00	76	59·16	136	105·32	196	151·48	256	197·64	316	243·80	376	289·96	436	336·08
17	13·80	77	59·96	137	106·08	197	152·24	257	198·40	317	244·56	377	290·72	437	336·88
18	14·56	78	60·72	138	106·88	198	153·00	258	199·16	318	245·32	378	291·48	438	337·64
19	15·32	79	61·48	139	107·64	199	153·80	259	199·96	319	246·08	379	292·24	439	338·40
20	16·08	80	62·24	140	108·40	200	154·56	260	200·72	320	246·88	380	293·00	440	339·16
21	16·88	81	63·00	141	109·16	201	155·32	261	201·48	321	247·64	381	293·80	441	339·96
22	17·64	82	63·80	142	109·96	202	156·08	262	202·24	322	248·40	382	294·56	442	340·72
23	18·40	83	64·56	143	110·72	203	156·88	263	203·00	323	249·16	383	295·32	443	341·48
24	19·16	84	65·32	144	111·48	204	157·64	264	203·80	324	249·96	384	296·08	444	342·24
25	19·96	85	66·08	145	112·24	205	158·40	265	204·56	325	250·72	385	296·88	445	343·00
26	20·72	86	66·88	146	113·00	206	159·16	266	205·32	326	251·48	386	297·64	446	343·80
27	21·48	87	67·64	147	113·80	207	159·96	267	206·08	327	252·24	387	298·40	447	344·56
28	22·24	88	68·40	148	114·56	208	160·72	268	206·88	328	253·00	388	299·16	448	345·32
29	23·00	89	69·16	149	115·32	209	161·48	269	207·64	329	253·80	389	299·96	449	346·08
30	23·80	90	69·96	150	116·08	210	162·24	270	208·40	330	254·56	390	300·72	450	346·88
31	24·56	91	70·72	151	116·88	211	163·00	271	209·16	331	255·32	391	301·48	451	347·64
32	25·32	92	71·48	152	117·64	212	163·80	272	209·96	332	256·08	392	302·24	452	348·40
33	26·08	93	72·24	153	118·40	213	164·56	273	210·72	333	256·88	393	303·00	453	349·16
34	26·88	94	73·00	154	119·16	214	165·32	274	211·48	334	257·64	394	303·80	454	349·96
35	27·64	95	73·80	155	119·96	215	166·08	275	212·24	335	258·40	395	304·56	455	350·72
36	28·40	96	74·56	156	120·72	216	166·88	276	213·00	336	259·16	396	305·32	456	351·48
37	29·16	97	75·32	157	121·48	217	167·64	277	213·80	337	259·96	397	306·08	457	352·24
38	29·96	98	76·08	158	122·24	218	168·40	278	214·56	338	260·72	398	306·88	458	353·00
39	30·72	99	76·88	159	123·00	219	169·16	279	215·32	339	261·48	399	307·64	459	353·80
40	31·48	100	77·64	160	123·80	220	169·96	280	216·08	340	262·24	400	308·40	460	354·56
41	32·24	101	78·40	161	124·56	221	170·72	281	216·88	341	263·00	401	309·16	461	355·32
42	33·00	102	79·16	162	125·32	222	171·48	282	217·64	342	263·80	402	309·96	462	356·08
43	33·80	103	79·96	163	126·08	223	172·24	283	218·40	343	264·56	403	310·72	463	356·88
44	34·56	104	80·72	164	126·88	224	173·00	284	219·16	344	265·32	404	311·48	464	357·64
45	35·32	105	81·48	165	127·64	225	173·80	285	219·96	345	266·08	405	312·24	465	358·40
46	36·08	106	82·24	166	128·40	226	174·56	286	220·72	346	266·88	406	313·00	466	359·16
47	36·88	107	83·00	167	129·16	227	175·32	287	221·48	347	267·64	407	313·80	467	359·96
48	37·64	108	83·80	168	129·96	228	176·08	288	222·24	348	268·40	408	314·56	468	360·72
49	38·40	109	84·56	169	130·72	229	176·88	289	223·00	349	269·16	409	315·32	469	361·48
50	39·16	110	85·32	170	131·48	230	177·64	290	223·80	350	269·96	410	316·08	470	362·24
51	39·96	111	86·08	171	132·24	231	178·40	291·	224·56	351	270·72	411	316·88	471	363·00
52	40·72	112	86·88	172	133·00	232	179·16	292	225·32	352	271·48	412	317·64	472	363·80
53	41·48	113	87·64	173	133·80	233	179·96	293	226·08	353	272·24	413	318·40	473	364·56
54	42·24	114	88·40	174	134·56	234	180·72	294	226·88	354	273·00	414	319·16	474	365·32
55	43·00	115	89·16	175	135·32	235	181·48	295	227·64	355	273·80	415	319·96	475	366·08
56	43·80	116	89·96	176	136·08	236	182·24	296	228·40	356	274·56	416	320·72	476	366·88
57	44·56	117	90·72	177	136·88	237	183·00	297	229·16	357	275·32	417	321·48	477	367·64
58	45·32	118	91·48	178	137·64	238	183·80	298	229·96	358	276·08	418	322·24	478	368·40
59	46·08	119	92·24	179	138·40	239	184·56	299	230·72	359	276·88	419	323·00	479	369·16
60	46·88	120	93·00	180	139·16	240	185·32	300	231·48	360	277·64	420	323·80	480	369·96

5

TABLE B

TAX DUE ON TAXABLE PAY FROM £1 TO £360

Total TAXABLE PAY to date	Total TAX DUE to date	Total TAXABLE PAY to date	Total TAX DUE to date	Total TAXABLE PAY to date	Total TAX DUE to date	Total TAXABLE PAY to date	Total TAX DUE to date	Total TAXABLE PAY to date	Total TAX DUE to date	Total TAXABLE PAY to date	Total TAX DUE to date
£	£	£	£	£	£	£	£	£	£	£	£
1	0.25	61	15.25	121	30.25	181	45.25	241	60.25	301	75.25
2	0.50	62	15.50	122	30.50	182	45.50	242	60.50	302	75.50
3	0.75	63	15.75	123	30.75	183	45.75	243	60.75	303	75.75
4	1.00	64	16.00	124	31.00	184	46.00	244	61.00	304	76.00
5	1.25	65	16.25	125	31.25	185	46.25	245	61.25	305	76.25
6	1.50	66	16.50	126	31.50	186	46.50	246	61.50	306	76.50
7	1.75	67	16.75	127	31.75	187	46.75	247	61.75	307	76.75
8	2.00	68	17.00	128	32.00	188	47.00	248	62.00	308	77.00
9	2.25	69	17.25	129	32.25	189	47.25	249	62.25	309	77.25
10	2.50	70	17.50	130	32.50	190	47.50	250	62.50	310	77.50
11	2.75	71	17.75	131	32.75	191	47.75	251	62.75	311	77.75
12	3.00	72	18.00	132	33.00	192	48.00	252	63.00	312	78.00
13	3.25	73	18.25	133	33.25	193	48.25	253	63.25	313	78.25
14	3.50	74	18.50	134	33.50	194	48.50	254	63.50	314	78.50
15	3.75	75	18.75	135	33.75	195	48.75	255	63.75	315	78.75
16	4.00	76	19.00	136	34.00	196	49.00	256	64.00	316	79.00
17	4.25	77	19.25	137	34.25	197	49.25	257	64.25	317	79.25
18	4.50	78	19.50	138	34.50	198	49.50	258	64.50	318	79.50
19	4.75	79	19.75	139	34.75	199	49.75	259	64.75	319	79.75
20	5.00	80	20.00	140	35.00	200	50.00	260	65.00	320	80.00
21	5.25	81	20.25	141	35.25	201	50.25	261	65.25	321	80.25
22	5.50	82	20.50	142	35.50	202	50.50	262	65.50	322	80.50
23	5.75	83	20.75	143	35.75	203	50.75	263	65.75	323	80.75
24	6.00	84	21.00	144	36.00	204	51.00	264	66.00	324	81.00
25	6.25	85	21.25	145	36.25	205	51.25	265	66.25	325	81.25
26	6.50	86	21.50	146	36.50	206	51.50	266	66.50	326	81.50
27	6.75	87	21.75	147	36.75	207	51.75	267	66.75	327	81.75
28	7.00	88	22.00	148	37.00	208	52.00	268	67.00	328	82.00
29	7.25	89	22.25	149	37.25	209	52.25	269	67.25	329	82.25
30	7.50	90	22.50	150	37.50	210	52.50	270	67.50	330	82.50
31	7.75	91	22.75	151	37.75	211	52.75	271	67.75	331	82.75
32	8.00	92	23.00	152	38.00	212	53.00	272	68.00	332	83.00
33	8.25	93	23.25	153	38.25	213	53.25	273	68.25	333	83.25
34	8.50	94	23.50	154	38.50	214	53.50	274	68.50	334	83.50
35	8.75	95	23.75	155	38.75	215	53.75	275	68.75	335	83.75
36	9.00	96	24.00	156	39.00	216	54.00	276	69.00	336	84.00
37	9.25	97	24.25	157	39.25	217	54.25	277	69.25	337	84.25
38	9.50	98	24.50	158	39.50	218	54.50	278	69.50	338	84.50
39	9.75	99	24.75	159	39.75	219	54.75	279	69.75	339	84.75
40	10.00	100	25.00	160	40.00	220	55.00	280	70.00	340	85.00
41	10.25	101	25.25	181	40.25	221	55.25	281	70.25	341	85.25
42	10.50	102	25.50	162	40.50	222	55.50	282	70.50	342	85.50
43	10.75	103	25.75	163	40.75	223	55.75	283	70.75	343	85.75
44	11.00	104	26.00	164	41.00	224	56.00	284	71.00	344	86.00
45	11.25	105	26.25	165	41.25	225	56.25	285	71.25	345	86.25
46	11.50	106	26.50	166	41.50	226	56.50	286	71.50	346	86.50
47	11.75	107	26.75	167	41.75	227	56.75	287	71.75	347	86.75
48	12.00	108	27.00	168	42.00	228	57.00	288	72.00	348	87.00
49	12.25	109	27.25	169	42.25	229	57.25	289	72.25	349	87.25
50	12.50	110	27.50	170	42.50	230	57.50	290	72.50	350	87.50
51	12.75	111	27.75	171	42.75	231	57.75	291	72.75	351	87.75
52	13.00	112	28.00	172	43.00	232	58.00	292	73.00	352	88.00
53	13.25	113	28.25	173	43.25	233	58.25	293	73.25	353	88.25
54	13.50	114	28.50	174	43.50	234	58.50	294	73.50	354	88.50
55	13.75	115	28.75	175	43.75	235	58.75	295	73.75	355	88.75
56	14.00	116	29.00	176	44.00	236	59.00	296	74.00	356	89.00
57	14.25	117	29.25	177	44.25	237	59.25	297	74.25	357	89.25
58	14.50	118	29.50	178	44.50	238	59.50	298	74.50	358	89.50
59	14.75	119	29.75	179	44.75	239	59.75	299	74.75	359	89.75
60	15.00	120	30.00	180	45.00	240	60.00	300	75.00	360	90.00

22

TABLE B

TAX DUE ON TAXABLE PAY FROM £361 TO £720

Total TAXABLE PAY to date	Total TAX DUE to date	Total TAXABLE PAY to date	Total TAX DUE to date	Total TAXABLE PAY to date	Total TAX DUE to date	Total TAXABLE PAY to date	Total TAX DUE to date	Total TAXABLE PAY to date	Total TAX DUE to date	Total TAXABLE PAY to date	Total TAX DUE to date
£	£	£	£	£	£	£	£	£	£	£	£
361	90.25	421	105.25	481	120.25	541	135.25	601	150.25	661	165.25
362	90.50	422	105.50	482	120.50	542	135.50	602	150.50	662	165.50
363	90.75	423	105.75	483	120.75	543	135.75	603	150.75	663	165.75
364	91.00	424	106.00	484	121.00	544	136.00	604	151.00	664	166.00
365	91.25	425	106.25	485	121.25	545	136.25	605	151.25	665	166.25
366	91.50	426	106.50	486	121.50	546	136.50	606	151.50	666	166.50
367	91.75	427	106.75	487	121.75	547	136.75	607	151.75	667	166.75
368	92.00	428	107.00	488	122.00	548	137.00	608	152.00	668	167.00
369	92.25	429	107.25	489	122.25	549	137.25	609	152.25	669	167.25
370	92.50	430	107.50	490	122.50	550	137.50	610	152.50	670	167.50
371	92.75	431	107.75	491	122.75	551	137.75	611	152.75	671	167.75
372	93.00	432	108.00	492	123.00	552	138.00	612	153.00	672	168.00
373	93.25	433	108.25	493	123.25	553	138.25	613	153.25	673	168.25
374	93.50	434	108.50	494	123.50	554	138.50	614	153.50	674	168.50
375	93.75	435	108.75	495	123.75	555	138.75	615	153.75	675	168.75
376	94.00	436	109.00	496	124.00	556	139.00	616	154.00	676	169.00
377	94.25	437	109.25	497	124.25	557	139.25	617	154.25	677	169.25
378	94.50	438	109.50	498	124.50	558	139.50	618	154.50	678	169.50
379	94.75	439	109.75	499	124.75	559	139.75	619	154.75	679	169.75
380	95.00	440	110.00	500	125.00	560	140.00	620	155.00	680	170.00
381	95.25	441	110.25	501	125.25	561	140.25	621	155.25	681	170.25
382	95.50	442	110.50	502	125.50	562	140.50	622	155.50	682	170.50
383	95.75	443	110.75	503	125.75	563	140.75	623	155.75	683	170.75
384	96.00	444	111.00	504	126.00	564	141.00	624	156.00	684	171.00
385	96.25	445	111.25	505	126.25	565	141.25	625	156.25	685	171.25
386	96.50	446	111.50	506	126.50	566	141.50	626	156.50	686	171.50
387	96.75	447	111.75	507	126.75	567	141.75	627	156.75	687	171.75
388	97.00	448	112.00	508	127.00	568	142.00	628	157.00	688	172.00
389	97.25	449	112.25	509	127.25	569	142.25	629	157.25	689	172.25
390	97.50	450	112.50	510	127.50	570	142.50	630	157.50	690	172.50
391	97.75	451	112.75	511	127.75	571	142.75	631	157.75	691	172.75
392	98.00	452	113.00	512	128.00	572	143.00	632	158.00	692	173.00
393	98.25	453	113.25	513	128.25	573	143.25	633	158.25	693	173.25
394	98.50	454	113.50	514	128.50	574	143.50	634	158.50	694	173.50
395	98.75	455	113.75	515	128.75	575	143.75	635	158.75	695	173.75
396	99.00	456	114.00	516	129.00	576	144.00	636	159.00	696	174.00
397	99.25	457	114.25	517	129.25	577	144.25	637	159.25	697	174.25
398	99.50	458	114.50	518	129.50	578	144.50	638	159.50	698	174.50
399	99.75	459	114.75	519	129.75	579	144.75	639	159.75	699	174.75
400	100.00	460	115.00	520	130.00	580	145.00	640	160.00	700	175.00
401	100.25	461	115.25	521	130.25	581	145.25	641	160.25	701	175.25
402	100.50	462	115.50	522	130.50	582	145.50	642	160.50	702	175.50
403	100.75	463	115.75	523	130.75	583	145.75	643	160.75	703	175.75
404	101.00	464	116.00	524	131.00	584	146.00	644	161.00	704	176.00
405	101.25	465	116.25	525	131.25	585	146.25	645	161.25	705	176.25
406	101.50	466	116.50	526	131.50	586	146.50	646	161.50	706	176.50
407	101.75	467	116.75	527	131.75	587	146.75	647	161.75	707	176.75
408	102.00	468	117.00	528	132.00	588	147.00	648	162.00	708	177.00
409	102.25	469	117.25	529	132.25	589	147.25	649	162.25	709	177.25
410	102.50	470	117.50	530	132.50	590	147.50	650	162.50	710	177.50
411	102.75	471	117.75	531	132.75	591	147.75	651	162.75	711	177.75
412	103.00	472	118.00	532	133.00	592	148.00	652	163.00	712	178.00
413	103.25	473	118.25	533	133.25	593	148.25	653	163.25	713	178.25
414	103.50	474	118.50	534	133.50	594	148.50	654	163.50	714	178.50
415	103.75	475	118.75	535	133.75	595	148.75	655	163.75	715	178.75
416	104.00	476	119.00	536	134.00	596	149.00	656	164.00	716	179.00
417	104.25	477	119.25	537	134.25	597	149.25	657	164.25	717	179.25
418	104.50	478	119.50	538	134.50	598	149.50	658	164.50	718	179.50
419	104.75	479	119.75	539	134.75	599	149.75	659	164.75	719	179.75
420	105.00	480	120.00	540	135.00	600	150.00	660	165.00	720	180.00

TABLE B

TAX DUE ON TAXABLE PAY FROM £721 TO £1080

Total TAXABLE PAY to date	Total TAX DUE to date	Total TAXABLE PAY to date	Total TAX DUE to date	Total TAXABLE PAY to date	Total TAX DUE to date	Total TAXABLE PAY to date	Total TAX DUE to date	Total TAXABLE PAY to date	Total TAX DUE to date	Total TAXABLE PAY to date	Total TAX DUE to date
£	£	£	£	£	£	£	£	£	£	£	£
721	180.25	781	195.25	841	210.25	901	225.25	961	240.25	1021	255.25
722	180.50	782	195.50	842	210.50	902	225.50	962	240.50	1022	255.50
723	180.75	783	195.75	843	210.75	903	225.75	963	240.75	1023	255.75
724	181.00	784	196.00	844	211.00	904	226.00	964	241.00	1024	256.00
725	181.25	785	196.25	845	211.25	905	226.25	965	241.25	1025	256.25
726	181.50	786	196.50	846	211.50	906	226.50	966	241.50	1026	256.50
727	181.75	787	196.75	847	211.75	907	226.75	967	241.75	1027	256.75
728	182.00	788	197.00	848	212.00	908	227.00	968	242.00	1028	257.00
729	182.25	789	197.25	849	212.25	909	227.25	969	242.25	1029	257.25
730	182.50	790	197.50	850	212.50	910	227.50	970	242.50	1030	257.50
731	182.75	791	197.75	851	212.75	911	227.75	971	242.75	1031	257.75
732	183.00	792	198.00	852	213.00	912	228.00	972	243.00	1032	258.00
733	183.25	793	198.25	853	213.25	913	228.25	973	243.25	1033	258.25
734	183.50	794	198.50	854	213.50	914	228.50	974	243.50	1034	258.50
735	183.75	795	198.75	855	213.75	915	228.75	975	243.75	1035	258.75
736	184.00	796	199.00	856	214.00	916	229.00	976	244.00	1036	259.00
737	184.25	797	199.25	857	214.25	917	229.25	977	244.25	1037	259.25
738	184.50	798	199.50	858	214.50	918	229.50	978	244.50	1038	259.50
739	184.75	799	199.75	859	214.75	919	229.75	979	244.75	1039	259.75
740	185.00	800	200.00	860	215.00	920	230.00	980	245.00	1040	260.00
741	185.25	801	200.25	861	215.25	921	230.25	981	245.25	1041	260.25
742	185.50	802	200.50	862	215.50	922	230.50	982	245.50	1042	260.50
743	185.75	803	200.75	863	215.75	923	230.75	983	245.75	1043	260.75
744	186.00	804	201.00	864	216.00	924	231.00	984	246.00	1044	261.00
745	186.25	805	201.25	865	216.25	925	231.25	985	246.25	1045	261.25
746	186.50	806	201.50	866	216.50	926	231.50	986	246.50	1046	261.50
747	186.75	807	201.75	867	216.75	927	231.75	987	246.75	1047	261.75
748	187.00	808	202.00	868	217.00	928	232.00	988	247.00	1048	262.00
749	187.25	809	202.25	869	217.25	929	232.25	989	247.25	1049	262.25
750	187.50	810	202.50	870	217.50	930	232.50	990	247.50	1050	262.50
751	187.75	811	202.75	871	217.75	931	232.75	991	247.75	1051	262.75
752	188.00	812	203.00	872	218.00	932	233.00	992	248.00	1052	263.00
753	188.25	813	203.25	873	218.25	933	233.25	993	248.25	1053	263.25
754	188.50	814	203.50	874	218.50	934	233.50	994	248.50	1054	263.50
755	188.75	815	203.75	875	218.75	935	233.75	995	248.75	1055	263.75
756	189.00	816	204.00	876	219.00	936	234.00	996	249.00	1056	264.00
757	189.25	817	204.25	877	219.25	937	234.25	997	249.25	1057	264.25
758	189.50	818	204.50	878	219.50	938	234.50	998	249.50	1058	264.50
759	189.75	819	204.75	879	219.75	939	234.75	999	249.75	1059	264.75
760	190.00	820	205.00	880	220.00	940	235.00	1000	250.00	1060	265.00
761	190.25	821	205.25	881	220.25	941	235.25	1001	250.25	1061	265.25
762	190.50	822	205.50	882	220.50	942	235.50	1002	250.50	1062	265.50
763	190.75	823	205.75	883	220.75	943	235.75	1003	250.75	1063	265.75
764	191.00	824	206.00	884	221.00	944	236.00	1004	251.00	1064	266.00
765	191.25	825	206.25	885	221.25	945	236.25	1005	251.25	1065	266.25
766	191.50	826	206.50	886	221.50	946	236.50	1006	251.50	1066	266.50
767	191.75	827	206.75	887	221.75	947	236.75	1007	251.75	1067	266.75
768	192.00	828	207.00	888	222.00	948	237.00	1008	252.00	1068	267.00
769	192.25	829	207.25	889	222.25	949	237.25	1009	252.25	1069	267.25
770	192.50	830	207.50	890	222.50	950	237.50	1010	252.50	1070	267.50
771	192.75	831	207.75	891	222.75	951	237.75	1011	252.75	1071	267.75
772	193.00	832	208.00	892	223.00	952	238.00	1012	253.00	1072	268.00
773	193.25	833	208.25	893	223.25	953	238.25	1013	253.25	1073	268.25
774	193.50	834	208.50	894	223.50	954	238.50	1014	253.50	1074	268.50
775	193.75	835	208.75	895	223.75	955	238.75	1015	253.75	1075	268.75
776	194.00	836	209.00	896	224.00	956	239.00	1016	254.00	1076	269.00
777	194.25	837	209.25	897	224.25	957	239.25	1017	254.25	1077	269.25
778	194.50	838	209.50	898	224.50	958	239.50	1018	254.50	1078	269.50
779	194.75	839	209.75	899	224.75	959	239.75	1019	254.75	1079	269.75
780	195.00	840	210.00	900	225.00	960	240.00	1020	255.00	1080	270.00

Weekly

A

Not contracted-out standard rate NI contributions

Before using this table enter "A" in the space provided on the Deductions Working Sheet P11 or substitute (see Instructions).

6 April 1991
to 5 April 1992

Use this table

- for employees who are over age 16 and under pension age (65 men, 60 women).
- for employees who have an appropriate personal pension (from 1 July) 1988).

Do not use this table

- for married women and widows who pay NI contributions at the reduced rate — see Table B.
- for employees over pension age or for whom form RD950 is held — see Table C.

Entries to be made on P11

- copy the figures from columns 1a, 1b and 1c to columns 1a, 1b and 1c of the P11.

If the exact gross pay is not shown in the table, use the next smaller figure shown.

Earnings on which employee's contributions payable 1a	Total of employee's and employer's contributions payable 1b	Employee's contributions payable 1c	Employer's contributions*
£	£	£	£
52	3·43	1·04	2·39
53	3·63	1·17	2·46
54	3·77	1·26	2·51
55	3·90	1·35	2·55
56	4·04	1·44	2·60
57	4·17	1·53	2·64
58	4·31	1·62	2·69
59	4·45	1·71	2·74
60	4·58	1·80	2·78
61	4·72	1·89	2·83
62	4·85	1·98	2·87
63	4·99	2·07	2·92
64	5·13	2·16	2·97
65	5·26	2·25	3·01
66	5·40	2·34	3·06
67	5·53	2·43	3·10
68	5·67	2·52	3·15
69	5·81	2·61	3·20
70	5·94	2·70	3·24
71	6·08	2·79	3·29
72	6·21	2·88	3·33
73	6·35	2·97	3·38
74	6·49	3·06	3·43
75	6·62	3·15	3·47
76	6·76	3·24	3·52
77	6·89	3·33	3·56
78	7·03	3·42	3·61
79	7·17	3·51	3·66
80	7·30	3·60	3·70
81	7·44	3·69	3·75
82	7·57	3·78	3·79
83	7·71	3·87	3·84
84	7·85	3·96	3·89
85	9·69	4·05	5·64
86	9·85	4·14	5·71
87	10·00	4·23	5·77
88	10·16	4·32	5·84
89	10·32	4·41	5·91
90	10·47	4·50	5·97
91	10·63	4·59	6·04
92	10·78	4·68	6·10
93	10·94	4·77	6·17
94	11·10	4·86	6·24
95	11·25	4·95	6·30
96	11·41	5·04	6·37
97	11·56	5·13	6·43
98	11·72	5·22	6·50
99	11·88	5·31	6·57
100	12·03	5·40	6·63
101	12·19	5·49	6·70

Earnings on which employee's contributions payable 1a	Total of employee's and employer's contributions payable 1b	Employee's contributions payable 1c	Employer's contributions*
£	£	£	£
102	12·34	5·58	6·76
103	12·50	5·67	6·83
104	12·66	5·76	6·90
105	12·81	5·85	6·96
106	12·97	5·94	7·03
107	13·12	6·03	7·09
108	13·28	6·12	7·16
109	13·44	6·21	7·23
110	13·59	6·30	7·29
111	13·75	6·39	7·36
112	13·90	6·48	7·42
113	14·06	6·57	7·49
114	14·22	6·66	7·56
115	14·37	6·75	7·62
116	14·53	6·84	7·69
117	14·68	6·93	7·75
118	14·84	7·02	7·82
119	15·00	7·11	7·89
120	15·15	7·20	7·95
121	15·31	7·29	8·02
122	15·46	7·38	8·08
123	15·62	7·47	8·15
124	15·78	7·56	8·22
125	15·93	7·65	8·28
126	16·09	7·74	8·35
127	16·24	7·83	8·41
128	16·40	7·92	8·48
129	16·56	8·01	8·55
130	19·32	8·10	11·22
131	19·50	8·19	11·31
132	19·67	8·28	11·39
133	19·85	8·37	11·48
134	20·03	8·46	11·57
135	20·20	8·55	11·65
136	20·38	8·64	11·74
137	20·55	8·73	11·82
138	20·73	8·82	11·91
139	20·91	8·91	12·00
140	21·08	9·00	12·08
141	21·26	9·09	12·17
142	21·43	9·18	12·25
143	21·61	9·27	12·34
144	21·79	9·36	12·43
145	21·96	9·45	12·51
146	22·14	9·54	12·60
147	22·31	9·63	12·68
148	22·49	9·72	12·77
149	22·67	9·81	12·86
150	22·84	9·90	12·94
151	23·02	9·99	13·03

* for information only — **Do not enter on P11**

6

Weekly Table A continued
6 April 1991 to 5 April 1992

Weekly

Earnings on which employee's contributions payable 1a	Total of employee's and employer's contributions payable 1b	Employee's contributions payable 1c	Employer's contributions*
£	£	£	£
152	23·19	10·08	13·11
153	23·37	10·17	13·20
154	23·55	10·26	13·29
155	23·72	10·35	13·37
156	23·90	10·44	13·46
157	24·07	10·53	13·54
158	24·25	10·62	13·63
159	24·43	10·71	13·72
160	24·60	10·80	13·80
161	24·78	10·89	13·89
162	24·95	10·98	13·97
163	25·13	11·07	14·06
164	25·31	11·16	14·15
165	25·48	11·25	14·23
166	25·66	11·34	14·32
167	25·83	11·43	14·40
168	26·01	11·52	14·49
169	26·19	11·61	14·58
170	26·36	11·70	14·66
171	26·54	11·79	14·75
172	26·71	11·88	14·83
173	26·89	11·97	14·92
174	27·07	12·06	15·01
175	27·24	12·15	15·09
176	27·42	12·24	15·18
177	27·59	12·33	15·26
178	27·77	12·42	15·35
179	27·95	12·51	15·44
180	28·12	12·60	15·52
181	28·30	12·69	15·61
182	28·47	12·78	15·69
183	28·65	12·87	15·78
184	28·83	12·96	15·87
185	32·34	13·05	19·29
186	32·54	13·14	19·40
187	32·73	13·23	19·50
188	32·92	13·32	19·60
189	33·12	13·41	19·71
190	33·31	13·50	19·81
191	33·51	13·59	19·92
192	33·70	13·68	20·02
193	33·89	13·77	20·12
194	34·09	13·86	20·23
195	34·28	13·95	20·33
196	34·48	14·04	20·44
197	34·67	14·13	20·54
198	34·86	14·22	20·64
199	35·06	14·31	20·75
200	35·25	14·40	20·85
201	35·45	14·49	20·96
202	35·64	14·58	21·06
203	35·83	14·67	21·16
204	36·03	14·76	21·27
205	36·22	14·85	21·37
206	36·42	14·94	21·48
207	36·61	15·03	21·58
208	36·80	15·12	21·68
209	37·00	15·21	21·79
210	37·19	15·30	21·89
211	37·39	15·39	22·00

Earnings on which employee's contributions payable 1a	Total of employee's and employer's contributions payable 1b	Employee's contributions payable 1c	Employer's contributions*
£	£	£	£
212	37·58	15·48	22·10
213	37·77	15·57	22·20
214	37·97	15·66	22·31
215	38·16	15·75	22·41
216	38·36	15·84	22·52
217	38·55	15·93	22·62
218	38·74	16·02	22·72
219	38·94	16·11	22·83
220	39·13	16·20	22·93
221	39·33	16·29	23·04
222	39·52	16·38	23·14
223	39·71	16·47	23·24
224	39·91	16·56	23·35
225	40·10	16·65	23·45
226	40·30	16·74	23·56
227	40·49	16·83	23·66
228	40·68	16·92	23·76
229	40·88	17·01	23·87
230	41·07	17·10	23·97
231	41·27	17·19	24·08
232	41·46	17·28	24·18
233	41·65	17·37	24·28
234	41·85	17·46	24·39
235	42·04	17·55	24·49
236	42·24	17·64	24·60
237	42·43	17·73	24·70
238	42·62	17·82	24·80
239	42·82	17·91	24·91
240	43·01	18·00	25·01
241	43·21	18·09	25·12
242	43·40	18·18	25·22
243	43·59	18·27	25·32
244	43·79	18·36	25·43
245	43·98	18·45	25·53
246	44·18	18·54	25·64
247	44·37	18·63	25·74
248	44·56	18·72	25·84
249	44·76	18·81	25·95
250	44·95	18·90	26·05
251	45·15	18·99	26·16
252	45·34	19·08	26·26
253	45·53	19·17	26·36
254	45·73	19·26	26·47
255	45·92	19·35	26·57
256	46·12	19·44	26·68
257	46·31	19·53	26·78
258	46·50	19·62	26·88
259	46·70	19·71	26·99
260	46·89	19·80	27·09
261	47·09	19·89	27·20
262	47·28	19·98	27·30
263	47·47	20·07	27·40
264	47·67	20·16	27·51
265	47·86	20·25	27·61
266	48·06	20·34	27·72
267	48·25	20·43	27·82
268	48·44	20·52	27·92
269	48·64	20·61	28·03
270	48·83	20·70	28·13
271	49·03	20·79	28·24

7

* for information only   Do not enter on P11

Weekly

Weekly Table A continued
6 April 1991 to 5 April 1992

Earnings on which employee's contributions payable 1a £	Total of employee's and employer's contributions payable 1b £	Employee's contributions payable 1c £	Employer's contributions* £
272	49·22	20·88	28·34
273	49·41	20·97	28·44
274	49·61	21·06	28·55
275	49·80	21·15	28·65
276	50·00	21·24	28·76
277	50·19	21·33	28·86
278	50·38	21·42	28·96
279	50·58	21·51	29·07
280	50·77	21·60	29·17
281	50·97	21·69	29·28
282	51·16	21·78	29·38
283	51·35	21·87	29·48
284	51·55	21·96	29·59
285	51·74	22·05	29·69
286	51·94	22·14	29·80
287	52·13	22·23	29·90
288	52·32	22·32	30·00
289	52·52	22·41	30·11
290	52·71	22·50	30·21
291	52·91	22·59	30·32
292	53·10	22·68	30·42
293	53·29	22·77	30·52
294	53·49	22·86	30·63
295	53·68	22·95	30·73
296	53·88	23·04	30·84
297	54·07	23·13	30·94
298	54·26	23·22	31·04
299	54·46	23·31	31·15
300	54·65	23·40	31·25
301	54·85	23·49	31·36
302	55·04	23·58	31·46
303	55·23	23·67	31·56
304	55·43	23·76	31·67
305	55·62	23·85	31·77
306	55·82	23·94	31·88
307	56·01	24·03	31·98
308	56·20	24·12	32·08
309	56·40	24·21	32·19
310	56·59	24·30	32·29
311	56·79	24·39	32·40
312	56·98	24·48	32·50
313	57·17	24·57	32·60
314	57·37	24·66	32·71
315	57·56	24·75	32·81
316	57·76	24·84	32·92
317	57·95	24·93	33·02
318	58·14	25·02	33·12
319	58·34	25·11	33·23
320	58·53	25·20	33·33
321	58·73	25·29	33·44
322	58·92	25·38	33·54
323	59·11	25·47	33·64
324	59·31	25·56	33·75
325	59·50	25·65	33·85
326	59·70	25·74	33·96
327	59·89	25·83	34·06
328	60·08	25·92	34·16
329	60·28	26·01	34·27
330	60·47	26·10	34·37
331	60·67	26·19	34·48
332	60·86	26·28	34·58
333	61·05	26·37	34·68
334	61·25	26·46	34·79
335	61·44	26·55	34·89
336	61·64	26·64	35·00
337	61·83	26·73	35·10
338	62·02	26·82	35·20
339	62·22	26·91	35·31
340	62·41	27·00	35·41
341	62·61	27·09	35·52
342	62·80	27·18	35·62
343	62·99	27·27	35·72
344	63·19	27·36	35·83
345	63·38	27·45	35·93
346	63·58	27·54	36·04
347	63·77	27·63	36·14
348	63·96	27·72	36·24
349	64·16	27·81	36·35
350	64·35	27·90	36·45
351	64·55	27·99	36·56
352	64·74	28·08	36·66
353	64·93	28·17	36·76
354	65·13	28·26	36·87
355	65·32	28·35	36·97
356	65·52	28·44	37·08
357	65·71	28·53	37·18
358	65·90	28·62	37·28
359	66·10	28·71	37·39
360	66·29	28·80	37·49
361	66·49	28·89	37·60
362	66·68	28·98	37·70
363	66·87	29·07	37·80
364	67·07	29·16	37·91
365	67·26	29·25	38·01
366	67·46	29·34	38·12
367	67·65	29·43	38·22
368	67·84	29·52	38·32
369	68·04	29·61	38·43
370	68·23	29·70	38·53
371	68·43	29·79	38·64
372	68·62	29·88	38·74
373	68·81	29·97	38·84
374	69·01	30·06	38·95
375	69·20	30·15	39·05
376	69·40	30·24	39·16
377	69·59	30·33	39·26
378	69·78	30·42	39·36
379	69·98	30·51	39·47
380	70·17	30·60	39·57
381	70·37	30·69	39·68
382	70·56	30·78	39·78
383	70·75	30·87	39·88
384	70·95	30·96	39·99
385	71·14	31·05	40·09
386	71·34	31·14	40·20
387	71·53	31·23	40·30
388	71·72	31·32	40·40
389	71·92	31·41	40·51
390	72·02	31·46	40·56

for gross pay over £390 see end of book

8

* for information only   Do not enter on P11

Index

All entries refer to coverage of these subjects in **Section 2: The Information Bank**.